Children and Pictures

DATE DUE

			PRINTED IN U.S.A.

To Lucy

. . . and to all my friends and family who will no longer have to ask, "are you *still* writing that book?"

Children and Pictures

Drawing and Understanding

Richard P. Jolley

WILEY-BLACKWELL

A John Wiley & Sons, Ltd., Publication

This edition first published 2010
© 2010 Richard P. Jolley

Blackwell Publishing was acquired by John Wiley & Sons in February 2007.
Blackwell's publishing program has been merged with Wiley's global Scientific,
Technical, and Medical business to form Wiley-Blackwell.

Registered Office
John Wiley & Sons Ltd, The Atrium, Southern Gate, Chichester, West Sussex, PO19
8SQ, United Kingdom

Editorial Offices
350 Main Street, Malden, MA 02148-5020, USA
9600 Garsington Road, Oxford, OX4 2DQ, UK
The Atrium, Southern Gate, Chichester, West Sussex, PO19 8SQ, UK

For details of our global editorial offices, for customer services, and for information
about how to apply for permission to reuse the copyright material in this book please
see our website at www.wiley.com/wiley-blackwell.

The right of Richard P. Jolley to be identified as the author of this work has been
asserted in accordance with the Copyright, Designs and Patents Act 1988.

Library of Congress Cataloging-in-Publication Data
Jolley, Richard P.
   Children and pictures : drawing and understanding / Richard P. Jolley.
      p. cm.
   Includes bibliographical references and index.
      ISBN 978-1-4051-0543-9 (hardback : alk. paper) — ISBN 978-1-4051-05446 (pbk.
alk. paper)   1. Children's drawings—Psychological aspects.   2. Child development.
3. Child psychology.   I. Title.

BF723.D7J65 2010
155.4—dc22
                                                                    2008044181

A catalogue record for this book is available from the British Library.

Set in 10.5/13pt Sabon by Graphicraft Limited, Hong Kong
Printed in Singapore by Ho Printing Singapore Pte Ltd

1   2010

Contents

Acknowledgements

Any student embarking upon a research journey needs supervision and mentoring by someone who has spent years treading their own journey in the same academic field. I have been fortunate to have had two excellent mentors, firstly Maureen Cox as my undergraduate dissertation supervisor, and Glyn Thomas as my PhD supervisor. It was with Maureen that I began my interest in children's representational drawings, and with Glyn I extended my interest and knowledge into children's expressive drawings as well as in children's comprehension of drawings and art. In many ways this book is a credit to both Maureen and Glyn.

Particular thanks go to the following reviewers of the book: Esther Burkitt, Robin Campbell, Alan Costall, Judy Dunn, Claire Golomb, and Kate Nation. For individual chapters the following academics and practitioners have given me useful feedback: Claire Barlow, Tara Callaghan, Maureen Cox, Mani Das Gupta, Norman Freeman, Jenny Hallam, Harlene Hayne, Clarissa Martin, David Pariser, Elizabeth Robinson, Ellen Winner, and Pete and Erica Woolley.

I would like to give special thanks to Sarah Rose, who has provided invaluable help in a number of areas during the book writing process. These include feedback on various earlier drafts, creating some of the graphs, compiling the references, and most notably, in trawling through my collection of thousands of children's drawing to find the best ones to illustrate my points.

The pictorial nature of the book meant that there were a lot of copyright permissions to be sought after, an onerous task for sure, so I am very grateful to Sue Collingwood who did much of this work for me. For technical support with all the figures I thank Paul Gallimore, and also to David Clark-Carter who has provided me with unrelenting statistical support over the years. Hannah Green also helped with some of the referencing.

Some authors' experience of their publisher is not always favorable, but I cannot speak highly enough of the development editors (Lindsey Howarth, Elizabeth Johnston, Peter Jones, William Maddox, Annie Rose) and commissioning editors (Sarah Bird and Andrew McAleer) at Wiley-Blackwell with whom I have worked over the course of writing the book, and thanks also to their production team. They showed an incredible amount of kindness and patience to me throughout every deadline that I missed.

This book was written while I have been a full-time lecturer in the Psychology Department of Staffordshire University, UK, and I thank my colleagues who have supported me in different ways. There are too many students to mention with whom I have had discussions, and benefited from, over the years, but Claire Barlow deserves a special acknowledgement in this respect.

Finally, I must not forget the assistance I have had from all the schools that have accepted me and my students into their busy lives, and above all the children themselves who have provided the drawings and responses that have shaped this book.

Credits

The author and publisher gratefully acknowledge the permission granted to reproduce the copyright material in this book.

Figures:

1.5 Drawings adapted from *The Pictorial World of the Child*, by M. V. Cox, 2005, Cambridge University Press. Reprinted with permission from Cambridge University Press.

1.7 Willats, John; *Art and Representation* © 1997 Princeton University Press. Reprinted by permission of Princeton University Press.

2.3 Adapted from "When children's drawings become art: The emergence of aesthetic production and perception," T. Carothers, & H. Gardner, (1979). *Developmental Psychology*, 15, 570–580. Permission granted by Howard Gardner/Harvard University.

2.4 From "Drawing's demise: U-shaped development in graphic Symbolisation," J. H. Davis, (1997). *Studies in Art Education: A Journal of Issues and Research*, 38, 132–157. Reprinted with permission from the National Art Education Association, Reston, VA-USA, copyright 1997.

2.6 From "The development of children's expressive drawing," R. P. Jolley, K. Fenn, & L. Jones, (2004). *British Journal of Developmental Psychology*, 22, 545–567. Reproduced with permission from the British Journal of Developmental Psychology, © The British Psychological Society.

tational change," 124–152, (2003), with permission from Elsevier.

6.5   Reprinted from *Journal of Experimental Child Psychology*, 86, C. M. Barlow, R. P. Jolley, D. G. White, & D. Galbraith, "Rigidity in children's drawings and its relation with representational change," 124–152, (2003), with permission from Elsevier.

7.1   From *Advances in projective drawing interpretation*, by E. F. Hammer, 1997, New York: Harcourt, Brace World. Reprinted with permission from Charles C. Thomas.

7.2   Reprinted with permission from Michelle Catte.

9.1   Adapted from "Some drawings of men and women made by children of certain non-European races," G. W. Paget, (1932). *Journal of the Royal Anthropological Institute*, 62, 127–144. Permission granted by Wiley-Blackwell.

9.3   Reprinted from "Types of child art and alternative developmental accounts: Interpreting the interpreters," B. Wilson, (1997). *Human Development*, 40, 155–168. Permission granted by S. Karger AG, Basel.

9.4   Reprinted from "Types of child art and alternative developmental accounts: Interpreting the interpreters," B. Wilson, (1997). *Human Development*, 40, 155–168. Permission granted by S. Karger AG, Basel.

9.5   Adapted from, "Social scalings in children's drawings of classroom life. A cultural comparative analysis of children's drawings in Africa and Sweden," K. Aronsson, & S. Andersson, (1996). *British Journal of Developmental Psychology*, 14, 301–314. Reproduced with permission from the British Journal of Developmental Psychology, © The British Psychological Society.

9.7   Reprinted from "Drawings of people by Australian Aboriginal Children: The Intermixing of cultural styles," M. V. Cox, (1998). *Journal of Art and Design Education*, 17, 71–79. Permission granted by Wiley-Blackwell.

Plates:
Plate 1: Photo J. Clottes

The author would like to gratefully acknowledge Greasby Infant School, Wirral, UK, for providing the three children's lion drawings in Plate 1, and Stockport school, UK, for providing two of the children's drawings in Figure 1.6 (top right and bottom right). These drawings were provided at short notice on request of the author for the direct purpose of illustration in this book, and were not part of a research study.

Every effort has been made to trace copyright holders and to obtain their permission for the use of copyright material. The publisher apologizes for any errors or omissions in the above list and would be grateful if notified of any corrections that should be incorporated in future reprints or editions of this book.

Introduction

Let me take you back to one evening during the 10th European conference on developmental psychology held in Uppsala, Sweden in 2001. After having spent a pleasant evening dining at a restaurant with my fellow contributors to a symposium on children's drawings held earlier that day, I joined a nearby table of other conferences delegates most of whom I recognized, except for two young ladies. They told me that they were Sarah Bird and Lindsey Howarth, that they worked for Blackwell Publishing, and that many of the people on their table wrote books for them. I excitedly told them that I had been thinking about writing a book. They appeared interested, despite looking as though they had enjoyed some quantity of alcohol, and enquired what it would be on. To keep it simple I said, "children's drawings". By this point most of those present on the table were listening to our conversation, and heard Lindsey's instant reply, "well, that would sell about three copies!" It was to my surprise, therefore, that soon after returning from the conference, Sarah emailed me to ask whether she and Lindsey could take me out to lunch during a British Psychological Society conference in England a month later to discuss further my book idea. I knew that if I got their full and undivided attention I could sell the idea to them. And I did and here is its fruition.

The point of the story is not so much to tell you how this book was conceived, as to highlight a view held by some, and encapsulated by Lindsey's initial reaction, that the study of children making and understanding of pictures has only limited academic and educational importance. Such a view cannot derive from a scarcity of pictures in the world. In fact, we live in a world that is proliferated with, and influenced by, pictures. We have what might be called "serious" art that is found in art galleries and museums, but we do not have to make a special visit to see pictures. They appear on just about everything we buy, advertising and informing us of the contents of our purchase. Pictures displayed in road signs enable us to travel safely from one place to another. Pictures are found in most books, magazines, newspapers and comics serving a variety of purposes that include their aesthetic communication, to illustrate the accompanying text, to express moods and ideas, and even to make us laugh. Through the creation of photography the ability to capture the visual likeness of our world is no longer restricted to some artists, but available to all who have access to a camera. Realism in pictures has been extended through the invention of "moving" pictures in film, where we can see on large cinema screens and television sets the finite incremental movements ingrained in real-life events or in animated stories.

So if the neglect of academic attention to children's picture making is not due to any paucity of pictures, could it be that *children's picture making is not worthy of study?* True, most of the influential pictorial examples I gave above are not typically made by children, but adults. However, although we live in a pictorial world it is created by relatively few adults (e.g., artists, illustrators, cartoonists, photographers, film makers). The engagement with pictures for the majority of adults is at the observational and interpretational level. In contrast, for most adults there was an earlier period in their lives in which they were very much engaged in the production of pictures. As children, we created a massive collection of pictures, particularly drawings. If we want to understand the development of the adult engagement with pictures then studying children's engagement with pictures is a necessity.

But what about studying children's drawing activity and their understanding of pictures for its own sake, as an exercise that contributes to the investigation of the psychology of childhood? It is not sufficient to argue for studying children's interaction with pictures that children do a lot of it. Children breathe a lot but few would be interested enough to research it. The study of children's making and understanding of pictures has to be informative, both in respect of issues within the subject of children and pictures per se, but also to more general aspects of the psychology and education of the child. The objective of the book, therefore, is to present an informative review of the key issues and research findings in the broad area of children and pictures, particularly drawings as they represent a significant contribution to children's picture making. In so doing I hope to encourage an appreciation of the importance of this aspect of children's lives, and provide insight to the developmental underpinnings of our pictorial world.

With this objective in mind I have written ten chapters that provide a detailed analysis of the literature pertaining to ten topics within this field of enquiry. In chapter 1 ("The Development of Representational Drawing") I provide an historical account of the early interest in children's drawings, and then discuss children's developmental progression in their representation of subject matter from life in their drawings, and also the range of psychological factors that influence that development. An account of the development of children's drawings would be incomplete, however, without an understanding of children's expression of their feelings and ideas towards the people, things and events that they represent. In chapter 2 ("The Development of Expressive Drawing"), therefore, I examine the expressive devices that children use, and discuss the nature of its developmental pattern and what may influence it. In each of these first two chapters the focus is on the drawings made by typically developing children. In chapter 3 ("Drawing by Children in Special Populations") we turn our attention to the drawings made by children with a variety of diagnostic conditions. A theme running through the chapter is whether their drawings follow a similar developmental pattern to that found in typically developing children's pictures, or whether qualitative differences are observed which can be linked directly to the etiology and symptomatic characteristics of the children's disorder.

In chapter 4 ("Production and Comprehension of Representational Drawing") we take our first detailed looked at children's understanding of pictures. In particular, I examine the relationship between children's understanding of pictures they see and the product of their own drawings. The chapter reminds us that children's engagement in pictures is not limited to their own drawings but extends to how they understand pictures in general. A key milestone in understanding pictures is to appreciate their dual nature: They are things in themselves as well as symbols that refer to some other reality. Children's development to gaining a fully mature conception of pictures' dual nature, and how this is influenced by the development of generic cognitive factors, is discussed in chapter 5 ("Children's Understanding of the Dual Nature of Pictures"). As children's developing cognition undoubtedly affects their pictorial understanding we might expect that by studying children's drawings we can gain some insight into children's minds. Consistent with this approach, I discuss the representational redescription theory in chapter 6 ("Drawings as Measures of Internal Representations") that claims that by studying children's representational drawings we can gain insight into the nature and development of the corresponding internal representations of the subject matter stored in children's minds.

There are a number of different practioners who have direct contact with children and their pictorial world. In chapter 7 ("Drawings as Assessment Tools: Intelligence, Personality and Emotionality") I evaluate the use of children's drawings in clinical practice, particularly in respect of the use and validity of the diagnostic drawing tests. In chapter 8 ("Drawings as Memory Aids") I assess the efficacy of asking children to draw as an aid for their memory recall of previous experiences; a practice that has potential implications for children's recall in clinical and eye-witness testimony settings, and of course as an educational tool.

In the final two main chapters I widen our attention to consider the cultural and educational influences on children's drawings. In chapter 9 ("Cultural Influences on Children's Drawings") I reflect upon children's picture making as a worldwide activity, the study of which gives us insight to the many and varied cultural influences on children throughout the world. The pervasiveness of children's drawing activity reminds us that it should be nurtured, and that there are a variety of educational practices and programs around the world. Hence, in chapter 10 ("The Education of Drawing") I discuss first the variety of pedagogical practices that have been used to teach Western children, and then widen the perspective to consider the Chinese approach to teaching children drawing. The chapter ends by taking a more holistic approach in considering the wider educational context on children's drawing experience beyond curricula influences. Finally, in chapter 11 ("Future Directions") I tie together some of the key threads covered throughout this book, and in so doing suggest important questions we should address in the future to further our understanding of this interesting and pervasive domain of activity in children's lives.

This book was not written quickly. It has been painstakingly researched and written over a 6-year period, at a time when a lecturer's workload is becoming increasingly demanding. But whether you are a student, academic, practitioner, artist, teacher, parent, or just someone simply interested in the subject, I hope you will find what I have written interesting and stimulating for your thinking about children's engagement with pictures. And finally, a big thank you if you have bought a copy of this book. I'm looking forward to telling Lindsey that it has sold more than three.

1

The Development of Representational Drawing

The chapter begins by considering the sources of the initial historical interest in studying children's drawings, and some of the key debates that drove this interest. These include the question of whether children's drawings provide an insight into understanding prehistoric art, and the development of art thereafter, and also the differing focus and appreciation artists and scientists had when they first began to take children's drawings seriously. I then present an in-depth examination of two theories of children's drawing development, that of Luquet (1927/2001) and Willats (2005). These two theories stand out as providing a detailed and innovative analysis of the developmental progression in representational drawing, and have been considerably influential to other researchers studying this area. The chapter ends by presenting an up-to-date overview of more specific debates and questions found in recent research into what develops and why in children's representational drawing.

Prehistoric and Child Art

We do not know when the first instances of mark-making occurred among our ancestors. It is likely that the earliest "pictures" were painted on their bodies, and in the open on wood, stone, sand and mud which are subject to decay from outside elements. Consequently, they have long since perished with the "canvases" upon which they were made. Nevertheless, there is evidence that colored pigments may have been used up to 400,000 years ago (Barham, 2002; Cox, 2005). Although it is not clear whether such pigments at this time were used intentionally to make either decorative or symbolic marks, discoveries have been made of such activity dating around 77,000 years ago (Henshilwood et al., 2001; Spivey, 2005). The earliest forms of representational pictures we have remaining today are cave paintings that are dated from 40,000 to 35,000 years ago (Spivey, 2005).

One might imagine these early paintings to display very simplistic representational forms, revealing a skill similar to a young child's drawing nowadays whose pictures have begun to develop from scribbles to marks and shapes from which we can recognize something from life. We might also think that if we looked at how art has developed since these early cave paintings that it would portray a gradual progression in representational skill not dissimilar to that typically observed in the development of drawing throughout childhood. In fact, such a view was suggested and discussed widely at the turn of the 20th century,[1] and encouraged a belief that by studying child art we can gain an insight into the development of art among our ancestors. But commentators of cave art such as Bahn (1996) and Clottes (1996), as well as experts in the field of child art such as Golomb (2002) and Cox (2005), have argued persuasively against this view. Cave paintings that have been discovered do not show a linear progression towards realism over the time periods they have been dated. Instead, similar pictorial conventions reappear across different historic periods. The recent expressionist movement in art, with its focus on the communication of moods and ideas rather than visual realism, further attests to the nonlinear progression of artistic styles in art history. Nor do many of the early cave paintings that have been discovered suggest our ancestral artists were struggling with representational techniques, as we can see from a cave painting of a "lion panel" found in Chauvet, France, dated around 32,000–30,000 BC (see Plate 1). When one considers the remarkable visual likeness of the lions' faces, and also other animal cave paintings that were commonly painted around this time, we can only stare in wonder at the representational skills of our ancestors. For comparison purposes see three 4- to 5-year-olds' pictures of lions I recently collected (see bottom of Plate 1). Although delightful, their representational skills have some way to go before they can compare with our ancestral artist.

Despite a close connection between developments in child and primitive art being largely unfounded,[2] this debate around the turn of the 20th century did help to elevate child art to a wider audience. And this was long overdue. Considering that the historical engagement in picture making of one sort or another is unlikely to have been restricted to only adults, and that children surely would have been participants too, it is surprising how late an interest in children's picture making began. So when did adults begin to take child art seriously and for what further reasons?

Early Interest in Child Art

The study of child art came from two disparate sources. First, from the Romantic artists in the late 18th and early 19th centuries, and second, the scientists of the late 19th century. Fineberg (1997, 1998; see also Golomb, 2002) notes that artists in the Romantic tradition marveled in delight at the apparent simplicity and innocence of how children's drawings appeared. The Romantic artists rejected the previously learned conventions of making pictures look like copies of reality, valuing instead inventiveness and expressive creativity that appeared to be embodied in the drawings of young children in particular. Such children's drawings seemed to be uncorrupted by representational conventions, and were considered to reflect a direct access to the expressive creativity the Romantic artists strove for. This artistic appreciation of children's drawings received a new impetus around the turn of the 20th century with the growth of the modernist movement in art. The modernist approach also rejected the prevailing practice at the time of using pictorial conventions that captured the objective nature of reality, in favor of using formal properties such as line, color and composition for expressive and creative purposes. During the 20th century some of these modernist artists even studied and collected children's drawings in order to draw inspiration for their own art, and this can be seen clearly in the artistic works of Dubuffet, Kandinsky, Klee, Miró, and Picasso, among others (see Fineberg, 1997).

The later scientific interest in children's drawings needs to be seen in the context of a growing awareness of studying origins and change in the second half of the 19th century, an awareness that was very much stimulated by Darwin's theory of evolution (Darwin, 1859). This interest led some to keep diaries of babies and infants, noting key developmental changes that were observed, such as can be found in Darwin's longitudinal study of his own son (Darwin, 1877). By the turn of the 20th century there were a number of baby biographies, articles and child development books that included a commentary on children's drawings (e.g., see Barnes, 1893; Clark, 1897; Lukens, 1896; Maitland, 1895; Major, 1906; Perez, 1888; Ricci, 1887). A typical approach was to describe stage and age progressions in the different forms of representation observed in the drawings, and in some instances to relate representational changes to the mental development of the child. In some notable cases the researchers gathered a massive collection of drawings. For example, Kerschensteiner (1905) collected around 200,000 drawings made by around 6,800 German school children. Interestingly, Kerschensteiner was initially hampered in this monumental task by many of the teachers doing the drawings themselves![3]

The artistic and scientific interests in children's drawings differed in the standards by which the child art was evaluated (Golomb, 2002). While artists appreciated the freedom of young children's drawings from visual realism conventions, the scientific approach in effect measured these same drawings by the adult standard of visual realism. Put another way, the artists were inspired by the *expression* of the children's drawings while the scientists analyzed the *representation* of realism in the drawings. In the next chapter I shall focus on the expressive aspects of children's drawings, but in this chapter I discuss the development of children's representational drawing. To set us on our way I first introduce you to what I consider are the two main (macro-developmental) theories of children's representational drawings, that of Luquet (1927/2001) and Willats (2005), which although differing in a number of respects I shall argue are complementary.

Luquet's (1927/2001) Theory of Drawing Development

There are a number of reasons why examining the ideas of Georges-Henri Luquet (1927/2001) in some detail is justified. First, Luquet's ideas have had a widespread and significant influence on many of the subsequent researchers in this area (e.g., see Costall, 1995, 1997; Cox, 1992; Freeman, 1972, 1980; Golomb, 2002, 2004; Light & Barnes, 1995; Milbrath, 1998; Thomas & Silk, 1990; Willats, 1997, 2005). Second, despite being written some 80 years ago the first English translation of his main publication has only relatively recently become available (Luquet, 2001), thanks to the translation by Alan Costall. This not only allows a restatement of Luquet's ideas to a wider audience, but also provides this audience with a complete and definitive account of what Luquet actually said rather than having to rely on second- or multi-hand fragments in the literature that have sometimes been plagued with misunderstandings of some aspects of the theory. Third, and most importantly, Luquet's account provides us with a very useful introduction to the development of children's representational drawing.

Children's first experience of drawing is scribbling, or as Luquet calls it, trace making. Luquet claims that although very young children know that pictures can represent life they do not think initially that they can draw representations. They believe that they are making a creation when they scribble, and that is sufficient for their enjoyment. What then happens is that the child begins to notice a vague resemblance between some marks they have made and something from our world (Luquet called this experience "fortuitous realism"). For Luquet, once the child believes they can represent life then this belief will characterize their subsequent drawing development. Indeed, Luquet opens his chapter on "Realism" by saying, "nothing describes children's drawing in general better than the term realism" (Luquet, 2001, p. 77).[4] Our initial reaction to this assertion might be incredulity, as even drawings made by older children look far removed from how three-dimensional subject matter actually looks in reality. But Luquet argues that children's drawings develop through different types of realism, only the last of which is visual realism (which he recognizes only relatively few children succeed in producing anyway). I shall now describe Luquet's four types of realism which children progress through.

(i)   Fortuitous realism

As described above the child (fortuitously) notices a similarity between a mark or marks (which will look like scribbles to the adult eye)

Figure 1.1   An example of Luquet's fortuitous realism: a "bird" drawing made by a girl (aged 2¹/₂ years). Upon noticing a similarity between her scribble and a bird she then added two vertical lines for legs.

with something from life, such as a bird. Luquet refers to an Italian girl aged 2 years 6 months who upon noticing a similarity between her scribble and a bird then added two vertical lines for legs (see Figure 1.1). The child is therefore making a (post-hoc) realistic inter-pretation of her drawing that she had not intended when setting out to make the drawing. Luquet argues that in such cases the child will continue to happily scribble in subsequent drawings without having an a priori representational intention, but will increasingly notice such fortuitous similarities over time. There is no sudden shift to the child becoming an intentional realist. Rather, the growing willingness of the child to accept their "accidental" marks as representational leads the child to more frequently *start* a drawing with a representational intention. As adults we may still have difficulty in seeing the visual likeness referred to in the interpretations made by the child. For the child, however, they are gaining confidence in their ability to repre-sent reality.

(ii)   Failed realism

As the child becomes a more consistent intentional realist their draw-ings become characteristic of failed realism. Although their draw-ings now begin to take on a representational quality that adults can more easily recognize, there are a number of motor, cognitive and graphic obstacles the child is struggling to overcome. These lead to a number of "errors" in the drawing. Because the child is still trying to gain control over the motor movements of the hand as well as the drawing tool there can be a faulty use of line. A lack of attention

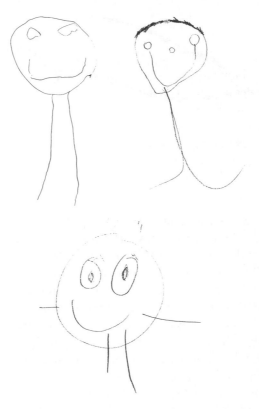

Figure 1.2   Three children's "tadpole" drawings of the human figure representing examples of Luquet's failed realism.

leads to only some of the details the child is thinking of to be included. Those details that are included may show technical graphic problems of poor position, orientation, and proportion. Furthermore, as the child's attention is concentrated on the detail currently being drawn there are apparent imperfections in the relations between the details. The "tadpole" form of the human figure (see Figure 1.2) is a good example of Luquet's failed realism. Although representational, a crucial element (the body) appears to be missing, and in some tadpole drawings the arms are omitted as well. Those parts that are drawn are aligned inappropriately (e.g., the arms and legs appear to be drawn from the head). Luquet used the term synthetic incapacity to characterize the lack of relations between the individual elements of the drawn topic.

With improvements in the child's attention the child is more able to consider other elements in the drawing rather than just the feature currently being drawn. This allows the child to remember to include more details and to draw them within more appropriate spatial relationships. It is through a gradual process that the number of elements of a topic increases (while synthetic incapacity diminishes), leading to the child's drawings becoming more characteristic of the next type of realism, that of intellectual realism.

(iii) Intellectual realism

The child's idea of realism is now to produce as many of the essential items of a topic (from the child's wider knowledge of all the details pertaining to the topic), and to represent each item in its characteristic shape. In the case of the human figure the body is now included, and over time an increasing number of further details appear (see Figure 1.3 for examples). The child is also more adept in synthesizing the parts. In the conventional human figure, for example, the arms and legs now extend from the body. As the child becomes more able to hold in mind the features he or she considers important to the topic, and in relating the parts synthetically, an increasing number of details are depicted. Clothing, for example, may be added to their human figure drawings.

Intellectual realism is not just characterized by an advance in detail and spatial arrangement, but also by the child's desires to draw the details in their usual, generic shape (described as "exemplarity" by Luquet). As we look at subject matter from life the shapes of its constituent parts change as we move around it (or because it moves). From some views certain parts will appear to us partially or even be totally occluded. But Luquet argues that children who draw in the graphic system of intellectual realism do not want to draw parts in atypical shapes, let alone leave them out altogether. Instead, they use various techniques to ensure that as many features as possible are shown and in their entire shape. These techniques include separation of the details, transparency, drawing some features from an air-view plan, and folding out certain parts of the topic (such as rooms in a

Figure 1.3   Examples of children's drawings of the conventional form of the human figure.

house or multiple sides of a cube). The use of these techniques (see Figure 1.4 for examples) often results in an "impossible" drawing, one in which the object or scene is drawn from a number of mixed perspectives. But according to Luquet, children are not drawing from a visual model (i.e. trying to capture how the topic looks from one particular angle) but from their internal model of the topic. This internal model is represented by the features the child regards as important or criterial for that topic (i.e. those they consider define that topic) and in their characteristic shape. Over time the child's internal model changes to include even more features.

Examples of intellectual realism are not only found in children's spontaneous drawings but can also be induced in experimental studies. As part of my undergraduate project that was supervised

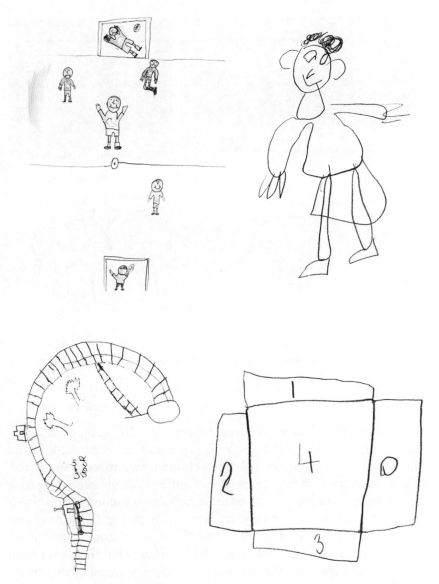

Figure 1.4 Drawings showing the use of separation of details (top left), transparency (top right), air-view plan (bottom left) and folding-out technique (bottom right) typical of Luquet's intellectual realism.

Figure 1.5   Seven-year-old girl's drawing of a "man-in-a-boat" and "man-on-a-horse" showing multi-perspective views and transparency, produced while viewing three-dimensional models (pictures of models shown above).

by Maureen Cox I asked children to draw a man riding on a horse and a man in a boat (Jolley, 1991; see also Cox, 1992, 2005). In one part of the experiment I showed children two three-dimensional models depicting these scenes (see Figure 1.5). In each case the model was presented so parts of the man were occluded by the horse and boat from the child's view, specifically, both legs in the "man in the boat" and the furthest leg in the "man on a horse". In Figure 1.5 we can see two drawings made by a girl approaching 7 years of age that are typical of the intellectual realism system. In the "man on a horse" drawing we see a side-on (profile) view of the horse but a frontal view of the rider. The child has used transparency so that no part of the horse or man is occluded by the other, and crucially both of the man's legs are depicted. Why does the child draw the horse in profile? The simple answer – that the child felt bound to reflect the same view as she saw of the model horse – will not do because she was willing to change from her profile view of the rider to draw him in frontal view. The child stays with the profile view of the horse because it is the best one to depict the optimum number of the features that define a horse, while a frontal view would result in features being distorted or omitted. In the "man in a boat" drawing the girl appears to have drawn the main body of the boat from air-view, with the funnel drawn in a side-on view. The man has been drawn with all the criterial features shown, including his legs, and separated from the lines of the boat. The use of these graphic techniques has allowed this child to show both the main features of the boat and man in their entirety. Thus, both drawings honor the child's knowledge of the main features of the topics and their characteristic shapes. In other words, the girl's internal model (or mental image as it is sometimes called) dictated how each scene was drawn, not what the girl could actually see from her view of the models. It may now be apparent to you that this stage is called intellectual realism because the child is drawing from what he or she *knows* about a topic not from what he or she *sees* from one viewpoint.

Luquet argues that children during the intellectual realism stage eventually become aware that although their drawings show the criterial features of topics in their full and complete shape, their representations are not good depictions of how they are often seen in reality. That is, they do not look visually realistic. This begins to bother children, which leads them to attempt to draw in a more visually realistic style.

(iv) Visual realism

Luquet argues that the development of the child's attentional capacities makes him or her aware that their mode of depiction (intellectual realism) is not representative of how things are seen in reality. Children begin to notice that the relations between elements change as we move our viewpoint of the subject matter. This leads to a dropping of separation, transparency, plan, and folding-out techniques, and instead they begin to get to grips with the graphic techniques of visual realism that include occlusion, suppression of details, and perspective (see Figure 1.6). The child now attempts to select only those details and how they are seen from one visual perspective for their

Figure 1.6 Drawings showing the use of visual realism techniques typical of Luquet's visual realism.

drawing. In essence, they are attempting to draw visual models (even if they do not have a physical model in front of them) rather than internal models. A related development is the drawing of particular examples of a topic rather than a generic version. Human figure representations, for example, begin to look like a particular individual rather than a generic example of a person (see Figure 1.6 for a very good likeness of Eric Cantona, the former French and Manchester United footballer).

Although children ultimately enter the stage of visual realism Luquet argues that this stage is more a stage of intention rather than achievement. The laws of perspective are as much a convention that has to be learned as the conventions of intellectual realism, and few children succeed in becoming very successful in acquiring the visual realism conventions. As Luquet points out, even many adults fail to draw in a visually realistic style. Luquet notes that many children stop drawing between 10 and 12 years of age (and this is still evident today), and that it is easy to find adult drawings similar to those produced by 12-year-olds and even those that use the intellectual realism system.

Evaluation of Luquet's Stage Theory

The popularization and incorporation of Luquet's "stage" account by Jean Piaget into his own stage account of children's thinking (Piaget & Inhelder, 1956, 1969) led initially to an assumption that Luquet conceived that children moved through his four forms of realism in qualitatively distinct stages. One criterion of traditional stage theory, at least as it is understood in psychology (e.g., see Flavell, 1963), is that children are "fixed" in a stage until some point whereupon they rapidly lose the characteristics of that stage in favor of the characteristics of the next stage. Consequently, a multitude of studies surfaced during the 1970s and 1980s testing whether children's drawings were fixed in a stage, or alternatively, whether children could easily be persuaded through simple contextual manipulations of drawing tasks and instructions to draw features that exemplified a higher stage (for reviews, see Cox, 1991, 1992; Freeman & Cox, 1985; Light & Barnes, 1995; Thomas & Silk, 1990). Much of the focus of this research was on the intellectual realism stage. Studies typically presented objects to children in a perspective whereby an important feature of a topic was partially or fully occluded (e.g., a cup with its handle hidden) or with one object behind another so that part of the behind object was hidden (e.g. two balls whereby only the top part of the "behind" ball could be seen). Early studies showed that children around the age of 5 to 7 years would, for example, include the "hidden" handle in their cup drawing and draw both balls in their entirety, providing evidence that children around this age do draw in an intellectually realistic style (Cox, 1978; Freeman & Janikoun, 1972). Researchers then asked whether children who typically drew intellectually realistic drawings in such experiments could be encouraged to draw in a more visually realistic style. An increasing body of research showed that such children could omit an occluded feature under certain contextual conditions (e.g., see Arrowsmith, Cox, & Eames, 1994; Bremner & Moore, 1984; Cox, 1981; Davis, 1983; Lewis, Russell, & Berridge, 1993). These conditions included asking the child to draw only what they could see of the model, not naming the identity of the model, preventing the child from touching the model, and presenting an occlusion scene that made more sense to the child (e.g., a robber partially hidden behind a wall). As children could be induced easily to draw different types of representations of a topic through simple experimental manipulations researchers rightly concluded that children's drawings do not develop in stages.

Costall's English translation of Luquet's original French text (and his introduction to it) confirmed what many had already begun to realize that there had been important misconceptions of Luquet's ideas in some parts of this historic literature.[5] By reading Costall's translation of Luquet's 1927 book (Luquet, 2001) it is easy to see that Luquet had never intended for his account to be a stage theory (although he does use the word "stage"). Luquet was at pains to point out that the transition between "stages" is gradual, frequently commentating that representations typical of a previous stage are still seen when the child adopts a mode of representation characteristic of the next stage. Furthermore, Luquet did not accept that visual realism was an advance on intellectual realism.[6] In his mind they were merely different systems of representation each having their own advantages and disadvantages.

If one reads Luquet's account without the prejudiced trappings of a stage theory one finds a number of gems. As I mention in my review of his book (Jolley, 2004), Luquet's opening chapter on intention represents a wealth of ideas on why children draw, an issue that is often strangely neglected by those working in this field. The second chapter on interpretation emphasizes how children's graphic mistakes can cue ideas for new topics to develop, which puts a more positive slant on how their production difficulties are normally considered. The third chapter on type has many ideas that reflect contemporary debates. For instance, Luquet's views on the conservative nature of children's repeated drawings (showing resistance to change) as relating to preference and habit, indicate an alternative position to the recent theory of representational redescription (RR) which states that such drawings occur due to an underlying cognitive constraint of not having explicit access to the elements of a topic (see this book, chapter 6). In the graphic narration chapter Luquet discusses the different techniques children use in showing action in their drawings, and could form a useful basis to a developmental account of children's representations of dynamic events.

It is important to recognize that Luquet's account was derived from the "monographic study" approach in which he directly observed the child creating their drawing, while listening to the child's comments. He was interested in studying the drawings children initiated for themselves, rather than drawings created on request as is typical of experimental studies. In that sense his account refers to children's *natural* drawing development. As Costall (2001) notes, Luquet was so serious about children's drawing development that he observed the development as it naturally occurred. For that reason alone any reader serious about understanding the development of children's representational drawing development would do well to begin their study with Luquet.

You can find descriptions of the graphic changes found in children's drawings in the many subsequent books on this topic (e.g., see Cox, 1992, 2005; Gardner, 1980; Golomb, 2002, 2004; Thomas & Silk, 1990; Winner, 1982). Although many of these descriptions are intended to provide only an overview of children's drawing development, rather than a formal theoretical account in the sense that Luquet proposed, they are consistent with the graphic changes Luquet described. That is, researchers agree that children's drawings initially develop from a period of scribbling to representations that become increasingly lifelike. This gradual progression is served by the use and improvement in detail, spatial alignment, proportion, depth, partial occlusion and on occasions even perspective. As in Luquet's account, this literature also discusses the psychological processes (e.g., cognitive, motor, spatial understanding) that shape these graphic changes (summarized later in this chapter). A notable and alternative approach in which the primary focus is on the graphic changes themselves can be seen in the work of John Willats (1977, 1985, 1987, 1992a, 1992b, 1995, 1997, 2005), which I shall turn to now.

Willats' Representational Drawing Systems

John Willats was educated in mechanical sciences and psychology, and until his recent death was a practicing artist with an interest in projective geometry. In work spanning across four decades he has set about analyzing the different drawing systems used in a wide variety of pictures that are created by artists, engineers, photographers, mapmakers, as well as by children. Although his theory is therefore a general theory of picture perception, part of his work has been devoted to children's drawings, and he recently dedicated a whole book on the subject (Willats, 2005). Willats argues that because children's drawings are often studied by developmental psychologists, their developmental accounts are influenced by their analysis of the child's mental processes involved in drawing. In reference to Luquet's account, for instance, he states that children drawing what they know rather than what they see is a way of describing the child's mental state not of the drawings themselves (Willats, 1997, 2005). Willats considers that mental processes can only be inferred from the picture, and that the validity of such interpretations cannot be attained without first gaining an accurate description of the developmental representational systems that children use.

Nevertheless, Willats was in agreement with Luquet in his view that children intend their drawings to represent realism, "what children look for in their drawings is realism, and what they want to produce are what I have called 'effective representations'" (Willats, 2005, p. 18). Over a series of publications Willats' aim, therefore, has been to describe the different drawing systems that children use to make effective representations of topics and scenes from life. In his experimental studies he has asked children of different ages to draw tables and unfamiliar rectangular objects. From the drawings Willats has formulated a developmental progression of drawing systems that represent different ways in which the spatial relationships in the real-world scene are mapped on to the spatial relationships of the lines in the picture. By interpreting the drawings Willats has derived five drawing systems that can be summarized as follows:

1 Topology
2 Orthogonal projection
3 Horizontal and vertical oblique projections
4 Oblique projection
5 Perspective

It is easier to understand these drawing systems of spatial relationships if we look at Figure 1.7 taken from one of Willats' earlier studies (Willats, 1977) in which 5- to 17-year-olds were asked to draw a table (with a variety of objects on it) from a fixed vantage point. Drawing (a) displays what the children saw, whereas drawings (b) to (g) represent children's drawings of the table and contents that corresponded to Willats' five drawing systems. In his commentary on the different drawing solutions the children came up with, Willats (2005) stated that drawing (b) is an example of a topological system in which the spatial relations between the objects on the table and the table itself are incoherent. The rest of the drawings reflected different (projective) drawing systems of displaying the front-to-back spatial relations of the scene. Drawing (c) is of orthogonal projection where the front-to-back relations are ignored (e.g., notice that only the front edge of the table is shown). The depth of the table in drawing (d) is shown by up-and-down lines typical of vertical oblique projection (in horizontal oblique projection depth is shown by side-to-side lines). But this results in the picture looking "flat" because one direction on the picture has been used to represent two different directions in the three-dimensional scene. This problem is solved in drawing (e), Willats notes, by using a more complex rule where the front-to-back sides are shown by oblique lines (oblique projection). Nevertheless, Willats argues, such drawings did not correspond to the view that the children actually saw of the scene. This is achieved by drawing both sides with converging lines. In drawing (f), called "naive" perspective by Willats, is an example of this, whereas drawing (g), Willats argues, is more or less true perspective because the converging lines lead to a suitable "vanishing point." As the children's drawings fell into these categories according to an age-related sequence Willats argued that children's drawings developed through these drawing systems.

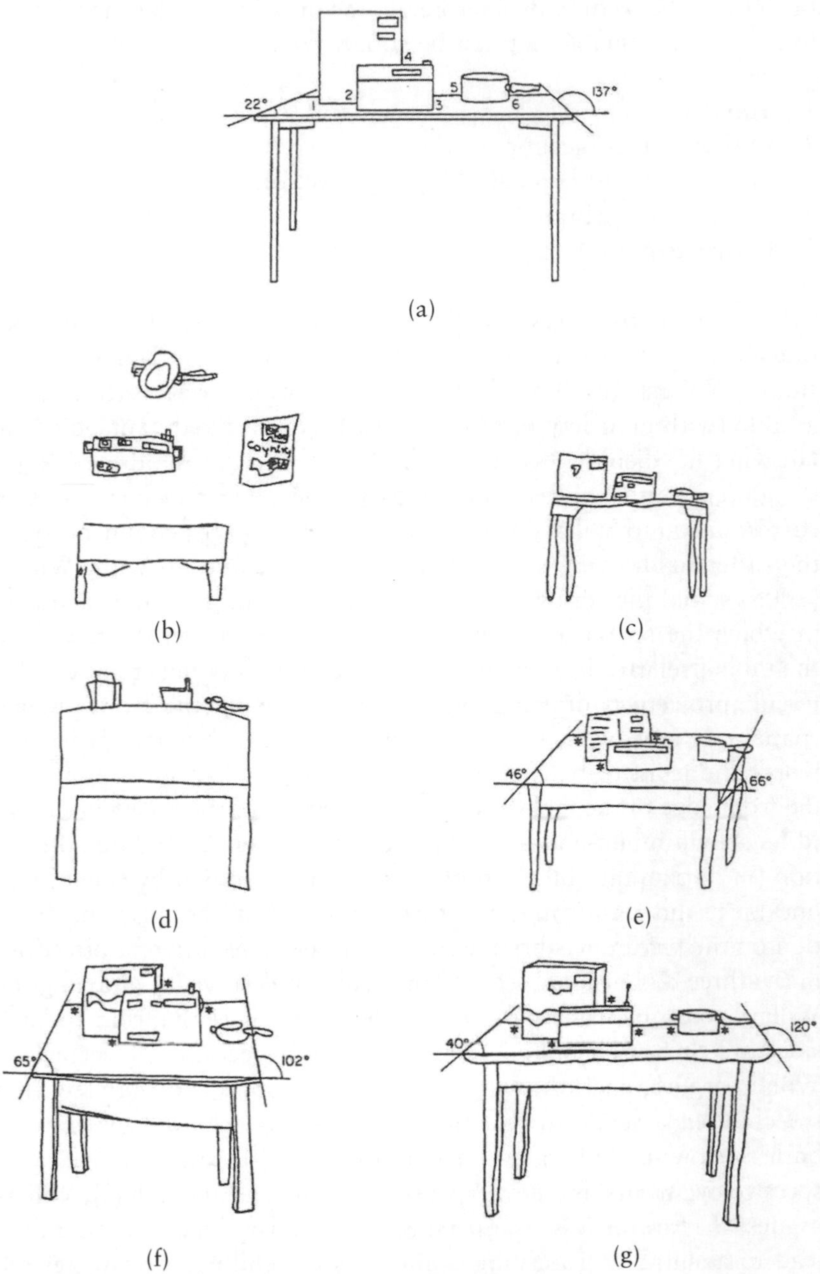

Figure 1.7   Children's drawings of a table depicting Willats' drawing systems: (a) the child's view of the table, (b) topological system, (c) orthogonal projection, (d) vertical oblique projection, (e) oblique projection, (f) naive perspective, (g) perspective.

While these drawing systems have extended our knowledge of the different ways children use line to represent spatial relationships, Willats (2005) notes that the systems are not adequate on their own in informing the viewer about what each line represents. Consequently, Willats has proposed and developed over the years an additional representational system, called denotational systems, in which lines denote the volumes, surfaces and edges of the topics drawn. Children's early representational drawings, according to Willats (2005), show enclosed two-dimensional shapes called regions that denote the volume of the topic, and accordingly are *not* the contours or edges of the drawn feature. In the case of a young child's drawing of a cube or a house that shows a singular circular or square shape, Willats argues this region represents the whole cube or house, and not the contours of their frontal face.[7] According to this analysis Willats speculates that in the tadpole form of the human figure (an early developmental representation of a person) the single enclosed area is a region probably intended by the young child to denote the volume of the whole (three-dimensional) head. Willats refers to the term extendedness to describe how the shapes in the drawing can be extended to reflect the relative dimensions of the elements in the real scene that the picture depicts. Specifically, Willats notes that young children use round regions for round volumes (e.g., heads) and long regions for long volumes (e.g., arms and legs). But of course most things in life are not purely round or long. In order to make more effective representations Willats argues that children further develop their drawings by varying the extent to which the shapes they employ are round and long, and also apply "shape modifiers" to these round and long regions. To cite two examples that Willats (2005) gives, a child may extend the body of her drawing of a horse longer than the legs to show this distinction in relative "longness" that is evident in the body and legs of horses. Further, a child will often modify their earlier "roundish" shaped enclosed area denoting a house to have straight sides. Willats comments on a range of other shape modifiers (e.g., corners, pointed line, bends in a line, dents, bumps, etc.) that children learn to use to make their denotations more effective representations of the features found in the three-dimensional scene.[8]

According to Willats, the developmental path of children's representational drawing temporarily diverges for topics that have flat faces with well-defined edges (e.g., houses) to those that have smooth and curved surfaces (e.g., people, animals, balls, fruit, etc.). For topics that have flat faces the child now attempts to draw some of the faces of the object (rather than just one enclosed shape standing for the object's volume). In the case of drawing a house, for example, the child may attempt to draw the faces of the house (rather than its volume), either in their true shapes or something approximating to them. The trouble with this approach, as Willats (2005) notes, is that it is difficult to make the faces of rectangular objects like houses join up properly, particularly if they have each been drawn in their true shape. Accordingly, such drawings give an impression of a fold-out drawing that is produced from a number of view-points (e.g., see the cube drawing in Figure 1.4).[9] Only with the use of more advanced drawing systems (such as perspective) and the acquisition of line junctions ("L," "Y," "arrow," and "T" – examples of which can be seen in Figure 1.6)[10] do the lines in children's representational drawings begin to denote the edges and contours of the objects drawn from a view (and not regions for the faces of a topic drawn each in their true shape).

The drawing of smooth and curved objects presents even more of a problem for children. Willats (2005) defines these objects in a strict sense as varying smoothly in three dimensions, without edges, creases or other abrupt abnormalities. Willats discusses how the representation of such objects is a particularly difficult graphic problem to surmount. Consequently, he argues that when children move from drawing the volumes of flat objects to the faces of such objects (as described above), they continue to use round and long regions (with varying extensions) to denote the volumes of smooth objects. But with the use of threading and further shape modifiers in their drawings of smooth and curved objects the child's use of line begins to denote regions in the visual field (i.e. the shapes of the elements in the scene from an actual view). In the case of threading (a term often attributed to Goodnow, 1977), for example, continuous outlines are used to join elements of a scene, rather than using lines for separate regions for each element. This developmental shift is most clearly displayed in the change one observes in children's human figure drawings. For instance, compare the segmented figures shown in Figure 1.3 (particularly the two top figures and bottom-left figure) with the threading of the arms to the upper body in the human figure drawing shown in Figure 1.6. Furthermore, Willats (2005) argues that children also start to use T and end-junctions in their drawings of smooth objects to illustrate points of occlusion and where contours end respectively. When the divergent paths for denoting flat and smooth surfaces come together Willats argues that the lines in the child's drawings are no longer denoting regions for volumes but true views of scenes.[11]

To summarize, the denotation system informs us about what the lines stand for (e.g., volumes or contours) while the drawing systems explain the spatial arrangement of the parts drawn. Willats not only encourages us to analyze each drawing in terms of the drawing and denotation systems but also to see the developmental connections between the two. For instance, regions denoting volumes is often accompanied by the simplest spatial arrangement, such as non-overlapping elements, that is characteristic of the topological drawing system. Similarly, drawings showing lines as contours and junctions are likely to show some evidence of a more advanced projective drawing system. For instance, the partial occlusion seen in a perspective drawing system is aided by the lines being used as contours and junctions between elements, giving an overall impression of a more view-specific drawing.

In Willats' lifelong work he has attempted to understand the "rules" of drawing in the same way as linguists (notably Chomsky) had previously set out to describe the rules of understanding language. Willats (2005) made a tentative comparison of his drawing and denotations systems with syntax and vocabulary respectively in language, and that shape modifiers served a similar purpose in drawing as adjectives do in language.

Evaluation of Willats' Representational Systems

Willats' drawing systems provide a more comprehensive and detailed graphic description of the variety of spatial relationships children use in their drawings than is available in Luquet's account. While he acknowledged Luquet's intellectual and visual realism styles of drawing, Willats' own drawing systems unpack the dichotomy of intellectual and visual realism. For instance, whereas topology can be associated with intellectual realism, the projective systems (orthogonal, oblique, and perspective) give more information on the developmental systems children move through between the extremes of intellectual and visual realism. Willats' approach of not being driven by the division of the mental processes from "draw what they know" to "draw what they see," but focusing instead on the drawings themselves, has allowed him to provide a more formal scheme for classifying drawings. Consequently, his account helps us to appreciate the variety of drawing systems children create as they get to grips with representing objects and scenes from nature. More generally, his thorough approach of analyzing the meaning and grammar of line before considering the psychological processes is innovative and largely absent in the previous literature on children's drawings. His account therefore acts as a timely reminder that we should not get carried away with making psychological interpretations to a drawing and its creator without understanding first what the lines represent and their spatial relationship.

Nevertheless, there are limitations to Willats' account. Because it is a relatively novel approach to studying children's drawings it needs further development. In respect of his drawing systems the experimental evidence that Willats provides is restricted to scenes and objects that are rarely found in children's drawings (e.g., tables, cubes, etc.). Studies into how well these systems of spatial relationships can apply to the drawings children spontaneously produce are needed to verify and extend Willats' drawing systems. Conducting such an analysis into the more natural drawings children produce, rather than collecting drawings of a single scene or object, may be less straightforward. For instance, some drawings no doubt display more than one projective system. Even in Willats' own studies his categorization of children's drawings of rectangular objects into different projective systems partly relied on his somewhat arbitrary coding of the angles of the lines (see Willats, 1977), which reminds us that even using systematic coding does not eradicate the subjective nature of interpreting children's drawings.

Although Willats' denotation systems are a vital supplement to the drawing systems, merely looking at a child's drawing will not always tell us unambiguously what the lines stand for. This is particularly relevant to the question of whether a single enclosed area denotes a three-dimensional volume or a two-dimensional contour of a surface (i.e. potentially a view). For instance, it is not usually possible to tell from looking at a tadpole drawing of a person whether the child intended the single enclosed outline to represent the entire volume of the head or the contours of the two-dimensional surface of the face. Similar problems are evident in interpreting a single enclosed line for a house. Willats acknowledged this problem, and presented some experimental findings that appear to indicate a developmental shift from children using line to denote volume and later line for contours of two-dimensional regions (see Willats, 2005). But unless you do further probing of the child, either through discussion or further experimentation, the interpretation as to what the lines stands for in some instances is left to speculation. For instance, Willats' (2005) opinion that children's early stereotyped drawings of houses with the windows attached to the lines of the house are indicative of the child intending the drawing to represent the whole volume of the house is definitely speculative, and requires further investigation. Perhaps because of Willats' approach to remove the psychology of the child from his or her drawing has given him at times too much freedom of interpretation of the lines. One must always be careful in becoming too exuberant in applying meaning to every aspect of a child's drawing. Willats acknowledged that some marks in children's representational drawings are accidental (see Willats, 2005, p. 122), and this should remind us that, particularly in young children's drawings, some marks just happen and are not meant to denote anything in particular let alone spatial relationships. To press this point further, perhaps some tadpole drawers do not give much thought about whether the enclosed region denotes the whole head or just the face?

By only recently giving some serious attention to the engagement of the child's mental processes in his or her drawing (Willats presented two chapters on this topic in his 2005 book) Willats' writings over the years on children's representational (drawing and denotation) systems ran the risk of appearing somewhat "dry" and bereft of context. Luquet's constant attention to the psychology of the child as it impacts upon drawing development gives his account a psychological richness that is lacking in Willats' representational systems. But Willats' account provides more information than Luquet's account on what the lines in a drawing stand for and in what spatial relationship. In this sense, therefore, Willats' and Luquet's theories complement each other, as each goes some way in providing what the other is lacking.

These two theories are relatively rare examples in the literature on children's drawings in that they attempt to provide a detailed analysis and holistic framework for understanding the developmental pattern of children's representational drawing. Most researchers, on the other hand, examine more specific micro-developmental changes in children's drawings and/or emphasize particular psychological influences on drawing and its development. In the next section I shall provide a brief overview of this approach.

Micro-developmental Accounts of Children's Drawing

Some questions have been directed to a particular developmental oint in children's drawings. For example, there is an ongoing discussion on developmental changes within the scribbling period. Some key questions are whether children intend their scribbles to be representational, what provides the child with insight that he or she can draw representationally, and what marks and forms children adopt from their scribbling period to make recognizable representations (e.g., see Adi-Japha, Levin, & Solomon, 1998; Callaghan, 1999; Cox, 2005; Golomb, 1981, 2004; Kellogg, 1970; Mathews, 1984, 1999; Yamagata, 1997). Luquet (1927/2001) considered trace-making (scribbling) to be activated by imitating adults' drawing (although he thought young children would do it anyway without adult models), and driven by the child's pleasure of their own creative power. For Luquet, children who scribble know that pictures can be representational, but they do not initially consider that they too can draw representationally. For Luquet it is through a gradual process of noticing vague resemblances of their marks to something from our world (fortuitous realism) which encourages the child to consider that he or she too can make representations.

Luquet's emphasis on the representational insight deriving from the child, however, neglects the role of representational suggestions coming from others. When a child presents an adult or an older child with their scribble they will often be asked, "What is it?" This no doubt sets up an expectation in the child that his or her drawing can be of something, rather than merely marks on the page. Adi-Japha et al. (1998) reported findings that confirmed the potential influence of adult questioning on scribblers' representational interpretations of their own drawings. They asked scribblers "What is this?" while pointing to the whole and parts of their drawing, as well as recording their spontaneous comments. Children tended to give representational meanings when the experimenter pointed to parts of the drawing rather than its whole. In particular, directing the child's attention to the angular curves induced representational interpretations from the scribblers, perhaps because angular curves give information to the contours of real objects. Furthermore, the frequency of such comments increased with age. However, these representational interpretations from the child occurred only after the drawing had been made, and usually in response to the interviewer's pointing rather than from the child's own spontaneous comments. Furthermore, such representational interpretations were not stable over time, as when presented with the same drawing a few weeks later the child was likely to attribute a different representational meaning to the angular curves. Nevertheless, these findings are consistent with Luquet's assertion that scribblers over time increasingly make post-hoc interpretations of representational meaning into their marks, and that the shift is gradual and interpretations flexible. But additionally they also suggest a potential role of the adult in provoking children to make representational interpretations into their scribbles.

The role of social interaction in the shift from scribbling to representational drawing was studied more extensively by Yamagata's (1997) longitudinal study in which she monitored the conversations between two mother-infant dyads on drawing activities. The interactions began when the infants were about 12 months old and continued for a further 18 months (the time of study covered therefore the period in which the children scribbled). Yamagata noticed that the infants from 12 to 15 months would regularly ask their mothers to draw for them, and by 18 months of age would suggest drawing themes to their mothers. After the mother had drawn these themes the child would add marks to their mother's drawings, and even draw particular parts of the topics by 22 months. Suggestions of drawing themes by the mother initially preceded those suggested by the child, but with older children the latter predominated over the former. One needs to be cautious in generalizing findings from such a small sample, but Yamagata's longitudinal study indicates the important role of social interaction in children's drawings becoming representational, and the developmental path in which this process may take place. The relative extent to which infants' representational interpretations of their scribbles derive from their own insights or are provoked by social interactions requires further research, but available data carries a consistent message that scribblers understand that marks on a page can refer to some wider reality (see chapter 5)

At the other end of drawing development there are investigations into children's acquisition of particular graphic techniques that allow a drawing to appear more visually realistic. These include integrating parts of a figure into a continuous contour (e.g., Fenson, 1985; Lange-Küttner, Kerzmann, & Heckhausen, 2002), depth and occlusion (Cox & Martin, 1988; Cox & Perara, 2001; Light & MacIntosh, 1980; Morra, Angi, & Tomat, 1996; Radkey & Enns, 1987), the use of spatial axes (Lange-Küttner, 2004), and the depiction of movement and action (Cox, Koyasu, Hiranuma, & Perara, 2001; Goodnow, 1977). A related discussion is to what extent children's drawings ever become truly visually realistic (Costall, 1995; Golomb, 2002; Luquet, 1997/2001; Thomas & Silk, 1990).

Another approach has been to describe the developmental pattern of drawing a particular topic, such as the human figure (e.g., Cox, 1993; Jolley, Knox, & Foster, 2000; Koppitz, 1968), houses (Barrouillet, Fayol, & Chevrot, 1994), cats (Richards & Ross, 1967), cubes, cylinders, sticks and disks (e.g., Bremner, Morse, Hughes, & Andreasen, 2000; Caron-Pargue, 1992; Cox, 1986; Deregowski & Strang, 1986; Freeman, 1986; Phillips, Hobbs, & Pratt, 1978; Toomela, 1999; Willats, 1992a, 1992b). In some cases researchers have taken an interest in a particular form of a topic typically drawn by children, such as the tadpole form of the human figure (e.g., see Arnheim, 1974; Cox, 1993; Cox & Mason, 1998; Freeman, 1975; Golomb, 2004; Willats, 1985, 2005). In the case of the tadpole form, theories for the apparent omission include the child having an incomplete internal model, having information processing constraints on attention and memory, having production difficulties, and that the single enclosed area represents both the head and body for the child.

Such theories remind us of another body of work that explains the many and varied factors involved in drawing and that bring about its developmental change. Some attempt has been made to relate theories of perception, most notably those proposed by Gibson and Marr, to intellectual and visual realism in drawing (Costall, 1995; Hodgson, 2002; Willats, 1987, 2005). There have been discussions on the nature of the internal model (Freeman, 1972; Cox, 1993; Golomb, 2002; Piaget & Inhelder, 1956). In chapter 6 we will look at a recent (representational redescription) theory that tries to explain children's developing flexibility in drawing in terms of an implicit to explicit shift in children's internal representations (see also Barlow, Jolley, White, & Galbraith, 2003; Karmiloff-Smith, 1990). Developmental changes in children's drawings have been related to other cognitive, conceptual and perceptual changes in the child, such as intelligence (e.g., Harris, 1963; Naglieri, 1988), symbolic understanding (Callaghan, 1999), a shift from to figurative to operative thought (Lange-Küttner & Reith, 1995; Milbrath, 1998), their understanding of space (Piaget & Inhelder, 1956, 1969) and visual attention to a scene (Reith & Dominin, 1997; Sutton & Rose, 1998). Factors involved in the process of drawing have been highlighted, particularly the information processing of attention, planning, monitoring, and memory (Freeman, 1972, 1980; Morra, 2002; Morra et al., 1996; Morra, Moizo, & Scopesi, 1988; Thomas, 1995). There are numerous papers on the graphic difficulties children need to overcome in translating three-dimensional subject matter onto a two-dimensional page (for reviews, see Cox, 1992, 2005). Children's metacognition of pictures, particularly their understanding of the developmental sequence in drawing and their preference for more advanced drawings than they produce themselves, may influence their own graphic development (Cox & Hodsoll, 2000; Jolley et al., 2000; see also chapter 4). A related debate is the extent to which children's drawings are influenced by children observing and getting ideas from other graphic models or inventing their own graphic schema (Arnheim, 1974; Golomb, 2002, 2004; Wilson & Wilson, 1977; see chapter 9).

One should also remember that drawing is an activity engaged in by not only typically developing children but also children from special populations with learning difficulties and deficits attributable to a clinical disorder. In chapter 3 we shall see that the study of such drawings raises some interesting questions, such as whether the drawing development from such children is similar but delayed to that found in the wider population, or shows signs of qualitative differences.

This is by no means an exhaustive review of all the lines of research into the graphic changes we see in children's representational drawings, but these factors remind us of the complexity of drawing and the multitude of psychological influences on it.

Summary

The early scientific interest in children's drawings around the turn of the 20th century focused on the developmental changes observed in the representations children made, and how the drawings may inform us in regard to the mental development of the child. Although another approach of identifying links between children's drawings and prehistoric art proved to be largely unfounded, it nonetheless contributed to raising the profile of studying children's drawings. Luquet's (1927/2001) account of drawing development has perhaps been the most influential during the 20th century and beyond in suggesting how children develop their drawings through various forms of realism, and how such changes are influenced by psychological changes in the child. Much of the subsequent research into more specific questions relating to representational changes in children's drawing, and the discovery of the many psychological factors that influence these changes, pays credit to Luquet's ideas either directly or indirectly. In work spanning four decades Willats has developed an alternative approach of studying children's drawings by analyzing what the lines in a child's drawing stands for and the spatial relationships that lie therein (Willats, 2005). Nevertheless, both Luquet and Willats were committed to the view that children's drawing activity is driven by the child's desire to make realistic representations of the world around them. Also, I have argued that the differences between the two accounts actually complement each other to provide us with a more complete and comprehensive framework for understanding the development of children's representational drawing. But Luquet's and Willats' allegiance to representational drawing in childhood neglected the clear *expressive* communication of moods, feelings and ideas found in children's art. It is children's expressive drawings that we now turn to in chapter 2.

Notes

1   This view was an example of the now discredited recapitulation theory (Haeckel, 1906) which argued that the physiology and mental growth observed from the embryonic period to adulthood repeats the evolutionary stages of forms and mental growth of the human race.

2   Although Cox (2005) agrees with this generally accepted view she does comment on some potentially interesting similarities between child and primitive art.

3   I am indebted to Robin Campbell's talk to the developmental section of the British Psychological Society on Kerschensteiner's work (Campbell, 2004).

4   Luquet distanced himself from the opposing views that children are idealists in their drawing (making nature more beautiful than it really is by adding additional features) or that their drawings are schematic (graphic inventions that "stand for" the topic referred to).

5   For earlier commentaries by Alan Costall alerting us that some key aspects of Luquet's ideas had been misinterpreted see Costall (1989, 1995, 1997; see also Cox, 1993).

6   A criterion of stage theory is that each subsequent stage is an advance on the previous stage.

7   This idea is very similar to Luquet's (1927/2001) assertion that children first draw lines to represent the whole of the topic (and only later unpack the parts).

8   Willats (2005) acknowledges that young children may initially use single extended lines for long volumes (as is the case of single lines for arms and legs) before using a long enclosed area. They also continue to use dots and patches of scribble that had been initially acquired while they were scribblers as they serve to make effective representations of certain elements (e.g., dots for eyes and a patch of scribble for hair).

9   Note that Luquet (1927/2001) also commented on fold-out drawings, although he saw it as one graphic technique of intellectual realism rather than an error (as Willats seems to conceive it).

10   Willats discusses lines as junctions as denoting corners and overlap. For example, an "L-shaped" junction is good for showing a corner while a "T-shaped" junction denotes where one foreground object meets a background object (the cross-bar of the "T" shows the foreground edge and the stem shows the edge of the rear surface; see also Kennedy, 1997, for his commentary on this).

11   Note the similarity with Luquet's stage of visual realism.

2

The Development of Expressive Drawing

Relative to the attention given to children's representational drawing, children's drawings as a means of communicating moods,
feelings and ideas in an esthetic sense has very much been an
under-researched area. This is despite the evidence of expressive techniques in children's drawings. This chapter discusses the
developmental pattern of children's expressive drawings; in
particular whether it progresses according to either a U-shape
curve or age-related increments, and how art values ingrained
in the rating criteria can influence how the drawings are evaluated. The chapter then goes on to present what evidence is
available on some of the abilities and skills that may be involved
in children making an expressive drawing.

Although the prevailing focus of the scientific research in the development of children's drawings has been on their representational communication (see chapter 1), the widespread intention in adult art is
to express moods, feelings, and ideas. Does this mean that children's
drawings are not expressive or that scientists, most notably academic
child psychologists studying children's drawings, are ignoring the
expressiveness of children's drawings? The former seems unlikely as
a number of artists' works have been likened to young children's
drawings, and that some artists acknowledge being influenced by children's drawings (see Fineberg, 1997, 1998). In a now famous quote,
Picasso said, "Once I drew like Raphael, but it has taken me a whole

lifetime to learn how to draw like children" (see Gardner, 1980, p. 141). Picasso's sentiments resonate with the earlier Romantic artists who saw in young children's drawings an expressive creativity that they desired to recapture in their own artwork. Consistent with these sentiments there has been a strong claim from some psychologists working in this area that the esthetic quality of young children's drawings in particular is comparable to that found in the drawings of adolescent and adult artists (Davis, 1997a; Gardner, 1980; Gardner & Winner, 1982; Rosenblatt & Winner, 1988; Winner, 1982).

You might be wondering what makes a drawing expressive, and isn't it down to the subjective opinion of the viewer anyway? I shall discuss at the end of this chapter how different art values may have influenced the reporting of diverse developmental patterns of children's expressive drawings in the literature. But first I want to consider the main graphic techniques that can make a drawing appear expressive, and then look at some individual children's drawings for evidence of these techniques.

Expressive Techniques

In essence there are three categories of expressive techniques: literal, content and abstract expression. In literal expression the mood/ emotion is shown by the depiction of the facial expression in people, or through personification if shown on animals, other living things, or inanimate objects. In content expression the artist is using subject matter from life to convey expressive meaning. For instance, a painting depicting a countryside scene on a summer's day with green, "rolling" hills and a "chocolate box" cottage may express a mood of serenity or peacefulness. Alternatively, a picture of a barren landscape on a cloudy and rainy day in winter may convey a depressing tone, while a thunder storm with fallen trees and wrecked buildings strewn across the ground could express anger or the force of nature. But without the appropriate use of what are called formal properties of the picture, such as line (its shape, thickness, direction, texture and shading), color and composition (the spatial arrangement of the elements on the page or canvass) much of the expressive potential of the chosen content would be lost. Of course, expressive formal properties can be shown in pictures independently of representational subject matter, in which case this is called abstract expression or more generally abstract art. For example, if we looked at a painting that displayed curved and uplifting lines, bright colors and a balanced composition we might interpret a positive mood from the painting. Both content and abstract expression are sometimes regarded as examples of metaphorical expression, either because they may be read on a similar basis to how we understand linguistic metaphors (e.g., see Kennedy, 1982; Thomas & Jolley, 1997) or simply to distinguish them from the directness of literal expression. Metaphorical expression is commonly considered an important esthetic property in pictures (see Goodman, 1976).

Do Children Use Expressive Techniques?

Very young children seem particularly adept at showing literal expression. In Figure 2.1 we see three drawings made by a 4-year-old when asked to draw a happy, sad, and angry picture. In each case the child has chosen to draw a person with a happy, sad, and angry face. In these drawings the mouth is doing much of the work to express the intended emotion (see also Buckalew & Bell, 1985). But what about children's use of other facial features to depict emotion? Both Golomb (1992) and Sayil (2001) compared primary school children's ability at using the mouth and eyebrows to convey basic emotions, and found more successful use of the mouth feature to express these emotions. Sayil (2001) also sought to discover the reason behind the mouth-bias effect by asking the children to copy pictures of happy, sad, angry, and surprised faces. Sayil found that children under 8 years of age had difficulty copying the oblique lines in the correct orientation to depict the eyebrows in their sad and angry pictures. The developmental delay in drawing expressive eyebrows may not only be due to children's difficulty with drawing this feature, but also may be a result of not understanding the expressive meaning of eyebrows (Sayil, 2001).

In respect of children's developing ability to draw facial features to signal different emotions Cox (2005) notes that happy is the most easily depicted, followed by sad, but the other four basic emotions (fear, anger, surprise and disgust) are poorly executed and seem not to follow a particular order of difficulty. Again, both a poor understanding

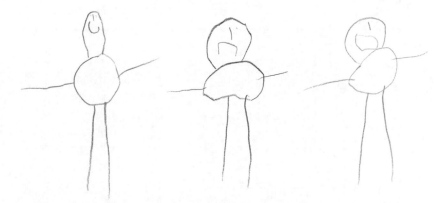

Figure 2.1   A 4-year-old's drawing of happy (left), sad (middle) and angry (right), showing the literal depiction of emotion.

of how facial features relevant to an emotion actually appear in its expression, and not having learned the pictorial conventions to display these features appropriately, are likely to contribute to children's difficulty in drawing these emotions.

Children's use of content expression is very much dependent on their developing repertoire of subject matter. In Figure 2.2 we see a 6-year-old's and a 12-year-old's drawing of a "happy" tree. In the 6-year-old's drawing we notice not only the literal (personified) depiction of a face on the tree but also that the tree appears to be in bloom by the use of a continuous curvy line for its foliage. This choice of the tree's season represents a simple example of content expression as it promotes a positive (metaphorical) mood of the tree. In the 12-year-old's tree drawing we see further examples of content expression that extend beyond the content of the tree, including the mood-appropriate use of weather, animals, fruit on the tree, and social activities.

Both "tree" pictures were drawn simply with a black pencil and hence have a limited range in their expressive formal properties, in contrast to the picture shown in Plate 2. When asked to draw a happy picture this 14-year-old girl has chosen mood-appropriate content of a countryside scene (hill and flowers), the (personified) sun and fluffy clouds, heart-shaped symbols, and two (smiling) people holding hands. But the positive mood is facilitated by the appropriate use of

Figure 2.2   A 6-year-old's (left) and 12-year-old's (right) drawing of a happy tree depicting a variety of expressive content themes.

formal properties (bright colors, balanced composition and curved lines) throughout the picture. In this drawing, therefore, the adolescent has used all three forms of expression: literal, content, and abstract.

Considering the ages of these child artists we may take the view that children in general become more sophisticated in their use of expressive techniques. But is this true? To answer this developmental question we need to examine the research evidence.

Research Studies on Children's Expressive Drawings

Research on the development of children's expressive drawings has been conducted by the Harvard Project Zero team on North-American children (Carothers & Gardner, 1979; Davis, 1991, 1997a, 1997b; Ives, 1984), and also in independent work on children from other countries (Jolley, Cox, & Barlow, 2003; Jolley, Fenn, & Jones, 2004; Morra, Caloni, & d'Amico, 1994; Pariser & van den Berg, 1997, 2001; Winston, Kenyon, Stewardson, & Lepine, 1995). In an early study in this area Carothers and Gardner (1979) showed 7-, 10- and 12-year-olds two line drawings of a boy going passed a shop (see Figure 2.3). Although the lines employed in the pictures may be regarded as only minimally expressive in themselves, the subject matter of the drawings conveys opposite positive and negative moods. The children were told that the child who drew the pictures had not finished them, and accordingly were asked to complete each scene

Figure 2.3 The two happy (top) and sad (bottom) "shop" scenes used by Carothers and Gardner (1979).

by drawing a tree and a flower as the child would have done. Although no mention of the mood in the drawings was made in the instructions, the children were encouraged to notice differences between the two presented drawings and to make their own drawings different in the same way. The pair of drawings each child produced was rated on a 3-point scale on the extent to which there was a perceptible difference in expression between the drawings. Although the authors did not test for significant differences between each age group, my own chi-square analyses on their categorical data show that there were significant developments between 7 and 10 years of age, and between 10 and 12 years of age. As the authors reported, however, only the 10- and 12-year-olds showed any evidence of variation in their pair of expressive drawings.

Although Carothers and Gardner's task served well in raising the profile of studying children's expressive drawings, the task has a number of limitations. For instance, because no mention of mood was made in the instructions some children may not have understood they were to draw expressively. Also, children may put less effort into tasks in which they complete another child's drawing than if the whole drawing had been their own (see Davis, 1991). Furthermore, the measurement of the drawings did not directly assess children's ability to draw expressively, reflecting instead how flexible children are in manipulating a topic to convey different expressive communications.[1]

In a more comprehensive assessment of children's use of expressive devices Ives (1984) sought evidence of literal, content, and abstract expression in 4- to 20-year-old's expressive (happy, sad, angry, quiet, loud, hard) drawings of trees and lines. The author reported that the percentage of children in each age group utilizing at least one of these three types of expression increased with age, but with a significant dip in performance between the 7- and 9-year-olds. Within this overall pattern the use of literal expression peaked among the 5-year-olds while evidence of abstract and content expression grew with age. It appears that the aforementioned dip in performance was accounted for by a less frequent use of literal expression among the 9-year-olds.

In contrast to Ives' scoring approach of merely identifying whether or not literal, content, and abstract expression appeared in the drawings, Winston et al. (1995) unpacked children's use of content and abstract expression. They scored Canadian 6-, 9- and 12-year-olds' pairs of happy and sad trees for the presence of six expressive content themes (personification, season of tree, aging/illness/death of tree, weather, attack, sociability). In respect of abstract expression the drawings were scored on whether each of line, color and size had been used expressively. Winston et al. reported that the number of expressive themes and formal properties in the drawings significantly increased with age, but subsequent analyses on individual themes and formal properties revealed that not all age groups differed significantly. It is difficult to ascertain from the paper whether there were any consistent slow periods of growth between age groups as the authors did not report further age comparisons on either the overall number of themes or total number of formal properties.

In addition to the problems peculiar to each of these three studies there are at least two common drawbacks that they share. First, that children were not allowed to make their own topic choices, and hence the findings may have underestimated children's ability to draw expressively. Second, none of the studies satisfactorily addressed the issue of quality of expression. Neither of these two drawbacks can be levied at the large-scale study reported by Davis (1991, 1997a, 1997b). She asked groups of 5-, 8-, 11-, 14-year-olds and adults in North America to make a happy, sad, and angry drawing, with participants free to choose the content of their drawings. The 14-year-olds and adults each consisted of two sub-groups, self-professed artists and non-artists. A variety of analyses were conducted but of most relevance to the quality of the drawings was two artist raters' judgments on the extent to which (on a 4-point scale) each drawing portrayed four esthetic properties (based on the work of Goodman, 1976). Three of these directly related to expression: overall expression (considering the use of subject matter, line, and composition), and the use of line and composition (separately) as agents to expression. The remaining property was the use of balance in itself. Excluding the two artist groups (14-year-old and adult artists) and using a composite measure of all the properties, Davis reported an L-shaped developmental pattern: the 5-year-olds scored higher than the other samples (all of which performed similarly). Independent analysis of each of the properties separately revealed close approximations to an L-shaped pattern. When the two artist groups were included, replacing the "non-artist" 14-year-olds and adults, a U-shape pattern was found: the 5-year-olds' drawings were rated similarly to the two artist

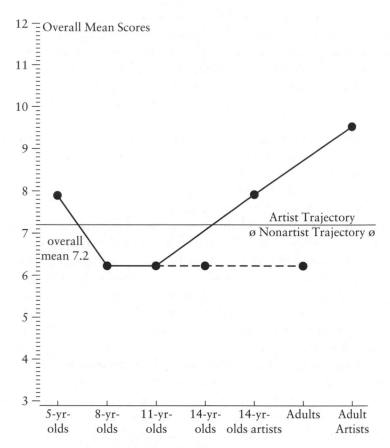

Figure 2.4   The L- and U-shaped developmental patterns of esthetic drawing reported by Davis (1997a).

groups, with the 8- and 11-year-olds representing the trough of the "U". Figure 2.4 shows the L-shaped and U-shaped patterns reported by Davis for all the properties combined.

We are beginning to discover that establishing a single and universal developmental pattern of children's expressive drawing might be elusive. Three of the studies discussed above reported age-related improvements but it is not clear from these studies if there was a reliable slow or even regressive period of growth. A more diverse finding is Davis's U-shape pattern. I will now present work I have carried out with colleagues on the development of expressive drawings among British children and adults (Jolley et al., 2003; 2004).

Our aim has been to provide a more comprehensive measurement of expressive drawing than adopted in the previous literature. In so doing we hoped not only to get a more complete picture of how children's expressive drawings develop, but also to gain some insight on why different patterns have emerged from the previous studies.

The British Studies

One important consideration in the two experiments we reported in Jolley et al. (2004) was to measure both the quantity and quality of expression. That is, to measure the number of expressive devices used in each drawing and the extent to which they contributed to the overall quality of expression in the picture. We sought to obtain these two measurements separately as a drawing may portray many expressive devices, but if the devices have not been used well the quality of expression may be limited (and vice versa). Furthermore, in the light of the distinct patterns reported by studies counting the number of expressive devices used (e.g., Winston et al., 1995) compared to Davis (1997a) whose concern was more with the quality of expression, it seemed prudent to examine the developmental patterns for quantity and quality separately.

There were two other considerations. First, we wanted to analyze the developmental patterns by mood. Although the previous literature had asked children to draw pictures of different moods (implicitly in the case of Carothers & Gardner, 1979), the authors have rarely reported the developmental findings by mood. This may be an important oversight as there is research evidence from children's interpretation of pictures that children tend to read more positive than negative feelings when viewing pictures (Jolley & Thomas, 1994, 1995; Parsons, 1987). In a rare case in which mood differences in children's expressive drawings have been reported, Buckalew and Bell (1985) noted a prominence of happy faces to sad ones among pre-school children's drawings of the literal depiction of mood. We might expect, therefore, that this positivity bias extends to children's drawing of content and abstract expression. The second consideration related to the nature of the tasks. We decided to provide topics for the children to draw in the first experiment and allow children to choose their own subject matter in the second experiment. This enabled us to investigate evidence for a consistent pattern of development across tasks or whether patterns are task dependent. Also, this approach allowed us to explore the possibility that the distinct findings reported by Davis (1997a) may have been due in part to her children having the freedom of choice about what to draw.

In the first experiment reported by Jolley et al. (2004) we asked 80 children (twenty 4-, 6-, 9-, and 12-year-olds) to make four expressive pictures: a happy and sad house, and a happy and sad tree. We developed a formal system of generating expressive subject matter themes by applying the procedure of content analysis used in analyzing written and spoken conversations (e.g., Krippendorf, 1980; Weber, 1990). We incorporated literal expressions within the "people" theme, but when appearing on non-human items they went under "personification." The content analysis of the tree drawings produced the following themes for both the happy and sad versions: personification, weather, season/state of tree and surrounding vege- tation, text, animals, vehicles/other objects, people and other (for the sad tree there was the additional theme of "action on tree"). The happy and sad houses revealed personification, state of house, state of surroundings in garden, weather, people, animals, text, vehicles/ other objects, and other. The content expression score for each draw- ing reflected the number of appropriately expressed subject matter themes judged by the raters. The abstract expression score was the number of formal properties (size, line, and color) that the raters judged had been used successfully to express the intended mood. Added together the content expression score and the abstract expression score provided an overall quantity score. The quality score was assessed by the same raters on a 5-point scale in respect of the degree to which they perceived the drawing expressed the intended mood.

The developmental patterns of the expressive tree and house drawings were essentially the same,[2] and accordingly I have presented the collated data in Figure 2.5. As is evident from the graph, similar developmental patterns were found for the happy and sad pictures, and for quantity and quality measures. Our data provided therefore consistent evidence across tasks, mood and measurements of a steady age-related incline in performance. There was one notable and reliable exception to the age-related statistically significant improvements: There was no significant improvement between the 6- and 9-year- olds for either the quantity or quality measures (there was also no

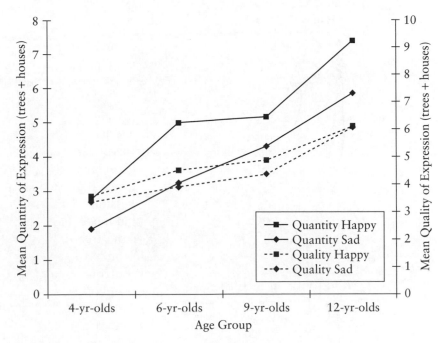

Figure 2.5 Mean quantity and quality of expression for happy and sad drawings of a tree and a house (combined data) by age group. Data from Experiment 1 reported by Jolley et al. (2004).

improvement in quality between the 4- and 6-year-olds). Although the patterns for the sad and happy drawings were similar, the happy drawings were rated significantly higher than the sad drawings for quality across both topics, and for quantity on the tree topic only. Representative examples of the tree drawings by age group and mood can be found in Figure 2.6.

In the second experiment we sought to establish whether the age-related developmental progression we had found in tasks where the topic of the drawings had been directed by the experimenters extended to tasks where children had freedom over the subject matter. One hundred and sixty children spread equally among the same four age groups sampled in Experiment 1 were asked to make a happy and sad picture. The themes generated from the content analysis were personification, weather, season/health of vegetation and countryside, vehicles/buildings, other objects, one person, more than one person, animals, text, thought bubbles, and other.

Figure 2.6   Representative examples of happy and sad tree drawings by age group in Experiment 1 reported by Jolley et al. (2004).

As was the case in Experiment 1, the quantity and quality of children's expressive drawing improved with age but with slow periods of growth (see Figure 2.7). The development in quantity scores was initially slow, with significant improvements from the 4-year-olds' level not shown until 9 years of age. A further development in quantity of devices was found in the 12-year-olds' drawings. The developmental pattern for the quality scores followed broadly the same progression as described for the quantity scores, particularly for the sad drawings where there was again a slow (non-significant) period of growth between 6 and 9 years. Happy drawings were scored significantly higher than sad drawings for both quantity and quality of expression. Drawings representing the scores for each age group and mood are shown in Figure 2.8.

In these two experiments we found a surprisingly consistent pattern of development in expressive drawing within the age range we tested (4 to 12 years) across tasks, moods, and measurements. Children's performance increased with age but with a reliably slow (and frequently non-significant) period of growth between the ages of 6 and 9 years.

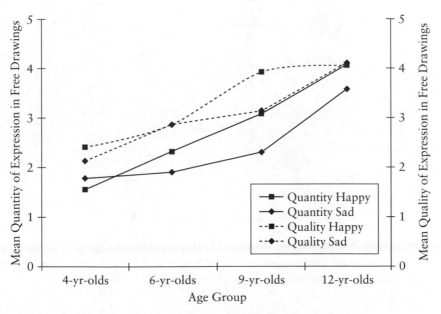

Figure 2.7 Mean quantity and quality of expression for happy and sad free drawings. Data from Experiment 2 reported by Jolley et al. (2004).

Figure 2.8   Representative examples of happy and sad free drawings by age group in Experiment 2 reported by Jolley et al. (2004).

At this point I began designing a study with Claire Barlow and Maureen Cox that included a number of improvements on my earlier work with colleagues, most notably to sample more developmental points and to generate a more sophisticated rating of the drawings. In Jolley et al. (2003)[3] children were sampled from the following groups: 4-, 5-, 6-, 7-, 9-, 11-, 12-, and 14-year-olds. As was the case in our earlier study, the 4-year-olds were tested to measure children's expressive drawing before they had received formal art training. The age groups of school children (5- to 14-year-olds) were selected to represent the start, middle, and end-points of each of the three Key Stages of the National Curriculum for Art and Design used in mainstream education in England (Key stage 1: 5–7 years; Key stage 2: 7–11 years; Key stage 3: 11–14 years). In addition to the 14-year-olds sampled from their final year of statutory art education, we sampled a further group of 14-year-olds who were taking a General Certificate of Secondary Education (GCSE) in Art.[4] We also tested two adult samples from higher education. One sample was represented by students doing a non-art based degree, the other sample were studying for an art degree. These three further samples not only allowed us to examine the developmental path beyond children's statutory art education but enabled us to make a direct comparison with the corresponding samples tested by Davis (1997a). Also consistent with Davis we asked children to produce an angry drawing as well as a happy and sad drawing. We decided to request "free" drawings only as we assumed "free" drawing tasks allow children the optimum opportunity to draw expressively. All participants were given their own set of ten colored pencils and an HB pencil (except the 4-year-olds who were given crayons), which they used to draw on a page of A4 white paper for each expressive drawing. Although we gave our participants a greater range of (colored) markers than were made available to Davis's (1997a) participants (they used a black felt-tip marker), the materials in both studies were similar in one essential detail, namely that fine point markers were used.

For the analysis of the drawings we had the benefit of two artist raters who had a wealth of experience in art, both in terms of practice and education. Their experience allowed us to develop the measurements, most notably in the formal properties and quality ratings. Through our extensive discussions with the artist raters, facilitated by drawings collected from a pilot study, we generated separate

7-point scales for each of the three formal property measurements under investigation (color, line, and composition[5]) and for overall quality. Each point on each scale had a detailed description of its defining criteria. The analysis of content themes was carried out in a similar way to that described in Jolley et al. (2004) but more themes were created reflecting the higher number of participants and the wider age range.

Scores for each of the five measurements by age group and mood are displayed in Figure 2.9. It was immediately evident to us that despite the range of measurements and mood in the drawings there was a consistent age-related trend, and furthermore, this was consistent with that found in Jolley et al. (2004). In Jolley et al. (2003) higher scores tended to be associated with each ascending age group for all five measures. The statistical analyses, however, threw up some reliable qualifications to this age-related pattern. First, there was a consistent lack of a significant improvement between the 5-, 6-, 7-, and 9-year-olds across all the measures (the only exception being a significant shift at 7 years of age for composition). Second, there was also a consistent lack of development between the 11-, 12-, and 14-year-olds (including the 14-year-old artist group), although these children were performing at a significantly higher level that the aforementioned 5- to 9-year-old group.[6] Explained in terms of the schooling systems in mainstream education in England there seemed to be a shift in performance between the primary school children (5- to 9-year-olds) and the secondary school children (11- to 14-year-olds). This shift was shown most clearly in the subject matter themes (content expression) scores (see relevant graph in Figure 2.9). Furthermore, inspecting the drawings revealed that whereas the primary school children performed the tasks by typically displaying a single person with the appropriate literal expression, the secondary school children often drew a scene or event that would be expected to evoke a mood (e.g., birthday parties, Christmas scenes, funerals, environmental abuse, road rage) as well as showing literal depictions of emotion in the "scene" drawings.

In addition to these two groups of children there was some less consistent statistical evidence for two further groups: the 4-year-olds and adult artists. For some of the measures and moods the 4-year-olds performed significantly more poorly than all other groups, and the adult artists performed significantly better than all other groups.

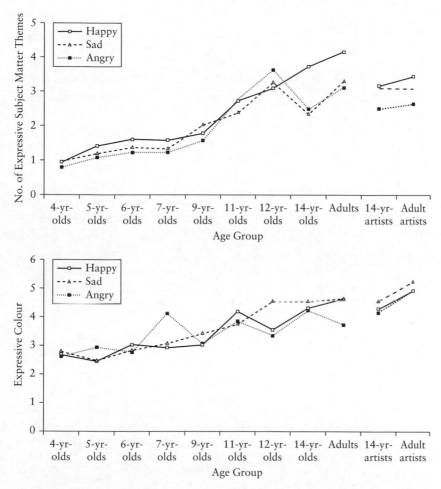

Figure 2.9 Mean scores of content expression, expressive use of color, line, and composition, and overall quality of expression by mood and age group reported by Jolley et al. (2003).

In Plate 3 we can see the shifts in expressive drawing ability in some drawings made by a 4-, 7-, 11-year-old and an adult artist.

In respect of differences in performance between the three mood drawings there were on occasions significantly higher ratings for the happy drawings but this was not consistent.

The reliably higher ratings attributed to each subsequent older age group in our three experiments is broadly consistent with the

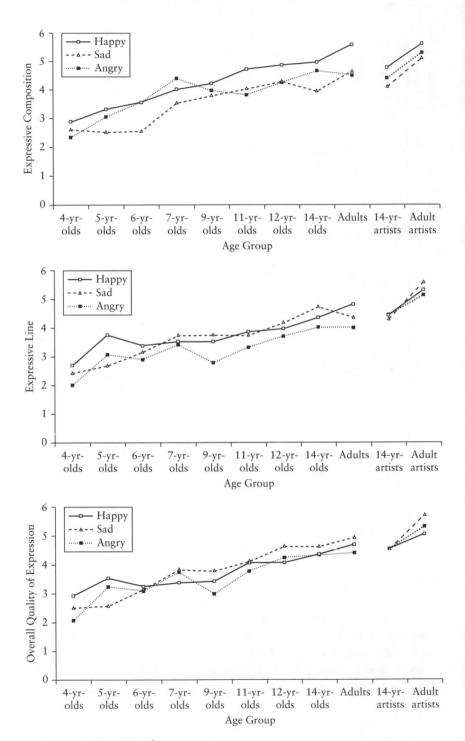

Figure 2.9   (*continued*)

age-related progressions reported by Carothers and Gardner (1979), Ives (1984) and Winston et al. (1995), but inconsistent with the L- and U-shaped patterns reported by Davis (1997a). I shall now attempt to tie these patterns together and provide explanations for their disparity.

Tying the Patterns Together

Age-related progressions in children's expressive drawing ability have been recorded in the majority of studies in this literature (Carothers & Gardner, 1979; Ives, 1984; Jolley et al., 2003, 2004; Morra et al., 1994, Winston et al., 1995). In addition, a number of these studies indicated slow periods of growth (or even regression). For instance, Ives (1984) reported a lack of improvement between the 7- and 11-year-olds tested which included a significant regression between the 7- and 9-year-olds. Jollcy et al. (2004) found a consistent lack of significant improvement between 6- and 9-year-olds for both quantity and quality of expression, and in some cases between the 4- and 6-year-olds. In Jolley et al. (2003), where there was a wide age range in the samples we tested with numerous developmental points, there was a consistent lack of significant improvement between the 5- and 9-year-olds and also between the 11- and 14-year-olds. Despite the variations in tasks and measurements this body of work does present a common developmental finding: Children's expressive drawings tend to improve with age but growth is not steady.

That finding stands in stark contrast to the U-shaped pattern reported by Davis (1997a) and claimed by other commentators from the Harvard Project Zero team (Gardner, 1980; Gardner & Winner, 1982; Rosenblatt & Winner, 1988; Winner, 1982). Recall from my earlier discussion of the Davis paper that the youngest group tested (5-year-olds) performed at a similar level to two artist groups (14-year-olds and artists), each representing the two high end-points of the "U," with the weaker expressive drawings made by the 8- and 11-year-olds representing the trough of the "U."

In trying to explain how these opposite patterns may be explained I first want to rule out some possible contenders by directly comparing the work I have been involved in (Jolley et al., 2003, 2004) with that reported by Davis (1997a), as both sets of work have similarities between them despite reporting differing patterns. In our work and that reported by Davis children were given the freedom to choose what to draw in the expressive tasks, and the drawings were rated on quality of expression. It seems improbable, therefore, that the two different patterns reported in the overall literature can be explained by either the nature of the task (free vs. predetermined topics) or whether one measures the drawings on quality or quantity of expression. I also feel confident in ruling out any suggestion that the children sampled by Davis drew differently, after having closely examined all the drawings collected in Davis's PhD thesis (Davis, 1991) which formed the basis for her published papers (Davis, 1997a, 1997b). As in our work, I noticed in Davis's drawings that the younger children drew people with emotional faces while older children increasingly depicted scenes that portrayed a mood-laden event. Indeed, Davis's own analysis showed that children progressed from using metonymic-physiological expressive connections (i.e. emotionally laden faces) to metonymic-narrative expressive connections (i.e. people being shown in an emotionally laden scene).

Comparing the rating criteria used in Davis's study with that used in our work, however, does provide us with a way forward to resolving the difference in patterns. The four esthetic properties Davis investigated (balance, line, and composition to express, overall quality of expression) were very much geared towards evaluating the expressive formal properties of the drawings. It appears that the raters saw these expressive formal properties more clearly in the youngest (5-year-old) children's drawings than the drawings from the children in mid-childhood. Not only that, but they saw an esthetic likeness between the drawings made by the 5-year-olds and the adult artists. In Davis's (1997a) discussion of her findings she explains this further. She presented two "happy" drawings from her study, one made by a 5-year-old and one produced by an adult artist (see Figure 2.10). The 5-year-old's drawing depicted a happy face whereas the adult artist's drawing appears to depict lines abstracted from a happy face, most notably the uplifting lines of the mouth. Davis (1997a) comments that, "because of a similar use of line and composition, from a distance at which the precise symbolic vehicle in each drawing could not be ascertained, the viewer would still recognise two happy drawings" (p. 155). It seems that Davis's artist raters (prompted by the rating dimensions that are biased towards expressive

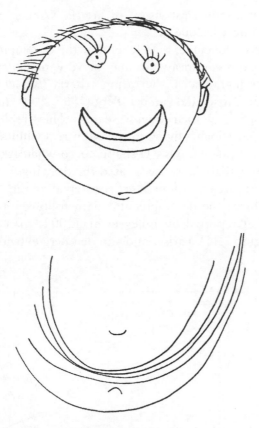

Figure 2.10 Two happy drawing made by a 5-year-old (top) and adult artist (bottom) reported by Davis (1997a).

formal properties) are viewing the drawings with "modernist" art spectacles. In the modernist tradition, artists eschew the search for realism, instead abstracting formal properties from representations (hence the term abstract art). Could it be, therefore, that the drawings produced by the 5-year-olds and those by the adolescent and adult artists in Davis's study were rated similarly because they both appeared to reflect a modernist approach to art? Davis herself seems to be agreeing when she said, "the celebration of the artistry of young children derives from and is unique to a modernist perspective" (Davis, 1997b, p. 152). Furthermore, Ellen Winner, a key proponent of the U-shape curve, confirmed to me that in her view, the U-shape curve depends upon a modernist vision of art (E. Winner, personal communication, July 19, 2006).

We are left to conclude, therefore, that the developmental pattern of children's expressive drawings may be very much dependent upon the art values ingrained in the rating criteria (see also Cox, 2005; Kindler, 2000). Pariser and van den Berg (1997, 2001) make this same point, supported by their own research. They replicated Davis's study on 55 participants living in the Montreal Chinese community. While they replicated Davis's U-shape curve when American artists (the same raters that Davis used) rated the drawings, when the same drawings were given to Chinese artist raters living in Montreal (but trained in China) the developmental path followed a more similar pattern to that reported by Jolley et al. (2003) than the U-shaped curve (see Figure 2.11). Pariser and van den Berg extended their work

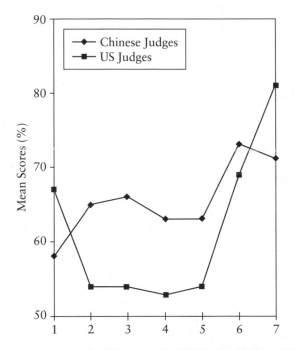

Figure 2.11   American and Chinese artists' ratings of Montreal Chinese esthetic drawings reported by Pariser and van den Berg (2001).
Age/Ability Groups: 1 = 5 years; 2 = 8 years; 3 = 11 years; 4 = 14 years; 5 = adult; 6 = 14-year-old artists; 7 = adult artists.

by having the drawings independently rated on graphic skill (including the skill of realistic rendering). These "skill" ratings were then correlated with the aforementioned Chinese and American judges' esthetic ratings. Interestingly, Pariser and van den Berg (2001) found a stronger positive correlation with the Chinese esthetic ratings than with the American esthetic ratings, particularly for the "non-artist" samples. Also, Pariser and van den Berg noted that when the Chinese artists were interviewed on the basis of their esthetic ratings they commented upon technical skill. Pariser and van den Berg (2001) concluded, therefore, that whereas the American judges took a modernist approach in the assessment of the drawings the Chinese raters were more inclined to evaluate the drawings on technical graphic skill.

It appears that from the work carried out by Pariser and van den Berg that different cultural art traditions and values influenced how the drawings were evaluated. In a further extension of this work Pariser and van den Berg, with colleagues, have subsequently set out to establish the proportion of judges who rate children's and adults' drawings according to a U-shaped pattern (Pariser, Kindler, & van den Berg, 2008; Pariser, Kindler, van den Berg, Dias, & Liu, 2007). In their large-scale "three-country" study, 5-, 8-, 11-, and 14-year-olds, adult art-novices and adult artists, from Canada, Brazil, and Taiwan, were recruited. All these participants were asked to draw a happy, sad, and angry drawing in one session, and in another session a map (the route from their home to school/work), a cartoon character, and people engaged in an activity. All drawings were sorted into three piles labeled, "good," "fair," or "poor" by 192 judges (64 each from Canada, Brazil, and Taiwan). The authors deliberately did not give the judges any further guidance on how to rate the drawings. Because the authors were also interested in examining how developmental patterns in the ratings may vary according to the judges' age and experience, they recruited an equal number ($N = 16$) of 8-year-olds, 14-year-olds, adult non-artists and adult artists within each of the three countries to rate the drawings. The most interesting finding relevant to the present discussion was that when they collated the ratings from all the drawing tasks, only about 29% of the adult artist judges (across the three countries) rated the drawings according to a U-shape curve, with barely any of the other groups of judges doing so (resulting in only 8% of all the judges' ratings producing a U-shape curve). Furthermore, approximately 60% of all the judges rated the drawings according to an upward-sloping line that reflected higher scores for increasing age of the drawer, a pattern more consistent with my own research conducted with colleagues.

Interestingly, David Pariser and his colleagues also found evidence for two more developmental patterns based on some judges' ratings: An inverted U-shape curve (called "anti-modernist") in which the drawings made by the 8- and 11-year-olds were valued most highly (representing 27% of all judges), and a flat line pattern where drawings from each group of drawer tended to be valued equally (5% of all judges). Although their study employed different drawing tasks rather than just those that assessed expressive skills, their findings suggest that within the population (i) only a minority evaluate young children's drawings on a par with adult artists, (ii) a majority consider that drawing skill improves with the age of the drawer, and (iii) there may be a number of developmental trajectories in children's drawings that are dependent upon the particular art values of the judge. In relation to this third point, Howard Gardner, a key figure in championing the U-shape curve over the years, more recently has acknowledged in a reply to Pariser's (2006) criticism of the U-shape curve that, "The U-shaped curve becomes not the universal, univocal story of children's artistic development, but rather one of a number of possible patterns (Gardner, 2006, p. 339).

But is it all in the "eye of the beholder"? Could not cultural art values also impact upon the drawings themselves, rather than just how they are rated? This is the question Zhang Zhi and I asked ourselves when we replicated the study reported in Jolley et al. (2003) on Chinese children and adults living in China. The next section discusses some brief and preliminary reflections on the drawings we collected.

Chinese Children's Expressive Drawings

Recently Zhang Zhi and I asked Chinese children and adults to draw a happy, sad, and angry picture using the translated instructions from Jolley et al. (2003). The same number of participants and eleven sample groups were employed as in the British study. Although we are awaiting a formal rating of the drawings we have been able to make some initial interesting observations. In particular, we noted frequent "scene-based" drawings depicting an event evoking a mood, even by the youngest children (for example, see a Chinese 4-year-old's drawing in Plate 4). Such drawings represented more complex and varied subject matter themes than the literal-only depictions of emotion typical among the young British children. As I mention in chapter 9 on cultural influences on children's drawings the traditional method of adult artists learning their profession in China has been to copy from other pictures, and this cultural artistic tradition is applied to young Chinese children as well. This approach may explain the larger repertoire of subject matter we saw in the young Chinese children's drawings compared to their same-aged British counterparts. Nevertheless, I felt the content in the Chinese children's drawings was not always drawn in an expressive way, particularly in the negative (sad and angry) mood drawings. It is possible that the focus on representing (by copying of) depicted subject matter within Chinese school art education at the time we tested the children may have given the Chinese children little opportunity to practice drawing their large repertoire of subject matter in expressive ways.[7] Even in the case of the literal depiction of emotion, it seemed to me that the expressions of sad and angry were not always as well differentiated as in the British drawings. I discuss other aspects of this project in chapter 9, but for now we simply need to acknowledge that differing cultural art values not only impact upon the criteria used in experimental studies to rate children's expressive drawings, but through education may also influence the drawings themselves.

So far in this chapter I have concentrated on the developmental pattern of children's expressive drawings. I now want to turn our attention to the particular skills that may explain individual differences in drawing expressively.

Individual Differences in Expressive Drawing

Investigating which skills are involved in expressive drawing not only has the potential to explain individual differences in performance but also to provide an understanding of the processes involved in a child making an expressive drawing. The research is in its early stages but the literature has indicated three skills or abilities that may play a role in children's expressive drawings: visual metaphor comprehension, working memory, and drawing skill.

For a drawing to be considered expressive of a mood or concept one might imagine that the child initially held an idea to communicate what he or she wanted.[8] At the beginning of this chapter I discussed different expressive techniques available to artists. Two of these techniques, content and abstract expression, have been given the term "metaphorical expression." As I stated then, the term "metaphor" may be applied in such instances merely to distinguish it from literal expression, that is, content and abstract expression is metaphorical because it is not literal (not displayed directly in the form of a human facial expression). However, it has been argued that the use of the term metaphor when applied to pictorial expression may have a more formal basis, as it does in the case of linguistic metaphor (see Kennedy, 1982; Thomas & Jolley, 1997). As metaphor is considered to be conceptual and can be communicated across symbol systems (see Kogan & Chadrow, 1986; Kogan, Connor, Gross, & Fava, 1980) we might expect that at least some instances of pictorial expression is understood on the basis of metaphor, and importantly for this discussion, that children who are more able to understand pictorial metaphor may be more gifted in generating expressive ideas for their drawings. Using Kogan et al.'s (1980) Metaphoric Triads Test (MTT), which measures children's comprehension of pictorial metaphor, Winston et al. (1995) gave 7- to 12-year-olds the MTT as well as asking them to draw a happy and sad tree. The correlations between children's use of expressive devices in their drawings and metaphor comprehension was somewhat mixed. When the influence of age was removed from the correlations only one subject matter theme (aging, illness, and death of tree) and one formal property (size/shape of the tree) were significantly and positively correlated to children's skill at detecting visual metaphors on the MTT. Nevertheless, Winston et al.'s findings indicated that metaphoric skill may play some role in the development of expressive drawing.

Once a child has generated his or her (metaphoric) ideas for an expressive drawing he or she needs to hold these ideas in memory. The role of memory and other information processing factors (e.g., attention and planning) in general picture production has been discussed in the literature (Freeman, 1972, 1980; Luquet, 1927/2001; Morra, 2002, 2005; Morra et al., 1996, 1998; Toomela, 2002). In a paper that directly examined the role of memory in expressive drawing, Morra et al. (1994) asked Italian 6- to 11-year-olds to draw three emotional drawings: a happy, sad, and scared topic (either a person, tree, or ship). The children were also administered "M-operator" tasks that measured their capacity of working memory. Morra et al. found that the ability to modify the shape of the tree and ship drawings across the three moods, but not for the person drawings, was positively linked to a higher capacity in working memory among the children. The authors argued that to produce metaphorical expression in a picture requires coordinating various pieces of information, and accordingly is a problem solving activity demanding attentional capacity. In contrast, the authors claimed that the literal depiction of emotion simply requires the recall of the appropriate emotional features rather than representing a problem-solving activity, and therefore is not dependent upon working memory. Consistent with this claim is that even very young children learn how to draw different facial expressions (see Figure 2.1).

While being able to generate and remember expressive ideas may represent important processes in expressive drawing, children still need to have the drawing skill to materialize their expressive ideas. As at least content expression depends upon a certain level of representational drawing skill children's drawing skill could be assessed on how able they are to draw life-like representations. Based on a task used by Cox, Perara, and Xu (1998) we asked children who participated in the second study reported by Jolley et al. (2004) to draw a figure of a man running (a 3D model was presented). Marks were awarded (on a 12-point scale) for the child's use of direction, overlap, partial occlusion, proportion, detail, and whether it was recognizable as a man. When the influence of age differences was removed we found a small, positive (but non-significant) association between their performances on this task and their expressive "free" drawings. Our study was very much a preliminary examination into the relationship between technical (representational) drawing skill and expressive drawing, and we noted that the relationship needed further investigation.

With this in mind Jolley et al. (2003) directly compared the relationships of visual metaphor comprehension, working memory, and technical drawing skill with that of expressive drawing. In contrast to the piecemeal investigation of these relationships in the existing literature, the advantage of testing these relationships within the same sample is that one can establish the relative strengths of these three factors on expressive drawing. After the expressive (happy, sad, angry) drawings tasks had been administered, the drawing skill tasks, working memory tasks, and the MTT were given in three further sessions to all of the 7-, 9-, and 11-year-old children. There were three drawing skill tasks: drawing a man running from a model (as in Jolley et al., 2004), drawing a man from imagination, and drawing a cube (a model was presented). Three "M" capacity tasks were administered (backward digit span, Mr. Cucumber, and counting span[9]) and also a short version of the MTT.

With the influence of age statistically removed, we found significant positive correlations between performances on the drawing skill and expressive drawing tasks of typically around a medium effect size[10] (0.11 < rs < 0.39). These were stronger than that found in Jolley et al. (2004), and indicated that technical graphic skill (as measured by realism techniques) is involved in expressive drawing. However, there was no link (positive or negative) between both the children's visual metaphor comprehension or working memory and their expressive drawing. One problem was that neither the performance on the MTT nor working memory developed between 7 and 9 years in our study. This is inconsistent with the literature and difficult to explain. However, if for whatever reason our measurements for visual metaphor comprehension and working memory failed to pick up the underlying abilities among the children we tested then the lack of relationships between these tasks and expressive drawing would not be surprising. Alternatively, we may be misconceiving what the underlying skills are in expressive drawing. For instance, it may be that divergent thinking plays a more central role in generating expressive ideas rather than visual metaphor comprehension, particularly if it was the case that much of pictorial expression is not communicated via metaphor. Recently, Debbie Martin and I compared 6-, 8-, and 11-year-olds' performance on an adaptation of the Unusual Uses Test[11] with their expressive drawing scores (Martin, 2003). The correlations were of at least a small effect size (0.15 < rs < 0.21) suggesting divergent thinking (or other similar measures testing for creativity) may be worth future research attention in its role in expressive drawing.

In respect of working memory I noted earlier that in Jolley et al. (2003) children younger than 11 years of age tended to draw literal expressions only (and also in Jolley et al., 2004), and according to Morra et al. (1994) the depiction of literal expression is not related to working memory space. Only when children draw more "scene-based" drawings, or when directly asked to manipulate subject matter expressively (as in Morra et al., 1994), may working memory become an influencing factor on performance. In any event, concentrating on tasks that tap into visuo-spatial working memory may reveal a stronger relationship with expressive drawing than administering a battery of tasks that test a broader range of working memory components. In the M capacity tasks used by Jolley et al. (2003), only the Mr. Cucumber task measured this potentially more relevant component of working memory to expressive drawing.

The literature addressing individual differences in children's expressive drawing is still in its infancy, and clearly more research is needed to understand what skills are involved in children's expressive drawing. But Jolley et al.'s (2003) finding of representational drawing skill being closely associated with expressive drawing raises another interesting question about the developing relationship between representational and expressive drawing, which I take up in the final chapter of this book.

Summary

It is easy to find examples of expressive drawing among children but it is not easy to describe the developmental pattern of children's expressive drawing. This is principally because of the subjective nature in evaluating an expressive work and the differing art values that may be employed in such evaluations. Despite this difficulty of assessment there is a surprising consistency in the literature that suggests an age-related incremental pattern with slow periods of growth. We are still some way from understanding the mental processes and skills involved in making an expressive drawing, but it seems likely that the drawing skills most relevant to making an expressive drawing play a leading role.

Notes

1   This is an interesting question in itself, and formed the basis of the Morra et al. (1994) paper in which 6- to 11-year-old Italian children were asked to draw a happy, sad, and scared person (or ship or tree). The study is commented upon later in this chapter.

2   Further support for this came from the statistical analyses that showed neither a significant topic main effect nor a significant age × topic interaction.

3   Although reported one year earlier than Jolley et al. (2004) my study with Maureen Cox and Claire Barlow was designed and conducted after that work.

4   In England, once children complete their National Curriculum education at 14 years of age they undertake two years of GCSEs across a range of subjects of their choosing.

5   Through our discussions with the artists it was decided to use composition as an expressive measure rather than size. Composition is a more comprehensive and inclusive measurement than size alone as it takes into account not only the size of the elements but also where they are placed and how they are balanced with each other in respect to the dimensions of the page. Composition was also analyzed by Davis's (1997a) so our inclusion of it was useful for comparison purposes.

6   The particular developmental point in which there was a significant shift between the 5- to 9-year-old group and the 11- to 14-year-old groups varied depending upon the measurement and mood of drawing.

7   The Chinese infant school art curriculum (3–6) has changed since we collected the drawings for this project; the new curriculum now includes the need for children to produce imaginative and expressive pictures (see chapter 10 for a detailed description of the current program).

8   That is not to say that ideas cannot develop during the process of drawing.

9   In the Backward Digit Span Test, series of digits are read aloud to the child who then is required to recall the digits in reverse order. In the Mr. Cucumber Test an outline of an extra-terrestrial figure is shown with round colored stickers placed in any number of eight positions. The figure is replaced by a similar figure without the stickers, and the child is asked to point to the positions on the figure where the stickers had been placed. In the Counting Span Test the child is asked to rapidly count aloud several sets of colored dots and then recall the number in each set.

10   According to Cohen's (1988) criteria for the magnitude of effect sizes.

11   The children were shown a plastic bowl, an empty milk carton, and a newspaper. After they confirmed what these items were and what they were used for, the children were asked to think of alternative ways in which they could be used, no matter how strange these ideas may be.

3

Drawings from Children in Special Populations

This chapter examines the research into the drawings made by children from a variety of special populations, in particular, children with learning difficulties, Down's syndrome, autism, Williams syndrome, attention deficit hyperactivity disorder (ADHD), developmental coordination disorder, and blind children. A consistent theme running through the chapter is whether the drawings from such children follow the same developmental pattern (either at a faster or slower rate), or develop in qualitatively distinct ways, compared to those produced by typically developing children. Where there are observed and reliable differences within a specific population of children can they be traced to the etiology and symptomatic characteristics of their disorder?

In the first two chapters I discussed the development of representational and expressive drawing, based on studies undertaken on typically developing children. But of course there are many children who through a variety of genetic, biological, or environmental causes show characteristics atypical to the norm. In that sense they may be said to belong to special populations of children, each population having its own common etiology and characteristic symptoms. A basic question we may first ask is what do the drawings of children from special populations look like? Taking a developmental perspective the literature has asked whether children's drawings from special populations develop in a similar pattern to that found in typically developing children (albeit at a slower or faster rate), or whether they appear qualitatively different. A related question is whether the differences we observe in the drawings from a given population of children can be attributed to the causes and symptoms that are characteristic of the disorder. With these issues in mind, I discuss the drawings made by children with non-specific learning difficulties, Down's syndrome, autistic spectrum disorder, Williams syndrome, attention deficit hyperactive disorder (ADHD), developmental coordination disorder (DCD), and blind children.

Children with Non-specific Learning Difficulties

In chapter 1 I referred to the early scientific interest in children's drawings around the turn of the 20th century that sought to map out the developmental course of children's representational drawing. A complementary approach around this time was to examine whether the quality of the drawings (measured broadly in terms of representational realism) was related to the child's general cognitive ability (measured initially in terms of their school work and teacher ratings). With the onset of drawing tasks being included in early IQ tests, and later with the creation of dedicated IQ drawings tests, the assumption was that children's drawings could be used to measure the child's intellectual capacity (see chapter 7 for a more detailed discussion of drawing as a measure of intelligence). In which case we would expect that children with learning difficulties would draw relatively immature drawings compared to those typically found in their own particular age group, but comparable to younger typically developing children of a similar mental age. Extending this idea further, we may predict the drawings of children of low cognitive ability would develop along the lines of the typical path observed in children without learning difficulties, but more slowly and in accordance with their mental age.

Cox (2005) comments that there were contradictory claims in the early literature as to whether intellectually disabled children drew like younger children of average cognitive ability (a developmental delay), or whether they drew differently (a qualitative difference). She notes that where observations of difference were commented upon these early researchers often referred to the drawings of intellectually disadvantaged children as showing unusual proportions, lack of spatial relationships between the parts, but including more details. However, it is only relatively recently that systematic controlled studies have been undertaken whereby the drawings from children with learning difficulties with no known cause have been compared to (younger) typically developing children matched on mental age (Cox & Cotgreave, 1996; Cox & Howarth, 1989; Golomb & Barr-Grossman, 1977). The two studies reported by Maureen Cox and colleagues are particularly interesting as each one concentrated on children with either mild (MLD) or severe (SLD) learning difficulties. Cox & Cotgreave (1996) collected human figure drawings made by 18 children with mild learning difficulties[1] of around 10 years of age but with a mental age of about 6 years of age. The drawings were compared with those made by 18 typically developing children in each of two control groups. Children in the CA group were matched to the learning difficulties group on chronological age (i.e. children of about 10 years of age), whereas children in the MA group were matched to the leaning difficulties group on mental age (children of around 6 years of age). We would expect that the drawings made by the MLD group to be developmentally inferior to those produced in the CA group, but the comparison with the MA group is critical to the developmental delay/difference debate. All the human figure drawings were scored using two methods. The authors used Koppitz's (1968) 30 developmental indicators to establish how developmentally advanced each figure was. Most of the indicators refer to the presence of a feature of a person (e.g., those relating to the head, body, arms, legs, clothing), but some referred to positioning, proportion and dimensionality. The drawings were also given to 12 teachers (that included 4 teachers who taught MLD children) to decide for each drawing which of the three groups of children it belonged to. According to the Koppitz scores, the drawings made by the MLD children and the MA group were developmentally inferior to those produced in the CA group, but were not statistically significant from each other. This finding was further supported by the teachers' categorizations. The CA group's drawings were categorized significantly more successfully than figures drawn by the MLD and MA groups' drawings, but with no significance difference in the number of drawings from the MLD and MA categorized correctly.

Cox and Cotgreave's findings that drawings made by children with mild learning difficulties are developmentally similar to younger typically developing children lent strong support to the developmentally delay hypothesis. But what about children with severe learning difficulties? Perhaps the severity of their intellectual disability makes them draw in ways that are not commonly found in drawings of children without disability? The findings reported by Cox and Howarth (1989) are informative to this question. In their sample of 15 children with severe learning difficulties[2] (SLD) there was no known cause in 12 of the children while the other three had Down's syndrome. The average age of the SLD group was 9 years 2 months with an average mental age of 3 years 9 months. These children were matched to one group of children on chronological age and to another group on mental age. The drawing tasks administered were more varied than the "draw a person" task used by Cox and Cotgreave (1996). As well as asking children to "draw the very best man you can," the children were also required to draw some arms on five pre-drawn (armless) human figures that differed in their head/body ratio (to see if they drew the arms on the body not the head), and to copy four lines of varying angles. The pattern of findings from the three drawings tasks indicated that drawings of the SLD group were similar but somewhat developmentally inferior to the MA group (the drawings made by the CA group were notably more advanced than those drawn by the two other groups). I also notice that the scores obtained by the MLD children in the Cox and Cotgreave (1996) study were lower than the MA group (in both measures), albeit non-significantly. How should we interpret the tendency for children with both mild and severe learning difficulties to draw somewhat less well than children of a similar mental age in the papers reported by Cox and her colleagues?

The most likely explanation is that in both studies the mental-aged matched controls had a slighter higher mental age than the learning difficulties groups (see also Cox, 2005). Additionally, there may be other sampling issues in relation to the SLD group reported by the Cox and Howarth (1989) paper. Children with exceptional drawing ability were excluded in the selection of children with severe learning difficulties, potentially underestimating the drawing ability of the SLD population. Also, the group included three children with Down's syndrome. As we shall see in the next section the drawings of children with Down's syndrome appear to be particularly delayed.

Despite these caveats in sampling, the two studies by Cox and her colleagues persuasively show that children with both mild and severe learning difficulties with no known cause produce drawings that are developmentally delayed to the point of their mental age level (or possibly just below). This finding was reliable across a range of different drawing assessments that included counting of features, assigning to categories of structural forms, and the judgment of teachers. There was little evidence of qualitatively different drawings made by these children with non-specific learning difficulties. We should not be surprised by the overwhelming consensus towards a developmental delay as these children's learning difficulties are likely to be due to be nothing more than having subnormal genes and/or being brought up in a poor learning environment. In effect this means that their learning capacity is like that of a typically developing younger child. Where differences in drawings might be expected are those made by populations of children whose learning difficulties have a known organic/biological cause. These disorders tend to have a specific pattern of behavior and symptoms which may impact upon drawings in qualitatively distinct ways associated with the characteristics of the disorder. I now turn our attention, therefore, to studies on drawings made by children with disorders known to have a specific cause.

Children with Down's Syndrome

Estimates of the prevalence of Down's syndrome vary but it is thought to be around 1 in every 1,000 births (Mash & Wolfe, 2005), and in most cases is due to an extra third chromosome on the 21st pair. As well as certain physical characteristics the deficits in Down's syndrome include mental retardation, memory, speech problems, limited vocabulary, and slow motor development (Berk, 2006). Particular problems experienced by children with Down's syndrome that are most likely to impact their drawings are deficits in vision, planning, and motor control.

A number of studies have compared drawings made by children with Down's syndrome with those produced by matched controls of typically developing children (Clements & Barrett, 1994; Cox &

Maynard, 1998; Laws & Lawrence, 2001; see also Barrett & Eames, 1996; Eames & Cox, 1994). Again, as in studies of drawings made by children with non-specific learning difficulties, the focus of these papers has been to establish whether the drawings of children with Down's syndrome are developmentally delayed or qualitatively different. In one of the first studies to systematically investigate this question, Clements and Barrett (1994) tested 29 children with Down's syndrome aged between 5 years and 7 months to 17 years and 10 months, with their verbal mental ages ranging from 3 years 2 months to 8 years and 3 months. Twenty-nine younger and typically developing children were selected to match the children with Down's syndrome on verbal mental age. All children were presented with four drawing tasks that measured their ability to draw a presented scene of one object partially occluded by another (e.g., a model of a 12 cm man standing behind a 10 cm wall). The performance of the children with Down's syndrome was consistently weaker than that of the typically developing children for all the drawing tasks, indicating that children with Down's syndrome are particularly delayed in their drawing ability (i.e. more delayed than children with non-specific learning difficulties). However, there was also evidence of a different pattern of drawing strategies being used by the children with Down's syndrome. In particular, there was a higher incidence of overlapping lines (i.e. fewer partial occlusions) than found in the typically developing children's drawings. Clements and Barrett suggested that the qualitative differences in the drawings produced by children with Down's syndrome reflected poor planning of the drawing, and attentional difficulties in relation to looking at the scene.

Clements and Barrett (1994) also reported that the children with Down's syndrome were poor on a picture selection task which required them to select a picture that best represented the spatial arrangement of the objects. This difficulty suggests a more generic difficulty in appreciating spatial relationships, than merely being able to draw them. Cox and Maynard's (1998) study investigated the drawing ability in Down's syndrome using tasks that were not dependent on the visual perspective taking skill of partial occlusion. In Cox and Maynard's tasks children drew a man in two conditions, one where a doll was present and one where no model was present. Seventeen children with Down's syndrome participated in the study, aged 8 to 10 years of age with a mean verbal mental age of around

4 years. Each child was individually matched to a typically developing child either on chronological or verbal mental age. All the drawings were scored on Koppitz's (1968) developmental indicators of human figure drawings. Unsurprisingly, the drawings made by the CA control group in both tasks were scored significantly higher than the drawings from the Down's syndrome and MA control group. Children with Down's syndrome and the MA group performed similarly in the free human figure drawing task, but whereas the MA group improved on the model task the Down's syndrome group did not.

Considering the findings reported by both Clements and Barrett (1994) and Cox and Maynard (1998) the drawing performance of children with Down's syndrome appears to be particularly delayed in tasks where children are required to draw from a model, presumably because of the additional visual attentional demands in such tasks. If the model displays depth information, as in a partial occlusion scene, then this presents even further difficulty for the Down's syndrome child. Could a particular difficulty in drawing partial occlusions among children with Down's syndrome be indicative of a problem with understanding spatial relationships per se? Laws and Lawrence (2001) tested children with Down's syndrome and typically developing children on spatial drawing tasks, and also on their understanding of spatial terms. In the drawing tasks children were asked to draw from scenes in which a toy bear was placed either beside, inside or behind a transparent or opaque pot. In the spatial concepts task children were tested on their understanding of the terms "in front," "by the side," "inside" and "behind." Seventeen children with Down's syndrome participated in the study, ranging in age from 7 years 7 months to 13 years 9 months (with verbal mental ages that varied from 3 years 2 months to 8 years 3 months). The mental ages of these children were closely matched to a sample of 17 younger and typically developing children. A different pattern of performance between the two groups was revealed for the representational quality of the "bear" drawings compared to how the bear was spatially aligned to the pot. Whereas the bear drawings were significantly more advanced in the Down's syndrome group, the authors noted the children with Down's syndrome produced more overlapping drawings of the bear and pot. Although their difficulty in drawing the spatial relationships of the bear and pot echoed the findings reported by Clements and Barrett

(1994), performance on the drawing tasks was unrelated to the children's understanding on the spatial concepts tasks. For example, the authors noted that an understanding of the term "behind" did not guarantee drawings correctly depicting the teddy behind the pot.

The studies reported by Clements and Barrett (1994), Cox and Maynard (1998), and Laws and Lawrence (2001) provide consistent pointers to both developmental delay and qualitative differences in the drawings of children with Down's syndrome. In free drawing tasks that are not especially demanding on attention and partial occlusion strategies the drawing performance may be similar to mental aged controls. Drawings of models requiring spatial relationships, particular partial occlusion, indicate a pronounced developmental delay, although there is some evidence that there may also be a qualitative difference in the drawing strategies that children with Down's syndrome use in such drawings (e.g., more overlapping lines). Further strong evidence of a qualitative difference comes from the reliable finding from each of the three studies that drawing ability in Down's syndrome is unrelated to mental age (see also Eames & Cox, 1994), whereas such an association was found in the samples of typically developing children. Laws and Lawrence's finding that the drawing performance in the Down's syndrome group was unrelated to their chronological age, mental age, language comprehension, and fine motor skills, is particularly persuasive of an atypical developmental pattern in the drawings of children with Down's syndrome.

Future research using tasks that tap into a greater range of drawing skills would inform us more clearly what aspects of the drawings of children with Down's syndrome are developmentally delayed and which are qualitatively different. Golomb's (2004) reference to drawings made by some children with Down's syndrome reported by Max Klager may be suggestive. They show remarkable artistic talent of expression and have been exhibited in many countries, despite the overall poor intellectual ability of the children. It reminds us that there is more to drawing than the display of representational skill, and comparisons of drawings made by special populations to typically developing children should be more comprehensive. Despite the evidence of qualitative differences in the drawings of children with Down's syndrome it is still unclear how these might relate to what is known about the deficits of the disorder. This small body of literature has suggested a number of explanations to account for the differences that have been observed in their drawings, such as poor visual skills, poor planning, attention and motor control, as well as a weak understanding of spatial relationships. But as yet these associations are merely speculative and require empirical support.

Children with Autistic Spectrum Disorder

Estimates of the prevalence of autism in children vary up to around 60 per 10,000 (Baird et al., 2000; Chakrabarti & Fombonne, 2001), and is more frequent in males to about 3 to 4 times (Fombonne, 2003). The etiology of autism has not yet been firmly established but is likely to include a range of causes including genetic influences, brain abnormalities, and environmental factors. Autism is a disorder characterized by qualitative impairments in social interaction, communication, and restricted repetitive and stereotyped patterns of behavior, interests, and activities. In addition to these core deficits there are further associated deficits, including intellectual disability, sensory/perceptual impairments, and cognitive deficits. It is called a spectrum disorder because the symptoms are expressed in different combinations and degrees of severity between individuals with autism. Nevertheless, the general profile of abilities in autism tends to portray an uneven but typical pattern. For instance, in terms of their IQ performance people with autism tend to score poorly on verbal tests but relatively well on non-verbal tests such as memory of number strings and spatial tasks. Furthermore, there are a notable number of individuals with autism who have "islets of ability" that stand in stark contrast to their overall profile of impairments. In a few of these cases, called autistic savants, these abilities are so advanced that they exceed even those of typically developing children of the same age. The particular and outstanding ability of the autistic savant will usually be either numeric calculation, memory, music or one of a number of spatial tasks including drawing.

One such example of an autistic savant with exceptional visual realism drawing skill is the famous case study of Nadia documented by Lorna Selfe (1977), which stimulated a wide interest across a number of disciplines including child psychologists, neuropsychologists and artists. From around $3^{1}/_{2}$ years of age Nadia produced drawings of horses from a variety of perspectives and poses, each displaying remarkable photographic realism. This ability was especially outstanding as they were largely drawn from memory of seeing a picture of a horse from a single viewpoint and pose, indicating that she was able to rotate this image in her mind. One popular explanation that linked her impressive drawing ability directly to autism was that due to her almost non-existent language ability Nadia lacked the conceptual knowledge of what she was drawing (e.g., see Costall, 1997). Accordingly, she was able to produce drawings representative of the images of what she had seen, and conjure new perspectives and poses in her mind, without these images being "distorted" by a deep understanding of the subject matter. Drawing from an outstanding eidetic (photographic) memory stands in complete contrast to a discernible phase in the drawing development among typically developing children whereby drawings are said to reflect children's knowledge of the subject matter (most clearly illustrated in Luquet's stage of intellectual realism, see chapter 1), rather than an attempt to capture its visual likeness from a given perspective. There followed further accounts of other cases of extraordinary depiction of visual realism in the autistic population (e.g., Selfe, 1983; Wiltshire, 1987). The clear lack of relationship between the highly visually realistic depictions in these case studies of autistic savants with their mental age stimulated speculations of a qualitative difference in drawing development in the autistic population.

But are the reported case studies of exceptional visual realism in autistic children's drawings typical of the drawings made by children with autism in general? A number of experimental studies were reported in the early 1990s on groups of children with autism, comparing their drawings with matched controls (Charman & Baron-Cohen, 1993; Eames & Cox, 1994; Lewis & Boucher, 1991). In a study that used particularly tight and comprehensive matching of children, Eames and Cox (1994) matched thirteen 13-year-old children with autism to two samples of typically developing children (chronological and non-verbal mental aged matched controls respectively), as well as a sample of Down's syndrome children also matched on non-verbal mental age. The authors presented a wide range of 11 drawing tasks in which children were asked to draw from visual models of objects (e.g., cups, cubes, wedges, a table) in a variety of spatial relationships. An overall visual realism score was calculated across the tasks. Inconsistent with the aforementioned case studies the drawings from the autism sample were scored significantly *lower* than those produced by the two groups of typically developing children.[3] Furthermore, Eames and Cox's data was supported by similar experimental studies cited above showing no visual realism drawing advantage in autistic samples. Of particular note is Lewis and Boucher's (1991) finding that children with autism displayed a similar level of drawing skill to children with learning difficulties over 20 "free" drawings where the choice of topic in each drawing was left to the child. It is clear, therefore, that the highly photographic drawings of some autistic savants are not indicative of the drawing ability of the wider autistic population.

Not only is there a consistent lack of evidence of any notable drawing ability across the autistic spectrum, there is the suggestion from Eames and Cox's (1994) data that drawing among the autistic population may actually be particularly delayed. However, as is the case in Down's syndrome, there is also evidence of a qualitative difference as Eames and Cox found that the visual realism scores of the autistic sample were not significantly correlated with either their chronological or mental age, whereas the respective correlations within the two samples of typically developing children (chronological and mental aged matched) were significant. Additionally, I discuss below aspects of the drawings made by children with autism that appear to be different than seen in the typically developing population.

If an exceptional ability to draw is not common across the spectrum of autism how should we interpret the isolated cases of remarkable photographic realism in the drawings of some autistic savants? Is such skill related in any way to the autistic disorder? Also, is there a common developmental path among these exceptionally gifted autistic drawers which is different to that found in typically developing children? In her analysis of the developmental paths of drawings made by six artistically gifted children with autism, Selfe (1983) concluded that they followed a similar path to that found in typical development but at a much faster rate (see also Golomb, 2004). The exceptional representational drawing ability in cases of autism may be due to advanced skill in visual imagery and visual memory (Selfe, 1983; Winner, 1996), not to mention drawing skill. It has been speculated (e.g., see Cox, 2005; Winner, 1996) that visual/spatial skills have become particularly enhanced in these children because their right side of the brain (which takes the major role in visuo-spatial processing) compensates for deficits in their left side of the brain (which is more responsible for language and verbal tasks). Alternatively, it may be more appropriate to understand their exceptional representational drawing ability as an artistic talent they possess rather than a result of a cognitive deficit associated with their autism (see also Golomb, 2004). However, their obsessional practice in drawing a limited range of topics may be symptomatic of the autistic characteristic of repetitive behavior.

So far my discussion of the drawings made by children with autism (from both the artistically gifted and non-gifted) has concentrated on the visual realism of drawings. But what about other aspects of their drawings, and can they be linked to deficits in the disorder? In chapter 2 I discussed expressive drawing in typically developing children, and in particular, their developing ability to use artistic devices to express mood in their pictures. Considering the difficulty children with autism have in communicating and interpreting emotion (Hobson, 1986), and also their lack of imagination (Wing and Gould, 1979), one would predict that their expressive drawing would be even more delayed than their representational drawing. In a study I carried out with Rachael O'Kelly and Claire Barlow we asked 15 children with autism to draw a happy and sad picture. Each of these children were matched to three other children: A typically developing child of the same chronological age (CA group), a younger typically developing child with the same verbal mental age (MA), and a child with mild learning difficulties with the same chronological and verbal mental age (MLD). Verbal mental age was assessed by the British Picture Vocabulary Scale (2nd edition). The happy and sad drawings were evaluated on two measures of expression, quantity and quality of expression, that had been developed by Jolley et al. (2003) in discussion with two artists for a large-scale study on expressive drawing in typically developing children (see chapter 2 for more details). The quantity measure referred to the number of content themes displayed in each picture that was appropriate for the intended mood (e.g. for the happy drawings there were 15 themes that included people, personification, social/leisure activities, animals, vehicles, buildings, countryside/landscape, weather, speech bubbles, text, etc.). Quality of expression was measured on a 7-point scale, with defining characteristics given for each point on the scale. The same two artists who helped generate these criteria in our earlier study also

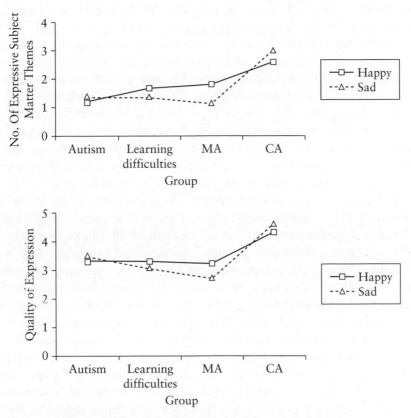

Figure 3.1 Mean quantity of expressive subject matter themes (top) and quality of expression (bottom) of happy and sad drawing by group (taken from a study by Jolley, O'Kelly and Barlow, in preparation).

rated the expressive drawings from the autism group and their matched controls, but were unaware of the different populations represented in the study. The mean quantity and quality scores for the happy and sad drawings by group are presented in Figure 3.1.

In respect of the number of expressive content themes depicted in the drawings (quantity of expression) the chronologically matched children produced significantly more themes in their sad drawings than children in the other three groups, and significantly more themes in their happy drawings than children in the autism group. For quality of expression, drawings in the chronological group were rated more highly than those made in the other three groups. These findings, as they relate to the typically developing chronologically matched children are unsurprising, as we would expect such children to be the best performing group. What is surprising is that the expressive drawings made by the children with autism were no worse than found in the two mentally aged matched groups. This is particularly noteworthy as an understanding of emotion and an ability to generate creative ideas are important in drawing expressively, but both skills are deficient in autism. Furthermore, the artists noted cases in drawings where an inappropriate theme had been shown (e.g., rain in a "happy" drawing), and the infrequent incidence of these were no greater in the autism group than in the control groups.

In Figure 3.2 we can see examples of sad drawings made by some of our children with autism that show a range of expressive devices. These included the literal depiction of emotion in a face, an abstraction of downward-shaped mouth, a personified sad expression on a donkey (Eeyore?), a bereaving person by a gravestone, and two downwardly spiraled lines. As was the case in many of the drawings made by the MA and MLD groups, most of the children with autism depicted the intended mood literally in the facial expression of a person. The extensive training typically given in autistic units of schools to the understanding of key emotions such as happy and sad no doubt helps children with autism know how happy and sad feelings are expressed in the face, and their drawings indicate strongly that many are able to show this graphically. For some children with autism their understanding of emotion may extend to an appreciation of events that evoke primary emotions, such as illustrated in the bereavement picture. What is more surprising was the occasional picture showing an emphasis on abstract expressive line, such as the downward-shaped mouth (the same child drew an upward-shaped mouth in their "happy" picture) and descending lines (see Figure 3.1). Such drawings indicated the diversity of abilities in autism, and show what can be achieved by some individuals. It would be interesting to examine drawings of other basic emotions (e.g., fear, anger disgust, and surprise; see Ekman, 1982) in the autistic population, and of more complex emotions (e.g., pride), to establish where the autistic deficits in emotion and in generating ideas is communicated in their drawings compared to mental-aged controls. For now, our findings show that the ability to draw the basic emotions of happy and sad in the autistic population is consummate with their generally delayed learning

Figure 3.2   Five sad drawings made by children with autism showing different expressive techniques (taken from a study by Jolley, et al., in preparation).

ability, and not further burdened with the specific autistic deficit in emotional understanding.

As well as evaluating the quality of (representational or expressive) drawing in autism there are other features of their drawings that might be affected by the impairments found in autism. For instance, observation of children with autism in social environments often reveals a relative lack of interest in people. This was supported experimentally in a picture sorting task reported by Celani (2002). Unlike mental-aged matched control groups who preferred pictures of people to inanimate objects (and also pictures of a person interacting with another person rather than with an object), this pattern tended to be reversed for the selections made by the children with autism. Furthermore, authors such as Selfe (1983) and Cox (2005) have reported that autistic savants gifted in drawing tend not to draw people, preferring to draw inanimate objects such as buildings, vehicles, roads, and road signs. But is a lack of depicting people typical in the drawings of the wider population of children with autism? Lewis and Boucher (1991) did not find any evidence for differences in the number of drawings of people versus inanimate objects between a sample of 12 children with autism (not selected for their drawing ability) matched to 12 children with learning difficulties. Consistent with their finding, Rachael O'Kelly, Claire Barlow and I also found little evidence to suggest that drawings from the autistic group portrayed a different pattern of expressive themes to that of the two groups of mentally aged matched controls.[4] For instance, a particular liking for inanimate subject matter among some autistic savants was not borne out in our sample of more typical children with autism. In respect of the frequency in which people were drawn, Table 3.1 displays the number of children from each group who drew a person in the happy and sad drawings, and also the number who drew only a part of the human body, typically just the face ("disembodied body parts"). Although there was evidence that there were fewer people drawn in the autistic group, particularly in their sad drawings, when we include the data for the part-person drawings there were no overall material differences. The request to produce "mood" drawings may be an optimum method of encouraging children with autism to include people in their drawings, as mood is usually considered a

Table 3.1 Numbers of Children by Group Depicting a Person (Complete or in Part) in their Happy and Sad Drawings

	Happy		*Sad*	
Group	*Depiction of person(s)*	*Disembodied body parts*	*Depiction of person(s)*	*Disembodied body parts*
Autism	6	5	4	7
Learning difficulties	9	3	13	2
Mental-aged matched	8	–	8	–
Chronological-aged matched	9	5	9	3

human state. However, their social impairment may still reveal itself in other ways in their drawings. For instance, it was noticeable that not a single autistic child drew a social scene in either their happy or sad drawing.

Research carried out by Lee and Hobson (2006) suggests that the social interaction impairment in autism may also influence other aspects of human figure drawings. They found that in a sample of fourteen 8- to 15-year-old children with autism many drew figures of a male, a female, and themselves that showed little differentiation, unlike the human figure drawings of children with learning difficulties matched on verbal mental age. The lack of differentiation in the autistic sample was limited to human figure drawings as they were able to vary their drawings of houses to a greater extent than the children with learning difficulties. Lee and Hobson argued that children with autism have a restricted social awareness in which they are unable to properly conceive the differences between people, including themselves, and that this was communicated in the human figure drawings in the autistic sample in their study. Another impact of the socialization impairment (and also poor communication) is that among autistic savants gifted in drawing they rarely make their drawings for communicative purposes (e.g., by not showing their drawings to others) or talk about their drawings (see Cox, 2005; Selfe, 1983). I am unaware of whether similar observations have been made of the more general autistic population but if autistic savants gifted in drawing do not "show off" their highly impressive representational drawings (a notable exception can be found in Wiltshire, 1987, 1989, 1991), then we would expect it to occur even less so for the "delayed" drawings produced by most children with autism.

As was the case for our findings, Lewis and Boucher (1991) also found a similar range of topics in the drawings made by their autistic group compared to a learning impaired group. However, it may be that the restricted, repetitive, and stereotyped patterns of behavior seen in autism lead to a narrow range of thematic content across a number of drawings made by an individual child. Indeed, this was the case across 10 drawings produced by each child in the autistic sample reported by Lewis and Boucher (1991), and has also been suggested to be the case for children with autism gifted in art (Cox, 2005; Selfe, 1983). Further evidence for a lack of creative and imaginative drawing in autism has been shown in tasks requiring the drawing of impossible entities, such a "fish-mouse" (Craig, Baron-Cohen, & Scott, 2001; but see Leevers & Harris, 1998).

Some researchers have commented on the process and planning of drawing in autistic savants gifted in drawing. For instance Cox (Cox, 2005; Cox & Eames, 1999) noted a tendency among them to build up the drawing part by part, producing and finishing each part with much detail before moving on to the next section (see also Selfe, 1983). This process contrasts to that often found in artists without autism who first sketch out the whole drawing and then add the details in (Cox, 2005). This focus of the details of the parts has been linked to a weak or absent drive for global coherence in autism. Weak central coherence theory states that while people with autism process things in a piecemeal way rather than the global whole, typically developing individuals attempt to process things in context and try to see things as a whole (Frith, 2003). There is some suggestive evidence that high-functioning children and adults with autism also tend to draw in detailed parts (Booth, Charlton, Hughes, & Happé, 2003; Mottron, Belleville, & Ménard, 1999), but there were still many who did not use this approach, or did so for only the beginning of their drawing. Future research needs to examine the process of producing drawings in detailed sub-sections in children who are more in the middle and lower-end of the spectrum of autism. What is known, however, is that even autistic savant artists who use this style still produce coherent and integrated drawings (Cox, 2005), suggesting that they have a strong idea of the finished product (Selfe, 1983). For these reasons one must therefore be cautious in making too close a link between drawing process and weak central coherence in autism.

Consistent with autism being a spectrum disorder, with a mix of abilities and severity in individuals with autism, we see a great variability in the drawings made by children with autism. There are aspects of their drawings (e.g., visual realism, topics drawn, process of drawing, etc.) that can be linked to either the cognitive profile or impairments and deficits of autism in the few cases of artistic giftedness, but it appears such features on the whole are not found in the drawings of the general autistic population. Future research will no doubt lay down more precisely the relationship between characteristics of autism and drawing behavior, but we will always find variability in drawings of children with autism that reflect the variability in the autistic profile. As it stands at the moment it appears that for most children with autism their drawings are developmentally delayed, with some evidence of qualitative differences in certain aspects of the process and product of their drawings and also because the quality of the drawings is not closely linked to their mental age.

Children with Williams Syndrome

Williams Syndrome is a rare genetic disorder relating to the 7th chromosome. Its prevalence has been estimated at around 1 in every 20,000 births (Morris & Mervis, 1999). Among general learning difficulties there is a severe deficit in visual-spatial skills, but with a marked preservation in many language abilities. Based on their deficit in visual-spatial skills one would not expect to find artistic giftedness in Williams syndrome, unlike that shown in some autistic savants. Indeed, one would predict that in the general population of children with Williams syndrome their drawing ability would be particularly poor.

In a case study reported by Stiles, Sabbadini, Capirci and Volterra (2000) both spontaneous and requested drawings were collected from a girl with Williams syndrome between the ages of 3 and 6 years. In particular, her drawings of people, houses, and copied geometric forms were studied by the authors. They reported that although her drawing performance improved with age, her drawing development was slow despite her receiving continued training in drawing. The authors noted that the poor integration of elements in her house drawings and copied geometric forms in particular clearly showed her visuo-spatial deficit. The authors suggested on the basis of this single case study that the drawings of children with Williams syndrome are delayed but develop along a typical course.

In order to test this, further studies have compared the drawing performance of children with Williams syndrome with that of control groups matched on mental age. They have shown that copying geometric patterns in Williams syndrome is comparable to controls (Georgopoulos, Georgopoulos, Kuz, & Landau, 2004), or appears to be particularly developmentally delayed (Bertrand, Mervis, & Eisenberg, 1997; Dykens, Rosner, & Ly, 2001). Furthermore, both Georgopoulos et al. and Dykens et al. reported significant correlations in the Williams syndrome group between their performance on the copying tasks and their mental age. Accordingly, both sets of authors concluded that drawing in Williams syndrome is developmentally delayed rather than deviant. This was also the view of Bertrand et al. (1997) who noticed that the children with Williams syndrome made the same errors in integrating the shapes as shown in the drawings made by younger, typically developing children.

Where children with Williams syndrome particularly struggle in copying geometric patterns are those tasks that require integration of parts to form a whole. There has been a debate in the literature concerning whether one characteristic of Williams syndrome, as in autism, is a bias towards the processing of local rather than global information. If such a local bias is found in drawing, then one would expect it to present itself primarily in integrating elements. In a task that is relevant to this question Farran, Jarrold and Gathercole (2003) asked 21 individuals with Williams syndrome and 21 typically developing children matched on non-verbal mental age, to copy small letters arranged in such a way to form a large letter (in some drawings the smaller letters were the same as the large letter they illustrated). The participants' drawings were scored on both global accuracy (e.g., relating to the accuracy of overall shape of the large letter) and local accuracy (e.g., accuracy of representing and orientating the smaller letters). The individuals with Williams syndrome were significantly better at drawing the local form than the global figure, whereas the control group did not show a local or global bias in performance.[5]

But is there any evidence of incoherent pictures (due to poor integration of its parts) in more "natural" representational drawings made by children with Williams syndrome? Bertrand et al.'s (1997) analysis of flower, house, and elephant drawings made by children with Williams syndrome revealed more disorganized drawings than produced by the mental aged controls, but the difference in number did not reach statistical significance. Human figure drawing, in particular, is an interesting topic to investigate in Williams syndrome because although it might present an especially difficult topic to draw as it requires integration of parts, it may be a well-practiced topic as children with the disorder are known to display very sociable behavior, even to strangers. In Stiles et al.'s (2000) longitudinal study the girl with Williams syndrome spontaneously drew many people and by 6 years of age she was placing them in scenes. Furthermore, the developmental forms of her drawings of people were similar to those found in the drawings made by typically developing children. However, as this was a single case study of drawings produced in variable conditions with no control group's drawing for comparison, the authors felt unable to comment on the developmental point of the girl's drawings.

A study that goes some way to inform us on the relative quality of human figure drawing in Williams syndrome was reported by Dykens et al. (2001). They asked 28 children, adolescents, and adults with Williams syndrome (mean age of 14 years) to draw a person. Not only was it possible for the authors to categorize their drawings in the forms commonly found in typically developing children's drawings but performance also correlated with mental age. Interestingly, Dykens reported that their performance on the human figure drawing task was comparable to that of a matched control group of children with learning difficulties, unlike the relative poor performance on a copying task in the Williams syndrome group (see above). It may be that with topics that interest children with Williams syndrome, namely people, they are able to overcome some of their weakness in producing coherent spatial relationships between elements. In which case the human figure drawings of children with Williams syndrome may be an example of an enhanced behavior in Williams syndrome (socialization) going some way to compensating a deficit relating to the syndrome (poor integration of parts).

Research into the drawings made by children with Williams syndrome has consistently shown that the drawings are developmentally delayed rather than qualitatively deviant. The graphic forms they produce are characteristic of those made by younger, typically developing children, and furthermore, are related to their mental age. The drawings are particularly delayed for those topics requiring integration of parts, which may relate to a configural bias in local rather than global processing. However, in the case of drawing the human figure, an interest and practice in this topic may offset any difficulty with assimilating parts into a whole.

Children with ADHD and Developmental Coordination Disorder

Apart from drawing research conducted on populations of children with non-specific learning difficulties, Down's syndrome, autistic spectrum disorder and Williams syndrome, there has been very little research on drawing from other special populations of children. Although there are numerous known disorders in childhood, most of them would not necessarily have implications on drawing behavior. There are a few, however, that would merit more attention than currently received. For instance, in the case of ADHD, with its core deficits of inattention, hyperactivity, and impulsivity, one might expect children to produce poor drawings as a direct result of their difficulty to concentrate on any one task for any length of time. But there are other associated problems of ADHD, such as a difficulty with executive functions (e.g., planning) and motor coordination, which might also negatively impact upon their drawing. Kibby, Cohen, and Hynd (2002) gave 6- to 12-year-old children with ADHD and typically developing children of a similar age the clock drawing task. In this task, children are asked to draw a clock and set the time to one designated by the experimenter. The authors reported that the drawings of clocks and the setting of the hands was significantly poorer in the ADHD group, with these drawings showing poor positioning and sequencing of the numbers. The authors attributed this to poor planning, and an indication of the executive function deficit in ADHD (see also Booth et al., 2003).[6] Miyahara, Piek and Barrett (2006) also did not attribute inaccurate drawing in their sample of children with ADHD as a direct result of the core deficits in the disorder, but instead interpreted it as evidence of a separate motor deficit. Unfortunately, research on drawing performance in ADHD is scarce and has not addressed the fundamental question of how drawing might relate to the core deficits of ADHD. Furthermore, I know of no research investigating the development of drawing in this population, and whether the drawings and drawing behavior differ from the norm in any way.

There are a number of other disorders which are commonly found in children with ADHD. One of these is developmental coordination disorder (DCD, also known as "clumsy child syndrome"), which is characterized by marked motor incoordination that is out of proportion with the child's general development (and found despite the absence of any other condition known to affect movement, such a cerebral palsy). Children with DCD are noted for their delays in achieving motor milestones (sitting, crawling, walking) and having difficulties with fine motor tasks (e.g., tying up shoelaces, doing up buttons).

Accordingly, we would expect drawing development to be affected by children diagnosed with DCD. Indeed, clinicians may be alerted to a potential diagnosis when seeing a child draw (Hamilton, 2002). Barnett and Henderson (1992) compared the human figure drawings of a sample of 42 clumsy children aged 5 to 13 years, each matched to a well-coordinated child on verbal mental age and chronological age. The authors reported that the human figure drawings (scored on the Goodenough-Harris scale, Harris, 1963) produced by the clumsy children were significantly delayed according to the scale, and also compared to the human figure drawings of the control group. The authors commented that the drawings made by the clumsy children revealed poorer representation of proportions, lower scores for depiction and detail of features, and in particular weak motor control and coordination. They commented that on average the drawing scores of the clumsy children were delayed by 2 years, with some children's drawings up to 5 years delayed.

In a follow-up 18-month longitudinal study on 16 of the original sample of clumsy children, Barnett and Henderson noticed that while some of the children's drawings became more developmentally delayed, others improved. This finding reminds us that within any disorder children do not represent a homogenous group, and that this may be reflected in their drawings. One factor that may influence the developmental trajectory of drawings in DCD is that some children may be more able to use strategies to compensate for their motor problems. Barnett and Henderson commented that a motivation to practice, drawing smaller pictures, pressing the marker down hard on the paper or by sketching, and using the non-drawing hand to guide the marker, all might reduce the impact of their motor deficit on the developmental delay of their drawings.

Blind Children

On first consideration one might think that blind children would not engage in picture-making activities, particularly those blind from birth or the "early blind," because they would not be interested in representing things that they have not seen. And accordingly, that asking blind children to draw in an experiment would be pointless, and even unkind, as surely they could not have the first idea on how to represent things they cannot see in pictures. But as we shall see, this is far from the case, as blind children are very able to make respectable pictorial representations that show the same graphic techniques of realism found in sighted children's drawings. This finding raises some interesting questions as to what extent blind children are able to discover themselves these graphic conventions, and also the flexibility of the brain to interpret spatial information on touch and movement alone.

Pictures suitable for the blind are most typically made with the use of raised line drawing kits. The kits include a board covered with a layer of rubber upon which a plastic sheet is placed. Once pressure is placed on the sheet by a ball-point, raised lines are produced which the drawer can feel. When blind children are presented with pre-made pictures on these kits they can recognize the subject matter through touch and movement at least as well as matched sighted (but blindfolded) children presented with the same raised-line pictures (D'Angiulli, Kennedy, & Heller, 1998). Furthermore, this has been replicated cross-culturally (Kennedy, 1997). Such findings indicate that blind children can interpret lines in two-dimensional space as representations of their three-dimensional referents. But can they produce recognizable representations, and do the drawings follow a similar developmental path to sighted children?

An early study that addressed this question was reported by Millar (1975), who compared the human figure drawings made by blind and sighted children aged 6, 8, and 10 years. The blind children were either blind from birth or became blind before 2 years of age, and so they would have had minimal visual experience of pictures and the things they refer to. Each blind child was matched to a sighted child on age, gender, parental socio-economic status, and on forward and backward digit span performance (so the samples could be considered broadly of the same intelligence). All the children were asked to draw a human figure with the raised line drawing kit (each child had used the kit 3 weeks before the experiment). The authors reported that none of the blind children had drawn a human figure prior to the experiment. In fact, Millar commented that many of them protested mildly that they could not draw because they were blind, although with a little encouragement they soon began to enjoy the task. The sighted children made two drawings, first when blindfolded and then in normal sighted conditions.

Analysis of the representational quality of the drawings made by the blind children and blindfolded sighted children revealed relatively poorer quality of drawing among the 6- and 8-year-old blind children, in fact, many of their drawings were unrecognizable as a human figure. In contrast, the 10-year-old blind children produced a similar level of representational quality compared to their sighted (albeit) blindfolded controls, and furthermore, used similar shapes for the human figure parts as found in the sighted children's drawings. Nevertheless, a particular and common error among the blind sample (including the 10-year-olds) was the orientation of the human figure drawing, with as many as 53% of them drawing it inverted or horizontal (only two sighted children did so). Their verbal responses to being asked to indicate where the "floor" was in their drawing emphasized that most were not aware of the pictorial convention of it being represented by the bottom of the page, even in those blind children who drew a vertical figure.

Two questions come to mind when considering Millar's (1975) findings. First, what enabled her 10-year-old blind children to draw at a similar level to their age-matched sighted children, when other blind children only two years younger struggled to produce a representational figure? Second, are there some pictorial conventions that rely on blind children being taught, if they have had little or no past experience of seeing pictures? Millar provides no answer to the first question of the remarkable developmental shift, merely commenting that the older blind children had grasped the rules of translating the information of the body they had gained through touch to pictorial line. Millar also gives no information on whether the older children had previous drawing experience, but one can presume that increased experience touching haptic pictures (and also objects) provides insight into appropriate lines and shapes for representational purposes. In relation to the question of learning pictorial conventions, Millar notes that it took centuries for artists to adequately master how to depict the floor in scenes. It is perhaps too much to expect blind children, therefore, to invent themselves this pictorial convention, not to mention others that represent the three-dimensional world in two-dimensional space. In which case, blind children in particular may be reliant on being taught such conventions.

In a review of his several years of working with blind children drawing, Kennedy (1997) noted a number of cases of blind adolescent and adult drawings that show blind people can use many of the pictorial devices that sighted children use. In particular he lists lines to denote edges and surfaces, foreshortened shapes and converging lines for depth, evidence of a vantage point, motion, and even symbolic shapes for abstract messages. This is indeed an impressive array of pictorial conventions, as many of them were drawn by people who had neither seen pictures nor the things they represent. Kennedy argues that the blind are able to do this because it is possible to gain the relevant information about space and form from touch and movement. In which case blind children with increasing experience of haptic pictures may become surprisingly proficient in learning the same graphic conventions used in pictures made by sighted people, and may not require extensive teaching of graphic conventions from the sighted. Kennedy's position has implications for the plasticity of the brain, and in particular, how the visual cortex can be used to process tactile discrimination. In his book, *Drawing and the Blind: Pictures to Touch*, Kennedy (1993) discusses this question in some detail. In brief, Kennedy (1997) states that the area of the brain that takes in information such as foreground and background, occlusion, perspective, flat and curved surfaces, is amodal in the sense that it is not reliant solely on one particular sensory input, such as attained through vision.

Blind children's ability to recognize objects depicted in raised line drawings indicate that they, like sighted children, can easily appreciate the correspondence between two-dimensional shapes with their real three-dimensional referents. The fact that they take relatively longer than sighted children to produce recognizable representations is no doubt due to being deprived of the visual information sight affords. Nevertheless, blind children's drawings can reach a similar representational level attained in sighted children's products using the same drawing kits when blindfolded, but are likely to fall short compared to visually unimpaired children's drawings produced in normal drawing conditions (see Millar, 1975). It is as yet unclear what the respective roles of blind children's own graphic inventions and tuition of pictorial conventions plays in the development of their drawings. In any event, the ability to produce representational drawings by the congenitally and early blind is a testament to the flexibility of the brain in processing spatial information.

Summary

Research into the drawings of children from different special populations has tended to show that their drawings are developmentally delayed, using similar graphic shapes that are consistent with children matched on mental age. This indicates that their drawings are more likely to be associated with their general learning difficulties rather than the deficits characteristic of their disorder. Nevertheless, there are instances of qualitative differences in their drawings that can be linked directly to the disorder, but more research is needed to establish the precise associations between aspects of their drawings and the core/peripheral deficits that define the disorder. One should also bear in mind that although children suffering from any given condition will share common diagnostic criteria, they will also vary in their diagnostic profile as well as in other attributes, and this is communicated in the variability in the drawings we see across children with the same condition. In the same way that typically developing children are individuals so are children with a diagnostic condition, and consequently we should appreciate the individuality in their drawings too.

Notes

1 Although the IQ of the children were not stated in Cox and Cotgreave (1996), Maureen Cox (2005) commented that the IQ of the children ranged from 50 to 70 (the range typically considered to reflect mild learning difficulties).

2 The IQ of children with severe learning difficulties is typically considered to be below 50. Although Cox and Howarth (1989) did not state the IQ of their SLD group, the larger gap between the chronological and mental ages in the SLD group than reported in Cox and Cotgreave's (1996) MLD group at least indicates that these children were more intellectually disabled.

3 Although the drawings from the children with autism received significantly higher scores than those from the Down's syndrome sample this finding may be accounted for by the specific difficulty in drawing spatial relationships by Down's syndrome children (see section on Down's syndrome children). Also, the children with Down's syndrome tested by

Eames and Cox (1994) had a slightly lower non-verbal mental age than the autistic sample.

4   The statistical differences we found in the use of individual themes between the groups were almost always due to relatively more children from the CA group displaying certain themes, which is entirely predictable.

5   There is evidence that the local bias in Williams syndrome appears more in tasks which require constructing a whole form from its elements, as shown by the performance on block design tasks and drawing, than in perceptual tasks that call for the identification of the global form of objects and other stimuli from its elements (Deruelle, Rondan, Mancini, & Livet, 2006; Farran et al., 2003). This suggests that the deficit is not visual perceptual per se, but configural (i.e. arranging parts spatially to represent a form or figure).

6   The clock drawing test is consistently used in adult neuropsychological evaluations as a measure of, among other things, visuospatial skills, graphomotor abilities and executive functions (of which planning is considered one component).

4

Production and Comprehension of Representational Drawing

It is generally true that the development of children's understanding of performance in domains of ability predates that of their own performance ability. Research that has compared the development of children's production and comprehension of representational drawing, however, has thrown up conflicting findings: either production and comprehension develop concurrently or production lags behind comprehension. After discussing this literature, and some methodological concerns I have with it, I present my own work with colleagues that compares children's cognitive and affective choices from a developmental array of drawings with their own drawings. While the findings are consistent with understanding the developmental lag in drawing being due to children encountering difficulties in production, there are also consistent with the view that children have different intentions and graphic models for comprehending and producing representational pictures. These two possibilities have implications for whether children are satisfied with their drawings or not, as does the tendency for younger children to overestimate the representational standard of their drawing ability. The chapter then considers deeper levels of children's comprehension of pictures, namely their understanding of what develops and why in drawing, that suggests a potentially interesting relationship with the child's own production level.

Only a few moments' reflection is needed to consider examples of domains of ability where our knowledge of human performance outstrips our own performance ability. For example, if given the inclination most of us can learn about art history, the artists that have shaped that history and the varying styles they have created, and even the meaning of individual paintings. But only a relative few are able to paint to the same standard as the Masters we can study, even if a lot of effort and tuition is engaged in trying to do so. In contrast, there are other practical activities that occupy many of us on a daily basis where we show great competence in, but if asked about our understanding of the processes involved most would struggle to answer. Recently I was in a situation where I had to direct eight car drivers back to my house from a central location where we had met up. I was rather unprepared for this task and found it quite difficult to visualize the map of roads and landmarks from where we were currently to my home, even though I had no trouble driving back home myself (everyone made it despite me underestimating the distance by half and misjudging the number of roundabouts!). It seems that for some skills, therefore, our production of them is more fluid and automatic compared to our understanding of their underlying processes.

The relationship between production and comprehension is particularly important and interesting to study in children as marked developmental changes in both occur in childhood, and are likely to influence each other in complex ways. For children it is generally the case that comprehension develops before production. A clear example of this is in their early use of language. Babies and young infants can understand a considerable amount from what is said to them long before they can speak those same words (see Jusczyk, 1997). As production lags comprehension in children's early development of language we might assume this to be the case for other symbolic systems as well, especially pictures. In producing a picture the child first has to extract from his or her wider knowledge of the topic to be drawn which features to depict in the drawing. During the process of drawing the child not only has to use appropriate graphic schema for those features with the required motor control of wrist and marker, but also monitor each line within an organized plan for the whole drawing. This necessitates planning, memory, and attention. In contrast, when viewing a picture the child is not required to engage in any of these processes. Instead, the subject matter of representational pictures can be recognized by noticing the similarity of the graphic conventions to the object or scene referred to. As representational pictures often represent an iconic similarity with their referents, unlike language, then we would expect recognition of pictorial content to be particularly straightforward in contrast to the performance of drawing that same content.

But recognition of the content in pictures is not the same as comprehending that content (see Sigel, 1978). Before we can establish the relationship between the child's production and comprehension of drawing we first need to define (and operationalize) what we mean by comprehension, and to distinguish it from recognition.

Recognition and Comprehension in Pictures

If we take recognition as being able to identify a similarity between a depicted object and its referent then habituation studies show that such recognition ability may be gained within the first few months of life (DeLoache, Strauss, & Maynard, 1979). Furthermore, with the onset of early spoken language infants can name objects in pictures much earlier than they can draw them, even if brought up in an environment with very minimal exposure to pictures (see Hochberg & Brooks, 1962). These lines of research are covered in depth in chapter 5, but for the purpose of the present discussion they confirm what is clearly evident from observing young children naturally: that they can recognize familiar content in pictures prior to being able to represent the same subject matter in their pictures.

Comprehension is more than mere recognition though, and involves both a cognitive and affective response. For instance, if we asked an art critic for an interpretation of the famous Renoir painting, *The Charpentier Family* that shows a girl looking at a dog as the central characters, we would be somewhat disappointed if we were only told it was of a girl looking at a dog (i.e. a recognition response)! We might expect to hear at least some of the following: what meaning the painting is conveying (expression of ideas and feelings), the process in which the materials had been used to create the picture, whether the painting is representative of a certain style or art tradition, and something about the painter's intention and how this particular painting is placed in respect of his other work (such as its style and subject matter).

The nature of comprehension becomes more complex when we consider that the above examples of knowledge of paintings are cognitive responses only. Let us not forget that a painting is largely created to be appreciated, and people may vary in their opinions of a work of art even though they may have a similar (cognitive) understanding of it. To give a trivial example from popular music, there are many people who understand that the Beatles fare well when measured against potentially important and objective criteria for assessing the worth of a pop or rock 'n' roll band (e.g., musicianship, creativity, record sales, influence on pop music and on the wider culture) but not everyone likes to listen to them very much. In such cases their comprehension of the Beatles includes a cognitive understanding of their achievements but an affective response that is rather negative. Although a trivial example, it highlights the need to include both the cognitive and affective responses in our construct of comprehension. But both responses are not independent from each other. If we asked our art critic for his personal opinion on the Renoir painting no doubt his liking or disliking of it would be explained at least in part by his understanding of the painting (see Goodman, 1976, for his discussion on the complex interplay between our cognitive and affective responses to art).

So how can we apply this discussion to measuring children's production and comprehension of drawing? As a starting point we need to measure children's cognitive and affective responses to pictures and in some way compare this with their own productions. But how? There is no point showing children fine art made by adult artists and then ask them about the same deep understandings of paintings that are held by art critics. They are largely unaware of such things. A more appropriate comparison is to ask children to respond cognitively and affectively to the types of depictions typically found in children's drawings, and compare these responses to the drawings they are currently producing themselves.

This approach is supported by research evidence that children's production and comprehension of pictures develop along very similar broad paths. We saw in chapter 1 that children's drawings develop from basic scribbles to representations of increasing visual realism. There is evidence from comprehension studies using a wide variety of methodologies (selection tasks to semi-structured interviews) and art forms (from colored line drawings to paintings) that there is a similar developmental shift. That is, children initially focus on the non-representational property of pictures and later attend to the subject matter with a growing interest in realism (e.g., Jolley, Zhi, & Thomas, 1998a; Machotka, 1966; Parsons, 1987; Rosenstiel, Morison, Silverman, & Gardner, 1978). Furthermore, in his semi-structured interviews of children on their opinions of a selection of works of art, Parsons (1987) found that children's interest in realism developed from a preference from the depiction of "schematic realism" to "photographic realism." This shift mirrors the development from intellectual to visual realism Luquet (1927/2001) described in his account of drawing development.

The striking commonality in the broad developmental paths found in children's production and comprehension of pictures provides further justification for comparing the respective points children are at in their performance and understanding of drawing. I shall now discuss the body of research that has done just that.

Comparing Children's Production and Comprehension of Drawing

The methodological procedure used by researchers has been to ask the child to draw a topic, and also to select a drawing from an array of pictures of that same topic. In this selection task the drawings present different representational standards that are said to reflect the developmental range typically found in children's drawings of the topic. Although some of the studies reported have been designed to pursue other research questions relating to children's attitudes towards pictures and their own drawings, by comparing the drawings the children select with the ones they draw themselves we can gauge whether comprehension or production is in advance of the other, or whether they develop concurrently. While some studies have reported that selections are in advance of productions (e.g., Fayol, Barrouillet, & Chevrot, 1995; Golomb, 1992; Jolley et al., 2000; Jolley, Knox, & Wainwright, 2001; Kosslyn, Heldmeyer, & Locklear, 1977; Lewis, 1963a), others found that children selected the same level of drawing as shown in their own picture (e.g., Brooks, Glenn, & Crozier,

1988; Moore, 1986; Taylor & Bacharach, 1981). Research has therefore thrown up two contradictory findings: production and comprehension develop concurrently or production lags behind comprehension.
I shall now present the evidence from these two camps.

(i)   The case for production and comprehension developing
      concurrently

Taylor and Bacharach (1981) showed 3- to 5-year-olds three cardboard formulaic representational drawings of a man (tadpole, transitional, and conventional figure[1]), and asked the children to pick the
one which looked most like a real man. Children were then asked
to draw a man with the conventional drawing left in view as a model.
The most frequent choice made by the tadpole and conventional drawers was the figure similar to the one they drew, although this choice
did not represent a high percentage (around 45% of the tadpole
drawers chose the tadpole drawing, and 60% of the conventional
drawers chose the conventional drawing). The study provided some
evidence, therefore, that young representational drawers are more
likely to consider a form of the human figure similar to the one they
currently draw as the most realistic. In contrast, the scribblers picked
the most advanced (i.e. conventional) drawing but their choices are
difficult to interpret as they were not provided with a similar (scribbled) drawing to choose from in the selection task.

Moore (1986) asked 4- to 9-year-olds to select the best drawing
of a house from an array of formulaic drawings of houses that varied
in the position of the chimney and windows, and whether the house
showed one or two sides (see Figure 4.1). The children were also asked
to draw a house (no model was shown). Moore argued that children
of all ages preferred drawings that had most features in common with
their own productions. Further support for this position came from
Brooks et al. (1988) who applied a similar methodology to 4-year-
olds' drawings and "best" choices of people and houses.

Despite using a different topic of the drawings (house and human
figure) and the variation in instructions for the selection task (the
best/the most realistic) these three studies converge on the view that
representational drawers produce drawing forms that they consider
as ideal. Furthermore, the authors of these three papers used a similar explanation to account for their consistent data. They stated that

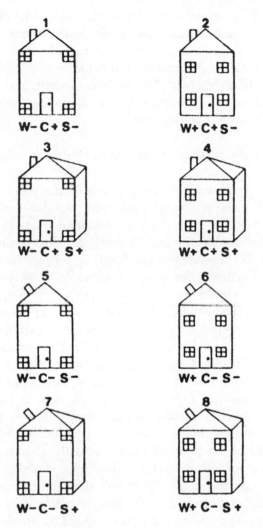

Figure 4.1 The house drawings presented by Moore (1986) in her selection task.

children have a (developmentally changing) conception of what the important features of a topic are, and these important features for the child are extracted from their wider knowledge of the topic. Clearly this argument is in essence Luquet's (1927) notion of the child's internal model (see chapter 1), and indeed both Moore (1986) and Brookes et al. (1988) refer to Luquet, while Taylor & Bacharach (1981) refer to the child's metaknowledge of the topic. The child's internal model (or metaknowledge) drives their choice of drawing, whether it is one they make themselves or select from an array of drawings. The implications for the relationship between production and comprehension is that they both develop concurrently, and are driven by the child's (changing) conception of the salient features of the topic and how they should be depicted.

(ii)   The case for production lagging behind comprehension

One of the early studies suggesting that children select developmentally more advanced representations than they draw themselves was reported by Kosslyn et al. (1977). They showed 4- to 11-year-olds three-dimensional objects which the authors called a cube, house (but shaped more like a warehouse or barn), a prism, and a flat surface with sticks protruding upwards. All four objects were presented at an angle to the children so that the depth of the objects would be visible to them. The children were then shown an array of drawings of each object, prepared by the experimenters, each showing a different method of representing the topic (e.g., front face only, diagrammatic or "fold-out" drawings, different types of perspective). The children were asked to pick the "best picture of what we saw" (the three-dimensional objects remained in view in half the trials). Children also drew each object while it was placed in front of them. Many children drew diagrammatic pictures that displayed the components of the object (but not from a visually accurate perspective) but chose one of the perspective drawings in the selection task. The authors concluded that children's drawings do not reflect an internal representation of an object but are affected by production deficiencies (i.e. opposite to the view provided by Brooks et al., 1988; Moore, 1986; Taylor & Bacharach, 1981).

Closer inspection of Kosslyn et al.'s (1977) data reveals that it would be too simplistic to conclude that all children's drawings were developmentally inferior to their chosen selections. For instance, it appears that many of the older children drew and chose "conventional" perspective drawings. The possibility that the gap between production and comprehension declines with age was tested by Fayol et al. (1995). They asked 3- to 10-year-olds to draw a man and a house, and three weeks later were asked to judge from pairs of other children's drawings which one was done by the older child. The authors suggested two hypotheses. First, that children's internal models are similar to those held by adults but that production difficulties lead to the child's own drawing to be developmental inferior to those drawings they choose. The tendency to select more advanced drawings than they draw themselves declines with age as children improve their production performance. Second, if both children's selections and drawings are dictated by their internal model of the topic, then there would be no production lag. Consistent with the first hypothesis, and as indicated by Kosslyn et al.'s data, the inferiority of the children's own drawing compared to their choices on the judgment task decreased with age. These two studies appear to support the view, therefore, that although production lags comprehension in drawing, the lag diminishes in older children as they become more accomplished in reproducing their visual intention.

Making sense of the opposing findings is hindered by the number of methodological problems ingrained in the studies reported from both camps. I will first discuss these methodological issues in detail and then present some of my own research with colleagues that has addressed these issues.

Methodological Issues

(i)   Topic of drawings

Using novel and unfamiliar topics that children have had little or no previous experience drawing is likely to result in inferior productions, relative to their choice of drawing in the selection task. This was the case in Kosslyn et al.'s (1977) study, and indeed the authors noted the frustration of the children during their frequent revisions as they struggled to produce representations similar to the presented models. By requesting drawings of novel stimuli the experimental tasks become an assessment on how well children can create "on the spot" solutions rather than a valid measurement of the child's current representational drawing ability. The latter is better served by asking children to draw well-practiced and familiar topics, such as people. Furthermore, there are likely to be known developmental patterns of children's drawings of frequently drawn topics from which experimenters can more reliably measure the developmental points of the child's production and comprehension.

(ii)   The production task

In some studies the child has been asked to draw from a two-dimensional model (Taylor & Bacharach, 1981) or a three-dimensional model (Kosslyn et al., 1977). In such cases the child does not have complete freedom to draw the topic as they please due to the demands of having to represent the model as accurately as possible. Consequently, the product may be far removed from how they typically draw.

(iii)   The selection task

Many studies in this literature have presented children with adult-generated formulaic reproductions of the topics that are so rigidly and heavily controlled (for examples, see Brooks et al., 1988; Kosslyn et al., 1977; Lewis, 1963a; Moore, 1986; Taylor & Bacharach, 1981) as to lose their connection with the reality of children's drawings. A clear example of this is in the house drawings presented by Moore (1986) (see Figure 4.1). The drawings vary only on placement of windows and chimney, and whether an additional side was shown. The variation in these depictions is far removed from the range of house drawings that children actually produce (see Barrouillet et al., 1994). The stimuli presented by Brooks et al. (1988) of a person and house was a better attempt to display a developmental range but even these drawings vary only in number of details, which is only one property in which children's drawings develop. Presenting experimenter-produced formulaic drawings may be advocated if the purpose of the investigation is to establish which properties of drawings (e.g., color, detail, proportion, perspective, etc.) children of different ages focus on (for this approach see Golomb, 1992). But where the purpose is to compare production and comprehension then using child-generated drawings in both tasks allows a more valid and direct comparison.

Even when actual children's drawings have been used in the selection task they have not covered the full developmental range of forms children produce. The eight drawings of a man presented by Fayol et al. (1995) were all conventional figures (taken from Goodnow, Wilkins, & Dawes, 1986, whose relevant paper to this area is discussed later in this chapter), even though Fayol et al.'s youngest children (from $2^{1}/_{2}$ years of age) would have undeniably drawn simpler forms, such as the tadpole form or even scribbles. As mentioned earlier, this same problem applied to Taylor and Bacharach's (1981) selection task where no scribbled drawing was presented even though scribblers formed part of the sample. In respect of the other end of the developmental scale it is important to present the most advanced drawers with at least one drawing in the selection task that is more advanced than their own. Only by doing so can we test whether production lags behind comprehension or both are at similar developmental points for these advanced drawers. For this reason we must be cautious in Fayol et al.'s (1995) conclusion of a declining lag in production as the oldest children they tested were 11 years of age but the children who provided the sample of drawings in their selection tasks were no more than 10 years of age.

The instructions in the selections tasks have varied from asking children to choose the best drawing (Brooks et al., 1988; Kosslyn et al., 1977; Lewis, 1963a; Moore, 1986), the most realistic drawing (Taylor & Bacharach, 1981) or the drawing made by the older child (Fayol et al., 1995). The instruction of "best" drawing is ambiguous and hence open to interpretation as it may cue a cognitive (e.g., the most realistic drawing) or an affective (e.g., the one you like the best) response. Moore (1986) and Brooks et al. (1988) appear to interpret their instruction of "best" as which one the child liked the best because they concluded from their data that children are satisfied with their drawings. The instruction to pick the one made by the older child implicitly cues a cognitive response, that is, the most advanced drawing. As Fayol et al.'s study adopted this instruction we may interpret their findings as showing that most children were aware of a more advanced (visually realistic) version of a topic than they actually drew.[2] This presents an intriguing possibility, therefore, that there may be more coherence in this literature than suggested by first appearances. That is, children are aware of more advanced forms that they produce themselves but they are satisfied (or even prefer) forms similar to those they depict in their own drawings. It is interesting to note the early work of Lewis (1963a, 1963b) who although reported that most children preferred drawings at a high representational level than displayed in their own drawings, choices made by lower levels of representational drawers tended to be for drawings one or two levels above their own standard rather than the most advanced drawing in the arrays (see also Trautner, Lohaus, Sahm, & Helbing, 1989).

The possibility that children may comprehend pictures differently in the selection tasks depending on whether they are responding cognitively or affectively underlines my earlier comment on the need to assess both aspects of comprehension. The next section presents a series of studies carried out by my collaborators and I that set out to do just that, and which also addressed the other methodological concerns I have discussed here.

Unpacking the Cognitive and Affective Responses

In the two studies reported by Jolley et al. (2000) children were initially asked to draw a picture of a man. The drawings were classified into one of four drawing categories (scribble, preconventional, simple conventional, and advanced conventional). These broadly represented the main developmental points of children's human figure drawings, and also the categories were consistent with the application of Luquet's (1927/2001) account of drawing development to human figure drawing (see chapter 1 for more details). Drawings considered nonrepresentational were assigned to the scribbling category. Preconventional drawings were representations of the human figure in which only some of the main parts were included, and furthermore, those parts represented were not spatially coordinated in the appropriate relationship. A typical example of this category was the tadpole form, with its omission of the body, and the arms and legs protruding from the head (see Figure 1.2). In the simple conventional category (see Figure 1.3) the main constituent parts of the human figure were displayed (head, facial features, body, arms, and legs). Although the spatial arrangement of the parts is accurate, the whole figure is drawn simply and out of proportion (often with a noticeably oversized head). Some of the drawings assigned to this category also showed transparencies. In the fourth category, an advanced conventional drawing (see the advanced figure in Figure 4.2), the human figure consisted of more details and a higher standard of proportion

(a) Scribble   (b) Pre-Conventional

(c) Simple Conventional   (d) Advanced Conventional

Figure 4.2   One set of drawings used in the selection task from the second experiment reported by Jolley et al. (2000).

and occlusion than seen in simple conventional drawings, giving an impression that it could represent a particular person (rather than the generic form of the simple conventional category). These four categories formed a workable number of drawings to present in the comprehension task.

In the comprehension task the standard presentation was of four drawings whereby each represented one of the four drawing categories described above. A number of sets of drawings were used, and Figure 4.2 illustrates one of the sets used in our second study. All sets were of children's drawings made in the production task, but no child saw his or her own drawing in the comprehension task. Consistent with our aim of unpacking cognitive and affective responses children were asked, "which picture looks most like a real man?" (the cognitive question), and "which picture do you like the best?" (the affective question). An estimation question, "which picture looks most like how you draw a man?" was also asked, the findings of which I shall discuss at the end of this chapter.

In the first study 61 children aged 2–9 years participated in the production and comprehension tasks. In response to the realism question none of the scribblers and only one each of the pre- and simple conventional drawers selected a drawing from the same category of human figure as they had drawn. The rest of the children in these three categories of drawer ($n = 46$) chose a more advanced drawing. This pattern was broadly replicated for the preference question, although there was evidence that a small minority of scribblers (2 of the 13), preconventional drawers (4 of the 18) and simple conventional drawers (2 of the 17)[3] preferred their own standard of drawing. The data conclusively showed, therefore, that for most scribblers, preconventional and simple conventional drawers the children's cognitive (understanding of most realistic version) and affective (most preferred version) selections were in advance of their own drawing level of the human figure. Although the data supported the view that comprehension is in advance of production in drawing, the children's selections threw up some interesting variations depending upon the children's own drawing level. For the scribblers and preconventional drawers, some chose the simple conventional drawing, particularly in response to the preference question (where a majority did). In contrast, the simple conventional drawers almost exclusively chose the advanced figure for both questions.

The advanced drawers almost without exception chose the advanced figure as their preferred and most realistic drawing. But interpretation of this selection is problematic as they were not given the opportunity to select a more visually realistic version than they produced themselves. Accordingly, in the larger scale second study ($N = 103$), the advanced drawers were shown a set that included an artist's drawing of a man (see Figure 4.3 for one of the six artist drawings used in the study). The age range of participants was extended to include those up to 14 years of age, enabling us to sample a larger

Figure 4.3 One of the six artist drawings presented in the selection task to the advanced conventional drawers in the second experiment reported by Jolley et al. (2000).

number of advanced conventional drawers than in our first study. Finally, we improved the reliability of the measures by asking all children to draw two human figures in two separate sessions, as well as repeating the comprehension questions over multiple sets of drawings.

Table 4.1 describes the number of children selecting each standard of drawing (including children who responded inconsistently across

Table 4.1   Numbers of Children Selecting Four Levels of Human Figure Drawing in Response to the Realism, Preference and Estimation Questions by the Category of the Children's Own Human Figure Drawings (Jolley, Knox, & Foster, 2000; Study 2)

Comprehension performance	Production performance				
	Scribblers	Pre-conventional drawers	Simple conventional drawers	Advanced conventional drawers	
Realism					
Scribble	–	–	–	–	–
Preconventional	–	1	1	–	2
Simple conventional	19	11	–	–	30
Advanced conventional	10	13	25	20	68
Inconsistent responders	1	2	–	–	3
	30	27	26	20	103
Preference					
Scribble	–	–	–	–	–
Preconventional	3	2	–	–	5
Simple conventional	15	7	3	1	26
Advanced conventional	9	17	22	19	67
Inconsistent responders	3	1	1	–	5
	30	27	26	20	103
Estimation of own drawing level					
Scribble	–	–	–	–	–
Preconventional	15	4	–	–	19
Simple conventional	12	17	19	–	48
Advanced conventional	1	3	7	20	31
Inconsistent responders	2	3	–	–	5
	30	27	26	20	103

the sets of drawing) for their realism and preference responses (but does not include responses to sets that included an artist's drawing). The data clearly supported the main finding from the first study: The overwhelming majority of the scribblers, pre- and simple conventional drawers chose a more advanced drawing in response to both the cognitive and affective questions than they produced themselves.[4] The data on the advanced conventional drawers again showed that they chose the advanced conventional figure. When shown the set that included an artist's drawing, however, almost all the advanced conventional drawers chose the artist's drawing in response to both questions. This indicated that comprehension is in advance of production at even the top end of representational drawing ability in children, a finding that argues against Fayol et al.'s interpretation of their data.

Closer inspection of Table 4.1 further supported the finding from the first study that the drawing category children choose in the comprehension task varies according to their own standard of drawing. Generally, the scribblers and preconventional drawers' selections are split between the simple and advanced conventional forms, whereas the (simple and advanced) conventional drawers choose the most advanced drawing available to them.

Recall at the end of the previous section I presented the possibility that the apparently inconsistent findings reported in the literature may potentially be explained by children *recognizing* higher levels of realism in drawing than their own standard but *preferring* drawings similar or slightly above their own production level. Our data, however, provided at best only weak evidence for this proposition. In two further studies I have conducted with Emma Knox and Rachel Wainwright we found a slight tendency for some children's preference selections to be nearer their own drawing standard than their realism selections (Jolley et al., 2001).[5] For instance, in Study 1 reported by Jolley et al. (2001), 5 (out of 30) scribblers and 7 (out of 29) preconventional drawers chose the same or one standard above their own production category for the preference question, whereas 3 scribblers and 2 preconventional drawers did so for the realism question. In Study 2 we sampled only representational drawers (preconventional, simple, and advanced conventional)[6] and again found a tendency among some of the preconventional drawers to prefer a drawing closer to their own standard than the drawing they considered to be the most realistic (see Table 4.2). From this table you can see that whereas only 3 of these children (from a total of 24) chose a drawing at the

Table 4.2   Numbers of Children Selecting Five Levels of Human Figure Drawing in Response to the Realism, Preference and Estimation Questions by the Category of the Children's Own Human Figure Drawings (Jolley, Knox, & Wainwright, 2001; Study 2)

| | Production performance | | |
Comprehension performance	Pre-conventional drawers	Simple conventional drawers	Advanced conventional drawers
Realism			
Scribble	–	–	–
Preconventional	2	–	–
Simple conventional	1	–	–
Advanced conventional	3	2	–
Artist	13	32	18
Inconsistent responders	5	–	–
	24	34	18
Preference			
Scribble	–	–	–
Preconventional	3	–	–
Simple conventional	5	–	1
Advanced conventional	3	8	–
Artist	7	22	15
Inconsistent responders	6	4	2
	24	34	17
Estimation of own drawing level			
Scribble	–	–	–
Preconventional	5	–	–
Simple conventional	4	7	–
Advanced conventional	2	21	16
Artist	5	4	2
Inconsistent responders	8	2	–
	24	34	18

same or one category above their own drawing level for the realism questions, 8 did so in response to the preference questions. For the first time I saw this same tendency extend to the simple conventional drawers. Some of the simple conventional drawers (8 out of 34) still preferred the child's advanced conventional figure even when a highly realistic drawing from an adult artist was on offer (whereas only 2 of them considered the child's advanced conventional drawing to be the most realistic).

Considering all the realism and preference data that we have collected across four experiments (Jolley et al., 2000, 2001) it seems there is a tendency for a small minority of drawers, particularly among the younger and more immature drawers, to prefer a drawing closer to their own standard than the drawing they consider the most realistic. One should state, however, that this tendency is represented by relatively few children and not always reliably shown. What is clear is that children of all ages and drawing abilities prefer, and consider the most realistic, those drawings depicting a higher level of visual realism than they draw themselves.

But what is the basis of the children's selections of drawings? By asking children to justify their selections we can confirm whether their responses to the realism question are indeed based on their comprehension of realism. Their preferences, on the other hand, may be deriving from an interest for features or properties of pictures unrelated to realism, and there may be developmental differences in these responses. In Study 2 reported by Jolley et al. (2001) the children sampled (categorized as either pre-, simple and advanced conventional drawers) were asked to justify their selections. The reasons given for both preference and realism choices revealed a similar developmental pattern for both types of response. Most preconventional drawers merely named a body part or article of clothing in their chosen drawing.[7] There was still some evidence of commenting upon local features among the simple conventional drawers but we also saw among these drawers references to the realism of the whole drawing, while almost all the advanced conventional drawers made holistic comments based on the visual realism of the drawings (e.g., overall detail, proportion, posture, and movement). For conventional drawers at least, therefore, their justifications confirmed that they did indeed recognize the highest level of realism in response to the realism question. The similar basis we observed for their preference selections is consistent with Parsons' (1987) claim that once children focus on the subject matter in pictures they have a value system that judges pictures on realism.

Production and Comprehension Models

The conclusive findings of a developmental delay in children's representational drawing, compared to aspects of their comprehension, adds further weight to the view that we cannot take children's drawings as print-outs of their mental images of the topics drawn. Furthermore, our own research has shown that children's selections of their most preferred and most realistic drawing indicate that at least some children hold different cognitive and affective comprehension models. While the complex processes that are specific to picture making must play a significant role in the developmental delay of production from such models, we should refrain from the (rather negative) view that children's drawings are merely adulterations of their mental models of topics due to production difficulties (see also Golomb, 2002). There is much evidence from the variability of graphic forms children can produce to stand for a topic at any given time point that children's drawings are a product of their *intentions* as well as subject to production processes. For instance, it is not difficult to find examples in children's drawings where the child has shown different versions of the same topic, such as a tadpole and a conventional figure (see Figure 4.4). Also, children can produce different drawings for themselves than they do for teachers, parents, and experimenters (Anning, 2002; Goodnow et al., 1986). It appears, therefore, that children on occasions produce different graphic models depending on the purpose of the drawing and for what audience. Furthermore, children may be well aware of their limitations in production and accordingly invent a graphic representation that is within those limitations (Arnheim, 1974) and be satisfied with their invention (see also Golomb, 2002). In other words, children may have mental models for their own drawing that is nearer to the final product than would appear from the judgments they make of drawings made by others.

I am not saying, however, that children are fully satisfied with their drawing efforts, as seems to be suggested by some authors (Brooks

Figure 4.4 Child's drawing showing both tadpole and conventional forms of the human figure.

et al., 1988; Moore, 1986; see also Trautner et al., 1989). Their preference choices in our studies undermine this possibility. Rather, that children develop a graphic equivalent that works for them but still prefer drawings typically made by older children that show a higher degree of visual equivalence to their referents. The extent to which children are content with the disparity between their production and comprehension models may vary with age, with older children tending to be more dissatisfied. Jolley et al. (2001) asked children whether they liked, disliked, or considered their human figure drawing they had just made alright/okay. We found that all of the pre-conventional drawers ($n = 27$) and the majority of the simple conventional drawers (27 out of 34) liked their drawing. In contrast, of the 18 advanced conventional drawers only 4 liked their drawing, with 7 disliking it and a further 7 saying it was okay/alright. When asked what they liked and disliked about their drawing the advanced conventional drawers liked those parts of their drawing they considered were detailed and drawn visually realistically, but disliked those parts that they felt were not. It is generally considered among researchers that older children become increasingly dissatisfied with their drawings (e.g., see Cox, 2005).[8] This may also reflect a general developmental shift towards children becoming more self-critical of their abilities, in contrast to young children being overly optimistic of their abilities and skills. In the next section I discuss how these two contrasting self-evaluations may impact on children's estimations and attitudes towards their own drawing ability.

Children's Self-evaluations of Drawing Ability

A contributory influence on older children's dissatisfaction with their perceived lack of realism in their drawing is a more generic and growing tendency for children to become more self-critical of their abilities (Blatchford, 1997; Plumert, 1995; Stipek, 1984; Stipek & MacIver, 1989). In contrast, younger children may be overly optimistic in the assessment of their abilities. I mentioned earlier in this chapter that as well as asking children to make preference and realism selections we also asked them to pick the drawing which looked most like how they draw a man (Jolley et al., 2000, 2001). Children's estimation data from Tables 4.1 and 4.2 show that only the advanced conventional drawers consistently choose a drawing from the same category as their own drawing ability, while younger drawers frequently overestimate their standard of their drawing.[9] The development towards accurate estimations in older children is consistent with other research showing that children have an increasing competence in perceiving their own abilities correctly (Harter, 1982; Newman, 1984; Spinath & Spinath, 2005), even though they may be self-critical of them (see above). Younger children's overestimation of their drawing ability is consistent with their general tendency to overestimate their ability (Schuster, Ruble, & Weinert, 1998). Cognitive factors and an engagement of "wishful thinking" has been suggested to account for younger children's overestimations (Schuster et al., 1998; Stipek, 1984; Stipek & MacIver, 1989). If young children do intend their drawings to be more developmentally advanced than they turn out to be then this may also augment their general tendency to overestimate. In either case we have an interesting explanation for why younger children may be more content with their drawings – they are deluded into thinking that they are better than they are!

Going Deeper into Children's Comprehension

Although asking children to make a single selection from sets of drawings enables the researcher to compare their understanding, preferences, and estimations with the children's own drawings, it does not allow an assessment of the deeper levels of comprehension one can have about drawing. For instance, what is children's awareness of the developmental pattern in children's drawings and the factors that influence its progression? And is their knowledge of what develops and why in children's drawings related to their own drawing level? I shall now turn our attention to these questions.

(a)   Children's knowledge of the "what" in development

The realism question in the selection tasks not only assesses children's recognition of the most visually realistic figure but can also be conceived as measuring children's understanding of the end-point of children's typical drawing development up to the onset of adolescence. But what about children's understanding of the whole developmental sequence in drawing? Can they seriate the drawings according to their correct age-related pattern and does such ability relate to the children's own production level?

There has been some previous research addressing these questions. Goodnow et al. (1986) tested five groups of children ranging from 4- to 11-year-olds on whether they could distinguish between a younger and older child's drawing, and whether this ability related to the child's own drawing skill. They presented pairs of human figure drawings from a total of eight drawings commonly seen in drawings made by 4- to 10-year-olds according to the Goodenough-Harris scale (Harris, 1963). All possible pairs of drawings were shown, and in a previous session the children were asked to draw a man. Goodnow et al. reported that the 4- and 5-year-olds' ability to distinguish between the younger and older child's drawings was not above chance levels. In contrast, the 7-year-olds' judgments were well above chance levels, with the 9- and 11-year-olds at ceiling. To examine whether the children's judgments were related to their own production performance the authors correlated the two measures for two groups of children: The 4- and 5-year-olds, and the 7- and 9-year-olds. In each case there was a significant positive correlation.

Goodnow et al.'s study is interesting as it not only highlights age-related changes in understanding developmental differences in drawing, but also that individual differences in differentiating the drawings is related to the child's own drawing ability, even for young children. What may be the nature of this relationship? One possibility is that as children progress in their own drawings they gain more knowledge of the developmental pattern up to their own level, but are less certain of future developments (as they have yet to directly experience such changes in their own drawing development). Consistent with this suggestion, the correlation reported by Goodnow et al. for the older age group ($r = 0.36$) was stronger than for the younger age group ($r = 0.13$). However, Goodnow et al. did not report where the developmental points of the errors in children's judgments occurred so we do not know whether they tended to relate to differences above the children's own production level or not.

Trautner et al. (1989) designed their study to directly examine this question. They presented 5- to 10-year-olds with eight sets of five human figure drawings. Each set included five drawings made by one child, collected in a previous longitudinal study by the authors, where children had been asked to draw a man and a woman once a year from 5 to 9 years of age. The sets of drawings may be regarded, therefore, as representative of the developmental changes seen in human figure drawings between those ages. For each set of drawings the children Trautner et al. tested had to arrange the pictures in the correct age-related sequence. The authors reported that even the youngest children (5-year-olds) ordered the drawings with an accuracy above chance levels, and that this skill improved further with age. Interestingly, Trautner et al. (1989) reported that the judgment errors for the youngest children were as high for drawings around their own age level as they were for older children's drawings. Their data cast doubt, therefore, on the suggestion I made above that children may be more knowledgeable about the development pattern up to, rather than beyond, the level they are currently at in their own drawing.

One difficulty with this interpretation is that the child's own drawing level was not assessed in Trautner et al.'s study. Accordingly, in the second study reported by Jolley et al. (2000) we asked 3- to 14-year-olds to seriate sets of human figure drawings in a developmental sequence task, and also to produce two human figure drawings. In the developmental sequence task children were asked to match four different forms of human figure drawing (scribble, preconventional, simple conventional and advanced conventional) to photographs of children aged 2, 4, 6, and 10 years – the ages in which these categories of drawing are typically drawn. We considered that providing photographs (with the ages written below each one and read out by the experimenter) communicated the task demands better than without using any developmental anchors (as in Trautner et al., 1989). The procedure was repeated for two more sets of children's drawings using two additional sets of children's photographs.

We correlated the performance on the developmental sequence task with the child's production level, while statistically partialing out potential age effects.[10] Removing likely age effects was important as both the studies reported by Goodnow et al. and Trautner et al. found seriating the drawings an age-related ability, and we wanted to know whether the child's production level was independently related to their ability to seriate the drawings correctly. There was still a strong, significant relationship between production and comprehension performance with age effects removed. Our data therefore confirmed and extended the earlier work by Goodnow et al. (1986) and Trautner et al. (1989), that is, children's knowledge of the developmental sequence in drawing is not only age-related but also related to the child's own production level. But were the younger (and poorer) drawers' errors related to points beyond their own drawing level?

On the whole the data did not support this view. The percentages of children who correctly matched the drawing to each photograph on at least two out of the three trials are shown in Figure 4.5. The only type of drawer showing a descending line of performance after the point of their own production level is the scribbler.[11] The scribblers showed a high degree of accuracy for matching the scribbled drawings to the pictures of 2-year-olds, but performed less well on matching the three representational drawings appropriately. Very young children may be more prone to focusing on the lines and colors for their own sake in their own pictures and the others that they see

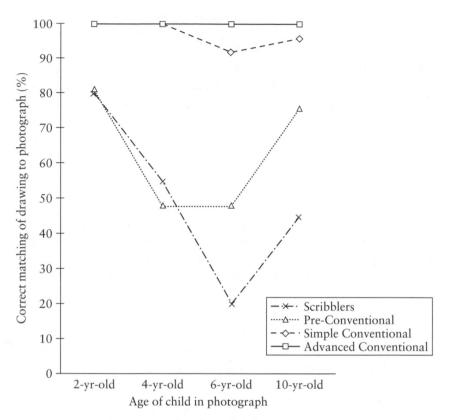

Figure 4.5 Percentage responses of matching each category of drawing to its appropriate position in the developmental sequence by four levels of drawer in the second experiment reported by Jolley et al. (2000).

(Luquet, 1927/2001; Parsons, 1987) that they give relatively little attention to representation and the different forms that representations take. Nevertheless, there were still many scribblers who were accurately matching the representational drawings to the correct developmental points.

Our findings, together with what we can surmise from Trautner et al.'s findings, indicate that although children's understanding of the developmental pattern of children's drawings is related to their own production level, such understanding is associated to developmental points both prior and beyond their own drawing ability.

(b)   Children's knowledge of the "why" in development

Children's understanding of the variety of causal influences of developmental change in drawing was investigated in the third study presented by Jolley et al. (2001). Sixty-seven children were categorized as either a preconventional (22), simple conventional (22) or advanced conventional (23) drawer on the basis of their drawing of a man. All children then participated in a semi-structured interview in which they were asked about (a) their preferences/dislikes in pictures, (b) their own picture making, (c) what they considered were easy/difficult things to draw, (d) what makes a good picture, and (e) how we get better at drawing. Content analysis was conducted on the transcriptions of the interviews. For the purposes of the present discussion I will refer only to the different reasons children gave for developmental change in drawing, but to point out that the whole transcript for each child was searched for such reasons. The following themes (with examples) were generated:

   (i)   Maturation. Age, getting bigger, intelligence, inherited skill.
  (ii)   Application/enjoyment (internal resources). Practice, concentration, trying hard, more experience, motivation.
 (iii)   Teaching/learning (external resources). Watching and being shown by others, seeing other drawings, education.
  (iv)   Knowledge. Knowing more about the subject matter.
   (v)   Motor development. Holding pen/pencil, better coordination.
  (vi)   Drawing related. Comments on how features in drawings change.
 (vii)   Miscellaneous. No response, don't know, they just get better.

    Table 4.3 gives a breakdown of the number of children citing each casual influence by the child's own drawing standard. The most popular themes cited were maturation, application/enjoyment and teaching/learning. We found that the number of themes cited varied significantly with production level, independently of age (age was partialed out in the correlation). That is, more thematic reasons were associated with increasingly higher drawing standards. The citing of two themes in particular differentiated the levels of drawer: application/enjoyment and teaching/learning. So children drawing more

Table 4.3 Numbers of Children Citing Theme of Change by Production Level (Jolley, Knox, & Wainwright, 2001; Study 3)

				Themes of change			
Production level	Maturation	Application/ enjoyment	Teaching/ learning	Knowledge	Motor development	Drawings-related	Miscellaneous
Preconventional (n = 22)	13	8	5	0	0	4	4
Simple conventional (n = 22)	20	10	15	3	3	2	1
Advanced conventional (n = 23)	23	18	20	4	5	4	0
Total	56	36	40	7	8	10	5

advanced forms of the human figure were more likely to comment on factors relating to internal (e.g., practice, motivation, etc.) and external (shown how to draw, looking at others' drawings, etc.) resources.

The relationship we found between children's knowledge of developmental causes and their production level provides an interesting and consistent adjunct to their knowledge of the developmental pattern. It appears that children's comprehension of what develops and why in drawing is related to their own production level. But the casual nature of this relationship is not straightforward and as yet not adequately understood. At the moment we can only speculate. Could children who are more aware of the (internal and external) resources available to them be more motivated to use them, leading to an advantage in their own drawing development? And conversely, might not improvements in the child's own drawings give insights to the child as to why this might have happened, and possibly provide the child with a clearer understanding of the developmental pattern of representational drawing? Understanding and production is a bi-directional relationship, and it is highly probable that in at least some respects progressions in production or comprehension of pictures mutually benefit each other.

We need more research, preferably longitudinal, to outline more precisely how the development of production and comprehension in drawing interact with each other. Whatever the nature of the interaction, I suggest that knowledge of the developmental pattern in drawing (and its causes) needs to be considered more holistically that just in terms of age-related changes. In Jolley et al. (2000) we noted that the subject of awareness of developmental change is derived from Piaget's discussion on diachronic thinking (Piaget, 1969), that is, children's knowledge that phenomena develop over time. As Montangero (e.g., Montangero, 1996; Tryphon & Montangero, 1992) has commented, however, diachronic thinking also incorporates an ability to explain a present situation from past events, and to predict future events from the present. Although Montangero (1996) explains the development of diachronic thinking by age, our data suggest that future research needs to examine independently the role of children's own production performance on their knowledge of what develops and why in drawing.

Summary

Research into the relationship between children's production and comprehension of drawing has produced somewhat inconsistent findings in the literature. However, by incorporating a number of methodological refinements, most notably presenting actual children's drawings and unpacking the cognitive and affective components of comprehension, we have consistently shown that children are aware of, and prefer, more realistic versions of the human figure than they are able to draw themselves (Jolley et al., 2000, 2001). As children probably draw the human figure more than any other topic, I would expect a greater production lag to be observed for other less-practiced topics. Nevertheless, we must not ignore the very real possibility that children intend to use different (less advanced) graphic models for their own drawings than those they consider as ideal from their observations of pictures made by others. If so, they may be reasonably content with their drawing level, particularly the younger, more inexperienced, drawers who think they produce more advanced representational pictures than they actually do anyway. When investigating children's understanding of what develops and why in children's drawings we find a potentially interesting relationship with their own drawing development. The nature of this relationship is unclear and requires further testing, but I would predict further investigations to reveal a complex reciprocal relationship between children's production and comprehension of drawing.

Notes

1   A tadpole figure (see Figure 1.2) displays a single enclosed area, usually filled with facial features, with legs (and sometimes arms) protruding from this "head." It appears that no body is shown. In contrast, the conventional form (see Figure 1.3) includes a separate area for the body, with arms and legs protruding from the body. The transitional figure is an intermediary form between the tadpole and conventional figures, and drawn by some children. There is an indication of a body, such as a small enclosed area drawn under the "head," or lines that are particularly extended down from the "head" which may denote the body

as well as legs (the top right drawing in Figure 1.2 could be considered a transitional figure).

2   With the aforementioned proviso that it is difficult to interpret the oldest children's selections in Fayol et al.'s study.

3   A further conventional drawer preferred the preconventional figure.

4   When the same children were shown a set of four stereotyped human figure drawings (scribble, preconventional, simple conventional and advanced conventional) drawn by ourselves the children again consistently chose a more advanced drawing than they produced themselves.

5   This paper refers to a conference presentation. A more detailed discussion of the three studies reported by Jolley et al. (2001) can be found in a book chapter written by Jolley and Rose (2008).

6   We did not test very young children (hence there were no scribblers) due to the language demands of asking children to justify their selections (see the reporting of this data later in the chapter).

7   It is interesting to note this focus on local features among the preconventional drawers is consistent with Luquet's (1927/2001) comments on children's drawing behavior in his failed realism stage, where the child tends to concentrate on each feature being drawn without attending to how it integrates with the whole drawing.

8   However, in a large-scale survey study on children's (and their teachers' and parents') views on children's drawing experience, Sarah Rose, Esther Burkitt and I found that most children of all ages sampled (5- to 14-year-olds) reported that they liked drawing and felt positive about their drawing ability, and also that a low drawing self-efficacy was not a commonly cited reason given by children, teachers, and parents for the decline in drawing activity among older children (see chapter 10 for more details).

9   It should be acknowledged that children's estimation of their own drawing standard in these tasks was requested in the same session as the cognitive and affective comprehension questions. Children's consideration of their more developmentally advanced cognitive and affective comprehension models may have contributed to an overestimation of the human figure drawings they themselves produce.

10   In a partial correlation the potential contribution of a third variable to the relationship between two other variables can be removed statistically. As we would expect children's performance on the developmental sequence task and in drawing both to improve with age (the third variable), partialing out age is useful to establish the strength of the relationship between seriating the drawings developmentally and the children's own production level without the contribution of their ages to that relationship.

11 I acknowledge that the overall weaker performance of the scribblers compared to the older children may be due in part to a poorer cognitive ability in simultaneously comparing differences between items. Also, I recognize that for the advanced conventional drawers the task did not test their performance at seriating drawings beyond their own drawing ability.

5

Children's Understanding of the Dual Nature of Pictures

Our knowledge and meaningful participation in the world in which we live is highly dependent upon an understanding of the concept of symbols. A fully mature understanding of pictures, for instance, requires an appreciation of their dual nature: Pictures are objects in themselves as well as referring to some other reality. This chapter outlines the developmental progression towards the child gaining this conceptual understanding of pictures. I present a resolution to the apparently conflicting findings from the two main methodological approaches reported in the literature, that of search tasks and false picture tasks. I then broaden the discussion to explore whether young children's difficulty in understanding simultaneously the two components of pictures' dual nature is symptomatic of a wider and more general cognitive limitation of holding in mind more than one representation of a given entity.

Introduction to Symbols

Much of what we learn is conveyed through symbols. The pervasiveness of language in our lives, in its oral and written form, enables us to understand facts, opinions and feelings relating to people and in the world more generally. Language is ably supported by other symbol systems, some of which have an iconic similarity to what they refer to, as displayed in pictures, television, and cinema films. Indeed, the variety of symbols seems endless when we further consider maps, mathematical and science notation, signs, miniature models, and gestures, to name but a few more examples. Just a moment's reflection tells us that without understanding the meaning of all these different symbol systems our knowledge of the world and people would be so impoverished that we would not be able to fully participate in society (see DeLoache, 2004). The sooner we understand these symbols, the sooner we begin to cognitively and socially engage in our environment. For this reason alone, the child's acquisition of a symbolic mind represents one of the most important milestones of the child's life.

The rapid developments and apparent ease with which infants acquire the meaning of a great range of symbols is quite astonishing. Most children across the world begin to speak words in the language they have been brought up in during their second year of life (Waxman, 2002). The fact that they do so, and rapidly expand their vocabulary with little formal training, is a testament to how the infant's brain is seemingly prewired for the job (Chomsky, 1986; Pinker, 1994). Further evidence that the period approaching two years of age is marked by the infant becoming symbol-minded is their use and competence with other symbol systems. In their play, for example, they start to pretend that objects represent other things or that something absent is really there, such as pretending to speak to someone using a toy telephone or pretending an empty toy cup contains liquid by sipping from it. Again, such symbolic play behavior seems to come naturally to the infant. Similarly, they can recognize familiar items in pictures, even if they have had very limited prior experience of pictures (see later discussion of Hochberg & Brooks, 1962). Of course there is still much that the infant has to learn about the variety of meanings symbols can communicate, as is evident by their increasing vocabulary, their more elaborate and complex associations in their pretend play, and their growing representational repertoire of graphic topics they produce. Although observation and direct training from others is important in the development of using and understanding symbolic meanings, which for many is a life-long endeavor (e.g., interpreting road signs when learning to drive a car), the underlying concept of symbols appears to be gained by most children during the second year of life. But what are the principles that define a conceptual understanding of symbols, and have children around 2 years of age really acquired an adult-like mature knowledge of these principles? I shall first outline in broad terms what these principles are, and then examine the question of what development, if any, there is in acquiring these principles.

The Dual Nature of Symbols

When we use symbol systems we usually concentrate on the meaning the symbols refer to, and give little attention to the physical properties of the symbol for their own sake. When reading a book, for instance, we attend to the meaning of the words rather than the print or feel of the page. Similarly, when viewing a picture we try to make some sense of what the picture is representing or expressing, and may only focus on the materials of the picture (e.g., frame, canvas, paper, lines, colors, etc.) if there is something particularly noteworthy about them. A child riding a stick as if it was a horse behaves as if he or she has cast aside any notion that it is a stick at all. This bias towards interpreting the meaning of the symbol, rather than attending to the materials of the symbol, is entirely appropriate as the function of symbols is to communicate meaning.

But there are exceptions to this attentional bias that remind us that the symbol is also a thing in itself. We notice the size of print if it varies substantially from the text we normally read (e.g., reading a book intended for an infant or young child), and the art of calligraphy attests to an interest in the esthetic properties of writing. We may spend some time choosing the frame for a picture, and art critics can marvel at the brush strokes in an original abstract painting.[1] A stick is a stick without it having to wait around for a child to pick it up as a horse to get its "reason to be," and of course children (and actors) bring their own personal characteristics to any part they play in a make-believe story.

At the most fundamental level, therefore, symbols have two main properties: The characteristics of the symbol itself and what it refers to. It is because symbols have these two properties that many researchers have commented on their dual nature (e.g., Beilin & Pearlman, 1991; Callaghan, 2000; DeLoache, 1987, 2004; Schwartz, 1995; Thomas, Jolley, Robinson, & Champion, 1999), and is a framework for conceptualizing pictures that can be traced at least as far back as Piaget (1929). When we consider specifically the dual nature of pictures, therefore, we are thinking of pictures being things in themselves (e.g., lines and colors on paper) which also refer to something else (from our world). Even nonrepresentational (abstract) pictures can refer to ideas and moods, and hence are more than just colors and lines. Of course understanding what abstract pictures are referring to (the symbolic meaning) is particularly challenging for the young infant who may instead focus on the colors for their own sake (see Jolley et al., 1998a; Parsons, 1987). In which case the optimum pictorial symbol to study children's concept of their dual nature is that which displays a representation of a familiar object or subject matter. For the most part, therefore, research has examined children's understanding of the dual nature of representational pictures.

Is this basic distinction between the picture itself and what it signifies all there is to understand about the dual nature of pictures? If so, it would not be surprising if young infants quickly acquire this distinction. In the next few sections I show that to have a fully mature understanding of the dual nature of pictures requires an appreciation of a number of characteristics of dual nature (see also Jolley, 2008), and that developmentally it may take longer to acquire these characteristics than that suggested by the infant's competence with symbols during the second year of life.

Early Understanding of the Dual Nature of Pictures

There is evidence that even newborns can recognize that real objects and pictures are different from each other, but that noticing the similarity between a picture and its three-dimensional referent may take a few months. When newborns are shown simultaneously a pattern in three- and two-dimensional forms they will prefer either one or the other indicating that a basic ability to discriminate pictures from their real referents is present at birth (Slater, Rose, & Morison, 1984). Using a habituation procedure, however, Slater et al. (1984) found that newborns may not recognize the similarity between the two stimuli. DeLoache et al. (1979), using a similar habituation procedure, reported that 5-month-old babies could recognize the similarity between a picture and its referent. They repeatedly presented a real doll over a number of trials and, as is typical of habituation to a repeated stimulus, the babies became less interested in the doll and consequently spent less time looking at it with each presentation. After the last presentation the doll was removed and the babies were shown two photographs, one of the doll that had been presented and the other of a different doll. The babies preferred to look at the picture of the new doll. The authors concluded that the babies recognized the previously seen doll from the picture of that doll, and because they had little interest in looking at it any further preferred to view the picture of the novel doll. Interpreted in this light DeLoache et al.'s findings suggest babies can recognize the similarity of a picture to its referent by at least 5 months of age.

Alternatively, the preferential looking of the pictured novel doll may be explained by the babies detecting more of a difference in this picture, compared to the picture of the familiar doll, to the actual doll. That is, we cannot be sure that the babies noticed a similarity between the doll and its picture. My interpretation of the subsequent research on babies' picture perception (for a review, see Bovet & Vauclair, 2000) is that we still have not designed studies that provide clear findings on when babies can recognize similarities between pictures and their referents. Some research shows impressive early cross-modal ability of, for example, matching the touch of a three-dimensional object to seeing its two-dimensional picture, but such cross-modal studies do not test directly the recognition of the picture-referent similarity within the visual domain. There is evidence that infants as young as 3 months old look longer at a picture of their mother than a picture of a stranger (Barrera & Maurer, 1981), but as neonates seem to have a particular interest and aptitude in recognizing faces (see Johnson & Morton, 1991) we cannot be sure whether this early ability to recognize familiar faces in pictures extends more generally to other visual stimuli.

What evidence there is of early recognition of picture-object similarity suggests that it may not require learning. The possibility that it is an unlearned ability was supported in the classic study by Hochberg and Brooks (1962) where a 19-month-old boy could name familiar objects and toys in line drawings and photographs when seeing the pictures for the first time. The boy had been brought up with very minimal experience of pictures up until the time of testing, and when such chance encounters with pictures had occurred at no point did the parents name the pictures. Presumably the basis of this unlearned ability to recognize pictures is the iconic similarity between the depicted and real object.

But is there also little need for experience or training to understand that pictures are distinct from their referents? There are numerous anecdotal accounts reported in the literature that young infants' first manual interactions with pictures are characterized by attempts to scratch or lift up the depiction as if it was real (e.g., Ninio & Bruner, 1978; Perner, 1991; Piaget, 1929; Werner & Kaplan, 1963).[2] Hochberg and Brooks (1962) made no mention in their study whether the boy they tested exhibited similar behavior when shown the test pictures. Experimental support for the anecdotal reports has been found more recently, however, by DeLoache, Pierroutsakos, Uttal, Rosengren, and Gottlieb (1998) who observed 9-, 15- and 19-month-old babies interacting with pictures. The authors noticed that the 9-month-olds touched the depicted objects as if they were unsure as to whether they were real objects or not, but pointed at the pictures (a conventional behavior towards pictures) much less. In contrast, the 19-month-old infants typically pointed at the pictures but rarely manually explored them. The 15-month-olds' exploring and pointing behavior fell someway between their younger and older counterparts.

DeLoache et al. (1998) were careful not to over-interpret the behavior of the 9-month-old infants as evidence that these infants thought that the pictures actually *were* the objects they depicted. On the basis of the video evidence of the infants' grasping of the pictures, DeLoache et al. (1998) concluded that they were merely puzzled by the pictures and were seeking further clarification that the objects depicted were not the objects themselves. Also, in another study from this paper they presented eight 9-month-old infants simultaneously with a set of toys and pictures of them, and found that the infants spent more time in contact with the toys. This behavioral preferential discrimination shows that 9-month-olds do not consider pictures and referents as the same entity, and is consistent with the visual discrimination between two- and three-dimensional stimuli shown by younger babies reported at the beginning of this section (DeLoache et al., 1979; Slater et al., 1984).

Where such confusion concerning a picture's contents does exist it is likely to be due to the infant's limited previous experience with pictures, and the level of realism in the pictures. DeLoache et al. (1998)

also tested eight infants from the Ivory Coast, ranging from 8 to 18 months of age. These infants came from the Beng community where there was very little exposure to pictures. The authors reported that six of these infants manually investigated the pictures they presented to them in similar ways to the American 9-month-old infants (described above). Infants may therefore be delayed in becoming sure that pictures are not the same as their referents if they have had little prior experience of pictures. The influence of realism in pictures was studied by Pierroutsakos and DeLoache (2003) who, as well as replicating their earlier findings regarding 9-month-olds' grasping behavior of pictures, found such behavior was more common with highly realistic pictures (see also n. 1 in relation to adults). Research carried out by Tara Callaghan (Callaghan, 2008; Callaghan, Rochat, MacGillivray, & MacLellan, 2004) indicates that infants during the second year of life may begin to behave towards pictures according to social conventions (i.e. looking and pointing at pictures) by model-ing adults' behavior towards pictures.

If children at least as young as 19 months of age can not only recognize familiar referents in pictures but also understand they are different from their real referents, have infants by this age acquired the conceptual knowledge required for understanding the dual nature of pictures? We shall see in the next two sections that infants have still more hurdles to cross, first in terms of understanding pictures as representations of particular referents, and second towards a deeper understanding of the independence of pictures to referents.

Pictures as Representations of Specific Realities

Although infants can recognize familiar subject matter in pictures with little training or pictorial experience, Judy DeLoache and her col-laborators have reported findings from a large collection of studies spanning the last 20 years (for a review see DeLoache, 2002) that suggests understanding the specific relation between a picture and its particular referent takes longer. In these studies 2- to 3-year-old infants are tested on a search task that requires them to understand the specific relationship between a symbol (picture, miniature model, map, or video) and its referent (a room). In a standard picture version of this search task (for example, see DeLoache, 1987) infants are presented with a picture depicting (some of) the contents of a nearby room. The infants are told that a toy has been hidden in the room and that it is hiding in the place the experimenter is pointing to in the picture (e.g., an item of furniture). The infant is then encouraged to find the toy in the room (and also to point to the place in the picture to ensure any failure in searching in the main room was not due to forgetting where the experimenter had pointed). This task (and versions where other symbols are used, such as a miniature model) is testing more than children's recognition of the referent conveyed by the symbol; it is assessing their understanding of the correspondence of the symbol (model/picture) to the particular room used in the experiment, and to use that knowledge to locate where the large toy is. Merely recognizing the subject matter of the picture or model is insufficient for successful searching in the room; the child needs to conceive the one-to-one-relationship between the symbol and the referent (the room), and consequently infer where the toy is and successfully locate it. Otherwise one would expect random searching in the room.

DeLoache (1987) reported around 70% of 30- to 33-month-olds successfully retrieved the toy from the room after being shown where it was hiding in the picture. Despite the majority of the infants understanding the specific picture-room relation, around 30 months is still considerably older than when they can recognize the subject matter of pictures. Can infants younger than 30 months successfully perform on DeLoache's search tasks using a picture? DeLoache and Burns (1994) employed a similar search task using pictures on a younger group of 24-month-olds, but only 13% of them succeeded. This poor performance was not due to any inability to recognize the topic in the picture as they had no difficulty naming the depicted topics. Nor had they any difficulty in remembering the place where they had been shown in the picture (as they pointed correctly to the corresponding place in the picture). They also understood that they were required to search for the toy as they went in the room and looked for it. But instead of going to the place pointed to in the picture they tended to go to the place where the toy had been hidden in the previous trial.

DeLoache and Burns (1994) argued that although these 2-year-olds can *recognize* topics in pictures they can not yet understand the *relation* between the depiction and the real referent. For DeLoache and Burns, infants around 2 years have decontextualized pictures from the real referents they represent to an extent that they are unable to consider the picture in the search tasks as representing the particular reality of where the toy is hiding in the room. To emphasize this point they argue that much of children's experience with picture books is that of seeing generic representations (e.g., a prototype example of a farm animal) rather than a representation of a specific example (i.e. a particular example of a real farm animal). I am somewhat skeptical about this explanation, as most 2-year-olds have had experience of photographs (such as of their family). It would be interesting to directly test for DeLoache and Burns' explanation by either testing 2-year-olds who vary in the extent of their natural experience of photographs, or (more feasibly) by observing the effects of training those who fail the search task by pointing out their relationship of photographs with their referents. Whatever the outcome of such research it is clear from DeLoache's work that understanding the relationship between a picture and its referent is a developmental step from being able to recognize the subject matter in pictures.

Independent research using DeLoache's search task has shown variability in the developmental point during the third year of life at which very young children come to understand the referential nature of pictorial symbols, and has also shed light upon some of its underlying factors (Salsa & Peralta de Mendoza, 2007; Suddendorf, 2003). Suddendorf (2003) claims that DeLoache and her colleagues have underestimated infants' ability in using a symbol to search for a toy. He argues that because infants are typically required to perform the search task over a number of trials the younger infants perform poorly because of a difficulty in disengaging from a previous successful search. When analyzing only first trial responses Suddendorf found that even 24-month-olds could search at above chance levels for a hidden object using a pictorial symbol of its location. In contrast, Salsa and Peralta de Mendoza's research showed that 30-month-olds' success depended, in particular, upon emphasizing the intentional function of pictures to represent referents (see also Callaghan, 2008), and that highlighting the perceptual correspondence between pictures and referents may also be beneficial (see also DeLoache & Burns, 1994). Callaghan (2000, 2008) has suggested that up until 3 years of age understanding of pictures as referential symbols is highly tenuous, and that success on DeLoache's search task is achieved only if the infants are able to use a verbal label for the hiding place.

Interestingly, infants can successfully search for the toy using information given from a picture at an earlier age than if a miniature model of the room is used instead of the picture (in this case the infant sees a miniature version of the toy being hidden in the model). Over a series of studies reported over the years, DeLoache (2000) comments that 36-month-olds shown the miniature model search successfully on their first attempt in the room between 75–90% without error, whereas 30-month-old infants do very poorly, making only 15–20% of errorless retrievals. The poor performance of 30-month-olds is directly due to not conceptualizing the dual nature of the model as when the need for dual representation is eliminated, by making the children believe that the scale model had been shrunk by a "shrinking machine," they can successfully search for a miniature toy in the "shrunken" room after seeing the large toy being hidden in the preshrunken room (DeLoache, Miller, & Rosengren, 1997).

DeLoache (1987) explained the earlier developmental success in searching on the picture version of the task by arguing that the infant is less likely to conceive the picture as an object in itself (compared to a three-dimensional model), and consequently focuses more on its representational relationship with the room. This explanation seems highly plausible but it does beg the question of whether even infants who successfully search for the toy using the picture understand fully the distinction between a picture and its referent (if they are so focused on the representational property of pictures). Indeed, in the next section I present evidence that suggests that even 3- to 4-year-olds have not learned all there is to know about the independence of pictures from their referents.

Understanding the Independence of Pictures

Beilin and Pearlman (1991) discuss three ways in which pictures are distinct from their referents: physical, functional, and existence. In respect of the physical and functional, a picture of an ice-cream, for example, feels physically different from a real ice-cream and also has a different function (to look at rather than to eat). Presumably, the nature of DeLoache et al.'s (1998) 9-month-olds' manual exploration of the pictures suggest that babies by this age are still unsure about the physical and functional distinctions between pictures and the three-dimensional objects they refer to. Existence refers to the fact that the contents of a picture remain stable despite any change made to the real object the picture depicts. For example, if we eat an ice-cream a picture of it does not disappear as well! Surprising as it may sound, there is consistent evidence from what are called "false picture tasks" that children up to around 4 years of age appear to show confusion over this existence principle.

The essence of the procedure in false picture tasks is to show to the child an object (usually a doll) and then produce a pictorial representation of the doll. A change is then made to the doll (either it is moved or something is altered on the doll). Typically the test questions ask the child about their understanding of the current position or appearance of the doll and of its pictorial representation. The focus of the research studies, however, is on the child's response to the picture question as this informs us whether the child understands the independent existence of pictures to their referents. A seminal paper using this procedure on 3-, 4- and 5-year-olds was reported by Zaitchik (1990). An instant Polaroid photograph was taken of a puppet at position "A." In most of the studies reported in her paper the children did not see the front of the picture (in the first study the children did see the picture as it developed). The children then saw the puppet being moved from "A" to position "B." Finally, each child was asked where the puppet is in the picture (at this point the child can only see the back of the picture so cannot merely "read off" the answer). Zaitchik found that 4-year-olds performed no better than chance with the 3-year-olds' performance worse than chance (the 5-year-olds were typically successful). As there are only two possible answers to the question there is a 50% likelihood of giving the correct answer by guessing alone. However, the authors noted little evidence of guessing among the two younger age groups, children were either getting the questions systematically right or wrong. It appeared, therefore, that many 3-year-olds (and some 4-year-olds) actually believed that the picture updated itself to represent the puppet in its new location, indicating that they have not yet grasped the independent existence of pictures.

Robinson, Nye, and Thomas (1994) sought to establish the reliability of this apparent misunderstanding while discounting two alternative explanations for Zaitchik's data. Robinson et al. drew a picture of the doll instead of taking a photograph of it as young children will be more familiar with the process of drawing than the processes involved in instant photography. Second, appropriate pointing accompanied the test questions to ensure the child knew whether the question referred to the picture or doll. In their procedure a doll was introduced wearing a sticker (e.g., of a sheep). A drawing was made by the experimenter of the doll wearing this sticker and then turned face down. The doll's sticker was then exchanged for a different one (e.g., a monkey) in front of the child, and the doll was turned face down (so the child could no longer see the sticker). The principal test question required the child to say what sticker was drawn in the picture (while the experimenter pointed to the face-down picture). The inclusion of Robinson et al.'s refinements to Zaitchik's procedure did seem to result in more correct responses among their 3- to 4-year-olds compared to those given by the similar aged children tested by Zaitchik, but there were still many children in at least one of the two trials who replied with the name of the sticker the real doll was now wearing. Furthermore, their experiments showed that children had little difficulty answering questions relating to the real doll, showing that the apparent difficulty with the existence principle related solely to their understanding of pictures.

The lower incidence of "picture" errors reported by Robinson et al.'s more optimal procedure cautioned these authors against the view that 3- to 4-year-olds actually believe that pictures update to match changes occurring in their referents. Instead, they argued that children who make errors have difficulty holding in mind and recovering the picture's features distinctly from those of the real referent. If this is the case and is due to young children's memory limitations then we would expect improved performance if children are helped in some way to disentangle the details about the picture and doll. This was one motivation behind the series of experiments reported by Thomas et al. (1999). We adopted a similar procedure to that reported by Robinson et al. (1994) except that we additionally asked "change" questions. For instance, in the first experiment we asked "remember this picture; has the sticker drawn in the picture changed?" prior to asking the typical question of what sticker is drawn in the picture (the "identity" question). We anticipated that if the previously reported errors on false picture tasks were due to memory difficulties, bringing the child's attention to whether any operations on the picture had taken place (since it had been drawn) would help them acknowledge that no such change had occurred. Furthermore, once correctly remembering no change to the picture had occurred we expected the child to then correctly state the sticker drawn in the picture (and not update it to match the new sticker on the real doll). To our surprise, as shown in Table 5.1, the children performed poorly on both (change and identity) picture questions (but as expected had little difficulty answering the change and identity questions addressed to the real doll).

In our second experiment we asked half of the children a modified change question: "remember this picture; did we change the sticker drawn in the picture?" By directing attention to the experimenter's actions to the picture (and also to the doll in a similar question addressed to the doll) we considered that this would be an even better facilitator of children's recall of the events (or nonevents as in the case of the picture) they had just witnessed. As can be seen in Table 5.1, however, errors were still apparent in responses to both the modified change question directed to the picture and to the identity question that followed, and also to another group of children who received the original change question (this group replicated the extent of errors found in the first experiment). Furthermore, both studies showed strong and significant correlations between errors on the change and identity

Table 5.1   Mean Scores (and Standard Deviations) on Change and Identity Questions Reported in Experiments 1 and 2 by Thomas et al. (1999)

Question	Doll	Picture
	Experiment 1	
Change	1.55 (0.82)	1.15 (0.89)
Identity	1.75 (0.59)	1.10 (0.87)
	Experiment 2	
Original change	1.50 (0.78)	1.15 (0.92)
Identity	1.80 (0.46)	1.15 (0.84)
Modified change	1.83 (0.45)	0.75 (0.81)
Identity	1.78 (0.42)	1.25 (0.84)

Note. Maximum score is 2.

questions: Children who reported that the picture had changed were likely also to update the identity of the sticker in the picture.[3]

The robustness of the children's picture updating errors led us to check that they only occurred for pictures that represented a doll whose sticker was subsequently changed. In our third experiment, therefore, we used a modified procedure to that described above to confirm that this was indeed the case. Two dolls (named Anne and Paul) were presented wearing identical stickers. Half of the 3- to 4-year-olds saw a picture of Anne (with sticker) being drawn, the other half saw Paul (with sticker) being drawn. The sticker on the doll called Anne was exchanged with a new one of a different subject matter. No change was made to the sticker on the doll called Paul. Thus, for half the children the drawing represented the doll (Anne) with an out-of-date sticker. Consistent with our expectation the children were more likely to assert that the sticker in their picture had changed if their drawing was of Anne rather than Paul.

The reliability of updating errors among 3- to 4-year-olds originally reported by Zaitchik (1990) has now therefore been established. Despite their reliability, however, the updating errors in false picture tasks are inconsistent with children's responses when directly questioned about the existence principle. Beilin and Pearlman (1991) asked 3- to 4-year-olds directly what would happen to a picture of a topic that it depicted if a change was made to the topic itself (e.g., "what would happen to this picture of a flower if we cut off the petals of this [real] flower?"). Most children answered this direct question correctly, indicating that 3- to 4-year-olds have understood the independent existence of pictures to their referents. Furthermore, there is no evidence from children's natural interaction with pictures, at least none has been reported as far as I am aware, of any children spontaneously behaving as if they think pictures update to match changes in their referents (children do not look at family photographs and wonder why the family members are not wearing the same clothes as they can see the family is now wearing!). So why do so many 3- to 4-year-olds fail false picture tasks? A second conundrum is how can we tally DeLoache's search tasks showing that children appear to have a fully mature understanding of the dual nature of pictures by $2^1/_2$ years, with false picture tasks showing that dual nature is not acquired until children's fifth year? These two questions are now dealt with in the next section.

Which Tasks are Testing the Dual Nature of Pictures?

Judy DeLoache has consistently interpreted performance on her search tasks in terms of children's understanding of the dual nature of the symbol presented, whether that symbol is a scale model, picture or video (DeLoache, 1987, 1991, 2000, 2002, 2004; DeLoache & Burns, 1994; DeLoache, Miller & Rosenberg, 1997; DeLoache, Peralta de Mendoza, & Anderson, 1999; Troseth & DeLoache, 1998; Uttal, Schreiber, & DeLoache, 1995). The age at which children successfully search for the hidden toy in the room depends upon the symbol used, the instructions, the physical similarity of the symbol and referent, and the degree of salience that is given to the symbol. Nevertheless, in standard conditions where the symbol is a picture, the majority of children around $2^1/_2$ years of age successfully search for the toy in the room (DeLoache, 1987; DeLoache & Burns, 1994). DeLoache argues that children who succeed on the task understand the dual nature of pictures because they understand that a picture represents a specific reality (as shown by their successful use of the information provided in the picture to locate the toy in the room), and that the picture is an object in itself (as shown by the children pointing to the place in the picture where the toy is hiding).

In contrast, the failure of many children of up to 4 years of age in false picture tasks has been claimed to reflect a less than complete understanding of the dual nature of pictures (Robinson et al., 1994; Thomas et al., 1999). Children do not appear to understand the picture as an independent object, in particular, that they lack an appreciation of the existence principle. This interpretation stands in stark contrast with DeLoache and Burns' (1994) claim that the cause of the failure of the 2-year-olds in their search tasks is that children have *overextended* their understanding of the picture being different from its referent. They argue that these young children have decontextualized pictures from the other realities that pictures refer to.

It is surprising that the apparent inconsistency in the findings and interpretations from the two tasks has not yet been addressed in the literature, and accordingly I would like to give some space here towards some resolution. Essentially I believe that the search task and the false picture tasks (in conjunction with the different test questions asked) each have their own bias towards one property of the dual nature of pictures. DeLoache's search tasks are primarily a test of children's understanding of the (specific one-to-one) representational property of pictures, and are only a limited measure of children's understanding of pictures as objects in themselves. In contrast, the false pictures tasks are principally measuring the child's understanding of the independent existence of pictures but less so of their understanding that pictures can represent specific realities (which children have long since been aware of by the age typically tested in these tasks).

Let me expand upon these points. When asked to point to where in the picture the toy is hiding in the room, DeLoache's children point to the appropriate place in the picture (rather than going into the room again), which indicates they have at least a basic understanding of the distinction between the picture and room. Even the 2-year-olds who cannot search successfully in the room point to the appropriate place in the picture (DeLoache & Burns, 1994). Indeed, DeLoache et al.'s (1998) observational study of infants interacting with pictures showed that 19-month-old infants understood this basic distinction between pictures and real referents by pointing at the pictures. But DeLoache's search task does not test whether children know that the contents of a picture remain stable if a change is made to the room (the existence principle) as there is never a mismatch between the picture (or any of the other symbols used in her tasks) and the room. Consequently, the search task is an incomplete test of children's understanding of the independence of pictures as it does not test for the existence principle.

It is this knowledge of the existence principle that is being tested by the false picture task. This is done by creating a mismatch between the doll and picture, and then asking test questions about the doll and the picture which are designed to address children's knowledge of the independence of both. But the false-picture task is only a basic measure of the children's understanding that pictures can represent particular realities. True, they are happy to acknowledge that the picture created is of the doll, but they are not asked to show their knowledge of the one-to-one correspondence of the picture-referent relationship as the search task does.

Although the findings from the search and false picture tasks may at first appear conflicting, seen in the light of my arguments they are in fact complementary. The search task shows that by 2$\frac{1}{2}$ years children understand that pictures can represent specific realities (and use that information to make successful searches) as well as showing a basic understanding that pictures are not the same as referents (which they have long since understood). Errors on false picture tasks indicate, however, that at least under this experimental context children may not have a complete understanding of the independence of pictures until their fifth year. Considering the findings from both tasks, therefore, children first acquire a complete knowledge of pictures' representational property before a complete understanding of the independence property of pictures. This should not surprise us as the primary purpose of pictures is to represent.

My explanation so far is fine except that we have a problem interpreting the errors on false picture tasks as a misunderstanding of the existence principle. As I mentioned above when directly asked whether a picture of a referent would change if an alteration was made to the referent most children around 3 to 4 years of age know it does not (Beilin & Pearlman, 1991). Also, there is no evidence of such misunderstanding from children's natural interaction with pictures. The key difference in Beilin and Pearlman's question with the false picture task procedure is that with the former the child is being asked to consider the picture principally in one way only, its independent existence (and explicitly so rather than implicitly as is the case in false picture tasks). In Thomas et al. (1999) we argued that children's errors on false picture tasks is due to being unable to *simultaneously* hold in mind the independent existence of a picture while attending to the representation of the picture to its referent. It is not the case, therefore, that children up to approximately 4 years of age do not understand the independent existence of pictures (they may well acquire the existence principal at much the same time as a picture's physical and functional independence). Rather, when presented with an experimental procedure in which they have to consider the independence of pictures *at the same time* as a representation of a referent, they cannot think about the picture in *both* ways, and respond according to a picture's representational bias.

You may now be thinking that children's performance on false picture tasks may have more to do with their flexibility of thought (being able to consider simultaneously one thing in two ways) rather than their intrinsic understanding of pictures. That is, are we really talking about a cognitive rather than a pictorial deficit here? In the next section I will outline some examples of children up to 4 years of age being inflexible in taking multiperspectives of a variety of entities, including symbols.

Flexibility of Thought in Children's Understanding of the Dual Nature of Symbols

In the appearance reality test children are shown an object which appears to look different from what it actually is (see Flavell, Flavell, & Green, 1983); for example, a sponge that is painted to look like a rock. When 3-year-olds are asked what it really is (a sponge) and what it looks like (a rock) they tend to respond to both questions with the same answer (usually a sponge). Thus, 3-year-olds are only able to conceive the object in one way, usually what it really is.[4] Similarly, in the case of ambiguous figures which can be seen as representing one of two things (e.g., a duck or a rabbit) depending on which features of the figure the perceiver is focusing on, 3- to 4-year-olds have difficulty perceiving both representations. Even when the representation that they have not spontaneously recognized is then pointed out to them they have difficulty reversing their recognition from one representation to the other (Gopnik & Rosati, 2001). In both tasks, therefore, the child is unable to hold in mind two meanings of the entity.

A similar cognitive deficit comes from studies testing inhibitory control where children are asked to switch between two pieces of information. For example, if young children are asked to use a rule for performing a card sorting task ("sort by color"), but then are required to sort the remaining cards using a different rule ("sort by shape"), children below 4 years of age tend to continue using the old rule in the postswitch trials despite correctly reporting both rules when directly asked (e.g., Zelazo, Frye, & Rapus, 1996; but see Deák, Ray, & Pick, 2004). Thus, although they know both rules they are unable to inhibit using the first rule when they are asked to switch. Applying this difficulty to children's failure on false picture tasks children may struggle to inhibit their focus on the representational property of the picture to attend to the independent existence of the picture to its referent (but see my discussion in the next section on Sabbagh, Moses, & Shiverick, 2006).

The pattern that is unfolding here is that children up to around the age of 4 years reveal a difficulty with representing simultaneously one thing in two ways across a range of tasks. In which case we would expect it not only to impact upon their performance on tasks testing for their (simultaneous) understanding of the dual nature of pictures, but other symbols systems as well. Indeed, evidence from "false word" and "moving word" tasks indicates that children up to around 4 years or even older struggle with thinking about words as things in themselves and as portraying referents. In the third experiment reported by Thomas et al. (1999) we wanted to see if children also made updating errors to written words, as well as pictures. In addition to those children allocated to the false picture task (see my earlier discussion of this experiment), we tested a further sample of 3- to 4-year-olds who instead of observing a drawing being made of the doll whose sticker was subsequently changed they saw the name of the doll and (original) sticker being written down. Although we made no statistical comparison between word and picture updating errors, more updating errors were made for words. The possibility that children are prone to updating words as well as pictures has been shown in research carried out by Bialystok (Bialystok, 2000; Bialystok & Martin, 2003). In her "moving word" task children are shown a card with a printed word (e.g., "cat") which is placed next to an object represented by that same name (a toy cat). Children were asked to report what the word said, both when it was in its correct position (i.e. next to the toy cat) and also when it had been "accidentally" moved to be adjacent to a different object (e.g., a toy bird). Even 4-year-olds tend to reply as if they believe the name has updated to correspond with the new object it is placed by.[5]

The question that is now emerging is whether young children's difficulty in understanding the dual nature of pictures (as shown by both DeLoache's search task and false picture tasks) is actually a fundamental picture-problem, or better understood as a cognitive deficit in representation per se. Evidence from the variety of tasks I have described in this section point consistently to children up to around 4 years of age having a difficulty holding in mind (i.e. representing) two pieces of information of a given entity. We might expect, therefore, that this leads them to perform poorly on tasks testing their understanding of the dual nature of symbols. In the next section I discuss the debate that has taken place in the literature about whether young children have a general representational deficit.

Do Children Have a General Representational Deficit?

We have seen that young children have a difficulty with tasks that require them to simultaneously attend to both the symbol as a thing in itself and to its referential communication. This has been shown for a variety of symbols, such as models, pictures, and written words. These symbols systems can be called external or public representations as they all have a physical form. There is another type of representation called internal or private that includes mental states, such as thoughts, beliefs, and desires. Of course these have no physical appearance (apart from what can be gleaned from brain activity via electrophysiology or brain imaging scans), but nevertheless represent the way in which we interpret the world. Furthermore, in the same way that a picture/word can misrepresent reality so can our mental representations, particularly our beliefs, misrepresent the truth about what they are attempting to refer to in the world. There has been extensive research over the last 20 years or so, from what have become known as "false belief" tasks, showing that children up to around 4 years of age lack an understanding that beliefs can misrepresent reality.

For example, in one version of the false belief task called the deceptive box task the child is shown a "smarties" tube and asked to state his or her belief about the contents of the box. Unsurprisingly, the child says smarties. However, when the tube is opened the actual contents are shown to be pencils. The child is then asked what they thought was in the tube (before it was opened). Many 3- to 4-year-olds state pencils (what the tube really contains) rather than smarties which they had only moments before stated (Perner, Leekam, & Wimmer, 1987). The same type of error is found in another version of the false belief task, that of the unexpected transfer task. In the classic version of this task (see Wimmer & Perner, 1983) the child witnesses a doll (Maxi) place a piece of chocolate in a blue cupboard. Maxi then leaves the room and while he is out Maxi's mother (another doll) moves the chocolate to a green cupboard. The child is asked to say where Maxi would look for the chocolate when he returned to the room. As in the deceptive box version many children up to 4 years of age mistakenly state the green cupboard (where the chocolate is now) despite being able to remember where Maxi had put the chocolate (measured by a separate question). They are seemingly unable to use this knowledge to attribute a false belief to Maxi (in the same way as they were unable to attribute their own false belief of what the smarties tube contained).

The updating errors found in these false belief tasks seem very similar to the updating errors reported on false picture/word tasks. In each case the child has updated the (false) representation (picture, word, or belief) to match the new or actual reality (doll with new sticker; the actual contents of the smarties tube; the current location of the chocolate). Similarly, in the appearance/reality tasks I mentioned earlier the child responds to the question of what the object (e.g., a sponge) appears to look like (e.g., a rock) with the answer of what it really is (a sponge). In fact researchers have applied the generic term "realist errors" to all these tasks as the child cannot recognize a (false) representation (whether it is a picture, word, belief, or object) that he or she knows to contradict reality.

The realist errors on the false belief tasks found commonly in children up to 4 years of age have been interpreted as children's lacking a representational theory of mind (Gopnik, 1996; Perner, 1991; Wellman, Cross, & Watson, 2001). What this means is that children cannot simultaneously hold in mind different beliefs (representations) about any given situation. Having a theory of mind is crucial to understanding human behavior, and lacking a theory of mind has been suggested to lie at the heart of the autistic disorder (Baron-Cohen, Leslie, & Frith, 1985). The interesting question proposed by Zaitchik (1990) for the purposes of our interest in children's understanding of the dual nature of pictures, however, was that young children's difficulty in representing false beliefs is not particular to understanding beliefs but rather it is grounded in a wider and more general difficulty with understanding representation per se (i.e. private and public representations). Recall in my earlier discussion of Zaitchik's (1990) paper that 3-, 4-, and 5-year-olds were shown a "false-photo" task in which only the 5-year-olds consistently stated the correct contents of a photograph after its referent has been altered (a puppet was moved). Zaitchik also reported that children found the false photo task at least as difficult as false-belief tasks, and consequently argued that children around this age have a general representational deficit.

I mentioned earlier, however, that by using drawings and appropriate pointing to aid children's understanding of the test questions, Robinson et al. (1994) found fewer errors on their false picture task than Zaitchik's false-photo task. A direct test of whether children's errors on false belief and false picture tasks reflect a general representational deficit was reported by Slaughter (1998). After finding that 3- to 4-year-olds' performance on two false picture tasks was better than their performance on false belief tasks (with no correlation in scores between the tasks), Slaughter sought to train children on each task. Inconsistent with the general representational deficit hypothesis, she found that the training facilitated performance on the task directly associated with the training, without any beneficial carry-over effects to children's performance on the other task.

This differential performance with pictures and beliefs cautions against the view of a central cause (a representational deficit) as we might expect it to impact on all types of representation similarly. Further caution comes from studies testing children from special populations, such as those with autism or severe hearing impairment, showing that these children perform relatively poorly on false-belief tasks compared to false-photo tasks (Leslie & Thaiss, 1992; Peterson & Siegal, 1998). There is also neurological evidence of dissociation between brain activity employed on false belief and false photo tasks in adults (Perner, Aichhorn, Kronbichler, Staffen, & Ladurner, 2006; Sabbagh & Taylor, 2000; Saxe & Kanwisher, 2003).

On the surface these lines of evidence suggest that we should employ a broad private/public representation distinction in the particular processes involved in each form of representation, but recent research using "false signs" has indicated a more accurate and precise dissociation (Perner et al., 2006; Sabbagh et al., 2006). Signs are similar to beliefs in that they both are intended to represent what they refer to *all* of the time, even if reality changes (in the case of signs we would all get lost if they did not!), whereas a picture is intended only to represent the referent at the time it was made (and not to update to reflect changes in the referent).[6] So although signs and pictures of referents are both public representations, the processes involved in understanding signs, rather than representational pictures, may have a closer relationship with those implicated in beliefs (Perner et al., 2006; Sabbagh et al., 2006). In a typical false sign task, based on the unexpected transfer version of the false belief task, Sabbagh et al. presented 3- to 5-year-olds with models of two locations (a blue and a red cardboard house), and an arrow (the sign) that pointed to one of the two houses. Children were instructed that a character in the story uses the sign to let everyone know where he is residing. However, as the story unfolds the character changes houses but forgets to change the sign (hence it is now a "false" sign), and children were asked where the sign says the character is. Sabbagh et al. found stronger associations between scores on three executive function tasks (in which the children were required to inhibit a response) and scores on false sign and false belief tasks, than they did in correlations between each executive function task and the false photo tasks (the latter producing no significant associations).

Sabbagh et al.'s findings are particularly relevant to our understanding of children's errors on false picture tasks. They suggest that while inhibiting a response to the referent is likely to play an important role in understanding beliefs and signs, it may not be in comprehending pictures. As beliefs and signs are more intrinsically linked to their referents than pictures are (because of the function of beliefs and signs to always represent current reality), the requirement to disengage beliefs and signs when they do not represent them (i.e. when they are false) demands a greater ability to inhibit thinking about the referent than that posed by pictures. Accordingly, errors in appreciating the independence of pictures may have relatively little to do with a general difficulty young children have in disengaging from the reality to which representations refer. A further line of supporting evidence of a dissociation of the mental processing of beliefs and signs on the one hand, and of pictures on the other, was reported by Perner et al. (2006) who found similar areas of brain activity involved in performing false belief and false sign tasks, while performance on false photo tasks provided a different pattern of neural activity.

Despite the initial excitement that followed Zaitchik's study it is now accepted from studies on normal and abnormal populations that children's representational errors do not have a single common cause, that of a general representational deficit. Children's realist errors on false belief tasks are generally considered to be a result of lacking a representational theory of mind; an explanation that places the errors firmly in the mental domain. Children gain a theory of pictures much earlier, that they are both similar and different to the reality they refer to, no doubt aided by being able to experience directly the physicality of the symbol. The physical form of a picture is likely to place less of an executive demand of disengaging from the reality of the referent compared to thinking about a past (abstract) belief of a reality, further facilitated by pictures not having the function of reflecting the current reality of the contents they refer to (unlike signs). Nevertheless, children are still struggling with false picture tasks a long time after they understand that pictures can refer to a particular reality and are physically, functionally, and existentially different from their referents.

I have discussed a wide variety of tasks in this chapter showing that children up to 4 years of age have difficulty holding in mind dual identity, that is, thinking about something in two different ways. This leads them to fail false-picture tasks as well as laying a further burden on them when confronted with false belief tasks (i.e. in addition to lacking a representational theory of mind). That is, they fail false picture tasks because they cannot hold in mind two ways of thinking about the picture at the same time: as an object in itself and as a representation. During their fifth year many children acquire this (dual identity) ability and this is when updating errors on false picture tasks evaporate.

Summary

Much of what we understand about our world is conveyed through the many symbol systems that pervade it. Understanding the conceptual (dual) nature of symbols, that they are things in themselves and communicate meaning by referring to some other reality, is therefore a fundamental developmental milestone typically achieved in childhood. Using a variety of tasks from diverse lines of research we can patch together a developmental path from young babies to early childhood in understanding the dual nature of the pictorial symbol system. Newborns can visually discriminate between pictures and their referents, and within their first few months may be able to recognize the contents of a picture if they are familiar with the referent. By 9 months they may behave towards pictures as though they are not entirely clear that pictures are different from the reality they refer to, but any confusion has certainly gone by 19 months of age (and no doubt before this). By $2^1/_2$ years children can understand the one-to-one correspondence of a picture to its specific referent to the point that they can use information from a picture to search for a toy located in its referent. However, because young children have a general cognitive problem of dual identity (potentially compounded by being inflexible in switching their attentional focus between both identities), even 4-year-olds can still give the impression that they think pictures update to match changes in their referents in tasks that require them to consider at the same time the picture as a representation and a thing in itself. In effect, their attentional bias towards pictures as representations blocks their already acquired knowledge of the distinctive properties of pictures and their referents. As the afore-mentioned cognitive limitations decline, typically in the fifth year, children become able to simultaneously and fully consider pictures as representations and objects in themselves.

Notes

1   Schwartz (1995) reported research findings indicating that adults are more likely to reason about the referent a picture represents, rather than the features of the picture itself, if the picture is highly visually realistic. However, in the case of "three-dimensional moving" pictures there may be a point in which the picture is so visually realistic that even adults behave in such ways as to appear they think it *is* the referent. In a recent trip to Legoland, England, I saw a "three-dimensional" film shown in the "Imagination Theatre." During the film I noticed that there were many adults (including myself!) who, at certain points in the film where the subject matter appeared to come out of the screen towards you, put out their arms (or moved their head away) for protection or curiosity.

2   Some of my own students have confirmed such behavior in young infants they know.

3   Although we intended in the first two experiments to facilitate the need to disentangle the details relating to the picture from those of the referent by bringing the child's attention to the (experimenter's) operations, it may be important to consider the child's interpretation of the role of

the experimenter as a factor in their poor performance on false picture tasks generally. Bowler, Briskman, and Grice (1999) found that 3- to 4-year-olds were more likely to pass a false drawing task if a naughty puppet "drew" the picture and then prevented the child (and experimenter) from seeing the contents of the drawing after a change had been made to the drawing's referent. Referring to McGarrigle and Donaldson's (1974) use of a naughty teddy in Piaget's conservation of number experiment, Bowler et al. commented that a similar adaptation in their false drawing task gave a rationale for asking the child the test question about the contents of the drawing, and making the motives and intentions of the experimenter in the task less salient.

4   One exception to these "realist" errors on appearance/reality tasks is where a color filter is placed around an object, with children tending to respond that the object looks like and really is the color of the filter (e.g., see Flavell, Green, & Flavell, 1986).

5   It should be noted that Bialystok's interpretation of errors on her moving word task is that children believe words have multiple meanings (as opposed to a belief that the meaning changes).

6   For this reason Josef Perner and colleagues have argued that pictures which no longer reflect the current reality of their referent should be called out-of-date, rather than "false" (Leekam & Perner, 1991; Perner et al., 2006).

6

Drawings as Measures of Internal Representations

In this chapter I examine the representational redescription theory, originally proposed by Karmiloff-Smith (1990, 1992), that children's attempts to manipulate their graphic representations provide information on how the corresponding internal representations are stored in the child's mind. Specifically, the theory claims that children's internal representations are initially stored implicitly and then undergo a process in which its elements become more explicitly accessible to the child. The chapter discusses the validity of this theory in accounting for children's developing flexibility in manipulating their representational drawings, as well as suggesting some alternative explanations.

Children's representational drawings do not just happen; they are usually initiated by the child's desire to draw subject matter of the people and things in our world. Accordingly, a child's representational drawing can be considered as a process that can be traced back to the child's mental representation of the subject matter they have depicted. The idea of drawings reflecting the child's internal representations was originally proposed in the notion of the internal model, discussed more fully in chapter 1 in respect of Luquet's (1927/2001) intellectual realism stage. The experimental studies relating to the child's internal model taught us not to assume that children's drawings are print-outs of the internal representations that underpin the topics drawn (i.e. including the main criteria features of a topic each drawn in their characteristic shape). In this chapter, however, I discuss a different theory of children's internal representations that concerns how they are stored and developed in the mind. This is Annette Karmiloff-Smith's (1990, 1992) representational redescription (RR) theory, which was induced in part from studying children's drawings.

Karmiloff-Smith's Representational Redescription (RR) Theory

In her book, *Beyond Modularity*, Karmiloff-Smith (1992) described RR theory as a bridge between Piaget's constructionist theory and Fodor's nativist theory. Her particular interest in the theories proposed by Piaget and Fodor was the opposing implications each had on constraint and flexibility in the child's cognitive system. In Piaget's theory she comments that overarching changes in the way in which a child thinks occur more or less simultaneously across domains through biologically determined domain-general mechanisms.[1] Piaget's domain general theory proposed that children's cognitive development is slow, having to wait for overarching cognitive change to occur via the domain general mechanisms. But when it does occur it allows maximum flexibility due to a qualitative shift in thought across domains. In contrast, she refers to Fodor's (1983) position that the infant's mind is already pre-specified in terms of hard-wired special purpose modules which are genetically preprogrammed for processing different types of information, for example, letters and numbers. Consequently, the cognitive system proposed by Fodor allows learning to be more rapid than the model proposed by Piaget because incoming information from the environment is processed by tailor-made modules rather than generic mechanisms. But the cost of this rapid learning is that there is a constraint on the cognitive system as a whole because what is learned via a module-specific mechanism cannot be transferred to other modules.[2]

She accepted Fodor's notion that the brain is likely to be modular in structure, but that initially babies have only a limited number of innately specified, domain-specific predispositions (that are not necessarily modular in Fodor's sense), and that over time there is a process of modularization whereby more specific brain circuits will be formed for dealing with particular environmental inputs. Furthermore, she has argued for an innate general mechanism, called representational redescription, that impacts upon microdomains (e.g., pronoun acquisition within the domain of language). In contrast to Piaget's domain-general mechanisms, however, Karmiloff-Smith does not believe the RR mechanism causes simultaneous changes across domains. Instead, the RR mechanism acts recurrently at different times across different microdomains. Furthermore, Karmiloff-Smith argues it exploits information already held in the mind. An example she describes is her own experience of succeeding at solving the Rubik's cube (a three-dimensional square block made up of smaller squares of six colors in which the task is to manipulate the cube so that each of the six sides has its own uniform color). Even after succeeding on the task the procedure was initially only implicit to her; she did not know how she had done it. But through further successful attempts she began to see a pattern in the procedure, that is, her "representation" of solving the puzzle became more explicit to her. For Karmiloff-Smith the key role of the RR mechanism is that it enables children's existing representations to become more understandable to the child, and accordingly become increasingly flexible (for example, being able to solve the Rubik's cube from any initial spatial arrangement of the individual cubes). Thus, the RR process involves making implicit knowledge *in* the mind explicitly available *to* the mind. The basic premise of RR is that our learning is initially implicit, procedural, isolated, and inaccessible. Then we eventually access representations and link them up with other representations so that our behavior, knowledge, and thought can become meaningful, explicit, and flexible.

Karmiloff-Smith states there are four levels of representational redescription, one implicit level and three explicit levels. At the implicit level information gleaned from the environment is gradually acquired until the child possesses a complete representation which can be automatically and successfully demonstrated when required (e.g., singing a song, producing a sentence, making a representational drawing, etc.). Once the child is able to consistently demonstrate such a representation he or she has achieved "behavioral mastery" of the representation. But at the implicit phase of this representation it is demonstrated procedurally and inflexibly because the child only has access to the procedure as a whole, not the component parts.

Furthermore, all the child's implicit representations are stored separately and as such the child cannot make links between implicit representations. In the case of a child's implicit internal representation of the human figure, for example, the RR theory says that the child can only produce a sequential procedure of the human figure parts rather than manipulate the parts of the figure or integrate them with components of other implicitly stored representations. Knowledge then gradually becomes more explicit (and therefore more flexible to the child) through an endogenous process (of internal reorganization of the representation) driven by the domain-general representational redescription mechanism via a series of three levels within the explicit phase. The first level of redescription (level E1) involves the representation's components becoming available to the rest of the cognitive system, resulting in links being made with other explicit phase representations. Further redescription allows the representation to become consciously accessible to the child (level E2) and finally open to verbal report (level E3).

Evidence of RR Theory in the Drawing Domain

Karmiloff-Smith (1992) presented evidence of her domain-general representational redescription mechanism in the domains of language, physics, mathematics, theory of mind and drawing. Notational domains that leave a physical trace created by the child, she argued, are a particularly useful indicator of the corresponding internal representation's RR level. For instance, in respect of children's drawing she states, "an analysis of the types of modification that they produce makes it possible to capture essential facets of the constraints on representational flexibility" (1992, p. 157). Accordingly, Karmiloff-Smith set children tasks that required them to change their existing graphic representations to elucidate the development of flexibility in their internal representations.

In an earlier seminal paper showing representational redescription in children's drawings Karmiloff-Smith (1990) asked 54 children aged 4–11 years to first draw a house and secondly, to "draw a house that doesn't exist" (alternative wordings included, "house you invent," "pretend house," and "house we have never seen before"). The same instructions, with the same alternative wordings, were given for drawing a man and an animal. The rationale for asking children to draw a house, man and animal was that children by 4–5 years of age have normally acquired a representational schema of these topics (i.e. achieved behavioral mastery) that they can produce quickly and efficiently.[3] The second set of drawings required children to operate on their representations of these topics and in so doing allowed an examination into how constrained (or flexible) these (internal) representations were.

The manipulations drawings (X that doesn't exist, etc.) were analyzed in terms of the types of changes the children had made. Six categories were derived:

1   Shape and/or size of elements changed
2   Shape of whole changed
3   Deletion of elements
4   Insertion of new elements
5   Position/orientation changed
6   Insertion of cross-category elements (from other representations).

One example drawing from each category is reproduced in Figure 6.1. There were developmental effects for the types of changes the children made, as can be seen in Figure 6.2. The 4- to 6-year-olds almost exclusively made the first three types of changes (shape/size of elements changed, shape of whole changed, deletion of elements), whereas the 8- to 10-year-olds made changes across all categories. This distinction in the products of the manipulation tasks was not the only difference Karmiloff-Smith observed between the age groups. Using deletions as an example she explains, "younger children deleted at the end of procedures, involving no interruption in sequential order . . . older children tended to delete at any point in the procedure and to continue with the rest of the drawing" (Karmiloff-Smith, 1990, p. 72). Furthermore, she claimed that those few 4- to 6-year-olds who made changes corresponding to the last three types of categories made their changes at the end of the drawing sequence, whereas older children made insertions in the middle of their drawing procedure.

So how do these developmental differences inform us about the RR process? Her observations of the point at which children made changes during their drawing procedure of a house/man/animal, she argued, reflected different levels of the RR process. Karmiloff-Smith

Figure 6.1   An example drawing from Karmiloff-Smith's (1990) six categories of representational change from her manipulation tasks. Shape/Size of elements (top left), Shape of whole (top right), Deletion of elements (middle left), Insertion of new elements (middle right), Position/Orientation (bottom left), Insertion of cross-category (bottom right).

argued that because all the children in her study were able to make some changes to their representations then the internal representations (of a house, man, and animal) had all reached the explicit phase, but that the younger children's representations were largely at the E1 level. She argued that at both the (earlier) implicit level and the first explicit level the elements of a procedure are sequentially

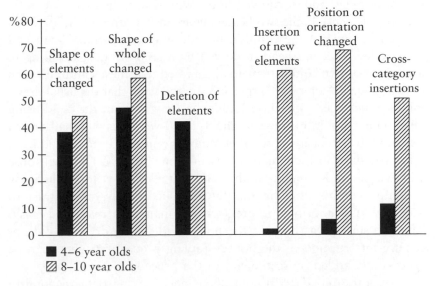

Figure 6.2   Percentage of children making each of Karmiloff-Smith's (1990) six categories of representational change by age group.

constrained, that is, they are produced as a sequentially fixed list. The changes the younger children typically made did not violate this procedural rigidity. For instance, size and shape amendments can be made without changing the sequence of elements drawn, and any deletions were made at the end of the sequence. In contrast, the representations produced by the 8- to 10-year-olds had proceeded further (beyond the E1 level), because the insertion of elements from within the representation (e.g., more arms and heads in the human figure), from other representations (e.g., wings on a house), and position/ orientation changes, were often made mid-procedure.

In a follow-up study Karmiloff-Smith (1990) checked that the few instances of the last three categories of changes found among the 4- to 6-year-olds were not simply because they had not thought of making these changes. Eight 5-year-olds who made changes that involved size, shape, and deletion (the first three categories) on the manipulation task (e.g., "draw an X that does not exist") in the first study were then asked to make changes typical of the spontaneous productions the older children had made. Specifically, these eight 5-year-olds were asked to "draw a man with two heads" (insertion of new element) and to "draw a house with wings" (insertion of cross-category element). In the two-headed figure task, Karmiloff-Smith found that all but one of the children first drew a conventional man and then added a second head, followed by a second body, resulting in a drawing of two complete men. She argued that these children's man drawings were "compiled" procedures in the sense that the usual drawing sequence was "tipped out" in its entirety without the child being able to interrupt it. In contrast, the 8- to 10-year-olds who had drawn a man with two heads in the first study had inserted the second head mid-procedure in their man-representation. In respect of the house with wings task Karmiloff-Smith found that all the 5-year-olds in Study 2 completed this drawing rapidly and successfully, in contrast to the slow and laborious progress on the man with two heads task. This she stated was because the house with wings drawing did not require interruption of the house-drawing procedure (wings can be successfully added on to the end of the procedure).

Karmiloff-Smith (1990) considered her drawing data to confirm the existence of the RR mechanism which activates on children's initial automated procedures to a flexible cognitive system. Summing up the shift from sequentially fixed elements to a flexible system she states,

> The present model . . . explains general developmental change in terms of a movement from an internal representation specified as a sequentially fixed list of core features . . . to an internal representation specified as a structured, yet flexibly ordered set of manipulable core features (pp. 76–7).

Challenges to Representational Redescription Theory

There have now been a number of studies investigating age differences in children's performance on drawing manipulation tasks (e.g., Barlow et al., 2003; Berti & Freeman, 1997; Morse & Bremner, 1998; Picard & Vinter, 1999; Spensley & Taylor, 1999; Zhi, Thomas, & Robinson, 1997). In Barlow's (2002) literature review of this body of research she notes that studies using the open-ended tasks (e.g., "draw a strange man") have supported the age-related developmental shift in the types of modification found by Karmiloff-Smith (Berti & Freeman, 1997; Morse & Bremner, 1998; Spensley & Taylor, 1999). But replication studies of manipulation tasks in which the instructions specifically determine what is to be drawn (e.g., the two-headed man task) have provided data inconsistent with those reported by Karmiloff-Smith (1990). For instance, Zhi et al. (1997) found as many as 15 of the 32 children aged 4–5 were able to draw a man with two heads (compared with only one of the eight 5-year-olds in Karmiloff-Smith's second study). In a direct comparison between performance on the two types of task Berti and Freeman (1997) found that when asked to draw a non-existent person (including Karmiloff-Smith's alternative wordings) over half of the 5-year-olds either refused to draw it (10 of the 62) or produced a drawing that was essentially the same as the drawing they had just produced when asked to draw a person (24 of the 62). In contrast, 76% (47 of the 62) of these children were able to draw a man with two heads when subsequently directly instructed to do so, with only 16% (10 of the 62) producing two bodies.

Could it be that young children find manipulation tasks that provide specific instructions as to what to draw easier because they are more aware of what is required of them (relative to the open-ended tasks)? Berti and Freeman (1997) commented that those young children who do include a second body in the "draw a man with two heads" task might mistakenly believe that they are being asked to draw two (complete) people. This suggestion was taken up by Barlow et al. (2003) who informed their sample of children that they were to draw a "silly picture . . . draw a man with an extra head – one man with two heads." This explicit instruction led to only five of the forty 5-year-olds drawing a second body, erasing the developmental shift on the man with two heads task altogether. Zhi et al. (1997) found that providing an illustration of a woman with two heads facilitated 3- to 4-year-olds' performance of a two-headed drawing task, further supporting the view that young children can manipulate their human figure drawings if the task requirements are made clear. It may also be that the relative poorer performance on open-ended tasks among the younger children is in part due to their poor imagination (Barlow et al., 2003; Spensley & Taylor, 1999) and being less willing to draw impossible representations that violate reality.

Subsequent literature to Karmiloff-Smith's (1990) paper has reported another piece of contradictory evidence to her theory, that relating to procedural rigidity. Karmiloff-Smith (1990) presented only anecdotal comments of the point at which children made their modifications based on her own observations. But does systematic coding of the process of children's drawings in manipulation tasks support her assertion that young children only make changes (such as deletions) at the end of the drawing procedure (because their internal representations when executed are sequentially constrained)? Berti and Freeman (1997) asked 5- and 9-year-olds to initially draw a person and then to make three further drawings of something missing (a person with something missing, a headless person, and a person with a body missing). The point in which any item was deleted was recorded, and the authors reported that the 5- and 9-year-olds were equally capable of interrupting their drawings. Most importantly, there was no evidence that the 5-year-olds were constrained by sequence as they deleted parts ranging over the entire sequence of their original person drawing. Further support that young children are not sequentially constrained can be found in the data reported by Spensley and Taylor (1999) and Picard and Vinter (1999). After obtaining a drawing of a man from twenty-eight 4- to 9-year-olds Spensley and Taylor (1999) asked the children to make three further drawings: a man which the experimenter interrupted mid-procedure, a man with a beard, and a man that doesn't exist. Children of all ages had no difficulty carrying on their picture after being interrupted and only two children drew the beard at the end. Although the "man that doesn't exist" drawing was more difficult for the children (which could be for any number of the alternative reasons to cognitive constraint as discussed above) those 4- to 6-year-olds who did make interruptions made them in the middle of their procedure. Picard and Vinter (1999) tested 5-, 7-, and 9-year-olds on their interruption ability using a deletion task and found that although 5-year-olds did make more end deletions than the older children, roughly 40% of 5-year-olds still made mid-type deletions. It appears, therefore, that Karmiloff-Smith's assertion that young children's deletions consistently come at the end of the procedure is not supported.

This body of independent studies has shown that, inconsistent with Karmiloff-Smith data and RR theory, a high proportion of young children can produce flexible representations in manipulation tasks (including those employed by Karmiloff-Smith), if the instructions and materials make it clear what type of manipulation is required. Furthermore, these children are also capable of making mid-procedure interruptions, a finding that is contradictory to Karmiloff-Smith's claim that their representations are procedurally constrained.

The Revised Representational Redescription Theory

Karmiloff-Smith had already become aware of contradictory evidence to her own data published in 1990 by the time she wrote her 1992 book. She had received drawings from independent researchers showing that young children can interrupt their drawing procedures. In her book she accepted this new evidence by saying, "it turns out that the sequential constraint . . . is, particularly in domains like drawing, considerably weaker than I originally predicted" (Karmiloff-Smith, 1992, p. 162). She now asserts (and more recently, see Karmiloff-Smith, 1999) that the permanent notational trace in drawing leaves a cue that facilitates interruption of the procedure. Her revised opinion is that procedural rigidity is most clearly seen in notational systems that leave no trace, such as spoken language, music, and counting. An additional influence on drawings being less procedurally rigid, she claims, is that drawings take more time to execute than those representations of a non-notational system such as language.

Despite her cooling towards the usefulness of drawing to support RR theory we can see in her most recent writing on the subject that she still considered the possibility of some procedural rigidity in young children's drawings. She suggested that procedural rigidity may relate to subroutines in drawing, and asked rhetorically, "Is there really a man-drawing procedure, or rather a series of subroutines for drawing the head, the body, and the limbs?" (Karmiloff-Smith, 1999, p. 325). Furthermore, the independent research has found supporting evidence for Karmiloff-Smith's age-related developmental shift in flexible representations (albeit weaker than she originally proposed). Even in manipulation tasks where contextual cueing has been provided, some young children still fail where older children do not. The tendency for younger children to experience greater difficulty in manipulating their representations in the experimental tasks may still be directly attributable to a high level of procedural rigidity in the way they normally draw the components in their standard drawing of the representation. RR theory, if it is to be informed and supported by the drawing domain, depends on this last proposition. In other words, is there a relationship between the child's tendency to maintain the sequential order of elements in how they typically draw a representation (the *process*) with a difficulty in manipulating that representation (the *product*)? In the next section I discuss some research my colleagues and I have conducted to seek whether there is evidence for any such relationship.

The Relationship between Procedural Rigidity and Representational Change

In Barlow et al. (2003) we commented that it was surprising that the relationship between procedural rigidity (due to a cognitive constraint of the internal representation) and representational change, being of fundamental importance to RR theory, had not been directly tested in the drawing literature. Barlow (2002) notes that only primitive attempts have been made to assess whether the elements in children's typical drawings are produced in a procedurally rigid sequence. There have been studies that have measured element ordering in only one premanipulation drawing (Morse & Bremner, 1998; Picard & Vinter, 1999; Spensley & Taylor, 1999), which of course cannot inform us to what extent children draw elements in a consistent order. However, Barlow (2002) does cite Zhi et al.'s (1997) assessment of rigidity levels across three human figure drawings (a Father Christmas, a postman and a man with two heads). Putting aside whether the two different premanipulation topics (Father Christmas and a postman) would represent children's usual drawings of the human figure, it is still interesting to note that Zhi et al. (1997) found that most children maintained the same sequence of core items in all three of their drawings, including the manipulation drawing of a man with two heads (25 of the 32 children aged 3–4 years). Zhi et al.'s findings suggest that young children's drawings of the human figure (the most common topic in children's drawings), may in fact show high levels of procedural rigidity. Unfortunately, the authors did not investigate the relationship between the degree of procedural rigidity on the Father Christmas and postman drawings with the representational change performance on the manipulation task.

In a series of studies we sought to establish the nature of the relationship between procedural rigidity and representational change in the drawing domain, and in so doing directly test whether children's drawings supported the RR theory. In the first of four studies (see Barlow et al., 2003) we asked children to draw themselves on three separate occasions within approximately two weeks. In the manipulation task, which was presented in the third session after the child had drawn their final drawing of themselves, the child was asked to draw a man holding a ball with both hands. This manipulation task was designed to meet fully the criteria outlined by Karmiloff-Smith (1990) as demonstrating a fully explicit representation. It required the inclusion of a novel element (the ball) that would disrupt the children's normal drawing procedure of a person as well as necessitating a position/orientation change to some of the usual (core) elements of the topic (the arms). The task also avoided problems of children misunderstanding the requirement of the task, having a lack of inventiveness or any unwillingness to draw something outside the bounds of reality that may be inherent in the instructions given in some of the literature (e.g., "draw X that doesn't exist"). To further ensure the children understood what the drawing should look like a three-dimensional model of a doll holding a ball in front of its torso was shown (see Figure 6.3 for an illustration of the doll presented to the children). The model was removed prior to the child commencing his or her drawing. In all the drawings the order of the elements drawn was noted by the experimenter during the child's drawing process, the reliability of which was checked by an independent judge viewing the video recordings of the children drawing.

To maximize the likelihood of testing children who may produce procedurally rigid and inflexible representations (either within the implicit phase or E1 level of the explicit phase) we sampled a group of forty-five 4- to 6-year-olds (fifteen 4-year-olds, fifteen 5-year-olds and fifteen 6-year-olds). An older group (fifteen 8-year-olds) was also tested for evidence of reduced procedural rigidity and more flexible representations (having moved on to one of the later explicit levels).

Each child's rigidity score was measured on the number of pairs of core elements that the child drew together (in the same order)

Figure 6.3 An illustration of the three-dimensional "man holding a ball" doll used in Study 1 reported by Barlow et al. (2003).

throughout all three premanipulation human figure drawings of themselves. Thus, if the body was drawn immediately after the head on all three drawings then this constituted a rigid pair. Seven core items were considered (head, facial features, body, two arms, and two legs) and the maximum rigidity score was 6. The child's performance on the manipulation task (the representational change measure) was assessed by both a product and process measure. The product measure assessed the extent to which the final product reflected the image described in the instructions and illustrated in the model. This was measured on a scale of 1 to 4 (see Figure 6.4 for examples of the scoring system) in which partial and full manipulations were allocated scores of 3 and 4 respectively. The process measure of the child's representation change ability related to the point at which the new item (i.e. the ball) had been inserted, and was recorded as start (first element depicted), middle, or at the end (the last item drawn).

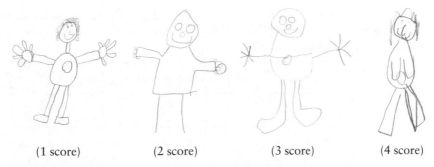

(1 score)   (2 score)   (3 score)   (4 score)

Figure 6.4 Illustrative examples of children's drawings showing the scoring range from the "man holding a ball" manipulation task (from Study 1; Barlow et al., 2003).

Forty-two percent of the whole sample produced a totally rigid sequence across the three premanipulation human figure drawings. Although the RR theory would have predicted higher levels of procedural rigidity among the younger children the level of rigidity was similar across all age groups. In respect of the representational change product measure there was a developmental progression towards higher scores by age (see Table 6.1). The numbers of children succeeding at making at least a partial manipulation of their human figure increased with age (40% of 4-year-olds, 47% of 5-year-olds, 67% of 6-year-olds and 93% of 8-year-olds). Consistent with the RR theory, chi-square analyses revealed that the 8-year-olds were more successful in comparison to the 4- to 6-year-olds. In our regression analyses, however, we found that only age, and not the rigidity score, predicted the "product" performance on the manipulation task (the analysis was performed only on the 4- to 6-year-old children as this was the age range most relevant to the proposed relationship; see Karmiloff-Smith, 1990). Furthermore, procedural rigidity was not related to the process measure of representational change. That is, children who produced higher procedurally rigid routines in their three human figure drawings prior to the manipulation drawing were no more likely to make end modifications in the manipulation drawing. The crucial finding from this experiment, therefore, was that levels of procedural rigidity in children's typical human figure drawings did not predict their representational change ability on the manipulation task.

Table 6.1 Numbers of Children in Each Age Group by Representational Change Score (1–4) on the "Draw a man holding a ball" Manipulation Task (Study 1, Barlow et al., 2003)

| Age (years) | *Representational change score* | | | | |
	1	*2*	*3*	*4*	*Total*
4	5	4	4	2	15
5	3	5	5	2	15
6	–	5	1	9	15
8	–	1	4	10	15
Total	8	15	14	23	60
4–6 Total	8	14	10	13	45

Recall that Karmiloff-Smith (1999) revised her opinion on procedural rigidity in the drawing domain, claiming that children may have rigid routines only in certain areas of their representations. Could it be, therefore, that procedural rigidity in these subareas constrains representational change in these areas of the representation? We tested this prediction in our second study by measuring 4- to 6-year-olds' rigid subprocedures (i.e. a pair of elements which was drawn together and in the same order on all three usual drawings) and then assessed their ability to manipulate one of their fixed subroutines.

In this second study seventy-five 4- to 6-year-olds were asked to draw a man three times over two sessions to establish which pairs of core elements were always drawn after each other in the same order. For each child one pair of rigidly ordered elements was then chosen by the experimenter to be the pair that the child would be required to interrupt in the manipulation task (all children had at least one rigid pair). Each rigid pair was assigned an item designed specifically to interrupt it, for example, a beard for the head to facial features pair. In a third session children were told that they were going to draw a man, "but with something added on" (i.e. the novel item assigned to their particular rigid pair). The novel item was displayed on a three-dimensional model of a man (as used in Study 1). The model was then removed and the child then asked to draw a picture of the doll that included the new item. Under these "free instructions" no direction was given as to when to draw the novel item. If the child did not interrupt their rigid subprocedure after this initial instruction they were then afforded a second attempt, with specific instruction to reorder their rigid pair (e.g., "can you draw the beard straight after you have drawn the head, and then draw the rest of the face such as the eyes, nose, and mouth"). The specific instruction was given to test whether any failure on their first manipulation drawing was due to being unable to reorder their fixed pair, rather than simply because they misunderstood the task requirements or chose to make the interruption elsewhere.

In the children's first attempt (the "free" instruction) only 17 of the 75 participants spontaneously modified their rigid subprocedure, but a further 49 did so after the specific instructions had been given. A total of 66 of the 75 participants, therefore, were successful at reordering. Even the majority of the 4-year-olds could do so (17 of the 25). We argued that as many children of all age groups could interrupt their rigid pair when directly asked to (albeit not spontaneously) suggests that it is not a cognitive constraint that accounts for fixed subroutines that appear in children's drawings. Rather, it is more likely to result from a preference that may be due to graphical ease, particularly in cases where the elements have a natural drawing order (see next section for an elaboration of this point).

Although even the 4-year-olds in our second study showed good evidence of re-ordering elements in a previously established rigid pair to include a novel item, they were less likely to do so than 5- and 6-year-olds. A possible interpretation is that the 4-year-olds were just in the process of redescribing their internal representation of the human figure (and hence relaxing their procedural rigidity in executing its drawing representation). In Study 3 we examined the possibility that even younger children may capture the procedural constraint that is characteristic of the implicit phase of the internal representation. We repeated the procedure used in Study 2 with a younger sample of thirty 3- to 4-year-olds and found, consistent with the data from Study 2, that the majority were able to insert the novel item between their rigid pair either spontaneously, or after being specifically told to do so (23 of the 30). Even the majority of those children who drew a tadpole person (a simpler form of the human figure that often precedes children's drawing of the conventional form) were able to manipulate their rigid pair to include the novel item. The conclusion from Study 3 was that the lack of evidence of procedurally rigid sub-routines in 4- to 6-year-olds (Study 2) extended to younger children (3- to 4-year-olds) and earlier developmental representations.

Our first three studies consistently showed, therefore, that even a watered down version of the RR theory in the drawing domain was unsupported. However, as I mentioned above, Karmiloff-Smith (1992, 1999) later stated that lack of rigidity in children's drawings may be due to the permanent external mark acting as a cue for procedural interruption. Presumably, we hypothesized, sequential constraint would be evident in young children's drawings if the marks made by the children left no visible trace, which in turn should inhibit interruption/manipulation ability. The removal of the notational trace in a drawing has not been used to test Karmiloff-Smith's (1992, 1999) explanation for the lack of consistent evidence for her original position.

Accordingly, in our fourth study, we asked 5- and 8-year-olds to produce drawings using an "artpad" (which left no external trace) linked to a computer which recorded the completed drawing. For comparison purposes another sample of similar aged children performed the same tasks using the standard pencil and paper. Consistent with our approach to monitoring the sequential order of children's usual drawings, all children produced three human figure drawings and three house drawings. The house drawings were requested partly to collect data that went beyond human figure drawings, but also because we wanted to replicate Karmiloff-Smith's (1990) original tasks. After children had produced these drawings (completed over two sessions) they were asked to complete three manipulation tasks in a third session with the following instructions: "Draw a man with an extra head – one man with two heads," "draw a house with some wings on each side – a flying house," and "draw me a picture of a man holding a ball with both hands, with the ball placed in front of his tummy." In this final study we did not use models to complement the instructions to ensure that children were operating on their existing human figure representation rather than simply creating a new procedure based on the model. As in the previous experiments, the experimenter noted the sequence order for all drawings and each session was video recorded.

The children's rigidity score for their three usual human figure drawings were scored in the same way as in the first study (i.e. 0–6 pairs).

Similarly, the drawings of the house were scored on a 0–6 scale (the core elements of a house were deemed also to be made up of seven items: square outline, roof, two upstairs windows, two downstairs windows, and a door). Figure 6.5 provides some illustrative examples of the scoring system used for the man with two heads and the house with wings manipulation tasks. Only drawings allocated to a score of 3 were considered true manipulations. For example, repositioning the first head to accommodate the second so that both heads appear equally balanced at the top of the body, and integrating the wings into the house outline (see Figure 6.5). The man holding a ball drawings were scored in the same way as described above in Study 1 (see also Figure 6.4). Finally, a process measurement was taken for the manipulation drawings in respect of when the novel item (head, ball, and wings) was inserted during the man or house drawing (start, middle, or end).

Inconsistent with what the RR theory might predict, the level of procedural rigidity for the usual man and house drawings was actually significantly *less* in the non-notational group (who used an

Figure 6.5 Illustrative examples of children's drawings showing the scoring range from the "man with two heads" and "house with wings" manipulation task (from Study 4; Barlow et al., 2003).

artpad that left no visible trace) than the notational group (using a normal pencil on paper). The lower mean scores of rigidity found in the non-notational group can be seen in Table 6.2. In respect of the manipulation tasks (see Table 6.3) children in the notational group achieved statistically significantly higher scores than those in the non-notational group on the man with two heads manipulation task. Although this is consistent with what the RR theory predicts (leaving a trace acts as a cue for drawing flexible representations), we should note this finding was not extended to the other two manipulations. Furthermore, the majority of children inserted the novel item in the two human figure manipulations at either the start of or during the drawing, regardless of whether they were in the notational or non-notational group.[4] Although there were more end-point insertions for the house with wings task than the human figure manipulation tasks, the relative frequency of start/mid-point and end-point insertions of the wings did not vary between the notational and non-notational groups.

Table 6.2   Rigidity Score Means (and Standard Deviations) for Each Age Group in the Notational and Non-notational Drawing Conditions for the Man and House Drawings (Study 4, Barlow et al., 2003)

		Descriptive statistics for rigidity scores (0–6 pairs)					
Age (years)	*Drawing condition*			*Mean (SD)*			
		Man		*House*		*Total*	
5	Notational	4.7	(1.42)	4.15	(1.63)	4.43	(1.09)
	Non-notat.	3.75	(1.74)	3.45	(1.85)	3.6	(1.19)
	Total	4.23	(1.64)	3.8	(1.76)	4.02	(1.2)
8	Notational	5.1	(1.33)	3	(1.86)	4.05	(1.17)
	Non-notat.	2.6	(1.76)	3.35	(2.01)	2.98	(1.44)
	Total	3.85	(1.99)	3.18	(1.92)	3.52	(1.4)
Total	Notational	4.9	(1.37)	3.58	(1.82)	4.24	(1.13)
	Non-notat.	3.18	(1.82)	3.4	(1.91)	3.29	(1.34)
	Total	4.03	(1.82)	3.49	(1.86)	3.76	(1.32)

Table 6.3 Representational Change Score Means (and Standard Deviations) for Each Age Group in Both Notational and Non-notational Drawing Conditions on the Man with Ball Task (MB 1–4 score), Man with Two Heads Task (M2 0–3 score) and the House with Wings Task (HW 0–3 score) (Study 4, Barlow et al., 2003)

		Descriptive statistics for representational change scores					
Age (years)	*Drawing condition*	*Mean (SD)*					
		MB		*M2*		*HW*	
5	Notational	3	(0.92)	2.5	(0.95)	2	(0)
	Non-notat.	2.95	(0.89)	2.1	(1.17)	1.9	(0.31)
	Total	2.98	(0.89)	2.3	(1.07)	1.95	(0.22)
8	Notational	3.75	(0.55)	2.9	(0.31)	2	(0)
	Non-notat.	3.35	(0.88)	2.4	(0.94)	2.05	(0.39)
	Total	3.6	(0.75)	2.65	(0.74)	2.03	(0.28)
Total	Notational	3.38	(0.84)	2.73	(0.72)	2	(0)
	Non-notat.	3.15	(0.89)	2.25	(1.06)	1.98	(0.36)
	Total	3.26	(0.87)	2.48	(0.93)	1.99	(0.25)

The final and most important question for the RR theory was whether differences in procedural rigidity could explain the varying performances on the manipulations tasks, particularly for the non-notational group who had no trace to aid interruption. In our regression analyses on the non-notational group data we found no relationship between procedural rigidity and representational change (and nor did we find any for the notational group, replicating our findings from Study 1).

Our series of four studies reported by Barlow et al. (2003) failed to find any substantial support for the RR theory in the drawing domain. Although older children were better at manipulating their representations, this ability was not associated with less sequential rigidity in their typical representation of the topics studied. This was true when either rigidity for all the core elements of a representation (Studies 1 and 4) or for subroutines (Studies 2 and 3) was measured. Finally, Karmiloff-Smith's (1992) revised assertion that the visible trace in drawing allows children greater flexibility was also clearly unsupported. The consistent lack of evidence shown by Barlow et al. (2003) for the RR theory in the drawing domain, including Karmiloff-Smith's (1992, 1999) amendments, requires alternative explanations for representational change in children's representational drawings.

Reflections on RR and Alternative Theories for Representational Change in Drawing

If you want to find evidence for the RR theory in the drawing domain you will be disappointed. The problem starts with the indefinable notion of behavioral mastery from which Karmiloff-Smith argues that the important shift from implicit to explicit understanding of the internal representation in the child takes place. Whereas behavioral success in speaking a grammatically correct sentence, playing a tune, or balancing a beam of blocks is straightforward to define in terms of success/failure, there are simply too many possible contenders of behavioral success in drawing to know from which point the internal representation becomes redescribed (Spensley & Taylor, 1999). In the case of the human figure, for instance, we see structural changes (unconnected parts, tadpole, segmented conventional figure, outlined conventional figure), increases in detail (from core features to the addition of peripheral details), better proportion of parts in relation to each other (e.g., a more appropriate head/body ratio), and a shift from a generic form to representations of individual people. At what point along these developmental shifts should we draw the line between success and failure?

If we take children's early representational drawings as cases of behavioral mastery (as they are dependent on some form of internal representation) then according to RR theory the internal representation is stored implicitly. But we see very little evidence of children's drawing representations being examples of an implicitly stored internal representation. Recall that Karmiloff-Smith's (1990) 4- to 6-year-olds could all make at least shape, size, and deletion changes, indicating that they have some explicit access to the elements of the representation. Karmiloff-Smith acknowledged this, saying that the children may have reached the first level of the explicit phase of awareness where procedural rigidity may still act as a constraint. It seems reasonable to suggest that the vestiges of a behavior characteristic in an earlier (implicit) phase may still be evident (albeit in a weaker form) at a later phase. But there is no good evidence of the implicit phase, even in younger children's drawings. Studies that have looked at younger children (3- to 4-year-olds) show that many can vary the order of the components in their human figure drawings in tasks that encourage them to do so (Barlow et al., 2003; Spensley & Taylor, 1999).

Nevertheless, there is some evidence of procedural rigidity in children's typical drawings that requires an alternative explanation to a cognitive constraint on the internal representations. Barlow et al. (2003) did see evidence of a sizable minority of children producing the human figure topic in a sequentially fixed list (about 40% of 4- to 6-year-olds drew the core items in exactly the same order over three drawings). Zhi et al. (1997) stated that the human figure is so frequently drawn by children that they may form a habitual routine when drawing familiar topics. Barlow et al. concurred with this view but also noted that the human figure topic has a natural drawing order that promotes a habitual routine. Human figures have a simple vertical structure that is most easily executed by using a top-to-bottom procedure, and we noted that most of the children we tested used this procedure. It makes sense for the child to find a consistent way of drawing a topic that they regularly draw, particularly if the structure of the topic lends itself to be drawn in a procedural framework rather than use alternative, more awkward, approaches (for example, starting with the feet).

As we argued in Barlow et al. (2003), habitual/natural drawing routines are more of a choice made by the child for the sake of graphical ease rather than a cognitive restraint of the internal representation. The fact that we found many children did not spontaneously interrupt their rigid pair in Studies 2 and 3, but were able to do so if asked directly, is consistent with our view that where children can keep the habitual/natural drawing order of a familiar topic they will (by choice), but most can draw it differently from their preferred choice if the instructions require them to. Thus, they are not cognitively constrained in the sense that the RR model suggests – there is little evidence from their drawings of them having only an implicit access to the corresponding internal representation. Nevertheless, their preferred choice may be partly dictated by other cognitive limitations unspecified in the RR mechanism, namely those relating to information processing. For instance, young children may work within their limits of planning, attention, and working memory by, on occasions and in some experimental tasks, completing their normal drawing process and then adding the novel item at the end (and of course we must not forget that limitations in young children's drawing skill are relevant here too).

Information-processing factors (e.g., planning, monitoring, awareness, and working memory) have also been suggested to account for the developmental shift in older children being more able to manipulate and change their representations (Barlow et al., 2003; Berti & Freeman, 1997; Spensley & Taylor, 1999; Picard & Vinter, 1999). For example, Berti and Freeman (1997) argued that younger children are less able to plan their drawings or monitor closely their drawing as it emerges. This limitation they claim needs to be considered in the context of Freeman's model on the child's developing framework theory of pictures which incorporates their understanding of the relationships between the referent, picture, artist, and viewer (see Freeman, 1995, 2000, 2004; Freeman & Parsons, 2001). One component of this is knowing how to communicate to a viewer the referent to be recognized. When applied to the drawing tasks typically used in this literature, such as being asked to draw a man that does not exist, Berti and Freeman state that the child needs to produce a drawing that is both recognizable as a man but also one that displays fictionality (so that a viewer can recognize both elements). For Berti and Freeman, monitoring and planning are key components for the child to attain this dual purpose objective in their drawing, and limitations in this area (due to a primitive framework theory of pictures) is one factor that leads young children to fail on representational change drawing tasks.[5]

Also taking an information processing perspective, Spensley and Taylor (1999) note that the representational changes typically made by younger children on the drawing manipulation tasks require less information to be held in central processing (or attention) than the changes made by the older children. For example, they argue that the spontaneous changes made by younger children tend to relate to localized, individual parts of the drawings (e.g., changing the shape of an element or deleting it) whereas the changes made by older children require more of an overview of the drawing that involves a reorganization of at least part of the drawing. For Spensley and Taylor, it is the child's developing ability of chunking information (and perhaps also processing speed and working memory) that account for representational change. Spensley and Taylor's (1999) and Berti and Freeman's (1997) agreement on the influence of informational processing factors in representational change leads them both to accept that external resources, such as illustrations and other children's drawings, help children with developing the flexibility of their own representations. Presumably this is because external resources provide more efficient use of children's informational processing resources.

Summary

This chapter outlines a general learning mechanism, called representational redescription, which is claimed to impact across a wide range of domains of knowledge, including drawing (Karmiloff-Smith, 1992). In essence, RR theory claims that children's representational drawings, in particular the changes children are able to make to them, inform us about how the corresponding internal representations are stored. According to the theory, young children's sequential rigidity in drawing the elements of representations, and the relatively superficial changes they are able to make to them, are indicative of the child having only an implicit access to component parts of the mental representations from which the drawings are based. Older children's more successful and global graphic representational changes are accounted for by the child's growing explicit access to their stored internal representations. Although a general domain mechanism, research has provided very little evidence for it in the drawing domain. In contrast to the drawing data reported by Karmiloff-Smith (1990), subsequent research has shown that young children are much less procedurally rigid in element-ordering, and also are able to manipulate their drawings under certain experimental contexts. Furthermore, the series of studies by Barlow et al. (2003) conclusively show that, despite RR theory's claim, procedurally rigidity and representational change in drawing are not linked.

I have to say that one could have predicted the theory floundering in children's drawings from the outset. The fundamental objection is the original premise that drawings could act as behavioral indicators to how the internal representations are stored. Numerous factors influence how a drawing ends up the way it does, and the diversity of influence can make it very difficult to isolate the role of any one factor when viewing a drawing. This is particularly so for the child's internal representation of the subject matter to be drawn (in whatever way we specify it) because this factor impacts very early on in the process of creating a drawing. In other words, many of the other influences (intention, motivation, information processing, motor and graphic skill, etc.) impact upon internally stored representations to "adulterate" the pure relationship (if there ever could be one) between the internal and external representation. There are simply too many intervening variables that mist the window to viewing a graphic representation as a clear picture of how the internal representation is (implicitly or explicitly) stored. That is not to say that children's knowledge of what they draw is not revealed in their drawings, just that the drawings themselves cannot be a precise measurement of something as intangible as the implicit/explicit nature of the internal representation.

Notes

1   A domain can be defined as a specific area of knowledge such as language, number, or pictures. Piaget's domain-general mechanisms are assimilation, accommodation, and equilibration.
2   I should say at this point that subsequent to the time Karmiloff-Smith described her ideas in her 1992 book, *Beyond Modularity*, we have become more aware of how Piaget's ideas have been misunderstood and miscommunicated (e.g., see Smith, 2002) and that Fodor himself has since changed his own position (Fodor, 2000).
3   Karmiloff-Smith was keen to distinguish her tasks from those used by van Sommers (1984) who found different processes within the same children's drawings of novel objects like a light bulb, a tennis shoe, and a paper punch. Karmiloff-Smith says that it is precisely because they are unfamiliar (i.e., prebehavioral mastery) objects that different routines were elicited.
4   As well as midpoint interruptions Karmiloff-Smith also viewed start-point interruptions as evidence that procedural constraint has been relaxed (i.e. "this involves a subroutine interrupting the procedural sequence", Karmiloff-Smith, 1990, p. 73).

5 Although Berti and Freeman (1997) encourage the reader to consider the child's developing framework theory as a contender for children's early difficulty with representational change they still accept the influence of an "endogenous" factor in which children's internal representations are redescribed to a more explicit level (i.e. Karmiloff-Smith's position) as well as exogenous resources such as ideas gained from looking at other pictures.

7

Drawings as Assessment Tools: Intelligence, Personality and Emotionality

The view that children's drawings can provide important clinically relevant information has been debated in the children's drawings literature for around 100 years now. In particular, drawings have been used as measures of children's intelligence, personality, emotional state, and their emotional attitudes towards the subject matter drawn, with each approach having formularized its own diagnostic drawing tests. In this chapter I review each tradition of clinical application, and some of their associated tests, while reflecting upon the research evidence that supports or refutes this practice. I then turn to what the prevailing practice is in using diagnostic drawing tests in clinical practice and comment upon some global differences. Finally, I suggest that rather than treating drawings as diagnostic tools or dismissing them altogether as clinically irrelevant, using drawings to generate hypotheses requiring further exploration from other sources and assessment tools may turn out to be a fruitful practice in shedding light on the child's disturbance or trauma.

A casual observation of a group of children drawing will usually reveal how enjoyable and relaxing drawing activities are for many children. It is unsurprising, therefore, that when a child is placed into the strange and potentially anxiety-provoking clinical situation, the psychologist may ask the child to draw (Bekhit, Thomas & Jolley, 2005; Thomas

& Jolley, 1998). In addition, drawing activities help build a rapport between clinician and child, without which attempts early in the clinical meetings to assess the child by more formal means may be met with resistance from the child. Of more intrinsic clinical relevance is the use of drawings as a facilitator for getting the child to talk about their experiences that directly relate to the cause of the referral (e.g., Burgess & Hartman, 1993; Veltman & Browne, 2002).

A contentious claim, however, is that drawings are clinically informative in themselves. Specifically, it has been argued that the drawings inform us about characteristics of the child, in particular their intelligence (Goodenough, 1926; Harris, 1963; Naglieri, 1988), personality (Hammer, 1958, 1997; Machover, 1949), current emotional state (Koppitz, 1968, 1984) and emotional attitudes towards the topics drawn (Burkitt, Barrett & Davis, 2003a, 2003b; Lowenfeld, 1939; Thomas, Chaigne & Fox, 1989; Thomas & Jolley, 1998). I shall now discuss the research evidence for each of these claims in turn.

Drawing as Measures of Intelligence

We saw in Chapter 1 that the scientific interest in children's drawings began by attempts to categorize the developmental changes in children's representations. Some of these early researchers investigated potential links between children's drawings and their general ability, as measured by their school work and teacher ratings (Claparède, 1907; Ivanoff, 1909). A growing awareness of potential cognitive links to drawings led to a more direct connection being made between the child's drawing and their intelligence.

Initially, drawing was incorporated into general IQ tests, most notably by Burt (1921), but the first dedicated drawing IQ test was Florence Goodenough's (1926) "Draw-a-Man" test. Goodenough considered the human figure an ideal topic for a number of reasons, including its familiarity, interest, and appeal among children of all ages. In the Draw-a-Man test, children are simply asked to draw their best picture of a (whole) man.[1] Assuming a representation of the human figure can be recognized, the drawing is scored according to the number of human figure details present from a list of 51 items in the scoring manual, some of which relate to proportioning skill and integration of parts. By comparing the child's score with Goodenough's standardized scores for each age group (derived from human figure drawings of large samples of children), the child's mental age and IQ can be obtained.

As standardized scores run the risk of becoming outdated Harris (1963) revised Goodenough's test (now called the Goodenough–Harris Drawing Test) by providing updated standardization scores based on a new sample of children. Furthermore, Harris took up Goodenough's (1926) suggestion that future work should examine gender differences and created separate tables for boys and girls. Harris extended the age range for which the test applied and children were now required to make three drawings (a man, a woman, and a self-drawing). Separate scoring protocols were provided for the man-drawing (73 items) and woman-drawing (71 items); surprisingly the self-drawing was not scored. Harris recommended that the scores for the man and woman be averaged to gain the most reliable measure.

A more recent standardized drawing test of (non-verbal) ability, normatively sampled on 2,622 children aged 5 to 17, was published by Naglieri (1988), and called the Draw-a-Person: A Quantitative Scoring system (DAP). In keeping with Harris's revision children are required to draw a man, woman, and themselves, but in Naglieri's test the self-drawing is scored. Naglieri recommended that the three scores be averaged. The scoring includes 14 criteria (12 of which relate to body parts, the other two are attachment of parts and clothing). Each criterion has typically four items that relate to the presence of a drawing feature, its detail and proportion, and a bonus point for obtaining all three. Naglieri considered that the small gender differences he found did not warrant the need for separate standardized scores for girls and boys, and he also presented only one conversion table for all three drawings. For these reasons the Naglieri DAP is a shorter and simpler alternative to the Goodenough and Goodenough–Harris tests.

As with any test the usefulness of drawing tests as measures of intelligence rely on their reliability and validity. The reliability of scores for these tests does appear to be high. For example, Goodenough (1926) reported an average "split-half" reliability of 0.77 for children aged 5–10 years, and Harris (1963) reported that subsequent studies showed high agreement among raters, commonly 0.90 or above for the original Goodenough scale. Naglieri reported that the mean test–retest reliability (averaged over age and type of drawing) of the

DAP was 0.74. The validity of the drawing tests as measures of IQ is more problematic. Although Goodenough (1926) found that the average correlation of the Draw-a-Man test and the Stanford–Binet test was 0.74 for children aged between 4 and 10 years, further validity tests reviewed by Harris (1963) showed that correlations varied considerably (from 0.26 to 0.92) between the two tests. For Harris's revised test, independent studies have shown modest correlations with the Wechsler Intelligence Scale for Children-Revised (WISC-R). For instance, the correlations reported by Gayton, Tavormina, Evans, and Schuh (1974), Oakland and Dowling (1983), and Abell, Von Briesen, and Watz (1996) vary between 0.40 and 0.64. A similarly modest correlation of 0.51 exists between the Naglieri DAP and the WISC-R (Wisniewski & Naglieri, 1989). The overall message is that while drawings tests purporting to measure intelligence or related abilities have acceptable reliability, they have insufficiently low (albeit often significant) correlations with other standardized and commonly used intelligence tests. Consequently, they cannot be recommended as a diagnostic test for intelligence for most children.

Nevertheless, it has been suggested that drawing IQ tests are a useful quick screening device to rule out low intelligence for children who are unwilling or unable to take more accepted psychometric intelligence scales (Abell, Wood, & Liebman, 2001). Drawing tests can give the clinician a rough guide to the child's overall ability where poor concentration or linguistic ability prevent the child from engaging and understanding the psychometric tests more typically used for children, such as the WISC-R and British Ability Scales. When used as a screening device, which of the drawings tests is most recommended? Abell et al. (2001) addressed this question by simultaneously comparing the Goodenough–Harris and Naglieri scores obtained from one human figure drawing made by two hundred 6- to 15-year-olds with the children's WISC-R scores. Both the Goodenough–Harris and Naglieri DAP tests had similar correlations with the WISC-R (0.54 and 0.53 respectively); correlations that were consistent with previous research. As the Naglieri DAP is simpler and shorter to administer and score, the authors recommended the DAP over the older Goodenough–Harris Drawing Test as a screening measure.

In the early days of intelligence testing the drawing tests, most notably the Goodenough Draw-a-Man test, served a useful purpose

in providing a relatively quick and broad measure of the child's intelligence. But with the development of more sophisticated psychometric tests, drawing tests of intelligence now appear too narrow
and primitive in comparison. Also, drawing tests of IQ or other forms
of cognitive ability are mediated by the child's drawing ability. Some
"bright" children may not draw well, and conversely some artistically gifted children may have only an average intelligence. In fact,
drawing tests designed to measure IQ or related cognitive abilities
may be more appropriately seen as measures of drawing ability. Indeed,
a number of studies have used the drawing tests for intelligence
in this way. For instance, Cox and Catte (2000) matched groups of
emotionally and non-emotionally disturbed children on their drawing
ability using the Goodenough–Harris Drawing Test. This allowed them
to examine whether observed differences in the drawings between the
two groups were due to drawing ability alone (see later in this chapter for a discussion of their findings). The Naglieri DAP test has been
used to examine if children's verbal recall of an event after drawing
it correlated with their drawing ability (Gross & Hayne, 1998,
1999; see this book, chapter 8). Most recently, we used the Naglieri
DAP test as one measure of children's representational drawing
skill to investigate the developing relationship between children's
representational and expressive drawing skills (Jolley et al., 2003; see
this book, chapter 2). Used in these ways drawing tests originally
designed as IQ tests can still provide a very useful tool for researchers.

Drawings as Measures of Personality

Despite the growing acceptance in the first half of the 20th century
of children's human figure drawings as measures of their intelligence,
some practitioners began to believe that children's drawings should
be more appropriately conceived as projections of the child's personality. Taking this alternative approach, and appealing to psycho-
analytic theory, a number of tests were created to serve this purpose.
One of the first of these, and certainly the most well-known even
today, was the Machover "Draw-a-Person" test (Machover, 1949).
In this test the child is asked to make two "person" drawings, where
the second human figure drawing is of the opposite sex to that
produced in the first drawing. A description of the child's character

Plate 1 The "Lion Panel" of Chauvet Cave, France, c. 32,000–30,000 BC (top). Three lion drawings made by 4- to 5-year-olds (bottom).

Plate 2 A 14-year-old's happy drawing of a countryside scene showing literal, content, and abstract expression.

4-year-old (sad)

7-year-old (angry)

11-year-old (happy)

Adult artist (angry)

Plate 3 Representative free drawings made by a 4-, 7-, 11-year-old and an adult artist from Jolley et al. (2003).

Plate 4 A Chinese 4-year-old's happy drawing.

Plate 5 A 7-year-old girl's drawing of a tree with a circular shaded "scarring" on the trunk. Drawing provided by Clarissa Martin.

Plate 6 Children's drawings of media images: a "Simpson's" style (left), Pokémon (middle), Mickey Mouse (right).

Plate 7 Chinese children's drawings showing a "school performance" theme. Celebration of top score (top), a painful comparison of scores with a fellow pupil (middle), a boy being punished by his father for a low Maths score (bottom).

Plate 8 Chinese children's drawings showing a concern for the environment: 5-year-old's drawing of factory pollution (top), 14-year-old's drawing of litter dumped next to sign "Do not throw rubbish anywhere" (middle), 14-year-old's drawing of deforestation (bottom).

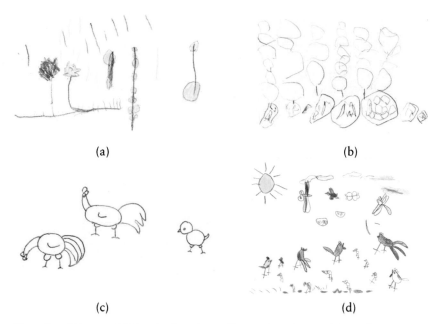

(a)

(b)

(c)

(d)

Plate 9 Chinese children's drawings illustrating the teaching of representational drawing in the Chinese infant school's art curriculum.

(a)

(b)

(c)

(d)

(e)

Plate 10 Chinese children's drawings illustrating the teaching of imaginative and expressive drawing in the Chinese infant school's art curriculum.

is formulated through subjective interpretations of a variety of features of the drawings (no objective or quantitative scoring method is provided, unlike that found in drawing IQ tests). The clinician or therapist will pay attention to whether the male or female was drawn first, the size, movement, distortions, and omissions in the two figures, as well as differences between the two figures. The details in the body parts and clothing are given close scrutiny, as are the formal properties of the drawings such as pressure and direction of the pencil strokes. The child's verbal comments and general behavior will also be noted, and upon completion of each drawing the child will be asked to give specific information about the person they have portrayed. The child may also be asked to make up a story about their drawings.

As Machover's Draw-a-Person test is typically administered in clinical and therapeutic settings the test is used mainly to assess the nature of a maladjusted personality (rather than the personalities in the normal population). Numerous case studies can be found in the literature, and I recommend those reported by Machover (1949) and Hammer (1958, 1997) as starting points to interested readers. Here I shall provide a summary of a case study reported in Hammer (1997) to illustrate the nature of the interpretations typically made using this projective approach.

Hammer (1997) discusses three drawings made by a 12-year-old boy (see Figure 7.1). As well as drawings of a man and a woman that are normally required by the Machover Draw-a-Person test, the child was asked also to draw a house. Before giving us his interpretation of the drawings, Hammer provides some background information about the boy. He had been brought up by brutal parents: the mother was persistently biting in her sarcasm to the boy while the father was physically abusive. The boy stayed away from school because he considered the teachers were picking on him, and his tensions were reflected in his facial expressions, language, and behavior. The boy's belligerence and refusal to abide by rules led to his referral. Although the child's human figure drawings in the Machover Draw-a-Person test are normally interpreted in respect of the child's expression of their personality (often cited as their body-image or self-concept), on this occasion Hammer considered that the male and female figures represented this child's perceptions of his father and mother, respectively. Furthermore, and consistent with the

Figure 7.1   Two human figure drawings and a house drawing made by 12-year-old boy (from Hammer, 1997).

projective approach, Hammer "saw" a variety of projections of the child's traumatic experiences with his parents in the drawings. In the "mother" drawing the opened mouth and teeth symbolized her verbally abusive nature. Furthermore, the lack of hands represented her ungiving and rejecting nature. In the "father" drawing (which the boy named "Stalin"), we see a man in uniform who expresses authoritarianism and severity. In particular, Hammer refers to the "scissor-like" hands as where the physically abusive nature of his father is seen. Hammer argues that this male figure, together with the house drawing in which the chimney is only tentatively attached to the house, reveals a castration anxiety of the boy. According to Hammer's interpretation of the drawings, the boy fears that his private parts are vulnerable to being cut off by his father.

As was the case for drawing tests of intelligence, accurate diagnosis of the child's personality disturbance depends upon reliability and validity. The reliability and validity of projective tests in general is a constant focus of debate and argument in the literature (e.g., see Anastasi & Urbina, 1997), and projective drawing tests have been very much a part of that debate (for a particularly heated discussion see the issue of the journal *School Psychology Quarterly*, 1993, volume 8, part 3).

As our personalities vary little over time then we might anticipate similar personality descriptions obtained over the sessions in which the Draw-a-Person test is administered (particularly if over a short period). Neither Machover (1949) and Hammer (1958, 1997) provide data to test this question of intra-reliability, but Hammer (1997) does make some comments relevant to this issue. In arguing against collecting only a small sample of drawings from the same projective drawing test, he says that different facets of the client's pathology may be displayed across a battery of projective drawing tests. The projective approach is then to formulate a profile of traits from a range of projective drawing tests, rather than to see if the same pathological personality was derived from repeated drawings of the same test or topic. Case studies are usually reported from the single perspective of the clinician assigned to the case, hence the issue of inter-rater reliability is left largely unaddressed. A cursory inspection of the case studies in the literature soon reveals, however, that clinicians interpret some features in a drawing differently. For example, the lack of hands in a human figure drawing is sometimes interpreted as a sign of helplessness, or an uncaring nature (as was suggested in the "mother" drawing cited above), or evidence of masturbatory guilt (always remember to put hands in your own drawings!).

The lack of consistency of interpretation between practitioners was tellingly revealed in a study reported by Wanderer (1969; paper reprinted in Hammer, 1997). Pairs of drawings (from the Machover Draw-a-Person test) made by five different participants representative of five groups (mentally defective, homosexual, schizophrenic, neurotic, and normal) were given to 20 experts (that included Machover and Hammer) for diagnosis. Wanderer comments that these groups were chosen on Machover's suggestion that they represented the five most appropriate groups to investigate the diagnostic validity of her test. The experts had to note which pair of drawings belonged to which diagnosis. Only the drawings made by the mentally defective participant were assigned to the correct group at a level significantly above chance. As this diagnostic group relates more to intelligence (and potentially drawing ability) than personality then the study's findings were particularly damaging to the diagnostic use of drawings as projections of personality. Wanderer concluded that clinicians often know something about the patient before viewing their drawings, such as information from the case history and clinical interview. Clinicians may therefore be attributing this extraneous knowledge to the drawings, making them "see" things they already know (see also Smith & Dumont, 1995).

In Hammer's reply to Wanderer's study (Hammer, 1969; paper reprinted in Hammer, 1997), he accepts that clinicians using projective drawings do tend to read into the drawings from their knowledge of the case, but argued they then read from the drawings significantly further. Consistent with Hammer's insistence on using a battery of projective drawing tests (see above), he argued that the Machover Draw-a-Person test, or for that matter any other projective drawing test, was never intended to be used as a sole measure for diagnosis, nor are interpretations made on isolated features. Hammer has argued repeatedly that projective drawings tests should be used in conjunction with other projective measures, information from the case history and clinical interview, and other available information (see also Hammer, 1958). A particular useful clinical tool, for Hammer, is when he sees certain themes appearing across a number of measures, and for this reason he argues that interpretations of projective drawing tests should not be carried out blindly.

Since the Machover Draw-a-Person test was published there have been many reviews over the years assessing the huge number of studies that have been carried out to address its reliability and validity (Falk, 1981; Farylo & Paludi, 1985; Klopfer & Taulbee, 1976; Motta, Little, & Tobin, 1993; Roback, 1968; Sims, Dana, & Bolton, 1983; Swensen, 1957, 1968; Thomas & Jolley, 1998). The reviews reported by Swensen (1968) and Roback (1968) are the most cited in the literature, both of which arrive at a similar conclusion that the reliability and validity of isolated drawing features expressing a particular personality trait is weak, and that the Draw-a-Person test may indicate only the drawer's overall level of adjustment. The crucial question is, can drawings provide the clinician with additional information about a child's personality to that gathered from other measures, such as psychometric tests and the child's case history? In Thomas and Jolley (1998) we suggested a way in which this question could be tested by giving clinicians vignettes of real cases histories with the children's drawings being included in some of the cases. It would then be possible to establish whether more accurate diagnoses were made for those cases where drawings were provided. As far as I am aware this remains an empirical question.[2]

If Hammer's most recent book (Hammer, 1997) is anything to go by, the debate between clinical practice and research evidence has been disappointing since Roback's (1968) and Swensen's (1968) influential reviews. The space Hammer gives to his section on "research studies and research issues" is relatively small, and contains mostly reprints of, and comments on, articles originally published in the 1960s and 1970s. I got the strong impression from reading the book that the external contributors, many of whom have been at the forefront of the projection tradition for decades (Buck, Gillespie, Hammer, Machover, etc.), are not particularly interested in engaging in the debate. They are absolutely certain children (and adults) convey a variety of forms of maladjustment in their drawings. Hammer's position is clear when he quotes Gordon Alport, "The problem facing psychology today is to prove that which it simply *knows* to be true" (Hammer, 1997, p. 298, his italics). In the other corner, some academics are so against the use of projective drawing techniques they say their continued use breaks ethical standards (e.g., Burgess & Hartman, 1993; Smith & Dumont, 1995). We need a more cohesive and informed debate between practitioners and researchers that works towards a more scientifically based interpretive framework for evaluating children's personality maladjustment from their drawings.

Drawings as Measures of Current Emotional Disturbance

Some of the interpretations of the child's personality projected into their drawings related in particular to the child's emotional disturbance.

An approach which concentrated on the emotional indicators in children's drawings can be seen in the work of Elizabeth Koppitz (1968, 1984). Koppitz considered that children's drawings reflected their anxieties, concerns and attitudes. In the Koppitz test, the child is asked to make one human figure drawing which is then examined for the presence or absence of 30 features or indicators of emotional disturbance. The 30 indicators fell into three categories. In the first category, items related to the quality of the human figure drawing (e.g., poor integration of parts, gross asymmetry of limbs, tiny/big figure, etc.). Items in the second category were special features not usually found in children's human figure drawings (short or long arms, inclusion of teeth and genitals, omission of hands, etc.). The third category consisted of omissions of items which would be expected to be seen in children's human figure drawings at a given age level (e.g., eyes, body, legs, etc.). Many of these features had previously been reported by practitioners in the personality tradition, such as by Machover (1949) and Hammer (1958). This is not surprising as Koppitz compiled an initial list of 38 indicators from this previous work, as well as from her own clinical experience. From a large sample of human figure drawings made by 1,856 American children, Koppitz found that 30 indicators met the following three criteria:

(a)   Be able to differentiate between those with and without emotional problems (i.e., clinical validity).

(b)   Be unusual and occur infrequently in human figure drawings (HFD) of normal children who are not psychiatric patients (defined as seen in less than 16% of the HFD of children at a given age level).

(c)   Must not be related to age and maturation (i.e. its frequency of occurrence in HFD must not increase solely on the basis of age).

The detailing of the 30 indicators and the further descriptive criteria given on how to assess some of these enabled reliable scoring. Koppitz (1968) also provided data reporting higher scores for clinically referred children compared with those obtained by children judged to be well adjusted, and also scores differentiating between clinical populations.[3] But subsequent independent work has been much less persuasive. Although a few studies have reported supportive findings (e.g., Sturner, Rothbaum, Visintainer & Wolfer, 1980), many have not differentiated between populations (e.g., Eno, Elliot & Woehlke, 1981; Forrest & Thomas, 1991; Fuller, Preuss & Hawkins, 1970). For instance, Forrest and Thomas (1991) found that bereaved children were no more likely to include emotional indicators in their human figure drawings than nonbereaved children and furthermore, the bereaved children produced on average only two emotional indicators in their drawing anyway.

The usefulness of the Koppitz test as a measure of emotional adjustment was seriously questioned in a large scale test of Koppitz's theory conducted by Michelle Catte and Maureen Cox (Catte, 1998; Catte & Cox, 1999; Cox & Catte, 2000). In their first paper, Catte and Cox (1999) obtained a clinical group of forty-four 7- to 11-year-old boys from special schools for children with behavioral and emotional problems, together with a chronological matched group (CA) and a mental age matched group (MA) of well-adjusted boys. Their design represented a more tightly matched sample than used by Koppitz (1968). All children were asked to draw a human figure according to the instructions outlined by Koppitz (1968). Consistent with much of the previous independent research, children from all groups produced only a small number of indicators in their drawings. Figure 7.2 shows a human figure drawing made by a 9-year-old boy from the clinical group that was scored as depicting five emotional indicators (no child produced more than 5 of the 30 indicators). For the purpose of comparing statistically the indicators produced by the three groups, children were allocated into two categories according to how many indicators they had depicted in their drawing: zero/one indicator or at least two. From Table 7.1 we can see that while the majority of children from the clinical group produced two or more indicators, the majority of the two control groups were found in the zero-to-one category. When children scores were statistically analyzed the clinical group did produce significantly more indicators in their human figure drawings than the children in both the CA and MA groups. Despite the statistical significance, however, the clinical group displayed on average only two indicators in their HFD.

With so few indicators being shown, even in the clinical group, Catte and Cox wondered whether the indicators derived from Koppitz's collection of American human figure drawings in the 1960s applied to British children at the turn of the 21st century. In

Figure 7.2 A 9-year-old boy's human figure drawing showing five emotional indicators (from the clinical group reported by Catte, 1998): poor integration, tiny head, no eyes, no nose, and no mouth. Drawing provided by Michelle Catte.

Table 7.1 Numbers of Children's Human Figure Drawings Showing 0 or 1 vs. 2 or More Koppitz's Emotional Indicators in Catte and Cox (1999)

	Clinical group	CA group	MA group
	Study 1		
0 or1	18	32	26
2 or more	26	12	18
	Study 2		
0 or 1	30	42	40
2 or more	14	2	4

their second study, therefore, Catte and Cox obtained a new sample of human figure drawings from 1,598 British 5- to 11-year-olds in mainstream schools to investigate which indicators still met Koppitz's inclusion criteria. Only 23 indicators met the criteria for both boys and girls, a further two for girls only, and in some cases the age in which the indicator became valid was different to that specified by Koppitz. When they rescored the drawings from the three groups of boys collected in Study 1 using this new set of indicators, the effect was to reduce the number of children scoring two or more indicators, with the majority from all three groups scoring between zero and one (see Table 7.1). Although the re-analysis still showed that the clinical group produced significantly more indicators, we need to ask the question, as Catte and Cox did, whether the Koppitz test can be a useful tool for diagnosing emotional disturbance when so few indicators were produced by the clinical group (on average about 1!).

In an interesting follow-up paper to their first publication, Cox and Catte (2000) introduced a new control group matched on drawing ability (as assessed by the Goodenough–Harris Drawing Test). When Cox and Catte (2000) compared the emotional indicators produced by the clinical group and the drawing ability matched group the significant differences disappeared. Even art therapists, blind to the group to which each belonged, were no better than chance in differentiating drawings made by the clinical group and those from the drawing control group (Catte, 1998). Cox and Catte concluded that differences reported in the literature between emotionally and nonemotionally disturbed children's drawings may well have been due to the emotionally disturbed children having developmentally delayed drawing ability.

In conclusion, the work undertaken by Catte and Cox offers very persuasive evidence that neither Koppitz's emotional indicators nor their own revised scale are valid tools for measuring children's emotional disturbance from human figure drawings. Furthermore, as practicing art therapists could not pick out the emotionally disturbed children's drawings, it is unlikely that there are additional emotional indicators not featured in either scale. Unlike the prevailing use of projective drawing tests, there appears to be a distinct lack of use of the Koppitz test, at least among British clinical psychologists (see later in this chapter). That is not to say that emotional disturbed children do not on occasions express their disturbance in their drawings; I return to this issue in my conclusions at the end of this chapter.

Drawings as Measures of the Emotional Significance of the Topic

The underlying assumption in the use of human figure drawings in both the personality and emotional disturbance traditions is that the disturbed child expresses themselves through drawing an unspecified person. An alternative approach used in some clinical tests, such as the Kinetic Family Drawing Test (Burns & Kaufman, 1970), is to ask the child to draw emotionally significant people known to the child. The assumption of this approach is that the child's emotional attitudes towards such people are displayed in these drawings, particularly in the use of size, placement, and color. This possibility may appeal more to the intuition of those who struggle with the idea that children project themselves when they draw people. There is also the additional advantage of assessing emotional significance as it may not be limited to clinically disturbed children but potentially applicable to all children more generally. It is principally typically developing children that I address in this section, as it is these children that there has been a notable number of studies undertaken on in the last 15 years or so asking whether their human figure drawings portray the emotional characterizations of the figures. Researchers have investigated whether children vary the size, placement, and color of the figure to signal emotional characterizations.

Size matters

Lowenfeld (1939) popularized the view that children increase the size of a figure to depict importance. But the link between size and importance can be traced much further back. A convention of drawing socially important figures relatively large compared to less important figures in society was evident in Ancient Egyptian art (Gombrich, 1995). In these early pictures, royalty was depicted larger than civilians, and the head of the household represented bigger than his servants and wife. More recent evidence of socially important topics being shown relatively large was reported by Aronsson and Andersson

(1996). In Tanzanian children's drawings of the classroom they depicted the teacher as a large, centrally placed figure compared to the much smaller figures of the children. These pictures were said to reflect the traditional child-rearing ideology that encouraged respect and obedience to teachers (for more details of this study see chapter 9). We should not forget that individual pictures have their own stories to tell, and size may be used to signal importance within the context of that picture. One of my students, Jacqueline Aspinall, told children a story of a man robbing an old lady of her purse. In Figure 7.3 we can see the exaggerated arms of the thief which appear to indicate the success of this theft.

Figure 7.3 A child's drawing of a "thief" after being told a story of a man stealing a purse from an old lady.

Nice and nasty men

In an interesting development to the claim relating importance and size in children's drawings Glyn Thomas and his colleagues investigated whether children use size to signal *emotional* significance of the topics drawn. Thomas, Chaigne, and Fox (1989) manipulated the emotional significance of a human figure drawing by providing 4- to 7-year-olds with differing character descriptions of a man (neutral, nice, or nasty). As the inclusion of details alone can change the size of a figure (see Henderson & Thomas, 1990) the instructions encouraged the children to draw only the outline of the men drawings, and an outline of a man filled in with black was presented to facilitate this instruction. They reported that drawings of the nasty men were drawn significantly smaller (in height) and nice men non-significantly taller than the drawings of the control (neutral) men. Thomas et al.'s findings indicated that Lowenfeld's (1939) importance hypothesis needed to be modified in respect of emotional importance. They argued that emotionally positive topics are subject to an appetitive/appetitive response whereby they are symbolically brought closer to the child by drawing them large on the page. In contrast, they claimed a defense response is activated by disliked/feared topics so that a small size in the drawn topic distances the potential threat. Nevertheless, the magnitude of the effects did not appear strong. For example, 6-year-olds drew the nasty man on average only 1 cm smaller than their neutral man drawing. At this point it was clear that further experimental work was needed to discover the reliability and strength of emotional importance size effects in children's drawings. Under Glyn Thomas's supervision, I conducted a series of studies for my PhD to do just that (Jolley, 1995).

Initially, I wanted to see how children would assign nice and nasty characterizations to pictures of differently sized men, using stimuli similar to the blocked-in stimulus presented by Thomas et al. (1989). The advantage of this approach is that it represents a more direct measurement of any consistent conception children may hold of the relationship between size and emotional character, without potential performance factors masking the relationship in their drawings. In the first of my picture perception tasks I presented two outlines of men varying in size only (see Figure 7.4), and asked children which was the nasty man or which was the nice man. Interestingly, children's

Figure 7.4 Two outlines of a man varying in size presented to children to choose which they considered to be either the nice or nasty man (from Jolley, 1995).

choices were opposite to what the appetitive and defense responses would predict. The *larger* figure was chosen for the nasty man, and the *smaller* figure for the nice man. Furthermore, this extended to pictures of pairs of large and small dogs and apples. I suggested that children may have learned pictorial conventions of large = nasty and nice = small. The basis for the large = nasty convention might be that large is powerful, and therefore a large nasty man can threaten his nastiness through his physical size. The children may have chosen the small figure for the nice man as someone more akin to their own size (e.g., a peer).

In an attempt to evoke the appetitive and defense responses, I then presented the two outlines of a man to a new sample of children and asked which figure they would prefer to meet if both were either nice and kind, or nasty and scary. Consistent with a defense mechanism, children chose the smaller figure if they were given the instruction of two nasty/scary men. However, equal numbers of children selected the small and large versions within the "nice/kind" instruction group. Perhaps half the children in this group chose the large figure to symbolically bring the nice/kind man nearer (consistent with the appetitive response) while the other half wanted the nice man to be more similar to their own size.

In conclusion, my picture perception tasks suggested that children consider a large size as best to portray a nasty figure (a pictorial convention), but if the instructions refer to a personal contact with the figure then the smaller figure is chosen (a defense response). The relationship of size to nice topics was less clear, particularly in conditions where the appetitive response might be activated, but recall the effect relating to children's drawings of nice men reported by Thomas et al. (1989) was nonsignificant.

Following on from the picture judgment tasks, I began a series of studies seeking evidence for the pictorial convention and defense/appetitive mechanisms in children's drawings of nice and nasty men. Initially, I adopted the same design and methodology used by Thomas et al. (1989). In contrast to their original findings, however, I found no significant differences in the size of drawings between the neutral, nice and nasty men (nor when I presented a stimulus figure of a man that was not blocked-in, or even when no stimulus was provided at all). I then emphasized the character descriptions of the men to increase the likelihood of the appetitive/defense responses being evoked, even to the extent that in some conditions children were asked to imagine that they would meet either the nice or nasty men. Still the men were drawn with very similar sizes. Finally, I wondered whether the nonsignificant effects I was finding were due to some children consistently using a pictorial convention (e.g., large = nasty), while others the defense or appetitive response (e.g., small = nasty, for the defense response), and that the two were balancing each other out. To test for this possibility, children were asked to draw both a nice and a nasty man on the same page, with the task repeated a couple of weeks later. There was no evidence that children were consistent in their size differentiation of the two figures (the reliability coefficient was 0.14[4]). It seems unlikely, therefore, that the lack of significant differences in my previous drawing studies could be explained by reliable but opposing emotional/size effects among the children.

In the six drawing studies that represented the first half of my PhD (Jolley, 1995) the effect that Thomas et al. (1989) reported had mysteriously disappeared (the topics covered in the second half of my thesis were more interesting and productive!). Furthermore, there were no published studies during the 1990s supporting Thomas et al.'s findings. I strongly suspect this was a result of the "file-drawer" problem, because anecdotal evidence I collected around this time from academics was of similar nonsignificant effects from their supervised student projects. Before I can write the obituary of the nice and nasty men in children's drawings I need to comment on their recent reappearance in the literature in a series of papers published by Esther Burkitt and her colleagues (Burkitt, 2004; Burkitt, Barrett, and Davis, 2003a, 2004).

Despite adopting a number of methodological improvements, including asking children to draw a range of topics measured by a variety of size measurements, the findings reported by Burkitt and colleagues were somewhat inconsistent. Burkitt et al. (2003a) found that, consistent with the appetitive response and defense mechanism, the nice and nasty topics were drawn significantly larger or smaller respectively, than the children's first (neutral) drawings. In Burkitt et al. (2004), however, the nasty drawings were not significantly smaller than the neutral drawings; in fact, the majority of the children tended to draw larger nasty drawings. In more recent work by Burkitt and her colleagues a similar picture emerged when the instructions referred to happy and sad men, or when the children drew themselves imagining they were either happy or sad. Only the happy characters were drawn significantly differently in size (bigger) to the neutral topic (Burkitt & Barnett, 2006; Burkitt, Barrett, & Davis, 2005).

It is particularly noteworthy that negative topics (either nasty or sad) in Burkitt's studies were frequently not differentiated in size to the neutral topics, as it is children's drawings of negative topics that have the most clinical relevance. Burkitt's methodological improvements allow us to see a clearer picture of the size/emotional import-ance effect in children's drawings, but what we see is not very much. In Burkitt et al. (2003a) the nasty drawings were only 0.39 cm smaller than the neutral drawings. Even in the case of area where one might expect large differences to appear, the nasty topics were only 1.33 cm^2 smaller than the neutral topics. Burkitt (2004) acknowledges that the size of negative figures is not as reliable in children's drawing as positive figures, and comments, "caution is urged when inferring negative feelings on the basis of drawing size" (Burkitt, 2004, p. 3). I am not convinced at all that clinical practitioners using drawings of children would even notice such small size differences, never mind consider them worthy of inferring a negative emotional importance for the child towards the figures drawn. One should be aware that statistically significant differences obtained in experimental settings do not automatically justify practical applications.

One lingering objection with the experimental manipulation of characterization on typically developing children, however, is that it is likely to be a poor indicator of the intense emotions that children can naturally feel (Thomas & Jolley, 1998; see also Burkitt et al., 2003a). In other words, do children who have experienced emotional upset communicate this in their human figure drawings of emotional significance that is not apparent from the experimental manipulations of emotional attitude? The next section reviews the small literature that is relevant to this question.

Real feelings and real men

Joiner, Schmidt, and Barnett (1996) obtained a variety of depression and anxiety measures from 80 child and adolescent psychiatric inpatients, and related these measures to children's use of size, detail, and line heaviness in three drawing tasks. At least one of the three drawing tasks (the Kinetic Family Drawing Test) is derived from the assumption that children express their emotional feelings towards people in their drawings. The authors reported, however, that ratings of the three graphic features under investigation (size, detail, and line heaviness) were consistently unrelated to the depression and anxiety measures that had been taken. The one statistically significant exception, that larger drawings were associated with higher levels of anxiety on one of the two anxiety scales used, was actually opposite to that predicted by a defense mechanism. One drawback of their study, however, was that we do not know whether the drawings requested reflected the source of their anxiety. The authors did not have access to any diagnostic information of the participants, but we can assume that the sources of distress were likely to be disparate and at least for some of the children unrelated to the topics of the drawings.

One method of obtaining a large group of children who have all suffered from the same source is to test children who have experienced war. With this in mind, Anita Vulic-Prtoric and I investigated drawings of soldiers made by 60 Croatian 7- to 10-year-olds, around 18 months after the cessation of the recent (former) Yugoslavian war in Croatia (Jolley & Vulic-Prtoric, 2001). We considered soldiers as the most likely topic to represent the war for the children, and hence be the best topic through which the children might express their feelings. Indeed, Kuzmic (1992) reported that Croatian children admitted to psychiatric clinics for war-related disturbances commonly drew soldiers, and cited examples of drawings in which Croatian soldiers were shown in a favorable light, while the enemy was shown under attack. All of the children tested in our study had witnessed war because their town (Zadar) had been continually attacked from land, sea, and air. Half of the children had lost their father in the war. Children were first asked to add details of an outline human figure to make it look like them. This drawing was then attached to an A4 page and the child asked to draw a (neutral) man within the remaining space. The self-portrait drawings was then removed and placed on a new A4 page. The children were asked to draw either an enemy or Croatian soldier, or another neutral man in the remaining space. We allowed the children to include details in their figures to enable the drawing task to be more natural to them (rather than just drawing an outline). Also, we not only measured the size of the figures but also their placement relative to the child's drawing of themselves.

Figure 7.5 shows the size and placement data for the three characterizations (neutral, friendly, enemy) by the two groups of children (with/without father). Statistical analysis revealed that neither characterization nor group had a significant effect on the size and placement of the figures. We did notice, however, one potentially interesting effect. There was some evidence that the "without father" group drew smaller soldiers (friendly and enemy) than their neutral man drawings. As is the case in studies that experimentally manipulate affect, however, the absolute height difference of the soldier and neutral man drawings in the "without father" group were not large (neutral/friendly: 1.19 cm; neutral/enemy: 0.47 cm). Nevertheless, these smaller soldiers occurred despite them containing more than twice as many details as shown in their neutral man drawings. As including extra details often increases the size of a drawing (Henderson & Thomas, 1990), these soldier drawings may have been even smaller if the number of items drawn had been similar to the neutral man

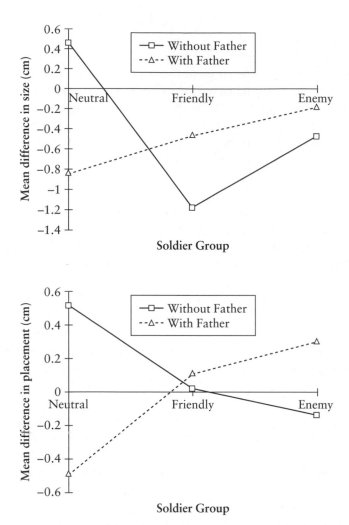

Figure 7.5   Mean differences in size and placement data between first drawing (neutral man) and second drawings (neutral man, friendly, and enemy soldier) made by Croatian children (with/lost father) reported by Jolley and Vulic-Prtoric (2001). Negative values of size should be interpreted as second drawings being smaller than first drawing. Positive values of placement should be interpreted as second drawings being relatively further away from the self-portrait drawing.

drawings. Jolley and Vulic-Prtoric (2001) suggested that the bereavement of losing one's father may have induced a broad negative affect towards soldiers per se. That is, a defense mechanism produced smaller drawings of soldiers regardless of what army they belonged to.

One limitation of our study, however, was that we did not obtain independent evidence of the children's attitudes towards the war, or more specifically the emotional attitudes they held to Croatian and enemy soldiers. Without this independent evidence the above interpretation is only speculative. A related point is that the chosen topic was generic to the children's emotional experience (i.e. not of any specific soldiers they had been in contact with). Stronger size effects may be seen in drawings of topics in which there is a personal and emotional link with the child, such as might be found in cases of sex abuse. In my literature search of research assessing drawings made by physically abused (including sexually) children I have not come across any study that has systematically compared abused children's drawings of the abuser with that of a control figure.[5]

Size is not everything: placement and color

At this point you may be thinking that only size matters to clinicians and researchers working in this area. Although size has preoccupied those of us testing the emotional significance hypothesis, there have been a few attempts to see if placement of figures, and most recently the coloring of the figures, signal emotional importance to the child. Jolley and Vulic-Prtoric (2001) found that the Croatian children did not vary the placement of the soldiers relative to their self-drawing. Our negative finding was consistent with that reported by Thomas and Gray (1992). They asked 4- to 6-year-olds to draw their "best friend" and a "child you don't like very much," next to a drawing they had made of themselves. When all three drawings were made on the same page, the friend and "not liked" child were placed at similar distances from the centrally placed self-drawing. On the basis of this (albeit limited) research evidence, interpretations of placement as signaling emotional importance to the child of the people drawn is unsupported, and questions the basis of such interpretations in the Kinetic Family Drawing Test.

Children's potential use of color as a signal of the feelings held towards the topic has frequently been cited by researchers (e.g.,

Alschuler & Hattwick, 1947; Arnheim, 1974; Golomb, 1992) and by clinicians and art therapists (Dalley, 1984; Hammer, 1997). As Burkitt et al. (2003b) note, however, many of the claims in this area have been based upon clinical observations, often from single case studies. In an attempt to provide experimental evidence, Burkitt et al. (2003b) conducted a large-scale study in which 330 children aged 4 to 11 were asked to color in three predrawn outlines of either a man, dog, or tree using one of the ten colored crayons provided. The outlines for each topic were first characterized as neutral, and then two more outlines were provided with the usual nice and nasty characterizations given in the instructions. In another session the children ranked ten color cards (same colors as the crayons) in order of preference. Burkitt et al. reported that all age groups use preferred colors for the nice figure, least preferred colors for the nasty figure, and colors rated intermediate for the neutral figure. While black was used predominantly for the nasty figures, a range of primary and secondary colors were used for the nice figure. Their results indicated, therefore, that both absolute differences and subjective preferences in color played a role in the children's choice of coloring in the affectively characterized topics. These findings were broadly replicated by Burkitt et al. (2004) where no graphic models were provided and no instructions given to omit details.

It appears, therefore, that children alter their choice of color in displaying affectively characterized topics in consistent and systematic ways. In two further studies Burkitt and her colleagues investigated the influence of culture (Finnish vs. English) and education (Steiner vs. mainstream) on color use in characterized figures (Burkitt et al., 2005; Burkitt, Tala, & Low, 2007). Although there were some cultural and educational differences in color choices use I was struck by the commonalities. In Burkitt et al. (2007) both Finnish and British children predominantly chose black to color in an outline drawing of a man characterized as nasty. In contrast, a wider range of colors represented the color chosen for the nice man (yellow, pink, red were the most frequent choices), but with a similar pattern of choices made between the Finnish and English children. Both Finnish and English children used a broad range of colors for the neutral character, although one noticeable difference was the popularity of green among Finnish children. When comparing color choices made by children from Steiner and mainstream schools for coloring in neutral, happy, and sad men,

Burkitt et al. (2005) noted no significant educational differences in the color choices for the happy and neutral drawings. The sad men, however, were more likely to be drawn in yellow by the Steiner children, while the mainstream children were more likely to use green, orange, and blue.

Esther Burkitt's work on the color choices children make in drawing positively and negatively characterized figures has revealed that children do vary their color choices between characterizations, and even between different descriptions of negatively charged characters (as shown by the different colors used to draw nasty and sad men). There appears to be a natural tendency to use black to depict nasty and a range of brighter colors for nice. But as Burkitt and her colleagues have found, personal preference also plays a role in precisely which color is shown, and this is most clearly shown in the range of colors found in children's drawings of positive figures. No doubt education and culture can act as a further mediating influence, but we need more research in other pedagogies and cultures to determine the extent to which children deviate from color universals in their drawings of emotive topics, and to understand more precisely the cause of any such differences. In the meantime, Burkitt's studies remind us of the role art education and culture on children's drawings, and cautions against assuming one-to-one correspondences between mood and color in children's drawings.

My interpretation of the available data on how children signal emotional importance in their human figure drawings is that size and placement are not used systematically, or to any large degree, to signal negative topics. Although more consistent effects have been reported for positively charged topics, these are still small and in any case less clinically relevant. In contrast, children may differentiate emotionally important topics using color that reflects both consistent choices between children and individual preferences. Future research should extend the analysis of the drawings to other features, such as content details,[6] as has been used in recent work on children's expressive drawings (see chapter 2). It would also be interesting to monitor the time children spend drawing positive and negative topics, as it may be that children spend proportionately less time drawing disliked or feared subject matter (and possibly a longer time to commence the drawing). Whatever the drawing measurements taken they may be more reliable indicators of emotional significance in drawings of topics known to be currently causing the child distress, such as in cases of abuse, or even in typically developing children who are asked to draw a child, such as a sibling or classmate, who has just upset them.

The Use of Drawings in Clinical Practice

The practice of making diagnostic interpretations of children's drawings to assess children's intelligence, personality, and emotional disturbance, and the emotional significance of the topic held by the child, is on the whole not supported by the research evidence. Does this mean drawing tests are no longer used by clinical psychologists?

Surprisingly, negative research evidence seems to have had little impact on the use of drawing tests among American and Chinese clinical psychologists. A number of surveys have now been conducted over the last 20 years that have asked American clinical psychologists to state how frequently they use a wide range of tests, such as the very popular Wechsler Intelligence scales and the Minnesota Multiphasic Personality Inventory, as well as drawing tests (Archer, Maruish, Imhof, & Piotrowski, 1991; Camara, Nathan, & Puente, 2000; Cashel, 2002; Kennedy, Faust, Willis, & Piotrowski, 1994; Lubin, Larsen, Matarazzo, & Seever, 1985; Piotrowski & Keller, 1989, 1992; Watkins, Campbell, Nieberding, & Hallmark, 1995). In Watkins et al.'s (1995) survey, projective drawing tests ranked 8th among the 38 tests listed in the survey. In surveys that allowed clinicians to respond to specific drawing tests both Lubin et al. (1985) and Cashel (2002) reported that the Machover Draw-a-Person test ranked 8th and 6th respectively, with the House-Tree-Person test ranked 10th in both surveys (the Cashel survey also included the Kinetic Family Drawing test which appeared 14th). Among the clinical psychologists surveyed by Camara et al. (2000) the House-Tree-Person test was ranked 8th (tests based on human figure drawings were 13th). As one might expect, drawing tests are particularly popular among psychologists working with adolescents and children. Archer et al. (1991) found that human figure drawings, the House-Tree-Person test and kinetic family drawings ranked 7th, 8th, and 10th respectively, while the school psychologists surveyed by Kennedy et al. (1994) ranked them 3rd, 5th, and 7th respectively.

The popularity of drawing tests is not restricted to America. Chan and Lee (1995) found that the House-Tree Person test and the Draw-a-Person test were ranked as high as 2nd and 7th respectively among the tests used by clinical psychologists working in Hong Kong. Earlier surveys conducted in mainland China reported the Draw-a-Person test ranked between 8th and 11th during the years 1979 to 1989 (Dai, Zheng, Ryan, & Paolo, 1993). As America and China contribute a significant part of the world's population it appears that the diagnosis of many children is still being informed in part by their drawings, despite such practice being largely unsupported by the research evidence.

To see if similar levels of unsupported practice were rife in Britain, Nawal Bekhit, Glyn Thomas, Simon Lalonde and I sent questionnaires to 270 British clinical psychologists, with 158 providing usable returns (58.5%). Of these 158 psychologists, 91 worked primarily in adult mental health, 33 with children, 18 with learning disabilities and 16 within older adults. In the part of the survey which is of most interest to this discussion, the psychologists were asked to state how frequently they used 44 assessment measures. Included in this list was a wide range of drawing tests, such as the Machover Draw-a-Person test, the Koppitz test, the Kinetic Family Drawing test, the House-Tree-Person test and the Goodenough–Harris Draw-a-Man test. We also asked clinicians to state how frequently they used drawings as an informal assessment aid.

The results of our British survey provided findings that were in stark contrast to those reported in America and China (Bekhit, Thomas, Lalonde, & Jolley, 2002; Bekhit et al., 2005). In respect of the drawing tests we can see from Table 7.2 that the majority of psychologists working with all client groups used the drawings tests only occasionally at best, with the majority never using them at all. Unsurprisingly, those working primarily with children used them more than other client groups, but in absolute terms even in the child client group drawing tests are used only sparingly. When we assessed the overall ranking of the drawing tests among all client groups combined, the highest ranking drawing test was the Goodenough–Harris Draw-a-Man test, but this appeared at a very lowly 27th. The House-Tree-Person Test (31.5 rank), Machover Draw-a-Person test (37) and the Kinetic Family Drawing test (39.5) all featured near the bottom of the table of the 44 assessment measures, with the Koppitz

Table 7.2 Percentages of British Clinical Psychologists use of Formal Drawing Tests by Frequency and Speciality Area

Drawing test	Never %			Occasionally %			Moderately %			Frequently %		
	A	C	LD	A	C	LD	A	C	LD	A	C	LD
H-T-P Test	97.8	72.7	88.8	2.2	21.2	11.1	0	6.1	0	0	0	0
K-F-D Test	100	90.9	94.4	0	6.1	5.6	0	3	0	0	0	0
D-a-P Test	100	78.8	94.4	0	15.2	5.6	0	3	0	0	3	0
Koppitz Test	100	100	100	0	0	0	0	0	0	0	0	0
D-a-M Test	97.8	54.5	83.3	2.2	30.3	16.7	0	12.1	0	0	3	0
Mean %	99	79	92	1	15	8	0	5	0	0	1	0

Note. A = Adult; C = Child; LD = Learning Disability; H-T-P = House-Tree-Person Test; K-F-D = Kinetic Family Drawing Test; D-a-P = Machover Draw-a-Person-Test; D-a-M = Goodenough-Harris Draw-a-Man Test. "Always" percentages were all zero for all client groups. Older adult excluded as 100% never used any of the formal drawing tests.

test never being used by any of the respondents. Although drawing tests were ranked higher among the child client group, they still appeared outside the top ten with the highest being the Goodenough–Harris Draw-a-Man test ranked at 11.5. Nevertheless, our inclusion of drawing as an informal assessment measure proved to be a useful addition to our survey, as our sample more frequently used drawings in this way compared to the formal drawing tests.

Table 7.3 shows that drawings were used informally to some extent by all client groups, with nearly half of those working with children using drawings frequently or always. Across all client groups, drawings as an informal assessment aid was ranked 9th, and as high as 4th in the child client group, when compared with all the assessment measures listed in the survey. Despite the relative high frequency of British clinical psychologists using drawings informally in their assessment procedure, very few mentioned drawings (either formal drawing tests or use of "free" drawings) as measures in which trainees should be competent. It appears, therefore, that British clinical psychologists hold drawings in much less regard as an assessment tool than their American and Chinese counterparts, and in this sense their practice (or lack of it) is more in keeping with the research evidence.

We found that the less frequent use of drawing tests by British clinical psychologists is consistent with the overall infrequent use of assessment per se in British practice compared to that reported in American surveys, and this disparity is particularly marked for

Table 7.3   Percentage of British Clinical Psychologists' Use of Free Drawing by Frequency and Speciality Area (Mean Percentages of Formal Drawing Test Usage from Table 7.2 in Brackets)

	OA	A	C	LD
	%	%	%	%
Never	50.0 (100)	74.7 (99)	18.2 (79)	55.6 (92)
Occasionally	6.3 (0)	12.1 (1)	18.2 (15)	22.2 (8)
Moderately	18.8 (0)	8.8 (0)	15.2 (5)	5.6 (0)
Frequently	18.8 (0)	4.4 (0)	36.4 (1)	11.1 (0)
Always	6.3 (0)	1.1 (0)	12.1 (0)	5.6 (0)

Note. OA = Older Adult; A = Adult; C = Child; LD = Learning Disability.

projective testing (Bekhit et al., 2002). If there is a lack of trust in projective techniques generally among British psychologists then this is likely to contribute to the infrequent use of formal drawing tests that rely on projective assumptions, in particular, those found in the personality tradition (Bekhit et al. 2005). This mistrust may also extend to other diagnostic drawings tests, such as those purporting to measure intelligence and emotionality. Although these other approaches often provide an objective scoring system rather than directly, and heavily, relying on the clinician's psychoanalytical interpretations, they nevertheless depend in some sense on the belief that a facet of the child (e.g., his intelligence) is projected in his or her drawings. In contrast, it seems that many American clinical psychologists have resisted the reliability and validity problems of projective techniques argued by academics (see Piotrowski, 1999; Watkins et al., 1995), instead believing such tests benefit an understanding of the client's clinical profile and in treatment planning (see Cashel, 2002). This resistance is most likely to come from those who practice psycho-dynamic approaches. According to Watkins et al.'s (1995) survey, 21% of the American clinical psychologists surveyed reported using a psychodynamic model as their primary therapeutic orientation (which was second only to the eclectic approach). Projective tech-niques such as found in some formal drawing tests fit in well with this psychodynamic approach, but not in the cognitive-behavioral and systemic models most commonly found in British clinical practice. Furthermore, projective tests are still being recommended on APA-approved internship programs (see Cashel, 2002), whereas my enquiries have suggested they represent a very minor part of British clinical training programs.

The greater expectation of American clinical psychologists to use assessment tests may be also influenced by health management organizations and medical insurance companies. The bias towards private health care in America means that American clinical psy-chologists are expected to provide assessment services so they can gain reimbursement from these private health care companies. A recent survey by Piotrowski, however, suggests that American health management organizations have begun to restrict the range and frequency of assessment tests in American clinical practice by not authorizing assessments and reducing the reimbursements for those tests that have been used (Piotrowski, 1999; Piotrowski, Belter, &

Keller, 1998). These financial constraints, Piotrowski argues, are leading clinical psychologists to use measures that are shorter and quicker to administer. To date there is no evidence that drawings tests are included in those that have begun to suffer in their frequency of use due to reimbursement issues. It may be that the comparative speed of administering, scoring, and interpreting drawing tests (relative to, for example, the Minnesota Multiphasic Personality Inventory, see Camara et al., 2000), will keep the use of drawings tests in America popular.

Wherefore Children's Drawings as Clinical Aids?

For any diagnostic test to be useful, its measurement, whatever form that may take, must be an accurate reflection of what the test is intended to measure. In the case of drawing diagnostic tests, the features of the drawing (although verbal and non-verbal behavior are also incorporated in some approaches) included in the assessment must lead to an accurate diagnosis. This is true whether the drawing tests have an objective scoring method (as is the case in tests devoted to assessing the child's intelligence, emotional disturbance, and emotional significance of the topic), or where clinicians and therapists interpret features as projections of the child's personality disturbance. A drawing diagnostic test relies, therefore, on most children who have the construct being measured to depict in their drawing(s) the features pertaining to the test. Apart from the possible exception of drawing features relating to intelligence, that level of consistency is simply not there in children's drawings. A single child may not even show his or her disturbance in the same way across a number of drawings, never mind other children portraying similar disturbances in consistent and reliable ways among each other. With such potential variability in how disturbance manifests itself in children's drawings, it is no wonder there is so much negative research evidence that has derived from comparing drawings from a clinical group of children to those of typically developing children.

It would be a fallacy, however, to conclude that children do not convey clinically relevant aspects about themselves in their drawings just because they do not do so in sufficiently consistent ways to support diagnostic decisions. A drawing is not made by a child independently of their psychological profile, in the same way it is not made independently from the child's motor and graphic skill. We saw in chapter 2 how children can use, at times, a range of esthetic devices to make expressive drawings. It would be very odd indeed if they did not use these and other expressive devices to communicate clinically relevant aspects of themselves. But how should the clinician interpret a child client's drawing if not to treat it diagnostically? I recommend that a form of hypothesis testing be used, based on the research evidence that we have available of the drawing features that are the most reliable in distinguishing between clinical and typically developing children.

To explain my point further, let me use an example of a child's "scarring" of a tree trunk. In the case of drawings of trees, for example, Hammer (1997) argues we are more likely to project both our unconscious feelings and conscious disturbance than in our human figure drawings. This is because, as Hammer explains, while a client may be less willing to scar and mutilate their person drawing for concern that the clinician will immediately "see" the client's disturbance, scarring may appear in their tree drawing because the client has put up fewer defenses when drawing that topic. In Plate 5 we see a 7-year-old girl's drawing of a tree with a circular shaded area on the trunk. This "scarring" of the trunk is typically interpreted by practitioners of projective drawing techniques as a sign of a trauma occurring earlier in the client's life. In this particular case the girl had been referred for constipation and its psychological effects on her. At the original onset of the constipation the child was admitted to hospital, an experience she found very traumatic. Furthermore, her parents reported that the situation was causing stress within the family, particularly as the parents disagreed about the strategies they should use to address the problem. Could the girl's scarring of the tree be a projection of the trauma of the onset of constipation and hospitalization, as well as her anxiety with the ongoing discussion in her family about her illness?

The way forward to answering this type of question is two-fold, and both research and clinical practice need to play their roles. First, research need to continue to establish which are the most reliable aspects of children's drawings, within the full array of individual and holistic features (e.g., items of content, proportion, placement, size, composition, color, pressure of stroke, etc.), that indicate clinically relevant characteristics of the child. In other words, which features, when they do appear in children's drawings, tend to be associated with a known disturbance in the child, but not found in normally developing and undisturbed children? For instance, does the "scarring" of a tree trunk (as shown in Plate 5) appear noticeably more frequently in the tree drawings of children who have experienced some sort of developmental trauma when they were younger than those children who have not? It does not matter if only a relatively few developmentally disturbed children scar their tree trunk, only that when one does see it in a tree drawing there is often independent evidence of a significant trauma.

The second step is for clinicians, armed with the knowledge of clinically relevant features from the research studies, to generate hypotheses of disturbance when they see such features in their child client's drawings. The clinician can then explore with the child, parents, and via other assessment tools the validity of any hypothesis. For example, upon seeing their child client draw a "scarred" tree the psychologist may hypothesize that the child is expressing a previously experienced trauma and then explore through other sources what this might be. For any child client, some hypotheses will be dismissed after being explored but some may remain, if they find external substantiation. Of course, such hypothesis testing will be particularly useful when the drawings allow positive lines of enquiry that had not been previously obtained from other sources of information. Drawing would also be additionally useful if they illuminate how the child is experiencing the trauma in his or her inner world, particularly if it involved some form of therapeutic effect for the child not enabled by other activities. Used in this way drawings may represent an important supplementary tool to formal standardized psychometric tests and the clinical interview.

Of course my suggestion of clinical practice is unlikely to be novel, and may well be adopted by at least some clinicians. Our survey of assessment in British clinical psychology (Bekhit et al., 2002, 2005) suggests many of those working with children are using drawings informally, and some of this practice may relate to the form of hypothesis testing suggested here. A further survey is needed to establish what benefits psychologists believe derive from using drawings informally in their clinical practice, and in what ways such practice is undertaken.

Summary

Children's drawings have traditionally been used in clinical settings to diagnose the child's intelligence, personality, emotional state, and emotional attitudes towards significant topics. The current research evidence on the whole seriously questions whether children's drawings should be used diagnostically. Nevertheless, diagnostic drawing tests remain popular in America and China, although much less so in Britain. Although children known to have a clinically relevant characteristic or disturbance appear not to produce consistent and reliable drawing features among themselves, it would be folly to believe that disturbed children do not at times communicate characteristics of that disturbance in their drawings. I suggest that children's drawings in clinical settings may still be useful to clinicians, if instead of either dismissing their relevance or treating them diagnostically, clinicians use drawings to generate hypotheses to be considered and explored in conjunction with other sources and assessment measures. On occasions this approach may shed light on an area of disturbance or trauma of the child that had not been initially evident from the other sources alone. It remains to be seen from future surveys whether this method, or indeed others, are employed by clinical child psychologists in their informal, rather than diagnostic, use of children's drawings.

Notes

1   Additional encouragement was given by saying that the aim was to see if drawings from their own school were as good as from children from other schools. It appears from Goodenough's (1926) instructions that children were to be tested in large groups, perhaps in their classes.

2   Even if such studies proved negative for including drawings in the diagnosis, I acknowledge Hammer's (1997) point referred to earlier in the chapter of the potential usefulness for the clinician of seeing themes recurring across a number of measures, including projective drawings.

3   However, Cox (1993) questioned the validity of some of Koppitz's emotional indicators in her reanalysis of the original data. Cox claimed that the repeated chi-square analysis adopted by Koppitz (1968) increased the risk of Koppitz mistakenly including indicators. When she applied

the appropriate probability (alpha) correction the number of items that differentiated clinical populations was reduced.

4 I note that Maureen Cox (2005) states that the correlation was 0.41. My apologies to her if I gave her the wrong figure!

5 In Veltman and Browne's (2002) review of studies assessing drawings from children who have been maltreated, they stated that there was inconclusive evidence regarding the usefulness of drawings to identify maltreatment.

6 In an interesting exploratory study, Sandow (1997) asked 8- to 10-year-olds to draw four pictures: a very clever person, a very stupid person, a very nice person, and a very nasty person. She describes a range of content-based features that were found in the drawings of each person, which indicates that researchers investigating how children communicate ability/character in their drawings of people should not limit themselves to size, color, and placement alone.

8

Drawings as Memory Aids

For children to lead a meaningful life it is necessary for them to remember previously acquired knowledge and experiences. There are other instances such as in judicial and clinical settings where children's accurate and complete retrieval is especially important. Considering children's limited retrieval ability compared to that found in adults, different techniques have been tested to facilitate children's recall, including asking children to draw while recalling. This chapter examines the research evidence for using drawings as memory aids by discussing the findings from four different methodological approaches: recalling staged/naturally occurring events, emotional memories, objects in item-recall tasks, and events presented in videos. The parameters in which studies have consistently shown drawing to act as a facilitatory cue for recall are outlined, and the explanations given to account for the effect are discussed. The chapter ends with some research ideas on how we may further improve the amount and range of information recalled by children who are asked to draw.

Memories are fundamental to living a meaningful life. Being able to retain information acquired from our past allows us to make sense of the present and plan our future. Having a competent memory is particularly important in childhood where there is so much new information to learn and retain, and it is increasingly assessed from a young age in school.[1] In addition, there are other occasions where adults require children to recall accurately and honestly a previous event they have directly experienced or observed, such as quarrels and misdemeanors perpetrated by other children or even adults. In serious cases of wrong-doing, some children may be required to provide eye-witness accounts within legal contexts, or to talk about their own trauma in clinical settings. The implications for providing accurate and error-free recall from children in such cases are far-reaching, as they may impact upon the freedom of other people, the child's own future safety, and potentially the therapeutic process.

Although historically children have not always been regarded as reliable witnesses there is an increasing recognition that they are more competent witnesses than previously assumed (Bull, 2001). Nevertheless, there are a number of generally accepted problems and issues specifically relating to children's memory and in accessing these memories in interviews. These include children's relatively incomplete memories compared to those of adults, their difficulty in structuring their recall, a lack of self-constraint in their imagination, children feeling intimidated by questioning from adults, and being susceptible to leading questions. There is the additional difficulty of being less willing to give evidence against a perpetrator with whom they have an emotional bond with, or are dependent upon, such as a parent.

In order to provide a context of the research that has examined the potential benefit of asking children to draw on their verbal recall of an event or experience, I shall first briefly outline the development of memory in childhood and its limitations, and then discuss the merits and drawbacks of other techniques that have been used to promote children's recall.

The Development of Children's Memory

The main problem facing interviewers of children is that children's memory of events is inferior to most adults, particularly so for young children. Evidence that older children recall more than younger children derives from standard tests of memory, as well as natural memory tasks such as recalling an event personally experienced by the child. In either case the consensus of the research evidence suggests that if children are given open-ended memory questions (e.g., "tell me all you can remember about . . .") a younger child's recall, compared to that of an older child, tends to be accurate but incomplete and vulnerable to increasing delay between event and recall (Baker-Ward, Gordon, Ornstein, Larus, & Clubb, 1993; Peterson & Bell, 1996; Steward & Steward, 1996).

Researchers in memory have been interested in how to account for the younger child's memory deficit. It is generally accepted that there are three phases in remembering information, and a difficulty in recall can potentially stem from any or all of these three phases. In the first phase, we attend to some of the information available to our senses (encoding), some of the attended information is transferred to our memory (storage), and finally, in the third phase, the stored information is accessed when we want to retrieve it (retrieval). Research has shown that although deficiencies in encoding and storage partly account for the young child's deficit in memory (see Howe & O'Sullivan, 1997), it is the retrieval stage that represents the primary cause of younger children's memory difficulties. There are at least two lines of evidence that support this view. First, when young children are repeatedly interviewed about a personally experienced event they often continue to report new information at subsequent interviews (Fivush & Hammond, 1990). This indicates that the new information recalled was initially encoded and stored but that there was a problem with retrieval in earlier interviews. Second, changing the conditions at retrieval can help children to remember more accurate information. For instance, creating an overlap between the recall and encoding conditions (Tulving, 1983), providing toys and props (Salmon, Bidrose, & Pipe, 1995), and giving directive questions as a framework for structuring children's recall (Hammond & Fivush, 1991) have all been shown to facilitate young children's recall. Further evidence that young children in particular have problems with recall is that they tend not to spontaneously generate retrieval strategies (e.g., rehearsal) for themselves (Flavell, Beach, & Chinsky, 1966). All these lines of evidence raise the question of what interviewers can do to help children with their recall.

How Can We Help Children's Retrieval?

Two ways in which the responsibility of the child's retrieval ability can be shared with the interviewer is in the style of questioning and the provision of nonverbal cues and props. Asking the child direct questions about an experienced event, particularly using questions that focus on certain episodes, has been found to increase the child's level of recall above that which is obtained from free recall only (e.g., see Poole & Lamb, 1998). Direct questioning provides an external cue to help children retrieve memories that have only a weak trace, and also provides them with a structure in collating their memories (e.g., see Eisen, Quas, & Goodman, 2002). Despite adding to the amount of correct information recalled, however, direct questioning is also prone to eliciting more *inaccurate* information recalled from children, particularly to questions that require a yes/no answer (Brady, Poole, Warren, & Jones, 1999; Peterson & Bell, 1996; Walker, Lunning, & Eilts, 1996). This unwanted consequence is closely related to the pitfalls of leading questions. Young children are particularly vulnerable to this style of questioning as they may give an answer they think the interviewer expects or wants. Such concerns are particularly pertinent in a court of law where one party may lead the child to give (false) information supporting their client. The opposite problem is when an interviewer knows so little about the event that the details in the question provide no cue for the child's retrieval at all, but the child still feels they need to provide an answer.

As a result of the drawbacks of verbal cues, crime and clinical investigators have supplemented their questioning with nonverbal props, such as dolls and toys. The provision of physical props may be beneficial for children who tend to focus more on sensory rather than verbal information when encoding an event (see Bjorklund, 1987; Salmon, 2001), and props allow some of the recall response to be displayed by a behavioral response (e.g., reenacting a scene with the dolls), therefore reducing the demands on verbal recall. Nevertheless, physical props may also encourage children to speak more about an event, including both accurate and false information, compared to a standard interview where props are not provided. In one study Salmon et al. (1995) investigated the extent to which actual items from an event (real props), or toy representations of the real items (toy props), or verbal prompts only (no props) facilitated 3- and 5-year-olds' verbal recall of a made-up medical event. This event had taken place 2 or 3 days earlier involving the child, the experimenter and a "sick" teddy bear. The real and toy props were both effective in enhancing the amount of information verbally recalled by the 5-year-olds relative to the no-props group, indicating that physical props can help some children's verbal recall of an event. However, Salmon et al. (1995) also found that the use of toy props led to more inaccurate information being recalled among both age groups.

Clearly props that resemble most closely the objects present in the original event will provide the most beneficial cues (see Salmon, 2001). Although this can be easily arranged in experimental studies (after all the experimenters designed the event!), in practice there is a genuine difficulty for the interviewer who is unlikely to be sufficiently knowledgeable of the event details to make appropriately informed prop choices. Furthermore, poorly chosen props can increase the likelihood of inaccurate information. If children do not see the link between the props provided and their memory of the event they may treat the props as play toys to fantasize with, resulting in verbal responses that are inaccurate to those in the actual event (Gross & Hayne, 1999; Salmon, 2001).

It would be much better, therefore, if the child was able to provide their own cues. As I mentioned above, however, young children in particular do not frequently generate their own retrieval strategies and cues. Nevertheless, recent research has suggested that asking children to draw a previously experienced event or experience prompts children to provide self-generated cues that aids their verbal recall. I now elaborate upon this idea as well as describing some potential nonspecific benefits of drawing on children's recall.

The Case for Drawing

A number of researchers have suggested specific and nonspecific recall benefits of asking children to draw (Burgess & Hartman, 1993; Butler, Gross, & Hayne, 1995; Davison & Thomas, 2001; Edwards & Fornham, 1989; Gross & Hayne, 1998, 1999; Kahill, 1984; Pynoos & Eth, 1986; Salmon, 2001; Thomas & Jolley, 1998; Wesson & Salmon, 2001). Most of these benefits relate to the drawing acting as a child-generated cue that facilitates retrieval of additional details about the event. As children normally draw topics and scenes that are of most interest to them, drawings are likely to stimulate the child to talk about the most interesting and salient episodes to them. As the drawing unfolds, the child may spontaneously talk about the details of what they are producing (and hence the event), cue the child to think about related items or episodes in the event, or refer back to features already drawn later in the drawing process. Furthermore, aspects of the drawing can be unobtrusively questioned about by the interviewer (e.g., "tell me more about this . . ."), which can include bringing the child's attention back to certain details due to drawings having a permanent record. A related specific benefit of drawing is that producing a drawing requires some level of structure and planning by the child (see Freeman, 1980). Young children's verbal recall of an event tends to be fragmented, and planning a drawing may help the child structure sequentially the event episodes.

In addition to these specific benefits of drawing on recall there are likely to be nonspecific advantages of asking children to draw. One must not forget that children between 2 and 12 years of age are prolific drawers, and for most children drawing represents an enjoyable activity. By inviting the child into an enjoyable activity the child's potential anxiety to the interview situation and/or previously experienced trauma is likely to be reduced. Furthermore, the child's awareness and anxiety at being questioned by an adult may become less salient as they start to focus more on the drawing activity and less on the interviewer. Within this relaxed atmosphere the bond between the child and the interviewer has a chance to develop. It is at this point that the child may begin to recall aspects of the memory. It has also been suggested that drawing the event prolongs the interview, thereby giving the child more opportunity to recall further details of the event. The drawing task itself will keep the child focused on the event, whereas in a standard interview based only on conversation the interviewer may need to frequently refocus the child to the event.

The specific and nonspecific benefits of drawing suggest that asking children to draw an event may be a very useful memory cue, and indeed there is evidence that drawings are being used in clinical practice to promote children's recall of traumatic events (Burgess, 1988; Oppawsky, 1991; Pynoos and Eth, 1986; Rae, 1991). But does the research evidence support this practice?

Drawings as Memory Aids: The Evidence

Four experimental approaches have been adopted to investigate whether asking children to draw an event facilitates their verbal recall of the event. The first involves children recalling information from either a unique event staged by the experimenters (e.g., a school trip to a fire station) or a naturally occurring routine event (e.g., a school medical examination). The second approach asks children to recall an emotional event they have personally experienced in the past. The third approach uses an item-recall task in controlled laboratory conditions. Finally, in the most recent (fourth) approach, children are shown a video and asked to recall the information presented. I now review the research evidence for the usefulness of drawings as memory cues within each of these methodological approaches.

(i)   Staged and naturally occurring events

In their seminal paper, Butler et al. (1995) used a staged event paradigm in which children were taken on a school trip to a fire station. During the visit the children were shown around the fire station by a confederate of the experiment, dressed in a fire-fighter uniform, who explained the duties of the fire-fighters. The children were allowed to climb on the fire engines and they saw the real fire-fighters practicing their drills. At two points two additional confederates of the research team, dressed as workers, interrupted the children's tour by acting out two pre-planned episodes (searching for a tool box and sliding down a pole).

This event formed the basis of two experiments. In the first experiment 5- and 6-year-olds participated in the event, and were tested for their recall one day later. In the second experiment a different group of 5- to 6-year-olds went on the trip together with a younger group of 3- to 4-year-olds; these children were tested for their recall one month after the trip. In both studies children were allocated to either a "draw-and-tell" group who were asked to draw about the trip and verbally recall what they could remember of it, or a "tell" group who were interviewed without being asked to draw. The recall for both groups was conducted in three phases, but only the first two will be described here as these are directly relevant to the present discussion. In the first phase (free recall) children were simply asked to recall (or draw and recall) anything that they could remember about the trip. At the point where the child was no longer providing additional information, the interview entered the second phase (direct recall) in which the child was asked four direct questions about specific episodes of the event (although a question was not asked if the child had discussed it already in their free recall). Those in the draw-and-tell group were asked to draw in response to each direct question (as well as verbally recall). In both phases, and for both groups, the interviewer kept the conversation going by making comments such as "uh huh" and "really," by repeating a part of a child's utterance, or asking the child if he or she could recall (or draw and recall) anything else. Only the child's verbal recall was coded (the children's drawings were not used as evidence of recall), and was recorded in respect of which phase of the interview it had occurred.

The two experiments carried out by Butler et al. (1995) reported positive, albeit restricted, evidence for the children's drawings acting as retrieval cues. On the one hand, the 5- to 6-year-olds remembered twice as much information if they drew the event. This was true both when the delay was one day or one month after the event, and furthermore there were only minimal recall errors. However, the facilitatory effect of drawing only occurred when the children were given direct questions. This does evoke a cautionary note because, as I have already mentioned, in real-life situations the interviewer may not have the knowledge to provide directly relevant questions for effective cueing. Although the direct questions used by the authors were very general (e.g., draw/tell where you went, how you got there, who went with you, what you saw there), and were therefore not dependent on the interviewer having prior knowledge of the event, it still raises the possibility that children may need some verbal guidance in addition to their drawings to recall additional information. The other potential limit on the supportive evidence for drawing on recall was that drawing did not benefit the younger group's recall, which the authors suggested may have been due to the poorer representational quality of their drawings.

Butler et al.'s (1995) findings that drawing an event one month later facilitated recall is interesting in the context of eye-witness testimony where interviews may occur some time after the event. But does drawing cue recall after longer delays? This question was examined by Gross and Hayne (1999) who investigated 5- to 6-year-old children's recall of a visit to a chocolate factory after delays of either one day or 6 months; both delay groups were also tested a year after the event. Gross and Hayne were able to extend the findings of their earlier study (Butler et al., 1995) in at least three important ways. First, children who were asked to draw and tell recalled significantly more accurate information (compared to the tell-only group) for all three delays, and hence using drawings as a facilitator for recall was supported for up to a year after the event. Second, children who drew in the interview a year later recalled significantly more new information compared to children who did not draw in the same annual interview (as much as 78% of the information recalled by the "draw-and-tell" group in the interviews held one year later was new, and highly accurate, to that reported in their previous interview). Third, although more information was recalled from direct questioning than free recall for all interview time points, drawing the event a year later also benefited free recall compared to the standard interview. However, the facilitatory effect of drawing only showed if the child drew at the time of the interview – merely showing the child their previous drawing had no effect.

Gross and Hayne's (1999) finding that drawing facilitates children's free recall after a one year delay is particularly noteworthy in relation to eye-witness testimony, but the overall retention levels found after one year may have been augmented by the children's previous interview acting as a form of rehearsal for them. In contrast, a study reported by Salmon and Pipe (2000) provided a more pure assessment of the effect of drawing on recall ability after a year's delay. They asked 5-year-olds to recall a standard school health assessment that had been given a year ago. Unlike the children tested by Gross and Hayne, the one-year interview conducted by Salmon and Pipe represented the first time some of the children had been interviewed (the other children tested by Salmon and Pipe had also been interviewed after 3 days). Children were given either verbal prompts (verbal group), prototypical medical items and a doll (props group) or asked to draw (drawing group). In contrast to the findings reported by Gross and Hayne, drawing was less effective than the standard interview (and also compared to props) in cueing recall for children who were interviewed for the first time one year on from the assessment.

Although Salmon and Pipe's study should act as a cautionary note to the positive findings reported in Hayne's studies, the two types of event adopted (a unique staged event and a routine health check) suggest that drawings may still be valuable recall cues but only for certain events. Salmon and Pipe (2000) noted that health checks are relatively common in the child's experience, and that young children in particular have difficulty in differentiating between a general script knowledge of an event and particular details relating to a specific occasion. They refer to work carried out by Hudson and colleagues who have shown that children's recall of an event that occurs routinely becomes confused after a delay of even one month (Hudson, 1990; Hudson, Fivush, & Kuebli, 1992). Salmon and Pipe argue that drawings may only help children generate their own retrieval cues of specific information if that information relates to a distinctive episode, otherwise a drawing will only cue the "gist" of the episode or the child's general script of the event (i.e. generic knowledge of the procedure of a health check). I shall shortly expand on how children's drawings may cue the child's general knowledge relating to the subject matter to which an episode relates. Suffice to say at the moment that reporting general knowledge lays the child open to recalling misinformation or errors compared to what actually happened in the particular episode that the child is trying to remember. Indeed, Salmon and Pipe (2000) found that the information reported by children in the drawing group after the one-year delay was highly inaccurate.

(ii) Emotional memories

The facilitatory effect of drawing on recalling unique events reported in the previous section is potentially relevant for utilizing drawings in children's eye-witness testimony, as the crimes children are asked to recall are likely to represent unusual experiences for the child. But some of these experiences will no doubt evoke emotions in the child. Furthermore, some of the events leading to clinical referrals will also have been emotionally traumatic for the child. It is important for the interviewer and clinician to know, therefore, whether drawing facilitates emotional memories. This is not only to establish whether drawings cue more reported details than in standard interviews, but also how the child has interpreted the experience from what they say (Pynoos & Eth, 1986).

Despite work in clinical settings indicating that drawings may facilitate children's ability to talk about traumatic events they have experienced, such as sex abuse, parental divorce, and illness (e.g., Burgess, 1988; Oppawsky, 1991; Rae, 1991), these studies have not compared recall with a nondrawing control group. Gross and Hayne (1998) addressed this methodological flaw in an experimental setting by asking children to recall (with and without the child drawing) emotional (happy, sad, scared, or angry) events from their past. Children in two age groups (3- to 4-year-olds and 5- to 6-year-olds) were tested, and the accuracy of their recall was checked by the children's parents. Consistent with Hayne and her colleagues' other work cited above, more than twice as much accurate information was reported if children drew their emotional experience. Furthermore, this was true for both age groups, across all emotional experiences, and with no increase in false information. These findings are important not only in extending the facilitatory effect of drawings to emotional experiences, but also because the drawing effect was found for 3- to 4-year-olds (where previous research had reported inconsistent findings).

Other independent work carried out by Karen Salmon and her colleagues (Salmon, Roncolato, & Gleitzman, 2003; Wesson & Salmon, 2001) has confirmed that asking children to draw a previous emotional experience helps them recall more details about it. In Wesson and Salmon (2001), 5- and 8-year-old children were interviewed about the times they felt happy, sad, and scared in one of three interview conditions: to verbally recall their memories ("verbal" group), to reenact and tell ("reenactment" group) or to draw and tell ("drawing" group). Wesson and Salmon found that both age groups recalled twice as much information for all three memories if they drew or reenacted their emotional memory compared to the verbal recall group.

Wesson and Salmon noticed that there was considerable within age group variability in the amount of recall, and the possibility that individual differences in the child's temperament and expressive vocabulary may be mediating factors in recall was investigated by Salmon et al. (2003). Interestingly, they found that 5- to 7-year-olds who drew about a time they felt happy and a time they felt scared not only recalled more information than the other two groups (reenactment and verbal), but neither expressive vocabulary nor temperament was associated with the recall from the draw group (whereas expressive vocabulary and temperament interacted with the tell and reenactment groups respectively). Salmon et al. explained that if drawing provides a memory cue for the episode as well as helping the child structure the narrative of the event, the child may be less dependent on their own expressive vocabulary in telling the story. In respect of temperamental differences, I suspect that if drawing does put the child at ease during the interview by, for example, giving the child a focus other than on the experimenter, then temperamental differences will have little influence on children's recall if asked to draw. Regardless of the extent to which either of these explanations are valid, the possibility that drawing facilitates recall of emotional information, irrespective of individual differences in the child's expressive vocabulary and temperament, suggests a potential application to children generally.

The Wesson and Salmon (2001) study, in particular, showed that drawing may not be a useful facilitator of eliciting the children's own affective commentary or evaluations of the event (e.g., comments on how they felt happy, scared, liked/loved an aspect of the experience, etc.). This may not matter in eye-witness testimony where the emphasis is on obtaining information about what happened rather than the (subjective) feelings of the interviewee, but in clinical contexts how the child interprets the experienced event is important for the clinician to know, for instance, in relation to decisions on therapy (Pynoos & Eth, 1986). Hence, Wesson and Salmon (2001) suggest that it may be necessary to prompt the child to talk about their emotional reactions to their experience.

Despite the apparent efficacy of drawing in promoting children's verbal recall of staged events and emotional event memories there are at least two outstanding concerns relating to this work. The first concern relates to the presentation and scoring of the information, and the second to whether drawing is particularly prone to cueing children's generic knowledge associated with the specific event knowledge. Due to the dynamic nature of the staged events we cannot be sure that each child sees the same information or for the same duration, and hence there is likely to be some variability in what each child encoded from the same event (see also Gross & Hayne, 1999). In studies assessing children's previous emotional memories the variability in the level of details relating to these memories will be even more pronounced, and furthermore it is difficult for experimenters to gather independent validation of the accuracy of the children's recall of such memories. In Gross and Hayne (1998) and Salmon et al. (2003) the children's reports were verified by the parents, but the parents' memory may have also suffered from the delay and in some cases, such as a child choosing to recall a nightmare, the parents have no direct access to the "event" details. In Wesson and Salmon (2001) no check was made as to whether the information children reported actually happened.

Although these issues of controlling event information and verifying children's responses need addressing they are not peculiar to children allocated to a draw-and-tell group (so we would not expect these problems to differentially impact upon these children). But the second concern is, at least theoretically, directly related to those children who are asked to draw. Davison and Thomas (2001) raised a potentially serious problem regarding the source of the information recalled by children who draw the event. They claim that children's drawings are often schematic in the sense that they tend to show the generic features typical of the category of the topic, rather than showing specific details relating to an individual example of that topic (e.g., "intellectual realism" is an example of prototypical information, see chapter 1). Accordingly, the depiction of generic information may cue children's general knowledge about the subject matter of the event (e.g., their existing knowledge of fire engines and fire-fighters), or their "script" knowledge of the sequence of events that normally occur in relation to this subject matter (e.g., their already held knowledge of bus journeys or what happens when there is a fire). This general and script knowledge will be scored as accurate recall where it coincides with the details relating to the actual event shown, thus giving the drawing group a spurious advantage. Furthermore, the need to disentangle generic knowledge from the children's reports in judicial and clinical interviews is clearly paramount, particularly where the generically driven information does not coincide with what actually happened.

The next methodological approach I shall discuss, that of presenting children with item-recall tasks, goes some way to addressing these two concerns.

(iii)   Item recall tasks

In a series of four studies Davison and Thomas (2001) presented children with items on a board, which the children were asked to recall after the items had been removed. Children were allocated to either a "tell" group or a "draw-and-tell" group (or in variations that resembled these two groups). This laboratory-experiment procedure allowed the experimenters, therefore, to ensure that each child was shown an identical visual presentation and length of exposure, with the additional benefit of unambiguous scoring considering the ease to which children's responses could be compared to the presented material. Furthermore, as children were simply asked to recall the items any general knowledge the child may have had about the items would not have gained any extra credit in the scoring of their recall, and it is difficult to see how any such general knowledge would have helped in recalling the items. Also, children would not have had a script knowledge of an item-recall task.

In their first study two age groups (5- to 6-year-olds and 7- to 8-year-olds) were presented with 25 familiar items on a board (5 unlinked items, 5 color-related items, 5 shape-related items, 5 rhyming-related items and 5 category-related items). Approximately 4 hours later each child was asked to recall (or draw and recall the items concurrently) as many of the items as they could remember. There was no significant difference in the number of items recalled between the groups.

The possibility that the cognitive demands of drawing and of recalling interfered with each other for children in the draw-and-tell group led Davison and Thomas to include a "draw-then-tell" group in their second study. In this group children were asked to recall the items only after they had completed *all* their drawings. For the 5- to 6-year-olds both drawing groups (draw-and-tell and draw-then-tell) recalled significantly *fewer* items than the tell group (there was no difference in recall for the 7- to 8-year-olds). Furthermore, in the two remaining studies reported by Davison and Thomas significantly fewer items were recalled by children drawing the items than in the recall-only groups. In conclusion, they found no evidence that drawing facilitates children's recall, and that in fact it often impaired recall.

How should we interpret the negative findings for drawings as memory aids in Davison and Thomas (2001)? There are a number of interpretations. First, that the positive data from studies using staged events and emotional memories is false because the recall scores of the children drawing had been inflated by the drawings cueing generic and script information that coincided with the specific event details. Davison and Thomas give an example of how this may have occurred in the studies conducted by Hayne and her colleagues in respect of children traveling by bus to the fire station and chocolate factory. If the children who drew utilized their general schema for a bus they would have included such typical features as the wheels and windows, which if commented upon would have been credited in the scoring. It is not possible in such cases to distinguish whether any accurately recalled item was evoked from generic and script knowledge or from event-specific information.

While Davison and Thomas's explanation is a serious one to consider there are at least two alternative possibilities for their negative findings. First, that drawing facilitates recall of event-based memories but not for singular and isolated items. Children's drawings often display narrative scenes and therefore may be a useful memory cue for the events presented in their day-trips (and emotional memories), but not for items that are not linked to a narrative or event. Second, and not unrelated to the first point, that laboratory-based item-recall tasks are unlikely to engage children in the same way as an interesting and exciting day trip, or in recalling personal and emotional memories. If item-recall tasks do not stimulate much interest from the child, then drawing the items may present an additional cognitive burden on the child to remembering the items. If this is the case we would expect drawing to actually hinder recall, and this is precisely what Davison and Thomas (2001) found. A similar point is made by Salmon and Pipe (2000) who argued that routine events, such as the standard school health assessment they used, may not engage the child as much as in their experience of unique and exciting day trips. For most children drawing is a pleasurable activity because it allows them to draw the things and events that interest them. Thus, the interaction of the enjoyment experienced in drawing and a captivating event may lead to drawing being a more useful recall tool for special events than for a mundane and typical experience.

The requirement of presenting information in an event that is both interesting to the child but not easily related to children's generic and script knowledge was taken up in some recent studies that have asked children to recall video information.

(iv)   Recall of video information

In an attempt to marry the advantages of both the staged event and laboratory item-recall studies but limit the disadvantages engrained in both methodologies, Amanda Apperley, Sophia Bokhari and I used a 10-minute video on "falling," chosen from a booklet of materials that publicizes teaching aids for the National Curriculum for Primary Science in England. We took two scenes from this video to use in our study. The first scene began with two puppet cats talking to each other. One of the cats had got stuck on an upstairs window ledge, the other cat was trying to coax the cat down. The story progressed into a series of chaotic events in which a man and a woman arrived and made novel but unsuccessful attempts to get the cat to jump. The second story was an information film on sky surfing. We considered that the information contained in the two video clips met a number of criteria we sought to meet. First, both scenes communicated narrative events, and second, were novel in their own ways. Accordingly, children would have had little general knowledge or have learned scripts of the episodes. Although the children would have understood the idea of a cat getting stuck (and so this video clip would have made sense to them) the novelty elements of the scene (puppet cats, silly people involved in a series of novel accidents, etc.) would have been sufficiently different from any previous experience they may have had of getting a cat unstuck. Similarly, in respect of the second video clip, although children would have known that people can fly through the air with aerodynamic support they are unlikely to have much general knowledge about sky surfing to help them in their recall. Third, both clips were interesting and entertaining. We noticed how the children concentrated throughout the video, finding certain parts amusing, and expressed afterwards how much they enjoyed seeing it. Fourth, a video more optimally allows children to witness the same information than an event directly experienced in life, and we showed the video to small groups to further ensure this. Finally, by a thorough frame-by-frame analysis of the video we were able to draw up a comprehensive list of all information presented in the two clips, categorized by items, their colors, what had been said and all actions.

We presented the video to sixty 5- to 6-year-olds in groups of 7 to 10 children (Jolley, Apperley, & Bokhari, 2002). The following day children were interviewed for their memory of the two "stories" described above. The children were allocated to one of three groups: a draw-and-tell group, a draw-then-tell group (they were asked to recall the events after they had completed their drawing of each story to separate the cognitive demands of drawing and telling) and a tell-only group. In the initial free recall phase all children were encouraged to mention all they could remember about each story, followed by a second phase in which they were then asked two direct questions (relating to particular episodes in each story). Finally, all children were given a last opportunity to recall anything further about each story. Drawings were requested from the two draw groups in the initial free recall phase, but not in the subsequent parts of the interview. In order to keep the child talking in the draw-and-tell group the interviewer made unobtrusive comments such as "yes," "no," "really?," "tell me more?," similar to the style of questioning that had been used in the staged-event studies (see Butler et al., 1995).

Figure 8.1 displays the mean recall for the three groups by type of information (items, colors, actions, and sayings). We found that both drawing groups recalled significantly more information than

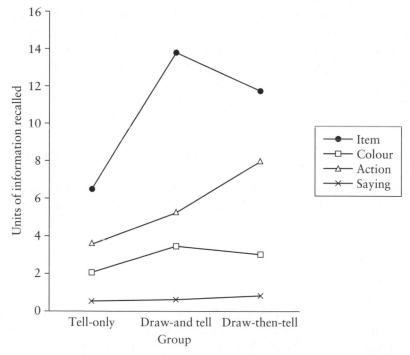

Figure 8.1   Units of information recalled by recall group reported by Jolley et al. (2002).

the tell-only group, but only for the "items" category. In addition, the draw-then-tell group recalled significantly more actions than the draw-and-tell and tell-only groups. Our findings indicated, therefore, that drawing facilitates recall of item information, and possibly actions in certain circumstances, but not colors or sayings. The drawing effect for items is consistent with Gross and Hayne's (1998) finding that drawing only facilitated children's recall for objects and descriptions. It is surprising that the colors of the items were not recalled more frequently by our draw groups as drawings communicate colors (and note that the children had access to felt-tip pens and crayons). Maybe the children considered it unnecessary to name the colors from their drawing as they were self-evident. In order to elicit this information from the child it might be necessary to directly ask them to comment on the colors of the items they have drawn. The lack of a "sayings" effect is less surprising as it is older children than those tested in our study who tend to include speech bubbles in their drawings (see Jolley et al., 2003; see also this book, chapter 2).

Anna Rowlands and Maureen Cox have also adopted the video approach in investigating drawings as a tool for event memory (Rowlands, 2003; Rowlands & Cox, 2002, 2003), and reported positive findings consistent with our own studies. They presented a video of a 2-minute theft scene, and hence represented material more closely related to the type of event memories children in eye-witness testimony might be asked to recall. In one of the studies reported by Rowlands (2003), 3- to 8-year-olds were interviewed the next day in either a draw-and-tell or tell-only group (matched on verbal and nonverbal IQ, and drawing ability) after seeing the video. Older children who drew reported significantly more accurate information than similar-aged children in the tell-only group, an effect that was also true for the younger children when their drawings, as well as their verbal transcripts, were also made available to the scorers. Furthermore, drawing did not increase the number of errors reported by the children.

Although further work is needed to test the reliability of these preliminary findings from video studies, they provide important support for the use of drawings as aids to children's recall. The effect reported by Jolley et al. (2002) was unlikely to have been obtained by children using generic or script knowledge, and Rowlands and

Cox's (2002, 2003) effect was obtained for an event pertinent to eye-witness testimony.

Drawing Inaccurate and Incomplete Reminders: A Cautionary Note

In cases where previous work has examined the errors in children's recall it has been consistently shown that drawing does not increase the incidence of misreporting compared to other groups. However, these experimental studies present interviews in ideal conditions where the interviewer does not provide misinformation. In real-life situations interviewers may ask questions that contain inaccurate or irrelevant information (due to a lack of knowledge of the event details), or even deliberately mislead the child into thinking that a fictitious event actually occurred (Gross, Hayne, & Poole, 2006). It is import-ant to establish, therefore, whether drawing misinformation protects the child from later reporting false information, or actually accen-tuates the likelihood of it being recalled. In a study relevant to this question Bruck, Melnyk, and Ceci (2000) presented children aged 3 to 6 years with a magic show. Between 2 and 4 weeks later the children participated in two "suggestive" interviews in which they were given true and false reminders. The false reminders referred to inaccurate details about an event that actually happened in the magic show. Half the children were asked to draw and recall these true and false reminders (drawing group), the other children were asked questions about the reminders without being required to draw them (question group). In a final interview held approximately 6 weeks after the magic show, children who had drawn in the previous two interviews had better recall of the true reminders than those in the question group, but they were also more likely to recall the mis-information provided by the experimenters. Gross et al. (2006) extended the drawing misinformation effect by showing that it also occurred if the misinformation referred to episodes that had never occurred in a children's visit to a police station, and that children would even invent further information themselves to these fictitious events. We know that drawings are notorious vehicles for the child's imagination, and both Bruck et al.'s and Gross et al.'s cautioned that interviewers need to be especially careful not to suggest possibilities of what occurred as any erroneous suggestions, if drawn, may well become part of the child's recollection of reality. Bruck et al. suggested that interviewers should ask children about what in their picture actually happened and what is made-up. An interesting adjunct to Bruck et al.'s study is the finding reported by Williams, Wright, and Freeman (2002) that drawing does not prevent the tendency for children to forget information from an event that had been omitted by an interviewer in a postevent discussion.

Summary of Findings

As a number of disparate methodological approaches have been adopted in this literature, some of which have reported conflicting findings, it is worth summarizing the main findings relating to the efficacy of drawings as memory aids for children's recall.

1 Drawings can have a substantial facilitatory effect on recall, with children recalling around twice as much information compared to those interviewed without being asked to draw.
2 Drawings tend to facilitate recall of events that are unique, interesting or emotional, but not for routine events or for isolated bits of information that are not part of a narrative.
3 The positive effect of drawing has been found across the age range of the 3- to 8-year-olds tested in the literature, although there is more consistent evidence of the effect in 5- to 6-year-olds.
4 Drawings can aid recall for up to a year after the event.
5 Drawings do not facilitate recall for all types of information. There is consistent evidence that they significantly improve recall for items/objects. There is only limited evidence that drawings may be helpful in cueing action memories, with as yet no supportive evidence for cueing recall for people, places, colors, sayings, and how the child felt towards the experienced event.
6 Although drawings do not increase the level of child-initiated errors in ideal interview situations where no misinformation is given by the interviewer, they do increase the reporting of misinformation where it is given.

Mechanisms of Influence

While knowing the circumstances in which drawing aids children's recall is practically important, it is theoretically interesting to know what it is about drawing that facilitates recall within these circumstances. I will now outline the various explanations cited in the literature as to why drawing might aid recall. As there has been relatively little published experimental work testing these claims, evaluations on their respective merits remain speculative.

(a)   Drawing helps structure recall of memory

Research that has investigated developmental changes in how children retell a story they have heard has shown that young children in particular are prone to reporting a story in an unstructured format (Hickman, 1985; Ilgaz & Aksu-Koç, 2005). Compared to older children, information may be missing or given at the wrong place in the story, with fewer explanatory links provided between the elements of the story. Asking a young child to draw a story or event, therefore, may help them structure the narrative in their minds which would otherwise be difficult to manage with thoughts alone (Gross & Hayne, 1998). Furthermore, as the drawing unfolds, the public record of what has been already drawn may further help the child keep the structure of the story in mind.

(b)   Representations act as memory cues

As well as drawing helping the child to structure the event, the drawing representations themselves may cue additional thoughts about the event in ways that I outlined earlier in the chapter in "the case for drawing" (see also Butler et al., 1995). Recently, Sarah Baxter and I tried to unpack the relevant influences of planning and representation in drawing on verbal recall. In addition to a tell-only group there were two further groups of children who were asked to draw a mock crime event they had seen from a video (the same video of the theft scene used in Rowlands & Cox, 2002, 2003). In an "invisible draw-and-tell" group children drew the event with an "invisible" pen that left no trace on the page. The purpose of this group was to remove any potential effects of making a representational record on recall, and consequently providing a more pure measure of the planning benefits of drawing. The other draw-and-tell group used a conventional marker. Interestingly, children in the invisible draw-and-tell group did recall more than reported in the tell-only group but not significantly so (whereas the standard draw-and-tell group recalled significantly more than reported in both of the other two groups). This study suggested, therefore, that planning alone cannot explain the beneficial effects of drawing, and that the permanent trace of the representations is an important factor in explaining the drawing effect.

It has been suggested that higher levels of representational quality of the drawings provide a better source of retrieval cues (Butler et al. 1995; Gross & Hayne, 1998, 1999). Representational quality has been assessed by raters' rankings or Golomb's Revised Compositional Scale of the drawings produced by the children of the event to be recalled (Butler et al., 1995; Gross & Hayne, 1998, 1999) or from an additional human figure drawing task, specifically the Naglieri DAP (Gross & Hayne, 1998, 1999). In almost all cases a significant positive correlation between the representational quality of the drawings and amount of verbal recall has been reported. But I am somewhat cautious about the relationship between representational quality and recall for a number of reasons. First, none of the above studies partialed out the child's age from the correlations. We know that with increasing age children recall more information and produce drawings of a higher representational quality. The reported correlations in this literature between representational quality and recall may therefore be accounted for by age differences in these two variables.[2] Second, some studies have not found a relationship between the representational quality of the event drawings and verbal recall (e.g., see Wesson & Salmon, 2001; Bruck et al., 2000). Third, my experience of the representational quality of drawings produced in my own studies is that children draw more poorly than would be expected from children of their age group. The drawing shown in Figure 8.2, made by a 6-year-old child tested in Jolley et al. (2002), is typical of the rather sketchy drawings one gets in these studies. Such drawings should not surprise us as the resources children are able to give to their drawings are being compromised by the verbal demands of recalling and responding to the interviewer. Indeed,

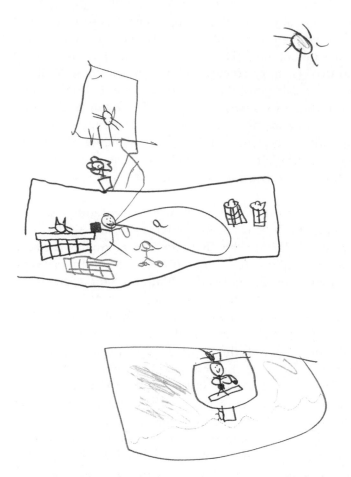

Figure 8.2   A 5-year-old's drawing of the "gravity" video reported by Jolley et al. (2002).

Gross and Hayne (1998) noted that the drawings themselves are difficult to interpret without the child's verbal recall, and that 38% of the drawings in their study were composed of shapes that could not be differentiated from each other. In any event, we know that children give more information than they actually draw (Butler et al., 1995), and so at least for some recalled information we know that it is not necessary for the child to have drawn the subject matter directly relating to that information.

(c)   Drawing removes conversational constraints

Butler et al. (1995) commented that drawing allows children to recall detailed information that would be considered too routine for normal conversation. In their example they noted that children who drew the bus they traveled on to the fire station gave elaborate details on its size, color, where the people sat, and even such level of details as the driver putting his jacket over the back seat. Children in the tell-only group tended to merely state that they arrived by bus. If you asked someone how they traveled to an event imagine how you would react if they replied with the level of detailed information given by the children who drew in Butler et al.'s study! But of course if this same person were being asked as an eye-witness to a crime that occurred on a journey then this sort of detailed information could be very important. Asking children to draw may be particularly useful in extracting detailed information that even children may know is considered inappropriate under normal conversational contexts. Children may learn that conventional conversational boundaries are broken when drawing as children are often encouraged to talk about their drawings to teachers and parents.

(d)   Drawing prolongs interview duration

Research that has measured the interview length has consistently found that the duration of interviews for children who draw are naturally longer than those interviewed without being asked to draw, and that interview duration and verbal recall are positively correlated (Butler et al., 1995; Wesson & Salmon, 2001).[3] Both these findings are unsurprising but it does suggest the drawing allows the child to keep focused on the event for longer and hence have more time to respond when drawing. As Gross and Hayne (1998) note, however, it is unclear whether this is a drawing-specific effect or would be found for any activity that keeps the child on task. There is also the related question of whether a drawing task unrelated to the memory event but given to prolong the interview would in itself have some facilitatory recall effect. This would be worth knowing as some children may be unwilling to draw a particularly traumatic experience but nevertheless report some details of the experience when asked to do some coloring, for example. If such a general drawing task does have

a positive influence it is presumably because making drawings unconnected to the experience is anxiety-reducing and non-threatening.

(e)   Drawing stimulates conversational and social support

In clinical contexts drawing is undoubtedly used on occasions to
make the child feel comfortable and to encourage a rapport with the
psychologist. But in the experimental studies it appears that the interviewers spend a considerable time with all the children tested (e.g.,
see Butler et al., 1995). Therefore, children in all interview groups
should have been at ease in the interview situation, and it seems unlikely
therefore that the act of drawing would have a significant additional
effect in this respect. But it does remind us of the importance of establishing a child-interviewer rapport, particularly in more threatening
circumstances such as clinical and judicial settings, and that drawing
is a useful means towards this goal.

Future Directions and Applications

Experimental work on typically developing children has on the whole
confirmed that children's drawings do indeed facilitate their recall
of events, and furthermore, it has specified more precisely the circumstances and types of information where the facilitatory effect is
evident. We should remember that in practical settings *any* increase
in accurate recall from asking the child to draw is beneficial, but it
is of course reassuring that much of the experimental work has reported
statistically significant improvements. The experimental research provides supportive evidence, therefore, of the application of drawing
on children's recall in clinical practice (e.g., see Burgess & Hartman,
1993; Edwards & Fornham, 1989; Kelley, 1985; Pynoos & Eth, 1986;
Rae, 1991; Sourkes, 1991). It is not clear to me to what extent, if
at all, children as eye-witnesses are asked to draw for the purpose
of stimulating their recall. Indeed, my literature search has failed
to highlight any studies reporting such practice. The criteria for
accurate recall is likely to be more rigorous in children's eye-witness
testimony than in clinical settings, so the efficacy of using drawings
as memory aids may need further research substantiation before they
can be safely used in court. Research findings that drawing does not

protect the child from reporting misinformation provided by the interviewer, but also may even increase the likelihood of it being reported, is clearly a concern for the use of drawing as a retrieval cue in legal settings, and remind us more generally of the dangers of suggestive questioning in child-interviews.

Nevertheless, the positive findings of drawing cueing accurate recall of actual event details from the experimental studies is particularly persuasive when one considers that it has been obtained by restricted conversational input from the interviewer. This input is usually limited to general non-directive content-free prompts (e.g., "Uh huh," "really?," etc.) that merely help keep the conversational flow, or general directive (but nonleading) questions that neither require experimenter knowledge of the event (e.g., "draw/tell me where you went," "how did you get there?") or refer to the child's drawing. For experimental purposes this ensures comparable interviewer input with that given to the standard interview group (where no drawings are collected), and negates the potential risk of the interviewer disclosing his or her knowledge of the event or asking leading questions. But such minimal input from the experimenter is likely to restrict the full potential of drawing on children's recall. Salmon (2001) notes that drawing tends to be a more effective cue in the recall phase of experiments when children are given non-leading prompts, compared to the free recall phase that is supplemented only by the interviewer's attempts to keep the conversational flow. As interviewer "scaffolding" appears to facilitate children's recall as they draw (see Butler et al., 1995; Lambert, 2007), the next step surely is for the interviewer to ask the children about aspects of their drawing. Such an approach may be particularly fruitful for aspects of the drawing not spontaneously commented upon by the child. Although Rowlands (2003) found positive effects of allowing judges to score recall from the drawings as well as the transcripts of the child's comments, it would be even more advantageous for the interviewer to ask the child at the time of testing aspects of the drawing not yet referred to in their recall.

In a preliminary investigation of this possibility we presented eighty 5- to 6-year-olds with video information, and then interviewed them individually the following day (Barlow, Jolley, & Hallam, submitted). One group of children were assigned to an "interactive draw-and-tell" condition where, in addition to their free recall with general conversational prompts from the interviewer, they were asked up to five direct questions about each accurate item displayed in their drawing ("what is it?," "what happened?," "what did it do?," "what color was it?," "what was said?"). We found that these children recalled significantly more than children allocated either to a tell-only group, a standard draw-and-tell group, or a cartoon strip draw-and-tell group. Also, our standard draw-and-tell group did not recall significantly more than the tell-only group, lending further support to the view that free recall alone may not be reliably sufficient in producing the drawing-cue recall effect.

The interactive interview approach may be particularly productive in cueing children to verbally recall those features of their pictures that the experimental work so far has found that children tend not to spontaneously comment upon, such as the colors, actions, and sayings relevant to the event. Furthermore, the interactive interview could include check questions about the authenticity of each aspect of the drawing in relation to that aspect in the event (see Bruck et al., 2000). For instance, the child could be asked to verify whether the colors depicted on the subject matter in their drawing reflected the actual colors in the referred subject matter in the event, and if not to state what they really were.

I mentioned in the mechanisms of influence section that one of the factors that may account for the drawing facilitatory effect on children's event recall is that the act of drawing helps children to structure their memory of the event details. If this is the case, then this could be capitalized on further by requiring children to draw the event in a series of progressive grids so that each new picture drawn shows a subsequent episode of the event. The task could be explained by encouraging the child to think about the series of pictures as being a comic strip. Although children do use a single drawing to communicate a series of episodes (e.g., see Luquet's [1927/2001] chapter on graphic narration), drawing the event in a comic strip might be easier for the child to communicate the sequential nature of the event. Furthermore, presenting the event in a comic strip format may be particularly advantageous in cueing actions and sayings because of children's familiarity with the typical portrayal of actions and sayings of characters in comics. As is the case of children reporting of color information, standard draw-and-tell groups in the literature have tended not to recall more action and sayings details compared to tell-only groups, so asking children to draw in a structured comic-style format may be necessary to elicit these types of information.

For the cartoon draw-and-tell group reported by Barlow et al. (submitted) we presented them with paper that had been divided into four sections. We first checked with them that they were familiar with cartoons, and showed them an example of a cartoon. We then asked them to initially think about how they could use the four sections like a cartoon to tell the interviewer a story about what happened in the video, and when they were ready they drew in the four sections. The interviewer used only general content-free prompts to keep the conversation flowing. We were surprised to find that the cartoon draw-and-tell group did not recall more than either the standard draw-and-tell or tell-only groups, as we had supervised a number of student projects in recent years which reliably had shown a positive facilitatory recall effect for children asked to draw in sequenced grids. We did note in our experiment that some children appeared apprehensive when asked to think about what they could put in the four sections, and so it is possible that the requirement to draw in a comic-strip structure placed a cognitive burden upon some children. Also, our example cartoon we showed children had been drawn by an adult and appeared in a national newspaper, which may have inadvertently communicated that we expected the child's drawing to be of a similar quality. We do still believe that a cartoon format is a potentially useful cue for eliciting event details in children's recall, but recommend that it is made clear to the child that they do not have to use all the grids, that the interviewer helps the child plan what they are going to include in each section based on the child's initial verbal narrative, that the interviewer provides more verbal support than merely conversational flow prompts during the drawing process, and that a simply drawn cartoon is provided as an example.

Recent work showing that individual differences in children's expressive vocabulary and temperament did not mediate the positive influence of drawing on recall (Salmon et al., 2003) suggests the practice of using drawings in interviews may be recommended for most children. The claim that those children who produce drawings of relatively high representational quality are particularly aided in their recall does suggest that drawing may be a less useful retrieval tool for children who produced poor representational drawings.

Related to this point, there is some evidence that girls tend to produce more details in their drawing (e.g., see Goodenough, 1926; Harris, 1963), so one might expect drawing an event to be particularly beneficial for recall in girls, although Hayne and her colleagues (Butler et al., 1995; Gross & Hayne, 1998) found no significant gender differences.

Finally, there is the tricky problem of drawing potentially cueing generic information due to children's drawings often displaying prototypical schema for subject matter. Our positive findings of drawing cueing recall of a novel and unusual event in a video (Jolley et al., 2002) is encouraging as it suggests that drawing can promote information specific to the event. But of course the positive effect of drawing reported elsewhere in the literature using other types of event may have been enhanced by the children's reporting of their general and script knowledge. To test this "generic" hypothesis more directly an event could be constructed based on a sequence of episodes that children have encountered before in their lives but where one version of the event is presented in a way that is inconsistent with how the event typically unfolds (with the more typical version shown to another group of children).[4] Until such research evidence is available interviewers in clinical and judicial contexts need to find ways of establishing what information provided by the child is generic and what is specific to the event.

Summary

Children's retrieval of memories is limited compared to adults. This presents a problem to interviewers of children where it is important to elicit as much accurate information from the child as possible. Although asking the child questions or using physical props in the interview often improves the child's accurate recall, both techniques can also lead to increased inaccurate recall fed by problems associated with leading questions and props cueing the child's imagination. Accordingly, research has investigated the potential benefits of drawing as an aid to recall. There are a number of reasons why asking the child to draw a previous experience may improve their verbal recall, such as drawing providing self-generated representational cues, helping the child structure their recall, and removing the conversational constraints inherent in more typical conversational contexts. Indeed, research evidence has consistently shown that asking children to draw a previously experienced event significantly enhances the amount of accurate information verbally recalled compared to a standard interview, without any accompanying increase in inaccurate recall. However, it appears there are limits and cautions to the effect. It tends to be found for event memories that are unique and interesting to the child, and then for only some types of information. The difficult issue of whether drawing in particular encourages children's use of their generic and script knowledge rather than event-specific information needs further exploration in the literature. Furthermore, if inaccurate information is given by an interviewer after the event, drawing appears to increase the likelihood of such erroneous information being recalled by the child. Nevertheless, the research evidence as it currently stands suggests that asking children to draw to aid their recall may be a useful tool for practitioners working with children in legal, clinical and educational settings.

Notes

1 In mainstream English schools, for example, the standard assessment tests (SATs) begin at 7 years of age.
2 But Rowlands and Cox (2003) did report a positive and significant correlation between judges' rankings of the representational quality of the event drawings and children's verbal recall separately for each of the four age groups they tested. Also, Harlene Hayne (personal communication, July 2, 2008) has informed me that in her work with colleagues significant correlations between verbal recall and representational quality are found within age groups. For an explanation of the statistical method of partial correlation, and its purpose, see n. 9 in chapter 4.
3 Bruck et al. (2000) kept interview time constant between children who drew in the interview and children who did not. Their finding that children who drew recalled significantly more accurate (and inaccurate) recall suggests that interview duration on its own cannot account for the positive effects of drawing on recall reported in the literature.
4 Although I am not aware of any such study using children's drawings, a potentially relevant study on children's recall of a video of a television crime investigation was published by Low and Durkin (2000). Children

either witnessed the five scenes in the order they appeared in the TV police drama and typically found in reality (crime, investigation, chase, arrest, court) or where the same scenes were jumbled up. The younger children tested (5- to 7-year-olds) were more likely to include additional (erroneous) information in the canonical version of the story than the children allocated to the jumbled version. Their findings indicate the possibility that when a familiar event is presented to children in a typical sequence they may use their script knowledge in their reporting.

9

Cultural Influences on Children's Drawings

Early work into describing age-related representational changes in children's drawings was conducted with little awareness of cultural variations in children's choice of subject matter and the forms in which they drew them. In this chapter I provide evidence from children's drawings collected around the world that such cultural variations exist, and consequently how they seriously undermine any view of a universal developmental pattern of drawing, and that standardized drawing tests are culture-free. As is the case of the drawings themselves the cultural influences on the observed differences are many and varied. I have categorized these influences as art in the culture and education, formal schooling, drawing models, environment, lifestyle, and cultural values. Caution must be applied at all times to casual interpretations of influence, however, as much of the work in this area is observational by nature, and hence our understanding of the precise cultural influence is often speculative. I close the chapter by a call to researchers to study the development of drawing within disparate drawing cultures to establish what principles of commonality and difference exist between cultures, and to investigate the developmental interaction of children's graphic inventions and borrowing from drawing models on their drawing development.

The Historical View of Cultural Universals

Much of the early scientific work on children's drawings, published around the late 19th and early 20th centuries, attempted to describe age-related changes in children's representational drawings (for further details see chapter 1). In these early developmental accounts there appears to have been little recognition of how children from different cultures draw. Even in Luquet's (1927/2001) influential book on children's drawings he did not give even one sentence to the issue of cultural variation. Such a lack of appreciation of cultural differences was more worryingly evident in Florence Goodenough's (1926) "Draw-a-Man" test which was designed as a measure of a child's intelligence.[1] The poverty of public collections of drawings made by children around the world led to an implicit assumption of a universal developmental pattern in drawing, and even as recent as 1970 DiLeo claimed that the "Draw-a-Man" test is still the best available culture-free test of intelligence.

When worldwide collections of children's drawings did become available it was apparent that there were marked differences in what children drew and how they drew them. In an early and important publication that highlighted cultural variations Paget (1932) reported findings from an enormous collection of over 60,000 children's drawings, mostly of the human figure, from around the world but particularly from children living in remote areas of Africa and Asia. In Figure 9.1 we see examples of the many variations of human figure drawings that Paget presented. For instance, Paget's collection included blocked-in figures (numbers 5–7), stick figures (14–17), and bi-triangular bodies (64, 65, and 69). These shapes are in contrast to the forms (oval, rectangular, triangle, and contoured) typically found in Western children's human figure drawing (see Figure 1.3). Paget also found drawings in which the facial features were not shown within a head contour (26, 29, and 29A). Even more different were the chain-like figures in which the features of the human figure are drawn in a list on a vertical axis (25). Genitalia and breasts were frequently found in Paget's collection (9, 10, 47, and 58). In another published collection, Fortes (1940) found that genitalia were commonly seen in drawings among the African Tallensi people. The presence of genitalia no doubt reflects the more open views (literally!) found in some

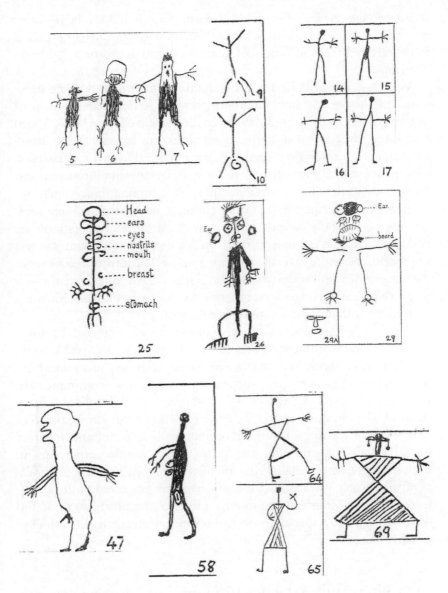

Figure 9.1 Human figure drawings from diverse cultures (from Paget, 1932). See text for references to numbers.

cultures to the display of sexual body parts, and should not be regarded as a sign of disturbance or sexual abuse as is commonly interpreted in the relatively rare instances of genitalia found in Western children's drawings.

As cross-cultural collections of children's drawings became more widely available the implicit assumption of a universal pattern of drawing development began to be challenged. As Cox (1993, 1998) states, the diversity of drawing styles shown in human figure drawings alone indicates that there is not a natural way of drawing a person and that the variety of structures represent different solutions. Furthermore, as I shall comment upon later, human figure drawings are not drawn frequently in some cultures, with other subject matter more commonly found that reflect the different interests of the children in those cultures. When we view drawings from around the world, therefore, we should not impose Western criteria in our assessment of what is drawn and how it is drawn, but instead use it as an opportunity to understand the diversity of cultural influences and symbols that impact upon children's drawings.

In the next few sections of this chapter I have categorized some of these cultural influences. As you read through each section you should bear in mind that the drawings referred to in the studies have often been collected in quite different circumstances (e.g., materials, instructions, use of adults in obtaining the drawings, etc.). Accordingly, direct comparisons are problematic. Similarly, the very nature of the variety of cultural influences that simultaneously act upon the child (e.g., art culture and education, schooling, environment, drawing experience, availability of pictorial models) often prohibits control of such variables. Consequently, any observed cultural differences in drawings may be due to a hybrid of cultural factors, and often we can only speculate on the respective strengths of influence of each factor.

Art Culture and Art Education

As one would expect there are different art education practices around the world, and these art education practices are in part a product of the predominant art values held within that culture at any given time. A notable example of contrasting art cultures is that of

Western and Chinese art. I discuss art education in Western and Chinese societies more fully in the chapter on education that follows, but here I give a broad overview of the key differences in their approaches. In Western cultures, such as in America and Britain, art education is presented as both a problem-solving activity for the child as well as a means of expression. Hence, Western children are typically asked to draw from observation of life (i.e. three-dimensional models) in which they have to invent their own graphic forms to represent a three-dimensional scene on a two-dimensional page. On other occasions they will be given more freedom about what to draw, allowing the children to utilize their own natural inclination to express their experiences of the world as well as their own "inner" world. There is a resistance in Western art education to providing the child with a graphic solution for either form of exercise, the emphasis being instead on what the child learns through the process of drawing. This approach to art education is most clearly seen in the writings of the well-known Western art educator Viktor Lowenfeld (1939, 1954; Lowenfeld & Brittain, 1987). He frequently pleaded with teachers not to let the child copy anything, whether it was a teacher's drawing or a drawing from another child. Lowenfeld's opinion, and many others involved in Western art education, derives from a belief that copying other drawings stifles the child's expression and creativity, and furthermore creates stereotyped drawings (see also Winner, 1989). An additional concern of art educators in America and Britain has been the continued undermining of the importance of art in a child's education in schools, with the increasing emphasis on the teaching of more "mainstream" subjects and skills such as numeracy and literacy (e.g., see Anning, 2002; Barnes, 2002; Fowler, 1996).

In contrast, there has been a long-standing high status given to drawing, painting and calligraphy in China (Cox, Perara & Xu, 1998; Gombrich, 1995). Gombrich (1995) says, "The Chinese were the first people who did not think of the making of pictures as a rather menial task, but who placed the painter on the same level as the inspired poet" (p. 150). Gombrich continues to note that Chinese artists were driven by a desire to paint their vision of nature that had formed in their mind through meditation, but that artists would first train themselves to paint by studying the works of renowned artists. It is perhaps this training period of studying existing pictures that accounts for the emphasis on copying in Chinese art education.

In a stimulating article by Ellen Winner (1989) she reported her observations on the teaching of drawing in Chinese schools, and confirmed that the Chinese child is required to master traditional Chinese and Western graphic techniques from copying drawings. In her visit to Nanjing, China in 1987 she gained first-hand experience of the formality in the art classes as the children obediently and with concentration learned to produce graphic schema by copying drawings either made by the teacher or from textbooks. In one class the children were taught how to draw a chicken, the teacher drawing it line by line with the children copying this graphic formula. Winner noticed a superior representational skill in the Chinese children's drawings compared to drawings typically made by Western children, commenting also upon the neatness of the Chinese children's drawings (hence the title of her paper, "How can Chinese children draw so well?"). I saw first-hand the neatness and life-like representations of a Chinese girl who drew for me when I visited Yunnan, China in the spring of 2004. On a tourist trip to the Stone Forrest of Yunnan I noticed a young girl on the trip and quickly seized the opportunity by prising a drawing pad and Chinese pencil from my traveling artist friend and gave it to this $4^1/_2$-year-old girl. The language barrier did not matter as she knew what I wanted. I was immediately struck by the care and attention that went into her very neat drawing of a bird and a rabbit (see Figure 9.2), as well as the level of control she had

Figure 9.2   A Chinese 4-year-old's drawing of a bird and a rabbit.

over the pencil and precise use of line. The slow and methodological process in which she drew was quite different from the care-free rapid drawings that I have seen many times by similar-aged British children. Furthermore, as you can see from the figure, the representational quality of the drawing is very impressive for a child so young. But are these impromptu drawings I witnessed from this little girl and those Winner observed indicative of superior Chinese children's drawings?

Cox et al. (1998) set out to experimentally compare the standard of drawings made by Chinese and British children. The samples of children were taken from British and Chinese mainstream classes, with an additional sample of Chinese children attending a special weekend art school. Cox et al. asked all the children (aged between 5 and 13 years) to draw a man and a horse both from imagination and from three-dimensional models. The imagination drawings were rated on a 5-point Likert-type scale (a very poor drawing, below average, average, above average, an excellent drawing) with no further criteria given. The drawings copied from the three-dimensional models were rated on representational realism criteria. Three raters (two British and one Chinese) rated all the drawings. Interestingly, although there were different styles of drawing between the cultures (see Cox, Perara, & Xu, 1999) there were no differences in the ratings between the drawings produced in the British and Chinese mainstream schools.[2] However, the tasks may not have provided either group of children with an advantage. The tasks may not have been typical of those normally given to Chinese children as they were not given a graphic solution to copy. Although the tasks set were examples of problem-solving drawing tasks, and therefore more akin to the drawing exercises experienced by the British children, Cox et al. noted these children may have rarely been asked in their art classes to copy objects as they see them or have received specific tuition on how to draw what they see. We need to see evidence from a greater range of tasks before we can be confident about the respective drawing skills of Chinese and Western children.

Another possible explanation for the lack of observed difference in ability as reported by Cox et al. (1989) is that the respective practices of teaching art in both cultures may not be as mutually exclusive as has been previously suggested (for example, Winner, 1989). Cox et al. (1998, 1999) observed art classes in China and in England, and noted that in both cases there was evidence of children copying from drawings, and drawing from imagination and from three-dimensional models. We require more systematic observational information on how drawing is typically taught in Chinese and Western schools. In respect of this it is relevant to note that the teaching program of art in Chinese infant schools has changed since Winner's and Cox et al.'s observations of art classes in China. During my visit to China in 2004 I interviewed an infant school teacher who explained to me in detail how drawing is now taught (since 2002) to Chinese children aged between 3 and 6 years. In the following chapter on education I discuss in full the developmental steps in this program, with drawing examples from Chinese children. Suffice to comment here that the traditional Chinese approach of predominantly copying from pictures has given way to a more eclectic approach that includes drawing from imagination and making creative drawings, as well as copying.

This discussion on British vs. Chinese children's drawings has so far focused on representational drawing, but what about their respective abilities at expressive drawing? From her observations of children drawing in China, Winner (1989) saw very little evidence that the children used drawing as an exercise for expressing their own emotional experiences, nor were they given expressive drawing exercises by the teachers. In chapter 2 I discussed a study in collaboration with Zhang Zhi in which we asked a large number of Chinese children and adults in the year 2000 to draw a happy, sad, and angry drawing. As I mentioned in that chapter I was immediately struck by the complex "scene-based" drawings of the younger children, particularly as when I had conducted the same study on British participants (Jolley et al., 2003) the British young children had tended to draw person-only drawings displaying the literal depiction of emotion. The narrative drawings of the young Chinese drawers were notable for their larger repertoire of subject matter (for example, see a Chinese 4-year-old's drawing in Plate 4) that may have been acquired in the requirement to copy a range of drawn topics from an early age in their art classes. However, I was not always convinced that the Chinese children had drawn their larger repertoire of content expressively, or even shown the literal depiction of emotion clearly. It may be that the teaching practice in Chinese schools provides the Chinese child with more content options to draw their expressive ideas, but that the Chinese child is not always particularly adept at drawing it expressively due to a lack of training in expressive drawing skills in Chinese art classes. As I noted above, however, there has been considerable shift of emphasis in art teaching practice in Chinese infant schools subsequent to our study. It would be interesting to reexamine the expressive drawing performance of young Chinese children now to see if the new teaching emphasis on imaginative and creative drawing is better reflected in their drawings compared to those I collected with Zhang Zhi in 2000.

The influence of art values on art education is not limited to geographical location as art teaching practices in one country can be derived from those that have originated in another country. In chapter 10 on the education of drawing I discuss in detail the Montessori and Steiner approaches to education. Traditionally, Steiner schools have emphasized the importance of developing the child's creativity and imagination, whereas the Montessori method has been to concentrate on teaching children practical and real-life skills. When applied to children's art activities Steiner children are encouraged to make imaginative and expressive drawings with much less focus on observational drawing from life, while Montessori children are expected to draw from the reality seen in our world rather than make-believe fantasy topics imagined within the child's inner world. Both educational philosophies have traveled further afield than the respective countries from which they originated. Rudolph Steiner set up his first school in Germany, and Childs (1991) comments that by the end of 1990 there were schools using the Steiner approach in 25 countries across the world (but a more recent estimate is 58 countries, see chapter 10). Maria Montessori, born in Italy, has schools accredited to her teaching ideas in an estimated 52 countries across 6 continents (Lillard, 1996). Interestingly, Lillard comments that Maria Montessori based her educational plan from ideas she gained from observing classes around the world, and as such is an example of how a variety of cultural practices can be combined into a coherent plan that is then translated back to children across the world.

The Effect of Schooling

We saw in the last section that a culture's art values and traditions can impact on the nature of the art education provision in schools found within that culture. Schools are in fact an environment through which many cultural art influences are seen in the children's drawing experience. I discussed above how in Chinese schools drawing models to copy from have been a central tool in the Chinese child's art tuition. But even in cultures where such copying is frowned upon, schools still provide ripe opportunities for children to observe and learn from other pictures, even though the teacher may infrequently ask their children to directly copy other pictures. Drawings made by other children, those found in art books, drawings and paintings brought in by the teacher, or even those made by the teacher, all represent drawing models that form cues and ideas for children to use in their own drawings. In this way the drawing models from a culture influence the development of children's drawing (see the next section for a further exploration of the influence of drawing models).

At a more fundamental level, schools also provide art materials resources that may otherwise be in short supply in the home. School art activities carried out regularly, therefore, allow the child to experiment and develop their own mark-making process in ways which may be difficult at home, particularly among economically poor societies. In addition to the opportunities afforded by art classes, schooling facilitates more generic cognitive developments that impact upon a child's picture making. For instance, schooling encourages children's understanding that symbols and signs stand for something else in a range of representational systems (e.g., numbers and letters). For children in remote parts of the world in which there is little evidence of symbol systems in the child's home life, schooling may provide the only real exposure to public symbol systems (Martlew & Connolly, 1996). We saw in chapter 5 that an important conceptual understanding of symbols is knowing the dual nature of symbols (that symbols are objects in themselves as well as referring to something else), and it has been suggested that such understanding may be an important milestone in children progressing from scribbling to representational drawing (Callaghan, 1999).

A rare and interesting insight into the effects of schooling on children's drawings was provided in a study of children from Papua New Guinea reported by Martlew and Connolly (1996). As there was little tradition and availability of art in the remote part of Papua New Guinea at the time the study was undertaken in 1982, this study provides a valuable opportunity for us to assess the effects of schooling on drawing development. In a large-scale study of 287 schooled and unschooled children, each child was asked to draw a person. Drawings made by children attending a school were categorized at a higher representational level than those made by the unschooled children. While all the schooled children drew conventional figures there was a much greater variety of drawings produced by the unschooled children, including scribbles and transitional forms, as well as conventional structures. The use of occlusion was only evident in the schoolchildren's drawings, which is consistent with Jahoda's (1981) claim that schooling may be particularly influential in exposing children to perspective drawings. Inventing drawing techniques related to perspective may be particularly problematic for the child without access to drawing examples and training to use those techniques. Interestingly, drawings of unschooled children who happened to live in a village that had a school tended to be of a higher representational quality than those produced by unschooled children with no school in their village. It may be that the unschooled children observed the drawings made by their schooled peers and gained indirect access to drawing models shown in the school.

Drawing Models

I noted in the last section that schooling provides pictorial models from a variety of sources, but drawing models are not restricted to those found in schools. For instance, the popular media provides further resources for graphic ideas through television, video games, and comics. In my own English collections of drawings I have seen evidence of cartoon characters, particularly from the Simpsons and Pokémon (see Plate 6 for examples).

Brent and Marjorie Wilson have done much work in a series of publications spanning over 25 years to emphasize the influential role of drawing models on the way children draw (Wilson, 1985, 1997, 2000; Wilson & Ligtvoet, 1992; Wilson & Wilson, 1977, 1981, 1984). In one of their earliest papers on this subject (Wilson & Wilson, 1977) they argued that subject matter from life provides a rather complex and infinite array of images to choose from to translate to a two-dimensional drawing. For example, consider the human figure in which there are as many exemplars as there are people, plus our numerous poses and positions, not to mention the immeasurable vantage points a viewer can take of a person. Instead of choosing from these infinite alternatives it is much easier to capitalize on an existing picture that has already made the translation from three-dimensional object to two-dimensional representation. Wilson and Wilson (1977) found that when interviewing 147 high-school children about their drawings they had previously produced and those made during the interview, almost all could be traced back to a previous existing source, such as drawings borrowed from parents, siblings, friends, popular media images, illustrations, and photographs. Furthermore, the Wilsons have shown in their subsequent body of research that drawings made by children from disparate countries such as America, Holland, Egypt, and Japan reveal differences between them that can be directly linked to the artistic models available in the particular culture the children are brought up in. Copying from other drawings may be actively discouraged in the teaching practice in some countries, most notably in the West, but children are very resourceful and they will do it anyway!

One clear example of the influence of media images on children's drawings is the manga style of drawing people found in Japanese children's drawings (Wilson, 1997, 2000). The manga comics are narrative stories told through a series of pictures presented in a framed structure typically found in comic magazines around the world. What is particularly noteworthy about the manga comics, however, is that there is a certain style in which the characters are drawn, and that they are hugely popular among Japanese children of all ages. Wilson (1997) comments that there are at least 1,700 manga publications representing one-third of all Japanese publishing, and that over 6 million copies of one particular manga comic are published every week. Furthermore, Japanese schools and even the children themselves set up manga clubs to share the comics and practice the style in their own drawings. Wilson (1997) notes that the manga style of human figure drawings often display well-defined features, such as heart-shaped faces, razor-cut hair and large "saucer-shaped" eyes (see Figure 9.3), and presents a 5-year-old's human figure drawing that clearly reflects this style (Figure 9.4). Wilson (1997, 2000) encouraged over a thousand 5- to 15-year-old children from different regions in Japan to invent their own story within pictorial frames typical of a

Figure 9.3 Manga comic drawings of the human figure showing heart-shaped faces, razor-cut hair and large saucer-shaped eyes (from Wilson, 1997).

Figure 9.4   Japanese 5-year-old's human figure drawing illustrating the manga style of heart-shaped faces, razor-cut hair and large saucer-shaped eyes (from Wilson, 1997).

comic-style, to explore to what extent manga-style drawings are adopted by Japanese children generally. From the several thousand narrative pictorial stories he collected Wilson (2000) noted that up to two-thirds of his sample showed evidence of the manga style.

The view that children obtain stylistic ideas from other pictures is opposed to Rudolph Arnheim's (1974) position, and also found in the writings of Golomb (2002, 2004), that drawing development occurs by children themselves continually inventing and adapting graphic equivalents that stand for the three-dimensional world. It is also inconsistent with Lowenfeld's plea that teachers and parents should not provide children with drawings to copy from as this, according to Lowenfeld, impairs the child's natural creativity. Wilson (1997, 2000) noted, however, that although the manga style was found commonly in his collection of Japanese children's drawings there was still much adaptation of the characters, as well as the children employing them in their own invented situations. Wilson is clearly persuaded by the benefits of the manga comics on Japanese children's drawing development, as shown evidently in the following quote: "I must express the awe I feel in the presence of children's manga-appropriating process. Because of manga models, Japanese children draw differently from children in other cultures – and far more skilfully than most" (Wilson, 2000, p. 176).

Let us remember, however, that similar claims regarding the copying of drawings have been made about Chinese children's drawings (see Winner, 1989), but experimental work did not find such claims substantiated (Cox et al., 1998, 1999). Are Japanese children's drawings really better than those produced by Western children? In a study set out to test for this possibility, Cox et al. (2001) compared human figure drawings in three different poses (no models were presented) made by 7- and 11-year-olds from the UK and Japan. The Japanese drawings were rated higher in at least two of those poses (a man standing and facing the viewer, a man running towards the right). Cox et al. noted that the drawings were not constructed differently between the two cultures (both cultures used techniques such as profile, symmetrical and angled limbs, occlusion, and foreshortening), but that the higher ratings among the Japanese drawings were due to the children's greater skill at executing these techniques. Consistent with Wilson's argument the authors attributed the Japanese children's skill to their exposure and practice of manga human figure drawings.

Whether one takes the view that the provision of drawing models produces unimaginative and stereotypical children's drawings or facilitates children's drawing development, we must recognize that children's drawings are products of both their own inventions and the ideas lifted from other drawings they see. Drawing is a problem-solving activity of depicting a three-dimensional topic onto a two-dimensional page (Freeman, 1980; Paget, 1932) and children will attempt to solve it with whatever internal and external resources are available to them.

Environment, Lifestyle and Cultural Values

Regardless of the extent to which children invent their own schemas or borrow from other sources it is accepted that children draw the topics that interest them and are important in their lives. Nevertheless, what is interesting and important varies between cultures. For instance, although the human figure has consistently been one of the most frequently drawn topics by children across the world there are cultural variations (Cox, 1993, 2000). Cox (1993) comments on Du Bois' (1944) finding that human figure drawings accounted for less that 10% of children's drawings from the former East Indies; the more common topics were plants, animals, building, and tools. Similarly, Anastasi and Foley (1936) found that African children were most likely to draw camels and Indian children cows. Furthermore, there is recent evidence that the human figure is still not a popular topic in some cultures. During the mid 1980s Court collected over 3,000 drawings of Kenyan children living in three areas (Court, 1989, 1992). Children were asked to produce four drawings including a free-choice drawing. Court (1989) noticed that houses were drawn more frequently than people in this free drawing. When asked to include a cow, person, and house in a drawing as many as 38% of the children from one area did not even include a person! Even when a person was drawn it was often not drawn in isolation but within a group of people. This is perhaps an indication of the communal lifestyle ingrained in the Kenyan culture.

Communal communities tend to be associated more frequently with cultures dependent on the cultivation of land, which if often accompanied by an emphasis on obedience and respect for elders from children (LeVine & White, 1986). In an interesting study reported by Aronsson and Andersson (1996), the authors capitalized on three samples of children that lived in cultures varying along a continuum in child-rearing ideologies and pedagogic practices. One sample was represented by Tanzanian children who were brought up in a traditional child-rearing ideology that encouraged respect and obedience to teachers. At the other end of the scale a sample of Swedish children were included to represent a typical Western society that promotes a liberal approach whereby inter-generational status is underplayed and children are seen more as individuals. Finally, a third sample was of children living in an African refugee camp in Tanzania in which the teachers had all been trained in Sweden, and therefore, can be considered an intermediate group between the ideologies of the other two groups. The authors explained how these ideologies impacted upon teaching practice, with the traditional Tanzanian children rarely moving from their seats, requiring permission to speak and then did so only softly. In contrast, the Swedish children would speak freely and loudly, while having more freedom to move around the classroom. The authors reported that this continuum of child-rearing ideologies and pedagogic practices were reflected in the children's drawings of a picture entitled, "when I am working in my classroom" that they were asked to draw (they were required to include both themselves and their teacher, and if they wished other children). Consistent with expectations the Tanzanian children receiving traditional teaching practice drew the teacher large, with much detail and central to the picture, with the children in the class depicted relatively small. In contrast, Swedish children's drawings were more child-centered as shown by a higher child-teacher size ratio, and the child drawing themselves more centrally with more detail and closer to the teacher (compared to the traditional Tanzanian drawings). Figure 9.5 shows two drawings that highlight the contrasting ways in which the Tanzanian and Swedish children drew the classroom scene. The refugee children living in Tanzania produced drawings showing features at an intermediate level between the Tanzanian and Swedish samples. The study indicates, therefore, that cultural child-rearing and teaching practice ideologies influence children's use of size-scaling, detail, placement, and distance between figures.

A further study by Karin Aronsson which complemented her earlier study reported above was her collection of Ethiopian children's drawings (Aronsson & Junge, 2000). Over 1,200 children of a mean age of 12 years were asked to draw a picture of "life where I live." Consistent with her Tanzanian children's drawings the focus of the picture was on adults, but in the case of the Ethiopian drawings it was of adults working. The drawings also showed consistent themes of recently created villages, and technological advances such as a watering taps and electricity (Court, 1989, made a similar comment in respect of Kenyan children's drawings of tables). Only 8% of the drawings were focused on child-centered recreational activities, a theme frequently found in Western children's drawings. Interestingly, Aronsson and Junge (2000) showed a child's drawing (see Figure 9.6) which although it presents a collection of children, shows them drawn in a simplified style compared to the drawing of the adult. Furthermore, the drawing portrays a context of a literacy lesson (another "work" theme). The authors interpret the picture as the "girl's pride in her community's collective efforts in fighting illiteracy" (p. 146). I could spend the rest of my life collecting English children's

Figure 9.5   Swedish and Tanzanian 10-year-old children's drawings of a picture entitled, "when I am working in my classroom" (from Aronsson & Andersson, 1996).

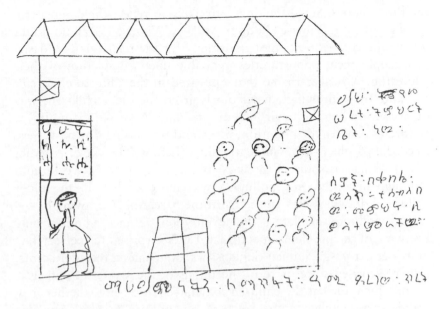

Figure 9.6 Ethiopian 10-year-old's drawing of her literacy class. The text describes efforts being made to eradicate illiteracy, and about the fact that it is "every learned person's duty to assist in the literacy campaign" (from Aronsson & Junge, 2000).

drawings and not find one eulogizing their daily lesson of the "literacy hour"!

School-related themes, however, were consistently evident in the Chinese children's expressive drawings I collected with Zhang Zhi. We asked 330 Chinese children and adults to draw a happy, sad, and angry picture (for more details of the study and its findings see my comments earlier in this chapter and also in chapter 2). A prominent theme in the drawings, which was rarely seen in the sample of British children's drawings (Jolley et al., 2003), was of school performance. For happy drawings depicting this theme, children displayed themselves in their picture with a beaming face while holding a mark sheet with a high score. For the sad drawings the child displayed sadness with a certificate showing a low score. In sad and angry pictures of this "school performance" theme the child was often being scolded by their father for getting a low mark. In Plate 7 we can see typical examples of how this theme was expressed in children's drawings across the three moods. Such drawings are likely to reflect the competitive spirit instilled in Chinese children (see also Winner, 1989), no doubt due to the competition among so many for the relatively few desirable employment opportunities available upon completion of their education. A further theme that appeared in the Chinese children's sad and angry drawings, particularly from the older children, was of a concern for the environment. In Plate 8 we see examples of children's concern for pollution, litter, and the cutting down of trees. According to the Rough Guide to China (Leffman, Lewis, & Atriyah, 2003) China has some of the most polluted cities in the world, and although a concern for pollution was more evident in the older children's drawings we can see from the 5-year-old's drawing of the factory pollution in Plate 8 that even young Chinese children may be aware of the problem. In contrast, I was surprised to see very few drawings expressing human rights issues, even among the adolescents. Either such issues are more in the minds of the Western's perspective of China, or that the children may have felt unsure whether they could express publicly in their pictures any political/freedom concerns they may have harbored.

I mentioned earlier in the chapter that I did not always feel the Chinese children's drawings were clearly expressive of the mood intended for the drawing. I wondered whether the emphasis of the Chinese art program prevalent at the time the drawings were collected on copying representations rather than making expressive pictures may have been a contributory factor. In some cultures, however, a lack of expression in children's pictures may be due to the culture's discouragement of public displays of emotion. In Japan, La Voy et al. (2001) noticed Japanese children displaying fewer emotions in their drawings compared to a comparative sample of American children, and attributed this to the relatively muted public displays of emotion in Japan compared to Western standards. La Voy et al. also noticed that Japanese children drew larger figures which the authors interpreted as indicative of the esteem to which they held their national identity. Although we need to be careful in assuming a strong link between size of drawing and self-esteem (see also my comments on clinical interpretations of size in chapter 7), it is likely that drawings can express children's feelings of national identity. In the writings of Brent Wilson that I referred to earlier in this chapter on the influence of manga comics on children's drawings (Wilson, 1997, 2000) he speculated that the manga style reflected how the Japanese as a nation see themselves or want to see themselves. For example, Wilson comments that the popular superhero "Doraemon" (an atomic-powered cat who typically solves problems cleverly on adventurous journeys) may be symbolic of the Japanese ceaseless journey in using their intellect and ingenuity to invent new technologies. I also wonder whether the disproportionately large eyes Wilson has noted in Japanese Manga and Japanese children's human figure drawings (I also noted the same style of eyes in the Japanese drawings included in La Voy et al.'s paper[3]), see Figures 9.3 and 9.4, is reflective of an increasing desire among the Japanese to have larger eyes typical found in Western people. I have seen more than one television program recently on the increasingly common surgical procedure undertaken by young Japanese adults to enlarge their eyes (see also Lewis, 1996).

Children's drawings not only reflect their culture's values but also, on occasions, depict current events of national significance. Magwaza, Killian, Petersen, and Pillay (1993) found that of the 184 pre-school black South African children who were asked to "draw a picture of something that had happened to them," 84% drew pictures with content associated with the violence that was prevalent in their country at the time the drawings were collected. Similarly, there are numerous collections of children's drawings collected during various wars that portray conflict (e.g., Geist & Carroll, 2002; Grant & Sendak, 1993; Volavkova, 1994). A recent study by Teichman (2001) showed the multiple ways in which children differentiate their human figure drawings of racial groups involved in conflict. A large sample ($N = 888$) of Israeli 4- to 15-year-olds drew "a typical Jewish man" of higher overall graphic quality than their drawing of "a typical Arab man" at all ages. They also drew the Jewish figures larger, with more complexity, more color, as well as showing the Jewish figures with less aggression and more positive attitudes, although some of these features were significantly differentiated among only certain age groups. Interestingly, the differences were least marked in children aged 7 to 9 years, which the authors interpreted as being due to the children's developing cognitive ability in being able to process information between different groups, and consequently tolerate the racial differences better. I also wonder if a desire for graphic visual realism that is typically found in this age group might have been partly responsible for muting any prejudice. Whatever mediating influence a desire for realism had on such children it appears from Teichman's findings that the early prejudicial views displayed in the youngest children's drawings resurfaced in the drawings made by children approaching and during adolescence.

When we consider the varieties of geographical and ideological variations embedded in the diverse cultures in our world it is not surprising that these are reflected in children's drawings. Whether children are brought up in a society that is individualistic or communal, child-centered or adult-orientated, focused on school achievement, proud of its national identity, or simply in the throws of a national event such as war, we see children's drawings reflecting these cultural values and concerns.

Historical Changes in Cultural Influence

We should remember that cultural influences are not static. The values and preoccupations of any given culture can change over time and this may be shown in children's drawings. Wilson and Ligtvoet (1992) found that trees drawn by Dutch children in 1986 revealed different schema than those found in a collection of Dutch children's drawings from 1937. In particular, the Dutch children in 1937 drew more detail, particularly in their depiction of the branches, leaves, and fruit. Furthermore, they noticed that the 1986 Dutch children's drawings of trees were more similar to American and Italian tree drawings made at the same time than they were to the tree drawings produced in their own country around half a century earlier. Among a number of potential explanations the authors speculate that at the earlier time point (1937) concentration and craftsmanship was encouraged by the art education specialists who taught the Dutch children. Fifty years on the authors noted a more laissez-faire approach to teaching art in the Dutch schools, and by generalist teachers not having had a professional education in art; a situation characteristic across many Western art classes in recent decades. The authors also suggested that different drawing models of trees may have been available between the two time periods, a point not necessarily independent from the different teaching practices between the periods where the drawings were collected.

Although Wilson and Ligtvoet found changes in the Dutch children's drawings I suspect that changes in children's drawings over time have been most marked in non-Western cultures. Through advances in transport and technology the world has become a place of global communication, through which cultures become transported to other lands. With the globalization of the world being more dominated by Western influences it is not surprising that researchers have found Western influences in non-Western children's drawings. Indeed, Fortes (1981) noted that Tallensi drawings have become more European in style, displaying more Western imagery and material than shown in his earlier sample (Fortes, 1940). Similarly, in a study on Aboriginal children's drawing by Cox (1998) there was evidence of Western human figure forms in their drawings together with the traditional Aboriginal "horse-shoe" shape for a person (see Figure 9.7). It is becoming increasingly difficult for researchers to gather drawings from truly isolated cultures that are not affected by images from other cultures, most notably through the increased provision of schooling and imported media and packaging. This is not a bad shift

Figure 9.7 Six-year-old Aboriginal girl's drawing showing both Western and Aboriginal human figure forms (from Cox, 1998).

in itself, as long as we do not find in years to come that a single style from one culture (e.g., Western) has dominated and overthrown traditional symbols from other cultures. If this was the case we would no longer see the marked and diverse styles of drawing found in Paget's (1932) huge collection, and consequently lose an important indicator of cultural boundaries.

Future Research

Cultural influence on children's drawings presents a difficult research area but I believe further studies would be usefully employed investigating two central issues that are as yet largely unaddressed in the literature. First, what commonalities and differences are there in the ways in which children develop their cultural symbols across the world? Second, what is the nature of the interaction between children's own graphic inventions and their borrowing ideas from the available drawing models on children's drawing development?

Considering the commonalities/differences question, some of the studies discussed in this chapter have reported different graphic structures across the world. The "horseshoe-shaped" person found in aboriginal children's drawings is one such example. An initial research question would be to establish whether within each of the cultural graphic forms and structures we see an age-related pattern in children's drawings? Or is it the case that a near-adult like version is acquired by young children with little subsequent adaptation? In cases where the drawing of cultural structural forms does develop with age are there any common principles of progression *between* cultures?

We have long since discovered that it does not make sense to argue whether a developmental phenomena is explained by nature *or* nurture. Similarly, we should be careful not to see drawing development as explained solely in terms of children's graphic inventions or borrowing from drawing models. After all, the drawing models have to be invented in the first place. Likewise, there may be few examples of radically new graphic symbols that are not in some way influenced by existing models. The really interesting question is the relative influence of invention and copying on children's drawing development and how the two interact with each other. As far back as the Wilson and Wilson (1977) paper we saw a promising line of research in which the authors interviewed children on the origin of their current and past drawings. Unfortunately, neither this or alternative approaches have been developed to provide empirical data to answer the question of how graphic inventions and borrowing from drawing models interact in children's drawing development.

Summary

In this chapter I have discussed many, but by no means exhaustive, diverse cultural influences on children's drawings. The extent and nature of the art traditions and art values within a culture, the impact these have on the child's art education not to mention the provision of art materials in schools, the availability of drawing models both inherent within the culture and imported from other cultures, and the child's environment, lifestyle and cultural/nationality values, all shape the choice and forms of subject matter found in children's drawings. Consequently, it does not make sense to conceptualize drawing development as a unitary and universal pattern, or apply drawing tests standardized in one culture to other cultures that use different drawing systems. A more appropriate and informative approach, I suggest, would be to investigate the commonalities and differences in how children's drawings develop between diverse cultures, and to understand better the interaction between the child's own graphic inventions and adoption of existing pictorial models on children's drawing development. These two issues are taken up in the final chapter, "Future Directions."

Notes

1 Goodenough (1926) does lament over a wordwide collection of children's drawings undertaken by Lamprecht that was never carried out to completion nor fully published.
2 Not surprisingly the (Chinese) children who attended weekend art classes did produce significantly superior drawings, but as a comparative British sample receiving additional art classes was not included by Cox et al. (1998), it is impossible to unpack the art education and cultural influences on these superior Chinese children's drawings.
3 Although Cox et al. (2001) also analyzed the way in which their UK and Japanese human figure drawings were constructed, their examination was not at the level of shape of facial features.

10

The Education of Drawing

This chapter first takes an historical perspective of the variety of pedagogical practices that have been used to teach drawing to Western children. I then consider the traditional Chinese approach to teaching drawing, and explain in detail the current drawing curriculum currently used in Chinese infant schools (3- to 6-year-olds) which illustrates a number of teaching methods within a highly structured developmental programme. The alternative approaches found in Steiner and Montessori schools as they relate to the teaching of drawing are described as examples of pedagogical practices that are found worldwide, and some experimental work is discussed that compares the drawings made by children attending these schools with those who are taught the National Curriculum for Art and Design in English and Welsh mainstream education. Finally, the chapter takes a more holistic approach to the child's drawing education by describing a recent large-scale survey/interview study that asked children, teachers and parents to comment on a wide range of educational issues relating to children's drawing experience.

A study of the history of educating children to draw (e.g., see Ashwin, 1975; Bell, 1963, Carline, 1968, Efland, 1990) reveals evidence of the practice dating back hundreds if not thousands of years. Prior to the turn of the 19th century, however, such education was largely restricted to academy schools set up to train students as artists, and private tuition for children within the cultivated classes. As Ashwin (1981) comments, the prevailing view at this time was that drawing was an accomplished skill, the learning of which was appropriate only for privileged children as part of their rounded and cultured education. Such children were typically taught to copy prints and drawings considered to be of artistic quality, in the hope they would attain some of the skills and insights of an artist.

A generally accepted view among art education historians is that the industrial revolution led to the teaching of drawing becoming more widespread among the child population. From the late 18th century and throughout the 19th century the need for design skills became increasingly important for the development of manufacturing activity. Consequently, children needed to be trained in drawing to support further industrial growth.[1] A further, less specific, justification noted in the literature took hold among educationalists during the 19th century, namely that a balanced education for every child should include the teaching of drawing.

If drawing was to be taught to a wider population of children it needed to establish its identity. Accordingly, art educators designed syllabi supported by a theoretical rationale. One such art educator, Heinrich Pestalozzi, had considerable impact on other European theorists during the 19th century. As Ashwin (1981) explains, in programs influenced by Pestalozzi children were initially given repetitious geometric exercises in which they learned how to produce various lines and shapes with precision. Pestalozzi believed children should be given drawing exercises of gradually increasing complexity, and not move on to the next exercise until the previous one was achieved. He advocated that young children should first draw on slate, a surface on which mistakes could be more easily rectified, and only once they had shown sufficient ability in their control of line were they allowed to draw on paper. His pedagogical practice was to break down the elements of subject matter into lines. Once the child had learned the technical skills for drawing lines then the child could start to represent subject matter from the object itself.

Although Pestalozzi's teachings can be considered an extreme version of the methods more typically adopted in European schools during the 19th century, the teaching of drawing in such schools during that time had an eye on the need for design skills for industrial innovation and manufacturing. Drawing tended to be taught by a prescribed teacher-centered approach in which the subject matter in representational drawing was reduced to linear outline. The initial stages in this teaching method involved the systematic practice of geometric exercises beginning with the straight line. The children copied lines and shapes from the teacher's drawings and from textbooks. If children did draw from a three-dimensional object it was not necessarily from concrete examples, as specially created models for the purpose of drawing exercises were used. Once children were allowed to make representational drawings, rather than mere line and shape, they were often directed towards forms of subject matter such as cubes, cones, prisms, and so on, whether copied from pictures or three-dimensional models. As Pasto (1967) comments, this geometric approach to teaching drawing found its way into American schools by the later part of the 19th century, supported by the view that design skills were needed for industry.

Much of the teaching of drawing in 19th-century schools is now perceived as being more akin to geometry than artistry. Indeed by the end of the 19th century this practice of teaching drawing began to be challenged. One of the influential challenges came from Ruskin (1857) who claimed that the real purpose of drawing is not to learn technical drawing skills but to see and appreciate nature through drawing. Accordingly, he advocated observational drawing directly from nature. A further influence came from psychologists, such as James Sully, who argued that the teaching of drawing should be geared more to what naturally interests the child rather than completing geometric exercises. During the later part of the 19th century, therefore, the teaching of drawing as the practice of learning geometric skills became less popular in favor of observational drawing geared towards a realistic rendering of subject matter from nature. Nevertheless, the teaching of drawing remained very much teacher-centered with little opportunity for the child to be imaginative or creative.

At the turn of the 20th century an important change of emphasis in the adult art world could be seen in the works of Van Gogh and Gauguin, for example, who produced works that dealt with feelings and emotions. Coupled with the later Expressionist movement during the early part of the 20th century that focused on art works conveying moods and ideas, some art educators such as Cizek (see Viola, 1936) and Lowenfeld (1939) argued that children should be encouraged in their art work to produce pictures involving imagination, creativity, and expression. The ideas of Marion Richardson in England during the early 20th century exemplified this approach in encouraging children to use their imaginations (see Richardson, 1948). She would vividly describe an event to children, asking them to engage their minds and imaginations with the details of the imagery. The children would then record their visualizations in their drawings. As a consequence of the shift in the art world towards expressive and ideas-based art, therefore, art education in Western schools during the 20th century began to encourage children's imaginative and creative drawing.

The belief that art education should encourage the child's creativity, imagination, and expression did not mean that all previous pedagogies were replaced. Drawing from nature through direct observation is still very much taught in Western schools today. For instance, in the National Curriculum for Art and Design that has been administered in schools in England and Wales since 1995, drawing from observation still represents a key component of statutory art education for children aged 5 to 14 years of age. Another technique that has been evident during the 20th century is drawing from memory whereby children are shown something and then draw it from memory alone. However, the 19th century teaching of drawing in the form of geometric exercises had virtually disappeared by the 1930s. Also, copying from other pictures is less practiced today as a formal teaching tool for fear of stifling the child's creativity and producing stereotyped drawings.

But drawing is taught very differently in non-Western countries, particularly in countries that have their own artistic styles and traditions which may in turn influence the way in which children in those countries are taught drawing. In the previous chapter on culture I commented that the traditional Chinese approach to becoming an artist is to study and copy paintings by renowned artists, and also that observations made by Winner (1989) on the teaching of drawing in Chinese schools confirmed the importance placed upon the children copying from other drawings made by the teacher and found in textbooks. Despite a considerable interest more recently in Chinese children's drawings and understanding of pictures (Cox et al., 1998, 1999; Jolley et al., 1998a, 1998b; Pariser & van den Berg, 1997, 2001; Rostan, Pariser & Gruber, 2002), there have been very few examples of further insights into how Chinese children are taught to draw. But in one notable exception relevant to the present discussion there have been doubts expressed to the extent to which copying dominates the Chinese art education in schools (see Cox et al., 1998, 1999). Furthermore, the implementation in 2002 of a new art curriculum for Chinese infant school children (3- to 6-year-olds) suggests a more eclectic range of differing techniques and practices, including copying, has now been adopted in the teaching of drawing. Potentially this represents a significant change of emphasis in Chinese art education in relation to drawing, and one that I have not yet seen commented upon in the literature. Accordingly, I present in the next section a detailed breakdown of this curriculum.

The Teaching of Drawing in Chinese Infant Schools

In China children start their formal and structured school education by 3 years of age in infant schools. It is from this age that Chinese children are taught their national curriculum, and this includes art. Furthermore, there are after-school art classes which are keenly sought after by parents on behalf of their children. At around 6 years of age children then move on to primary school. When I visited China in March 2004 I was fortunate to have the opportunity of interviewing a Chinese infant school teacher (Gao Fuzhen). She informed me that the infant school art curriculum that is taught throughout Chinese infant schools had recently changed in 2002. In response to my particular interest in drawing she provided me with very detailed knowledge of how Chinese infant school children are taught drawing within their art curriculum, and later sent me children's drawings to illustrate the various steps in the program. My Chinese academic collaborator and interpreter, Zhang Zhi, later confirmed the accuracy of these details with other teachers with whom she is in contact in Chinese infant schools.

Figure 10.1 displays examples of Chinese infant school children's drawings, collected by Gao Fuzhen, to illustrate the initial steps in the drawing curriculum. The first step of the program occurs between 2 years 5 months and 3 years where they begin by practicing drawing lines. Initially these scribbles are created by to-and-fro hand movements across the page (Figure 10.1a). Children are then taught to draw more controlled lines, such as vertical lines (Figure 10.1b). At

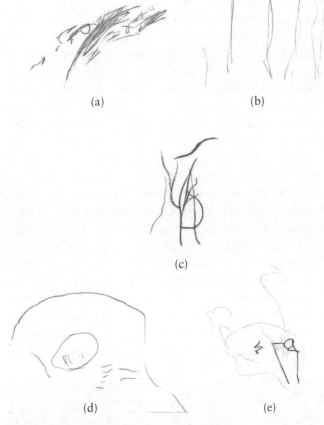

(a)

(b)

(c)

(d)

(e)

Figure 10.1   Chinese children's drawings illustrating the initial teaching of scribbling in the Chinese infant school's art curriculum.

this point they are also taught to draw enclosed forms in a circular shape (Figure 10.1c). To facilitate children's drawings of these vertical and enclosed forms examples from reality may be suggested by the teacher, such as watching raindrops fall.

In the second step children are taught further on how to draw curved lines (Figure 10.1d). Emphasis is given on how to hold the pencil and in gaining control over the mark-making process. The teaching of scribbling culminates with children being taught how to combine the different lines they have in their repertoire (as if depicting a row of beads joined by a thread). For instance, children may be asked to draw an enclosed shape with vertical lines (Figure 10.1e).

Now that children have mastered different lines and control over the marker they begin to draw representations (the third step) – see Plate 9. Initially, children are asked to draw topics from their imagination. Children's previously learned ability to coordinate enclosed forms with vertical lines encourages certain topics to be chosen, such as sweets (candy) on the end of sticks as well as flowers (Plate 9a). But this initial task of drawing from imagination is only a preliminary step to the copying of representations – a key teaching tool in Chinese art teaching. At this point the teacher draws a topic on the blackboard, for example, a bowl. The children are then asked to approach the blackboard and add to it by drawing sweets in the bowl. This activity is then followed by the children drawing the bowl and sweets on paper, copying from the illustration on the blackboard (Plate 9b). I asked Gao Fuzhen whether the children copy the teacher's drawing line by line (as stated by Winner, 1989), that is, the teacher drawing one line that is then copied by the children, followed by the teacher drawing the next line which is then copied, and so on. However, she said that children only copy the completed teacher's drawing. As well as copying the topics on paper the children at this time may also create the same images in sand with a stick. At the end of these three steps the children will be around 4 years of age.

Between 4 and 5 years of age children's drawing repertoire of topics is expanded along the same method as described above in the third step. For instance, the teacher may draw a chicken on the blackboard and the child asked to copy it. The child is then encouraged to add to their drawing by producing more chickens on the paper (a family of chickens) and then to tell a story about their picture. In Plate 9(c) Gao Fuzhen has drawn three chickens that represent the styles of chicken she would draw on the blackboard for children to copy. Here we see two graphic forms of chicken representing an adult and baby chicken (the former shows two different "postures"). In Plate 9(d) the styles of both graphic forms are shown in this child's drawing.

In the next step of the curriculum the children are encouraged to add subject matter from their imagination to their copied pictures (see Plate 10). In Plate 10(a), the child has copied the boat on the left-hand side of the page from the teacher and then added some of its decorations such as the stars, after which the child completed the rest of the drawing from her imagination.

From 5 to 6 years children's imaginative drawings are particularly emphasized. In one task children are asked to create a picture explaining where they come from. But they are discouraged from making literal interpretations (e.g., drawing their house or street). Instead, they are asked to produce pictures with symbolic and expressive meaning. For instance, in the city of Kunming where I was staying children might draw a rose which is symbolic of Kunming. In Plate 10(b), the boy announced while drawing, "I come from the flower, so my hair is covered with red pollen!" (see center of drawing). He then drew a brown mouse (far right of picture) and commented, "the mouse wants to eat the pollen, so it jumps into the flower where I was born", followed by, "then the mouse changes into a nice boy!" (see two flower drawings to left of centered boy). Other drawings children produce under these instructions will show different imaginative ways of being born. For instance, the boy who drew Plate 10(c) commented on his drawing, "I come from the stone under the sea, a small shark (showing his teeth) wants to eat me, but the dolphin plans to protect me from danger! My younger brother remains inside the stone." In addition to these imaginative drawings that do not involve any copying from the teacher, other drawing tasks will continue the aforementioned activity of children copying some subject matter from the teacher's drawing on the blackboard and then completing the picture, by adding additional subject matter of their choice from their imagination.

In the latter part of infant school the children are encouraged to make expressive pictures ($5^1/_2$ to 6 years). The teacher will take the children on an outside trip, such as along the streets or to a nearby park. The children are asked to observe the scenes around them. Once back at school they are asked to draw from their imagination something of their choice from what they saw on the trip. Consistent with the previous encouragement they received to draw imaginatively not literally, children are encouraged to draw their chosen subject matter creatively and not to produce a literal likeness. For instance, children may draw some animals in a strange way, such as an elephant with wings or eyes on a group of flowers. In Plate 10(d), the girl has drawn a picture expressing some nonliteral associations, such as herself with two heads, an unusual ginseng fruit tree depicting three ginseng fruits with faces and wings, and the sun with eyes and glasses. In Plate 10(e), although it might first appear a conventional drawing of the world under the sea, the girl has drawn the fish with different colored fins compared to those used for the fishes' bodies, and she commented that the two larger and centrally placed fish have in fact four eyes, the other two being on the other side of the fish.

Comparing the Teaching of Drawing in Chinese and Western Schools

In the Chinese infant art curriculum we see a number of techniques comparable to those that have been used in Western art education over the last 200 years or so. The Chinese children's initial training in gaining control over mark-making, particularly in respect of line and shape, has similarities to the geometric approach adopted in Western 19th century drawing education. However, unlike Western 19th century drawing education the Chinese teaching on line and shape is given to only the youngest children and is relatively short-lived. The teaching also is very much geared to providing a graphic repertoire for the children's subsequent representational drawing. The children's early representational drawings are produced by copying the teacher's drawings. Copying from other pictures was the main teaching practice pre-19th century in the West. Although it has long since fallen out of favor in Western art education due to concerns that it stifles the child's creativity and a belief that it produces stereotyped drawings, on occasions teachers in Western schools do informally draw for the child either on the blackboard or on the child's drawing. Furthermore, while copying is a more prominent teaching tool in Chinese art education it appears to be a building block to imaginative and creative drawing rather than an end-goal in itself. Chinese children are encouraged to add subject matter from their imaginations to their copied drawings. This part of the drawing requires children to draw subject matter from their memories, a teaching tool found in 20th-century Western art education. In the final steps of the Chinese infant art education children are not only asked to produce drawings from memory but to show the subject matter in inventive ways. The encouragement for the child to engage in the subject matter creatively is at least consistent with the Western art philosophy of allowing children the freedom to express themselves in their drawings, but also the details of the tasks may closely parallel the drawing activities advocated by some art educators, most notably Marion Richardson.

The Chinese infant art curriculum is interesting because, as in Western art education generally, it encourages both representational and expressive drawing. Also, as stated above, it adopts a variety of teaching techniques to children's drawing that have been used in the past, and currently, in Western art education. Where the Chinese curriculum differs is in its clearly defined drawing activities set within a very prescribed developmental structure (and also the role of copying from other drawings). Accordingly, it would be interesting to compare Chinese infant school children's drawings with their English counterparts to see what differences are observed in the drawings. In chapter 9 I discuss an experimental study reported by Cox et al. (1998, 1999) comparing the drawing ability of Chinese and British children, but this was conducted prior to the change in the Chinese curriculum. A more general point is that studies investigating the effects of different curricula found between countries on children's drawings are rare. Where studies are undertaken there is always a problem in attributing any differences in the drawings directly to the curricula. As I state in chapter 9, there are so many varying factors between cultures that any number of these may be contributing to differences between the drawings rather than just one factor, such as the art curricula. In cases where different art educational programs are practiced within the same culture, however, we can be somewhat more confident in assuming that the curriculum has contributed (albeit nonexclusively) to any observed differences in the drawings. In the next section I discuss some research comparing children's drawings collected from English schools that have widely different educational philosophies. Furthermore, these educational philosophies present some interesting predictions in relation to their respective influences on children's representational and expressive drawing.

Testing between Art Education Programs: Steiner, Montessori and the National Curriculum

In the previous chapter on cultural influences I commented briefly on the Steiner and Montessori approaches to education. Each of these have implications for how drawing is taught in their respective schools, and presents researchers with the interesting question of how children's drawing performance in these schools compares with that of children in mainstream schools who are taught according to the art curriculum set by the government.

The first Steiner school, following the ideas of Rudolph Steiner, was set up in Germany in 1919. Despite Rudolph Steiner's death in 1925 the philosophy and practices of a Steiner education continues to gain considerable support, and by June 2006 there were 921 Steiner schools found in 58 countries.[2] In Steiner schools art is integrated into all subjects resulting in a high proportion of the timetable being devoted to art or craft activities. Cox and Rowlands (2000) comment that the focus of the Steiner approach in general is to encourage the child's imagination and fantasy, and this expresses itself in the art teaching by developing the child's creative artistic ability. They go on to say that there is no observational drawing in Steiner schools, and coloring in of outlines is discouraged. However, this is only true for the ages of the children they tested in their study (around 6 years of age); observational drawing is encouraged in Steiner schools for older children.[3]

Current estimates of the number of Montessori schools suggest there are around 7,000 schools worldwide, but obtaining a definitive number is difficult as unlike Steiner schools there is little regulatory control over schools choosing to call themselves a Montessori school. In contrast to the Steiner education, Cox and Rowlands (2000) note that the traditional approach in Montessori schools has been to teach real life and practical skills. Accordingly, they state, children in Montessori schools were encouraged to copy from other pictures and make pictures from observing subject matter from life, while being discouraged from making free drawings from their imaginations. However, the traditional approach in Montessori schools has subsequently been relaxed. As Cox and Rowlands note, there has been a growing awareness in Montessori schools of the importance of allowing children to express themselves in their art.[4]

Since 1995, the art teaching in mainstream schools in England is taught according to the government's National Curriculum for Art and Design. The curriculum attempts to strike a balance between drawing from observation and encouraging children's expression and creativity. For instance at Key Stage 1 (5–7 years) the curriculum states, "pupils should be taught to represent observations, ideas and feelings" (Department for Education and Employment, 1999, p. 16), and this is developed further within Key Stage 2 (7–11 years) and 3 (11–14 years). Accordingly, the approach of encouraging observational and creative/expressive drawings adopted by English mainstream schools can be considered to lie in between the traditional approaches of Steiner and Montessori schools (Cox, 2005). However, when one reads the literature published by the Qualifications and Curriculum Authority (QCA), who regulate and monitor the National Curriculum in England, there appears to be a definite bias towards observational drawing.

Cox and Rowlands (2000) tested twenty 6- to 7-year-olds from each of the three educational systems on their drawing ability. Each child was given three tasks: a free drawing, a scene drawing and an observational drawing. In the free drawing children were encouraged to draw a picture from their own imaginations. In the scene drawing children were instructed to draw certain subject matter (the sun shining in the sky, birds flying, and a house on a hill with a garden that has trees and flowers), and to make the "best" drawing they could. In the observational drawing children were given a three-dimensional plastic model of a man running, presented in a side view, and were encouraged to draw exactly what they could see. The free and scene drawings were both rated by two independent raters on a 5-point scale in relation to how "good" they considered each drawing (very poor, below average, average, above average, excellent). The observational drawings were scored by the same raters on a 12-point scheme previously devised by Cox et al. (1998, 1999) that adhered to a realistic rendering of the model (e.g., detail, proportion, partial occlusion, etc.). Cox and Rowlands reported that the drawings produced by Steiner children were rated significantly more highly than children from Montessori and mainstream schools on all three tasks. The free and observational drawings of the Montessori and mainstream children were rated similarly, with the mainstream children scoring more highly on the scene drawing.

The overall superiority of the Steiner children is not surprising considering the greater focus on art within their education. In particular, their drawings were noted for their use of detail, color, and shading, and filling up the whole page. Consistent with the emphasis placed on fostering the child's imagination the Steiner children depicted more fantasy items in their free drawings. However, their advantage over the other children in the observational drawing task was unexpected in the light of their lack of experience of making observational drawings (and with the teaching of observational drawing in Montessori and mainstream schools).

It would be interesting to see if the Steiner advantage reported by Cox and Rowlands is replicated and extended across a wider range of ages and tasks. In particular, it would be useful to explore further the representational and expressive aspects of Steiner children's drawing ability. Cox and Rowlands' use of the words "best" and "good" to the children and raters respectively leaves a question over how the children and raters interpreted these words.[5] With this in mind I have recently conducted a study with Sarah Rose and Amy Irwin in which we presented tasks that were explicitly designed to test either the children's representational or expressive drawing ability. All children performed six drawing tasks. Three of these directly relate to representational drawing skill, that of drawing a man from a wooden mannequin, a house, and a free drawing. In these tasks children were encouraged to draw in a visually realistic style. The other three tasks, conducted in a separate session with the children, were geared towards children's expressive drawings. Specifically, children were asked to draw a happy, sad, and angry picture. The representational drawing tasks were rated according to visual realism criteria, and summated to provide an overall realism score for each child. The expressive drawings were rated on five measurements, and according to the scoring protocols developed by Jolley, Cox and Barlow (2003) discussed more fully in chapter 2. These measurements were expressive subject matter themes, use of expressive color, line, and composition, and overall quality of expression. The same two artists who developed the rating criteria for Jolley, Cox, and Barlow also rated the expressive drawings made by the Steiner, Montessori, and mainstream education children.

The sample included 135 children from Steiner, Montessori, and mainstream schools in England (six schools participated in the study, two from each educational establishment), and was made up of 45 children from each type of school, further split between fifteen 5-, 7- and 9-year-olds. Figures 10.2 and 10.3 show respectively the expressive and representational drawing scores by age of child and educational establishment. The statistical analyses of the expressive

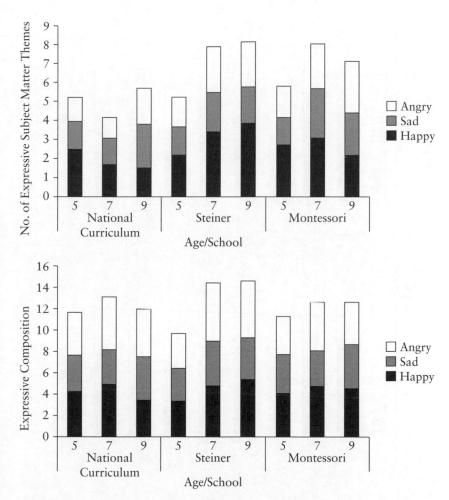

Figure 10.2 Mean expressive drawing scores of 5-, 7-, and 9-year-olds from mainstream, Montessori, and Steiner schools in England.

drawing scores revealed that where there were statistical differences between the schools they were shown at the 7- and 9-year-old age groups. The lack of significant differences in the 5-year-olds sample is unsurprising considering that the differing art education practices would have had little time to exercise their influence. In the two older age groups, however, Steiner pupils generally depicted more content themes, used formal properties more expressively and produced higher quality expressive drawings than Montessori and mainstream

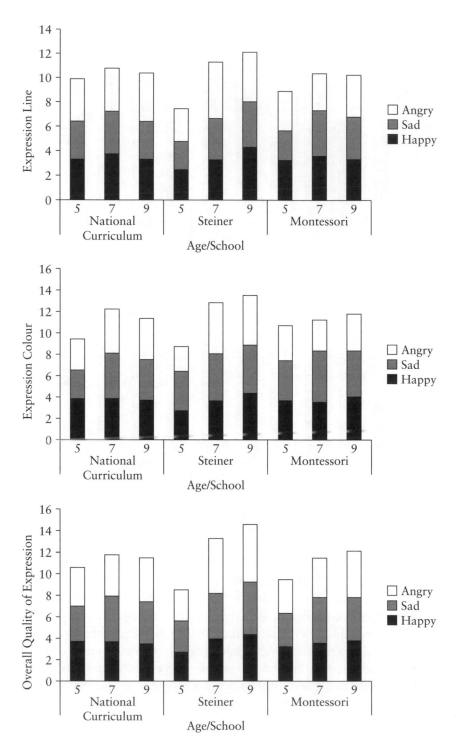

Figure 10.2 (*continued*)

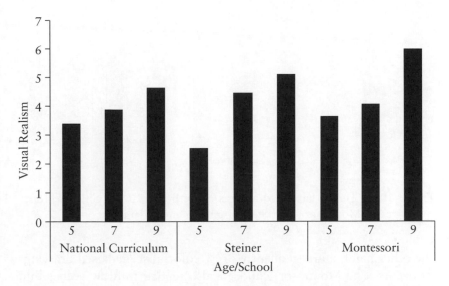

Figure 10.3 Mean representational drawing scores of 5-, 7-, and 9-year-olds from mainstream, Montessori, and Steiner schools in England.

pupils. These differences were found in drawings depicting a happy or angry mood, but were not always significant across all measures. There were no significant differences between the schools in the sad drawings. Little difference was detected in the expressive drawing ability of mainstream and Montessori pupils, although it was found that Montessori pupils depicted more themes of expressive content in drawings depicting an angry mood. With regard to children's representational realism drawing score there was little consistency in the observed differences. Although at age five Steiner pupils produced significantly poorer drawing than children from Montessori and mainstream schools, the Steiner 7-year-olds produced significantly superior drawings than those made by children from the other two schools. However, by age nine there were no differences between the three schools.

Inspecting the expressive drawings indicated to us that the drawings made by children in the Steiner and mainstream schools represent quite different approaches to the task. Consistent with the large-scale study of expressive drawings reported by Jolley et al. (2003)[6] children taught the National Curriculum tended to draw a single person depicting a literal (facial) expression. The Steiner children, on

Mainstream National   Montessori   Steiner
Curriculum

Figure 10.4   Three "happy" drawings made by 7-year-old children from mainstream, Montessori, and Steiner schools in England.

the other hand, more frequently drew colorful scene-based drawings of events. The Montessori children also tended to draw scenes, but less detailed and colorful compared to the Steiner children. The three happy drawings shown in Figure 10.4 made by 7-year-olds from the three different educational systems illustrate these differences.

Considering these findings and those reported by Cox and Rowlands (2000) it appears that Steiner children have a clear advantage in drawing expressively and imaginatively over their Montessori and National Curriculum counterparts. The data on representational drawing is less straightforward as differences are somewhat inconsistent. However, where differences do appear Steiner children's drawings are generally rated more highly. This is noteworthy, and surprising, because of the limited (or non-existent!) opportunities the Steiner children tested in these two studies would have had in observational drawing, and the relative lack of attention to drawing in a visually realistic style within the Steiner curriculum. Perhaps children generally have a natural and developing inclination to draw subject matter in some form of realistic style (cf. Luquet 1927/2001) and that this inclination develops without extensive formal educational support. In contrast, it may be that drawing expressively is more dependent upon external and expert support. In Jolley et al. (2003) we reported impressive representational drawing development in children up to 11 years of age taught in mainstream English schools (see Figure 11.1), but very slow progression in expressive drawing within the same period (see chapter 2 for further details). In Jolley et al. (2004) we commented that the teaching of expressive drawing in English primary schools may be limited due to the minimal amount of art education training received by the "generalist" teachers. In any event it appears from Steiner children's expressive drawings that a curriculum based on creativity does indeed facilitate expressive and imaginative drawing.

At the beginning of this section I argued that interpreting the effect of curricular differences on children's drawing abilities is more straightforward if the children tested come from the same culture. But even in such cases we should still be careful about not over-interpreting differences in drawing ability directly and solely to the children's school art education. As Cox (2005) comments, the superior drawings of the Steiner children in the Cox and Rowlands study may be due to a self-selecting sample. For instance, children sent to Steiner schools may have a higher proportion of parents who are artistically gifted because such parents may be persuaded to send their children to Steiner schools by the strong contribution the arts play in Steiner education. Thus, Steiner children may have benefited from a better genetic endowment towards the arts and from an artistically vibrant environment in the home.

The last point is a useful reminder that a child's art education is more holistic than the particular art curriculum they receive or how it is delivered by teachers. In the next section I consider the variety of educational influences that shape children's drawing development, including those emanating from teachers, parents, other children, and the media.

The Wider Art Education Context

There are many and varied educational influences on children's drawings and on how children experience their drawing activities. The school-based influences on drawing extend beyond art curricula, as there are a number of issues relating to the interaction of children and teachers in how the curriculum is delivered and experienced, and also the place of a child's art education within the child's wider school education. To gain a more comprehensive understanding of a child's art education, however, we should not look solely at school-based influences but take a wider perspective that incorporates influences in the home, and from the media. Children's art education is not limited to what they receive in school as many get instruction and encouragement in drawing in their home from parents and other family members. Children's drawing is also influenced by the media either directly through art programs on the television or images conveyed through comics, cartoons, and computer games. In addition, we should not overlook how children's drawing development is affected by children looking at and discussing between themselves their respective drawings.

One approach to understanding better how the variety of these educational influences shape children's drawing development is to observe, survey, and interview the three main players in the child's drawing experience, that is, teachers, parents, and of course the children themselves. While empirical studies using this approach present a wide and extensive literature on the attitudes and practices relating to art curricula (e.g., see Allison & Hausman, 1998; Danvers, 2003; Rayment, 2000) and on the training of art teachers (e.g., see Gibson, 2003; Grauer, 1998; Green & Mitchell, 1998), in a review by Rose, Jolley and Burkitt (2006) we commented that there have been only a few studies investigating wider educational issues on children's drawing experience (see Anning, 2002; Coutts & Dougall, 2005; Flannery & Watson, 1991; Potter & Eden, 2001; Richards, 2003; Rosensteil & Gardner, 1977; Thompson, 1999). Three of these papers concentrated primarily on the attitudes regarding drawing and support that parents (Anning, 2002), teachers (Anning, 2002; Coutts & Dougall, 2005) and children (Anning, 2002; Thompson, 1999) give to children drawing. The other four papers focused on how children's attitudes towards drawing may change with age (Flannery & Watson, 1991; Potter & Eden, 2001; Richards, 2003; Rosensteil & Gardner, 1977). This small literature represents an incoherent body of work due to having disparate aims and because the studies make little reference to each other. The very small samples in most of the studies also caution against being confident in generalizing the findings to the wider teacher, parent, and child populations.

Perhaps unsurprisingly considering the small literature it contains a somewhat limited set of questions, leaving some central issues relating to the holistic education of children's drawing as yet unaddressed. For instance, we have little empirical data on fundamental questions relating to children's experience of drawing, such as the amount of time they spend drawing, their level of enjoyment in drawing and perceived drawing ability, and also how these vary with age. Children have rarely been questioned about their perceptions of the help they receive with their drawing, or what further help they would like in their drawing. Similarly, we have not heard from teachers and parents regarding the help they report giving to children in their drawing, and consequently in what ways the educational support children receive at school and in the home vary. Furthermore, it would be interesting to understand what teachers and parents may perceive as barriers or difficulties they experience in the support they give. Children are likely to gain additional support from the wide variety of media resources that are available to them, but which are the most popular source of ideas? Finally, a fundamental issue which we have little empirical data on, but needs urgent attention, is the decline in drawing activity among children as they get older. This has often been commented upon by academics in the broad literature of children's drawings as occurring at around 10 to 12 years of age (Cox, 1989; Gardner, 1980; Golomb, 2002; Kellogg, 1969; Luquet, 1927/2001; Mathews, 2003; Mortensen, 1991; Thomas & Silk, 1990; Winner, 1982). However, there has been little investigation on the perception of the decline from those who have the most direct and regular contact with children's drawing activity, that of teachers, parents, and the children themselves. In particular, do they agree that a decline in the amount of drawing activity occurs, and if so, when? And what factors do they report as contributing to any decline, and what do they say should be done to address the problem (or even whether it is perceived as a problem).

In order to address these and other issues Sarah Rose, Esther Burkitt, and I have recently completed a large-scale study in which we have interviewed and surveyed teachers, parents, and children about children's drawing experience. Separate surveys for children, teachers, and parents were initially piloted and finalized, with appropriate adjustments in the questions made for the age of the child and whether the teacher taught at primary (5–11 years) or secondary (11–14 years) level. Children (5 to 14 years), and the teachers who had the main responsibility in delivering the National Curriculum for Art and Design (which includes drawing) to our sample of children, were interviewed individually with their respective surveys. The children's parents completed the parent survey in their own time. All surveys contained two types of questions, those requesting open-ended responses where the participants said/wrote their own replies, and Likert-type questions where the respondent was asked to pick from five options the one that best reflected the respondent's view. Content analysis was used to analyze the responses to the open-ended questions in order to generate themes of response. For the Likert-type questions the responses were analyzed by the percentage of responses per point on the scale, and for some questions they were analyzed further by Key Stage of the Art and Design Curriculum (Key Stage 1: 5–7 years; Key Stage 2: 7–11 years; Key Stage 3: 11–14 years). The analyzed data is made up of 270 children, 44 teachers and 146 parents,[7] with 29 participating schools from an English city. The children's sample included 30 children from each year group from year 1 (5- to 6-year-olds) to year 9 (13- to 14-year-olds).

A wide variety of issues were addressed in the surveys but for the purposes of this chapter I will focus on those where there are presently little empirical data, in effect those that I summarized above. I have categorized these under five topics, (i) children's experience of drawing, (ii) the help children receive in drawing, (iii) the extra help children report they would like, (iv) the difficulties teachers and parents report they experience in helping children to draw, (v) issues relating to the decline in children's drawing activity.

In respect of the themes generated by the content analysis of the respondents' replies to the open-ended questions please note that even in cases where the same or similar question was asked to more than one form of participant (child, teacher, parent) the titles of the themes generated between the groups of respondent may differ slightly. Although using identical themes for all three respondents in such cases would have made direct comparisons easier, we felt it more valid that the themes' labels should be generated solely to reflect the comments made by the particular group of respondents being analyzed (e.g., children) and not unduly influenced by the comments made by the other groups of respondent (e.g., teachers and parents). Each participant was credited with a theme if they made a comment that was later categorized under that theme; any additional comments relating to that same theme received no further credit (i.e. frequencies relate directly to the number of respondents citing that theme). In figures that display frequencies of respondents citing each theme by Key Stage, an analysis of the breakdown by Key Stage within an individual theme needs to bear in mind that the numbers of children participating in the survey by Key Stage were unequal (KS1 = 60; KS2 = 120; KS3 = 90). Comparing the popularity of themes cited within the same Key Stage is more straightforward. Finally, as one would expect, the older the children the more likely they would give more reasons that spread across a greater number of themes.

Children's experience of drawing

We asked children to estimate how much time they spent drawing in an average week at school and at home (see Figure 10.5). Due to concerns about the youngest children being able to estimate time, the school and home data for the Key Stage 1 children were provided by teachers and parents respectively. There was no evidence for the expected overall developmental decrease in the amount of time reported that children spent drawing. Children spent more time on drawing activities in the home than those engaged in school, signaling a positive message as children are more likely to have chosen to draw while being at home. Indeed, there were further positive data

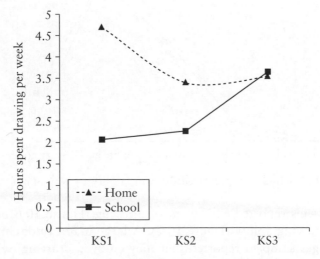

Figure 10.5   Estimated time spent drawing at home and at school by Key Stage.

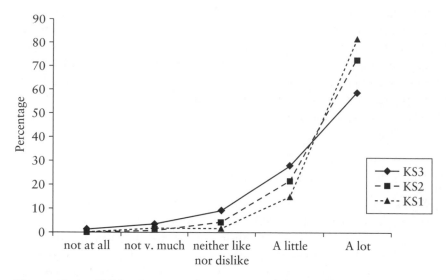

Figure 10.6   Children's reported enjoyment of drawing by Key Stage.

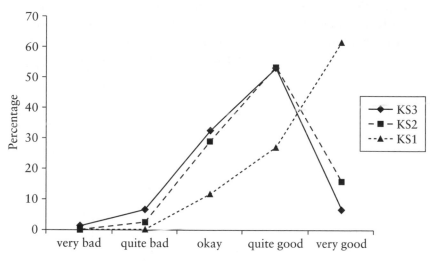

Figure 10.7   Children's perceived drawing ability by Key Stage.

on children's reported enjoyment of drawing (Figure 10.6) and perceived drawing ability (Figure 10.7). A large majority of children of
all the ages sampled reported that they enjoyed drawing, with little
evidence of a developmental decline. Although there was more reti-
cence among children in Key Stages 2 and 3 (7- to 14-year-olds) in

evaluating their drawing ability compared to Key Stage 1 children, most children of all ages considered their drawings to be good or satisfactory. This data on time spent drawing, enjoyment of drawing, and drawing self-efficacy presents a surprisingly clear and encouraging picture of children's drawing experience, and one that stands in contrast to the assumption generally held in the literature that these aspects of children drawing decline in the period approaching adolescence. Furthermore, statistically significant and positive correlations between time spent drawing at home, enjoyment and drawing self-efficacy indicated that children who spent relatively longer time drawing at home were also those children who enjoyed drawing more and were more satisfied with their drawing ability.

Help children receive in drawing

In our survey we asked children to report what help they received from teachers, parents, children, and other people with their drawing. We also asked teachers and parents what help they gave children, and also what other influences there are on children's drawings (e.g., the media). The themes children cited as help they received from teachers, and those that teachers reported as giving help to children, are shown in Figure 10.8. The most common theme in the children's responses was "Graphical and Spatial Demonstrations," and refers to children receiving guidance from a drawing shown on the board or on paper ("teachers draw something and I copy it"; "teacher demonstrates how to do things on the board, e.g., 3D shapes"; "they show me how to draw a man, not a stick man";), or where the teacher draws an outline or shape with their hand ("they show us with their fingers the shapes we need to do"). Children's second most commonly cited theme was "Verbal Suggestions" which refers to advice and tips children felt they received from teachers (e.g., "they give me ideas how to make the drawing better"; "they say what you can do when you get stuck"). In the theme "Directions," the children reported that the teacher gives specific and precise instructions on what to draw and how, with some children commenting that the teacher would also show them a drawing to facilitate their understanding of the task requirements (e.g., "teachers explain how they want things done"; "they tell me where to draw the things and how big to draw them"; "teachers tell me what colors to use"; "they show us other students'

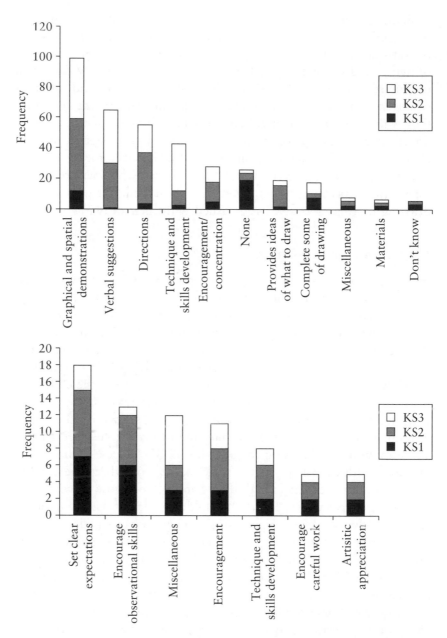

Figure 10.8   Frequency of themes relating to help children reported receiving from teachers (top), and to help teachers reporting giving children (bottom), each by Key Stage.

work, what they think it should look like"). There was an indication in these responses that children had little opportunity to negotiate with their teacher regarding the drawing task given to them. In a further theme, some children referred explicitly to teachers helping them with "Technique and Skills Development" (e.g., "they tell us about warm and cold colors"; "they point out the shadow to help us shade"; "they show me how to make the drawing look more realistic").

In respect of the teachers' responses to what help they give children to improve their drawing the most widespread theme was "Set Clear Expectations through Demonstrations and Instruction." In this theme teachers reported using both verbal instructions and demonstrations to communicate what was required in the drawing activity set by them. The teachers' comments indicated little opportunity for the child to experiment outside the boundaries of the task expectations set by the teacher ("show the children what I want and what I don't want"; "use pupils' work from previous years as examples of what is expected from the pupil"). This theme, therefore, relates closely to the children's theme of "Directions," although the teachers' references to both verbal and graphic assistance underlines children's own acknowledgement of these two forms of help ("Graphical and Spatial Demonstrations" and "Verbal Suggestions"). Teachers' comments that they "Encourage Observational Skills" ("encourage the children to look carefully and think about what they are drawing") was the second most frequently cited theme from the teacher's responses, despite very few children making any reference to this form of help. However, some teachers' reference to "Technique and Skills Development" was also reflected in some children's comments (see above), and both parties accepted there was the general provision of encouragement (teachers: "praise the children as they work"; "get the children to believe they can do the task"; "display the children's work in a positive way"; children: "teachers say our drawings are good"; "they tell me there is no such thing as can't").

The most frequent responses children gave for parental help in their drawing (see Figure 10.9) echoed those that they gave for help they received from teachers, namely "Graphical and Spatial Demonstrations" and "Verbal Suggestions." In the case of graphical and spatial demonstrations children reported that parents would make a drawing which the child would try to copy or use as a guide for their

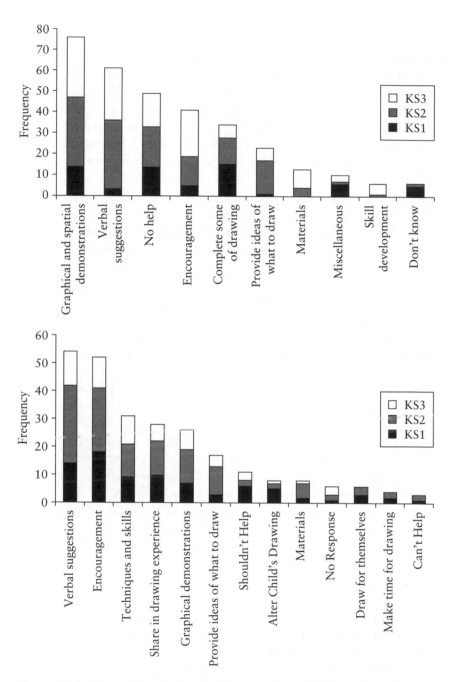

Figure 10.9 Frequency of themes relating to help children reported receiving from parents (top), and to help parents reporting giving children (bottom), each by Key Stage.

own drawing ("parent shows me how to draw things and I copy them"; "parents do it in rough to give us an idea of how we can do it"; "they show me which way to go with the pencil if I'm not sure"). Example comments for verbal suggestions were, "they sit down with me and give me ideas of how to improve my drawing", and "they help me choose which colors to use". The receiving of verbal help in children's drawing was very much confirmed by the parents in their two most popular thematic responses, "Verbal Suggestions" ("I suggest ways for the child to improve the drawing" and "Encouragement" (giving praise).

In our examination of the children's and parent's responses of graphic and verbal help we noticed that some of this help was suggestive of it occurring during a shared drawing experience, where the parent sat down with the child as the child drew. Other comments, particularly made by the parents, indicated this more directly as exemplified by the theme "Share in Drawing Activity" ("I draw with the child"; "I encourage the child to talk about their drawing," "have fun with the child"). Some parents referred directly to giving advice on "Technique and Skills" (e.g., on coloring, detail, proportion, perspective, etc.), and no doubt a proportion of these would have occurred during a shared drawing experience session.

When we reflected upon the differences in the responses between the school and home support for drawing it was apparent that children shared their drawing experience with their parents far more often than they did with their teachers. Parents are likely to have more time and opportunity to provide one-to-one contact with their child than teachers have. In a question related to this issue we asked parents how often they sat and/or talked with their child while their child drew, the responses to which are presented in Figure 10.10. An impressive 49% of parents of Key Stage 1 children (5- to 7-year-olds) reported that they did so. Although this shared drawing time decreased for parents with older children, 72% of parents nevertheless reported they shared in their child's drawing experience at least once a week with their Key Stage 3 child (11- to 14-year-olds). Furthermore, we found that an association between the more time spent by parents with their child during drawing activities with higher levels of the child's reported enjoyment of drawing and drawing self-efficacy. It is perhaps not only the direct help children receive in these shared sessions that children benefit from, but also the good feeling that comes from an adult showing enough interest in their

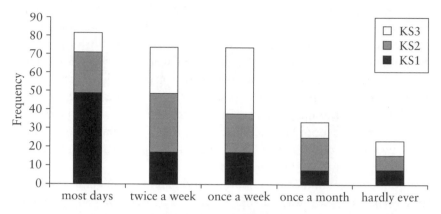

Figure 10.10   How often parents reported that they sat and/or talked with their child while their child drew, by Key Stage.

drawing work to spend time with them on a one-to-one basis. Indeed, the theme of "Encouragement" tended to be prominent in the responses of help received in the home (both from children and parents) than found in a school setting. A further difference we noticed in the educational support children received in the home compared with that at school was that parents appeared not to give firm directions in their child's drawing activities, indicating that children had more freedom in their drawing at home than at school. Even where parents gave the child a drawing to copy the child still had more freedom to use the drawing as a guide (there was no indication in the responses that children were expected to copy it exactly) than a teacher telling the child the task requirements, stipulating what they can and cannot do.

The most common response children gave as to what help they received from other children in their drawing was no help (see Figure 10.11)! Indeed a sizable number gave a similar response to what parental help they received (Figure 10.9), and perhaps surprisingly they were some children who reported they did not receive help from their teachers (Figure 10.8). The majority of children making these responses seem to be indicating that they did not *need* any help (and some appeared insulted at the suggestion!), or that their drawing was personal to themselves and that they liked doing it themselves. The particularly high frequency of such responses in relation to what help they receive from other children appears at first sight to cast doubt on some claims made in the literature on the extent to which

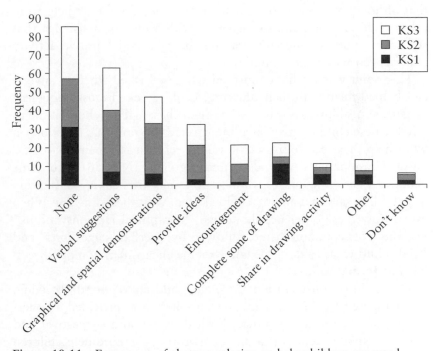

Figure 10.11   Frequency of themes relating to help children reported receiving from other children, by Key Stage of participating child.

children facilitate each other in their drawing (see Wilson & Wilson, 1977; also see "Drawing Models" in chapter 9). Nevertheless, there were a high number of responses in the themes children did cite as receiving help that suggested drawing is an activity children collaborate in. For instance, see the comments in the common themes of "Verbal Suggestions" ("they give me tips"; "they say if it needs more detail or color", "they help me get things more realistic by telling what to change"), "Graphical and Spatial Demonstrations" ("other children show me what to do and I copy it"; "they say I won't do it for you but I will show you and then you try", "if they have drawn something that I want to draw they help me draw that thing"), and "Provide Ideas" ("when we are drawing in class we use each others' ideas; "they inspire me with their drawings and gives me ideas of what I want to try"). It appears also that some children actually collaborate in the same drawing, as illustrated in the theme "Complete some of Drawing" ("they draw the line faintly and then I go over it"; "sometimes they draw for me and I color them in"). So it appears that although some children consider that they do not get help from other children, the majority report a wide range of assistance that strongly supports children's drawing being a collaborative activity experienced with other children.

This point was further confirmed when we asked whether anyone else helped them with their drawing. Children cited most frequently cousins and siblings ($N = 65$) as many of these will be children themselves (these children may have interpreted the previous question on what help they receive from children as referring to their classmates only). Grandparents were also cited regularly ($N = 58$) with some children mentioning uncles, aunts, and family friends ($N = 23$). Only five children said that an artist helped them with their drawing. When asked how these other people helped, "Graphical Demonstrations" was the most common theme, followed by "Verbal Suggestions" and "Tells child what to do" (the latter theme encapsulating more directive and formal tuition).

Taking into consideration the help children reported receiving, supplemented by the teachers' and parents' data, provided a coherent picture of verbal assistance (both directive and suggestive) and graphical/spatial demonstrations constituting the core help children receive in their drawing from other people. But there are other external influences on children drawing that are more media driven. We asked teachers and parents what other influences, apart from themselves, there were on children's drawings (see Figure 10.12). Television was the most cited response, including art programs for children as well as characters from cartoons. Similarly, computer (including playstations) and the internet were reported by teachers and parents as providing drawing inspiration for children. Books, magazines, and popular culture images were also cited, but not all the influences cited were pictorial. Parents, in particular, commented on the child's personal experiences (e.g. holidays, school visits) and general observations of their surroundings, and even internal psychological states (e.g., the child's mood, their interests).

Extra help children asked for

Considering the range of resources children have at their disposal to assist them with their drawing it perhaps was unsurprising that when asked what extra help they would like many children said they did

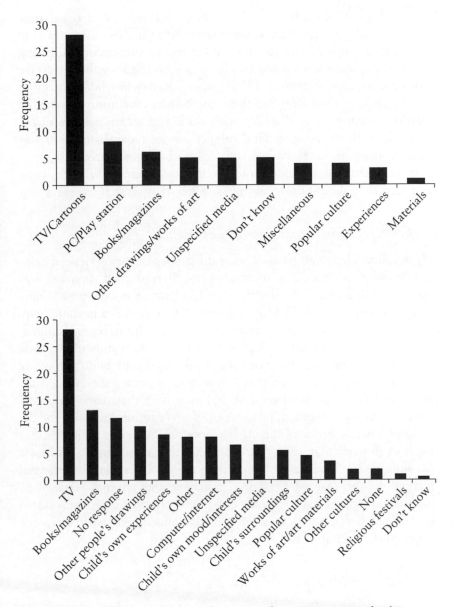

Figure 10.12 Teachers' (top) and parents' (bottom) reports of other influences (apart from themselves) there are on children's drawings.

not need any more help ($N = 73$). These children stated either they did not need any more help, were content with their own drawing performance, or preferred to have a go themselves (therefore mirroring many of the statements made by children who felt they didn't receive any help at all, see above). Of those children who did want more assistance with their drawing the most common request was having pictures to copy ($N = 37$), help with skills and techniques ($N = 29$), and help with drawing specific subject matter ($N = 28$). There was an indication in the responses that fell within these three categories that some children are not content with how their drawings appear, and that they would prefer graphic rather than verbal assistance.

Difficulties teachers and parents experience

We asked teachers and parents what difficulties they experienced helping children to draw. The most common barrier they reported was their own drawing skill (Teachers = 13; Parents = 28), which may be connected with the children's desire to receive more graphic help. For instance, some of the comments made by the parents included, "I have trouble expressing ideas on paper," "I find it difficult to draw with my child because I'm not very good," and "my child's drawing is better than mine." Some teachers and parents, therefore, may prefer not to supplement their verbal help with their own graphical illustrations, or if they do, produce ineffective representations for the children's needs. Some of the other responses, however, indicated that parents, in particular, didn't consider that they experienced problems (Parents = 83; Teachers = 8), or that the problems lay in external factors. In the case of the latter, teachers and parents referred to motivational problems within the child, unsupportive parents (as stated by the teachers), and a lack of material and time resources in the home and in school.

Decline in children's drawing activity

As I mentioned earlier in this chapter it is commonly agreed among academics who research children's drawing that the level of children's drawing activity declines around the ages of 10 to 12 years. However, such reflections tend to be anecdotal and observational, without direct supportive evidence from data. Inconsistent with the consensus, our survey study indicated that children's overall time spent on drawing does not decrease between 5 to 14 years of age, although this evidence relied upon estimates of time spent from children, teachers, and parents rather than actual recorded time. Also, academics rarely have direct contact observing children's drawing behavior outside the experiments they run on drawing. Do teachers and parents, who have day-to-day contact with children's drawing activities, believe that there is an age-related decline in children's drawing activity? In our survey we asked teachers and parents how much they agreed with the statement that the amount of time children spend drawing declines with age (apart from the drawing they are required to do in school). Figure 10.13 displays the percentage responses for each of the five response options. The majority of both teachers and parents either agreed or strongly agreed with the statement (86% and 57% respectively). The stronger belief in the decline held by teachers suggests that children may give the impression of being less interested in drawing while at school than they do at home. Also, parents have better access to the level of drawing activity that children initiate for themselves, as child-driven drawing is more likely to occur in the child's own time spent at home. Nevertheless, of those parents and teachers who agreed that there was a developmental decline in

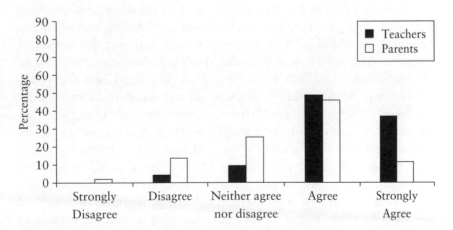

Figure 10.13 Percentage of teachers and parents who (strongly) agreed/disagreed to the statement that, "The amount of time that children generally choose to draw, outside what they are required to by their schools, declines as they get older".

drawing activity both groups gave a mean age of around 11 years of when it occurred, confirming the impression among academics.[8]

Those teachers and parents who agreed that there was a developmental decline in children's drawing activity were asked to state whether they considered that this decline mattered. Although 75% of teachers said that it did matter, only 40% of parents thought that it did. The majority of reasons given by these teachers and parents were that drawing develops creativity and imagination and is a means of self-expression and communication. Another common response made by teachers and parents was that a decline in drawing activity may result in losing a skill and having less confidence in drawing, and that children then will lose a way in which they can gain a sense of personal achievement. But other teachers and parents who also believed that a decline in children's drawing activity occurred stated that it does not matter (teachers: 21%; parents: 29%). Of the reasons given, the most popular was that it was up to the personal choice of the child whether he or she wanted to continue drawing, and that not all children enjoy drawing. Others took a philosophical view that it was a natural part of development to draw less, or that it did not matter as long as they develop other interests to express themselves.

We also wanted to know what children thought about a decline in drawing activity as children get older. When we asked them whether they thought it was a good or bad thing 43% said it was bad, with 45% saying it was neither good or bad. The overwhelming response the children gave for why it was bad was for a loss of drawing skill, which was considered both a shame at the level of the individual child and for society ("all the things that they have learned will be forgotten"; "wasted all the effort of learning how to draw"; "we need more artists"). Some also felt that by giving up drawing it would have negative implications on future career options, or that simply children would lose a means of enjoyment. In contrast to the teachers' and parents' responses, very few children commented on a loss of creativity, imagination, and self-expression. But of those children who stated that it was neither good or bad for children to draw less as they get older, many were in agreement with the reasons given by those teachers and parents who also felt that the decline did not matter, namely that it was down to the personal choice of the child, or that it was natural to draw less as you got older ("it is part of growing up"; "sometimes you think that drawing is really good but sometimes they might think it is a bit babyish").

An important issue that our survey study addressed was what factors our participants considered accounted for a decline in drawing activity in older children. When we asked children, teachers, and parents to give reasons for the decline (but only to parents and teachers who had agreed that there was a decline) each group reported a similar pattern of responses (see Figure 10.14). One common response from all three groups was "Interests and Relationships Diversify" where children develop hobbies and pastimes (social or solitary) to fill their free time ("they would rather do other things"; "busy social life"; "children go out more as they get older"; "express themselves in other ways"). A similar but subtly different response was that children become "Too Busy." In addition to generic comments about having less time to draw when one gets older, responses

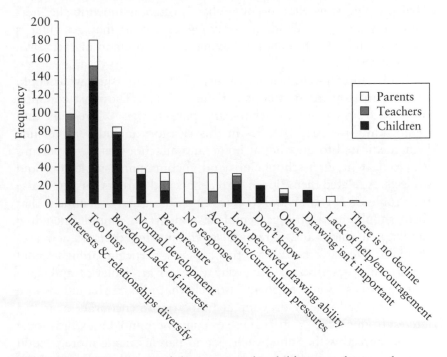

Figure 10.14 Frequency of themes given by children, teachers, and parents for why children's drawing activity may decline as children get older.

in this theme referred to jobs and chores that the child would have to do when he or she got older ("they have more homework"; "have to go to work" "might have to look after children"; "increased responsibility"). Teachers and parents in particular commented on the pressure from other subjects in the academic curriculum ("less drawing opportunity at high school"; "pressure from other subjects"; "pressure on passing exams"). Some children, teachers, and parents referred to peer pressure in the sense that older children might think that drawing is a childish or immature activity, and not considered "cool." A similar theme reported by the children in particular was "Normal Development" ("they think they have grown out of it"; "they watch grown-ups and see that they don't draw"). A high number of children felt that children may lose interest in drawing as they get older, or become bored, tired, and lack patience with drawing. But there were unexpectedly low numbers of children and teachers (and hardly any parents) who referred to "Low Perceived Drawing Ability," suggesting that, despite what is often assumed in the literature, any decline in children's drawing activity as they get older is not principally due to children having a poor opinion of their own drawing ability.

Finally, all children, teachers and parents were asked what could be done to stop the decline (see Figure 10.15). The most common response from children, teachers, and parents was "More Time and Opportunity for Art." Replies in this category included more time being dedicated to drawing at home and at school, more opportunities to draw in after-school clubs and in community workshops and projects. A related theme given by teachers and parents was to "Raise the Profile of Art in Schools." As well as the general comment that there should be a stronger emphasis on art in school (including funding), teachers and parents also commented that art activities should be integrated more into other subjects, particular at high school (11 to 16 years of age), have day trips to art galleries and have visiting artists. Some teachers also felt that children could receive more support for their drawing at home (more encouragement and interest from parents, restricted use of computers and TV), which some parents agreed with. Some teachers and parents made more general comments that children should be encouraged and confidence built in their drawing, a theme that was particularly strong in the children's responses which also included wanting more ideas of what to

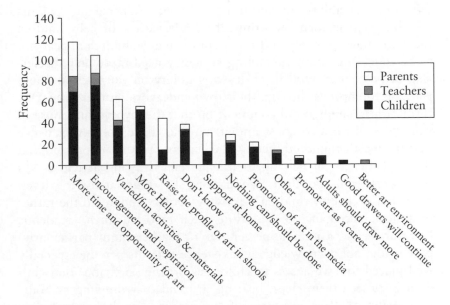

Figure 10.15 Frequency of themes given by children, teachers, and parents for what could be done to help stop the decline in children's drawing activity.

draw to inspire them (also acknowledged by some of the teachers). Some parents felt there was not enough emphasis placed upon making sure children had fun in their drawing activities. Similarly, within the same theme, many children remarked that their school art lessons should include more varied drawing activities that are exciting and fun to participate in. A number of children responded to the question by simply saying "More help" but did not, or were unable to, articulate more precisely what form this should take.

Summary of Survey Study

The large-scale survey study that Sarah Rose, Esther Burkitt, and I recently worked on provides a useful, pioneering, and potentially ground-breaking view of the child's holistic education of drawing. It presents a surprisingly positive picture of children's experience of drawing, particularly in the time spent on, and enjoyment of, drawing activities, as well as the encouraging attitude children have of their own drawing ability. In addition, children, teachers, and parents are consistent in their reporting of a wide variety of help children receive in their drawing, and furthermore, many children appear not to be clamoring and complaining that they need more help, preferring to be content with their drawing ability on the one hand and wanting to improve through their own endeavors on the other. One form of help children did comment on that they would like more of was more pictures to copy, and it may not have been coincidence that the most common difficulty teachers and parents expressed that they experienced in helping their children's drawing activities was their perceived lack of their own drawing skill. Our data on the developmental decline of children's drawing activity countered the rather pessimistic acceptance of a decline often reported in the academic literature. First, a notable percentage of teachers and (particularly) parents did not acknowledge its existence. Parents may be especially well placed to have access to children's drawing activities that children instigated themselves, bearing in mind that drawing at home is probably the best indicator of the extent to which children are interested in the activity. However, a worrying aspect of the "decline" data was the sizable minority of children, parents, and (perhaps most disappointingly) teachers who considered that any developmental decline in drawing activity was of little concern. Nevertheless, a wide range of useful and thoughtful points for actions were raised by all three groups regarding how to address the decline. These should provide a basis for those involved either in art education policy and its delivery to consider how to develop strategies further to encourage and inspire children in their drawing.

Future Directions

Throughout my discussions of historical perspectives on the teaching of drawing, the traditional approaches used in Western and Chinese art education, and pedagogies derived from the ideologies of Steiner and Montessori, we have seen a wide range of techniques and practices for teaching children how to draw. The Chinese infant school art curriculum is an example of how many of these can be incorporated into one program. But how do art education curriculum designers know which pedagogical practices to include in their programs, and how to integrate them into a cohesive framework? Without evidence-based research that tests the respective merits of different teaching methods, curricula are likely to be designed on ideology alone. It is not that ideology is in itself bad, far from it, but left unchecked by research evidence two problems accrue. First, many children may be disserviced by inappropriate or ineffective programs. Second, our knowledge of what works best and what does not will continue to stagnate, in effect the discipline of art education will continue to be dominated by ideas with insufficient evidence of which ones are good and which ones are of less worth. This is an issue I take up in the final chapter.

The teaching of drawing (and art education in general) for most children in mainstream education is presented as an activity subordinate to other subjects that are considered more "academic" and therefore more important. Whatever the rights or wrongs of this message, it undermines the many benefits that accrue to children by engaging in art-making activities. One of the questions Sarah Rose, Ester Burkitt, and I asked children, teachers, and parents in our survey study was to tell us what they considered to be the benefits of drawing. We were given a wide range of answers including developing children's analytical and problem solving skills, their observational and visualization skills, their creativity and imagination, and a means of expressing their ideas and emotions. Other more general benefits of drawing were mentioned too, such as improving hand-eye coordination, fine motor skills, improving concentration and patience, and of course building confidence and a sense of achievement and self-worth. While all of these appeal to our common sense, we need research evidence to support that drawing does actually provide these benefits. As I will argue in the final chapter, such evidence would be an invaluable weapon for the many who exhaustively champion the need for drawing and art more generally in the child's education.

As I have argued in this chapter, however, children's drawing education is not limited to a particular art curriculum or even other drawing activities they may engage in within a school context. The sources and resources of children's drawing education go far wider and deeper, and include what they receive in their home, from other children, the media, and wider culture. The account of our survey's findings gives testament to that, but there are at least four areas in which I feel our survey work could be extended. First, we need observational studies to examine the extent to which our participants' self-report responses are actually reflected in reality. There is always a risk in interview and self-report measures that some of the answers given may represent a more positive picture than is found in reality, particularly if the participants feel they need to give an answer that is expected by the interviewer. Video and tape-recordings of drawing-based class activities would establish whether the attitudes and practices expressed by the children and teachers in our survey are apparent in actual art classes. Similarly, children and parents completing "drawing diaries" would confirm the drawing activities engaged in the home. Second, longitudinal studies could examine the casual influence of many variables involved in children's drawing education. Third, it would be useful to extend the survey and observational work to those children engaged in non-compulsory school-based art-education, such as in Key Stage 4 in England (14- to 16-year-olds). This would enable us to see the extent to which there are similar or different issues at the end of children's mainstream school art education where children choose to continue art for a qualification. Finally, it would be interesting to extend the survey study to other educational practices, most notable within the Steiner and Montessori approaches, to examine how attitudes and practices differ in the diverse curricula found in privately funded education.

Summary

A study of the history of art education reveals a number of different pedagogical practices of the teaching of drawing, including the drawing of line and shape, copying representational pictures, observational drawing directly from nature or from memory, as well as techniques to encourage creative and expressive drawing. The current drawing program used in Chinese infant schools is one example of how some of these practices have been integrated into a detailed and prescribed curriculum. However, there are many other programs, some of which derive from a more global perspective of teaching ideology, such as found in the Steiner and Montessori approaches. Testing between these programs by comparing the drawings produced by children attending these schools provides a useful insight into the effects of different curricula and pedagogical practices on the children's artistic skills, but generally there is a paucity of experimental studies testing between different curricula and programs. We should remember, however, that children's drawing education is holistic, deriving from many external resources, such as from teachers, parents, other children and the media; all of which shape children's drawing development.

Notes

1   But see Romans (2004) for a dissenting voice to the view that publicly funded art tuition in Britain was driven by economic reasons.

2   Data obtained from the website http://waldorfschule.info/upload/pdf/ schulliste.pdf, accessed June 30, 2006. Steiner schools are also known as Waldorf schools.

3   A colleague of mine, Sarah Rose, who has received a Steiner education up to the age of 16 in three different countries, says that observational drawing is taught for children by the age of 12 years in Steiner schools.

4   This was confirmed when Sarah Rose spoke recently to a Montessori teacher who said that using drawing as a means by which children express their feelings is considered appropriate, as long as it does not include fantasy.

5   I made a similar point when discussing the ambiguous instruction of choosing the "best" picture in studies that have compared children's comprehension and production of pictures (see chapter 4).

6   See chapter 2 for more details.

7   This represented a 54% response rate from the parents which is considered very acceptable in the general survey literature.

8   There was a considerable range in estimates given by teachers and parents, with the standard deviation being between 2 and 3 years respectively.

11

Future Directions

At the turn of the 20th century scientific work was first undertaken on children's representational drawing. Since then we have developed a considerable body of evidence that confirms the existence of a broad developmental path. In this path initial scribbling precedes the representation of subject matter in graphic forms that increasingly reflect a visual likeness to their referents (see chapter 1). In more recent times, however, there has been a backlash by some researchers against the view, originally grounded in the historic work, that there is a single universal developmental pattern in children's drawings. For instance, Golomb (2002) argues strongly that there is evidence of multiple paths in case studies from disordered and artistically gifted populations. Furthermore, the variations in cultural graphic forms found in children's drawings collected from around the world caution against the assumption that a universal pattern exists (see chapter 9).

Nevertheless, I believe there is stronger evidence for commonality in the broad developmental pattern of children's representational drawing than for diversity. It is sometimes easier to see the exceptions that vary from the norm than the norm itself. Even where there are differences they may not be as widespread or as significant as they first appear. In respect of the developmentally delayed, their drawings tend to follow the normative path albeit at a slower rate (see chapter 3). In the case of cultural variations, Paget's (1932) enormous collection of children's drawings from non-European races needs an up-to-date replication to establish whether the wide range of graphic forms he reported are still as prominent today. On the basis of the available evidence that we do have (see chapter 9) the current influences peculiar to a culture appear largely to impact upon the style, skill, and subject matter of the drawings, rather than illustrating a diverse range of structural forms. I suspect the immigration of Western images that has taken place since Paget's (1932) study has reduced the frequency and variety of structural forms found in children's drawings around the world.

Where we do find evidence of distinct cultural graphic forms it would be interesting to examine whether they change developmentally and if so, whether there are common principles of progression across cultures. In other words, do children's early representations, whatever cultural form they take, later become differentiated and unpacked, with the inclusion of more detail and drawn in a style that increasingly resembles a visual likeness to the graphic model that is considered exemplary within that culture? The state of the research evidence at present has done well to describe the differences in children's drawings across cultures, and at times even provided explanations for these differences. But we lack a cross-cultural approach investigating the commonalities and differences in the development of drawings produced by children from diverse cultures. The question of any apparent universal principles of development, rather than of universal patterns of development, has yet to be adequately addressed in the literature.

Compared to the wealth of studies on children's representational drawing, and its cultural diversity, relatively scant research attention has been given to the expression in children's drawings and its development. Consequently, its developmental path is less well understood, and further hampered by the lack of objective and universally agreed criteria from which to judge an expressive drawing. But whether one favors the U-shape curve with its dipped performance in middle childhood, or the incremental (albeit sometimes slow) progression reported by the consensus in this small literature (see chapter 2), the consistent message from both claims is that the development of children's expressive/esthetic drawing is not as impressive as their representational drawing development. In the only study of which I am aware that has tested both representational and expressive drawing ability in the same sample of children Jolley et al. (2003) found disparate paths for the two skills. We presented three expressive drawing tasks and three representational drawing tasks to 11 groups of participants ranging from 4-year-olds to adult artists (see chapter 2 for more details of the study). Compared with the pronounced developmental progression of children's representational drawing from 4 to 11 years (see Figure 11.1) there was a very slow progression in their expressive drawing in this age range (see Figure 2.9).

Nevertheless, we should not allow such disparate developmental progressions to lead us to consider representational and expressive drawing independently from each other. Importantly, in the study described above we found a statistically significant and positive correlation between the two skills, suggesting a need for research to explore further how representational and expressive drawing skills interact with each other during children's drawing development.

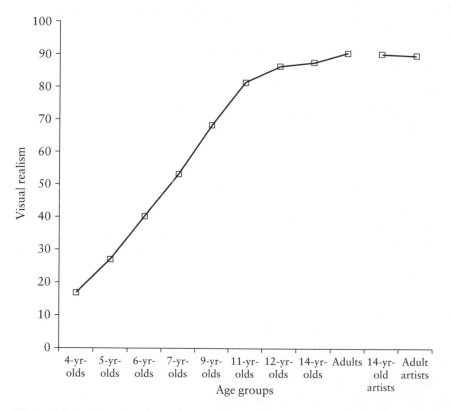

Figure 11.1   Visual realism drawing ability by age reported by Jolley et al. (2003).

A starting point would be to collect longitudinal data to confirm the developmental paths of the two skills, and then apply a detailed analysis of periods in which there is marked growth in one skill and examine what changes if any are observed in the other skill. This approach is similar to that adopted in microgenetic studies where there is a focus on developmental changes occurring rapidly over a short period of time (see Kuhn, 1995). It may well turn out that there is much individual variability among children, with no common pattern as to how representational and expressive skills interact with each other. But the significant and positive correlation between the two skills referred to above suggests that marked shifts in one skill may actually facilitate the other skill, rather than the U-shape curve proponents who argue that schoolchildren's attempts at making their drawings visually accurate are detrimental to their expressive drawing (Davis, 1997a; Gardner, 1980; Rosenblatt & Winner, 1988).

The nature of any interaction between representational and expressive drawing potentially has educational implications for how we should integrate the teaching of both skills in the art curriculum. The detailed and prescriptive drawing curriculum used in Chinese infant schools (see chapter 10) is an interesting attempt to integrate these and other skills, but research could contribute more to this issue to assist in the designing of art curricula (see also my comments below). From a theoretical perspective there needs to be more attention given to incorporating children's expressive drawing as well as representational drawing in accounts of children's drawing development. In any event it is certainly clear that continuation of the prevailing focus on representational drawing to the neglect of studying the expressive aspects of the drawings will not produce anything more than half the story of children's drawing development.

There is another danger to getting an incomplete understanding of children's drawings. This relates to how children's drawings are typically studied. Much of the psychological research into children's drawings has collected the drawings under experimental conditions in which the finished drawing products (and occasionally the drawing process) are analyzed by researchers who may not even have been present when the children drew them. There are at least two concerns with this methodological approach. First, we cannot assume that what children draw in our experiments adequately reflects what they draw for themselves (see also Goodnow et al., 1986). Second, by examining the drawings "cold" without knowing the context of the child's perspective on his or her drawing, we can lose the artist's meaning from the drawing. This is further compounded when researchers are unfamiliar with the culturally determined symbolic meaning of the subject matter depicted in the drawings. This concern was poignantly driven home to me when I recently visited China to collect nearly 1,000 "expressive" drawings made by Chinese participants ranging in age from 4 years old to adults (see chapters 2 and 9 for more details of this study). My initial intention to give only a cursory look through the drawings before bringing them home was soon rejected as I struggled to understand the meaning of many of them. My understanding, however, was greatly enhanced by my Chinese collaborator (Zhang Zhi), who had collected the drawings, as she explained to me what each child had said while making the drawing and, where appropriate, the symbolic meaning of the subject matter that was ingrained in the Chinese culture.

In the introduction to his translation of Luquet's classic 1927 book, Costall (2001) voices Luquet's reservations about drawing experiments. Luquet stands among the few who have made a persistent and concerted effort to directly observe children making their own drawings (see also Matthews, 1999, 2003). For instance, Luquet's earlier publication of his PhD thesis (Luquet, 1913) contains 1,687 drawings made by his daughter Simonne, that are precisely dated and often accompanied by carefully observed information about the context of what she was doing and saying at the time (Costall, 2001). By extending the principles of this approach to a wider set of children Luquet (1927/2001) was subsequently able to gather not only a rich understanding of the developmental changes occurring in children's drawings, but also of the psychological processes that underpinned those changes. Today, there is a pressing need for researchers of children's drawings to spend more time with their child participants while they draw, and gently to probe the child about his or her drawing to establish the context and motivation that has driven it. Those researchers who dedicate themselves to direct observation of children's spontaneous drawings, and who investigate their contexts, may provide us with a new theoretical framework for understanding children's drawing development in the 21st century. For too long now such an approach has been neglected, and our understanding of children's drawing has consequently not developed as it might have done.

Let me not be misunderstood here. Experiments in drawing research will always have a key role to play in our quest for understanding children's drawings. If we have a specific hypothesis to test we could wait an inordinate amount of time observing children in their spontaneous drawings before one child addresses our research question! We will always need to design drawing tasks for children in order to get the relevant drawing responses for our questions. Indeed, there are instances where we need more experimentation, not less. A clear case for this is the need for more evidence based research on the most effective ways to teach drawing in schools. I mentioned above how research into the developing relationship between representational and expressive drawing could help inform the drawing component in the designing of art curricula. Furthermore, in discussing the education of drawing in chapter 10, I outlined a number of different methods for teaching drawing that have been used since drawing began to be taught to the populace of children. These include precisely regimented copying of the linear outlines of abstract forms, geometric shapes, and representational figures; observational drawing directly from concrete examples or from memory; and the many varied practices of encouraging imaginative and expressive drawing. No doubt each of these pedagogical approaches enables the child to learn drawing skills specific to that approach. But how should these approaches, and others, be integrated into a holistic drawing program? Which skills should be emphasized more? How should a program be developmentally structured, with consideration given to the optimum ages at which certain skills are to be taught?

Unless research adequately addresses these and related questions the practice of teaching art and drawing will be subject to unproven ideology and subjective opinion, or worse, fail to arrest the all too common practice that is found in (at least) American and English schools of providing very little actual teaching of drawing (and indeed art). Psychologists, art educators, and artists can usefully work together towards this goal, a partnership that I believe is insufficiently developed at present but one that could potentially deliver a quality research-based discipline in drawing/art education. Such interdisciplinary work would provide a stronger claim for art education, particularly at a time when art education is being undermined by a number of sources. These include pressures to teach other subjects in the curriculum (e.g., numeracy and literacy), a lack of monetary resources for teaching art, and a perception that there is over-interference in some countries, such as in England and Wales, by government bodies in the designing and implementation of the curriculum. The status of art in our schools would be strengthened if research could help to dispel the myth that the purpose of art is not much more than a relaxing play-time activity for the children (not to mention the teachers!); a "filler" activity squeezed between the teaching of "proper" academic subjects.

With this aim in mind, some advocates of the arts have adopted a strategy of arguing that engagement in the arts has a positive transfer effect on general academic achievement. Indeed, correlational studies have consistently shown that there is a link between children's participation in arts programs and their higher scores in academic tests, such as those measuring verbal and mathematical ability. But do such programs *cause* more general cognitive rewards and academic achievements? A large research team led by Ellen Winner as the principal investigator, conducted a series of meta-analysis studies to address this very question in the Reviewing Education and the Arts Project (REAP). They examined the relevant research dating from 1950 to 1998, and came to the potentially damning conclusion that there was as yet no evidence that children's participation in the arts actually enhances academic achievement (see Hetland & Winner, 2004; Vaughn & Winner, 2000; Winner & Cooper, 2000). But as Winner and her colleagues argue, why should the arts have to be justified on the basis of what they might provide for other subjects? Why should the arts have to justify themselves on the grounds of transfer effects when this is not expected of the "academic" subjects?

A better strategy argued by the REAP research team for championing the arts is to consider what is learned within the disciplines of the arts themselves, without viewing the arts primarily as instrumental tools for facilitating learning in the "academic" disciplines. If I may translate this argument specifically to the visual arts, and in particular drawing, the benefits of drawing/art purported in the art education literature provides a long list indeed, and includes developing the child's visual thinking, creativity, imagination, expression, problem-solving, analytical, and observational skills to name but a few.[1] Although the range of all the benefits listed here, and no doubt many others, have an intuitive appeal, we need research to show conclusively that engaging in drawing directly leads to these benefits as they are found within the artistic domain, otherwise the claims are merely unsubstantiated advocacy. For instance, do children who are put through an intensive art program develop any of the skills listed above relative to a control group receiving a non-arts program? And if they do, but the skills do not generalize to other disciplines (e.g., if improvement in creative drawing has no knock-on effect in creative writing), then so be it. If research found that training in maths does not have any positive transfer effects on literacy learning would we then remove maths from the school curriculum (Winner and her colleagues give similar examples to this point)? A complementary approach is for research to address what skills are gained through artistic training that are not developed (or at least not to the same extent) by training in other disciplines. Art educators can then claim, backed up by the research evidence, that the dwindling of arts education is potentially disabling children from developing certain fundamental skills that are provided by the arts, as such skills are not compensated by their learning of other subjects.

Overall, the focus needs to be on the intrinsic value of drawing and art. Art education allows the children to appreciate, and to develop for themselves, unique competencies and understanding that are under threat from the erosion of dedicated time and other resources given to art. In the same way children need literacy lessons to develop their reading and writing, they need art lessons to develop their artistic skills. A supportive scientific research base towards the varied, intrinsic and peculiar benefits of drawing/art would provide a powerful argument for those involved in art education to champion their discipline as part of the wider education of children. And by complementing the skills and training of art educators, artists and psychologists, research can help pull the art discipline out of the shadows of literacy and numeracy in school curricula.

It is not just with the general education community that champions of art need to assert their cause but also with the children making the art, as we know that by early adulthood many are engaging very little in art activities. But first let me deal with the positive and surprising news regarding our survey data on children's drawing experience. Recall that Sarah Rose, Esther Burkitt, and I surveyed children (5- to 14-year-olds), their teachers and parents, on a wide range of issues relating to their drawing experience and education (see chapter 10 for more details). We found an unexpectedly positive picture of children of all ages reporting that they enjoyed drawing, felt good about their drawing ability, with no obvious age-related decline in the overall amount of time they reported engaging in drawing activities. Furthermore, when we asked children why children draw less or even stop drawing when they get older, relatively few reported that it was due to children having a low perception of their drawing ability. Similarly, few parents and teachers reported this explanation. These lines of data strongly indicate, therefore, that any decline in drawing activity is not principally due to children's holding a negative attitude towards their drawing. Our evidence stands in stark contrast to the numerous anecdotal comments in the literature that many children give up drawing simply because they become disillusioned with their drawings not turning out as they want.

The factor that did stand out as the main cause for the decline among the responses of all three participant groups was that older children have less time to draw. This came in two forms: children becoming too busy with things they have to do; and with the time they choose to invest in their increasingly diverse interests and relationships. In the first of these forms the responses illustrated the increasing pressure on children to commit to the "academic" subjects that are considered important for their employment opportunities, and the consequence this has on "non-vocational" activities, such as drawing, getting squeezed out. Furthermore, there was evidence in the participants' responses that older children are expected to take on extra responsibilities, such as household chores and employment. In the second of these forms we saw the increasing number of competing influences that attract adolescents' attention. With their growing maturity they are given more freedom in how they can spend their time, no longer being constrained by adult supervised activities (which are likely to include drawing/art) in the home (either with friends or not). Now they are given more freedom, they can go out and socialize with their friends, which may not necessarily involve a defined activity. But of course many adolescents do get involved in diverse social activities, with their cognitive, physical, social, and emotional development freeing up more opportunities for engaging in a wide range of sports, hobbies, and pastimes that were not accessible when they were younger. In either case they are socializing, and this is where I believe lies the main challenge if drawing is to continue throughout adolescence into adulthood. That is, drawing is often considered a solitary activity. And for the adolescent who wants to commit more time to forming deeper friendships it is simply not attractive.

So what is the answer for drawing, and art more generally? When we asked our survey respondents what could be done to arrest the decline in drawing activity we got answers that directly addressed the causes of the decline. They responded by saying there needs to be more art social clubs where children can make art but at the same time meet their increasing social needs. We heard from them that the activities need to be fun and varied, using different materials, with the children having more freedom and inspiration than they often find in the art experiences they get at school. In regard to their school activities, teachers and parents felt that the profile of art needs to be raised; in essence, art should be presented to children as being as important as the core academic subjects. If we present art to children as a peripheral pastime then is it surprising that many of them end up acquiescing to this view? In making this point I am reminded of the claim that children stop playing too young, due to a hurried lifestyle, changes in family structure, and increased attention to academic subjects (e.g., Ginsburg, 2007), and consequently lose the continued cognitive, social, physical, and emotional benefits of play. Similarly, parents and teachers (not to mention those involved in educational policy) should be mindful not to fill up children's time to such an extent they are left with little opportunity to develop their artistic skills, and consequently no longer receive the particular benefits that may only develop by engaging in art.

So far I have mainly discussing drawing production. But as commented upon throughout this book the pictorial world of children is not limited to the images they produce themselves but also extends to those they see and their understanding of them. One important question is, what influences do picture production and comprehension have on each other in the child's engagement with pictures? In chapter 4 I provided strong evidence that children of all drawing abilities are aware of, and prefer, more advanced drawings (in terms of representational realism) than depicted in their current drawings. Furthermore, my colleagues and I reported a consistent and statistically significant relationship between children's production level (i.e. representational quality) and their understanding of what develops and why in drawing, independently of age (Jolley et al., 2000, 2001).

Such findings indicate that we need to look more closely into the interacting and developing relationship between production and comprehension in drawing. One question relevant to such an investigation is, when does the influence of cultural drawing models that children see begin to bear on children's own productions? While Kellogg (1969) argues that only in older children's drawing do we see local cultural forms, Brent and Marjorie Wilson (Wilson, 1997, 2000; Wilson & Wilson, 1976, 1977) have argued that this occurs much earlier. Arnheim (1974), in contrast, argues that children's own drawings result from the child's own efforts to find graphic equivalents for the subject matter they draw (rather than borrowing ideas from other drawings).

As I argued in chapter 9 both resources (pictorial models and graphic inventions) are used by children in their own drawings. But research needs to examine how these two resources interact with each other in children's drawing development. For instance, to what extent do children of different ages copy and adapt seen graphic images? Wilson and Wilson (1977) reported an interesting line of enquiry by asking children where they got their ideas from for their current and past drawings. Among a number of questions the children were asked were, "Did the drawing originate with you?," "Is it a copy of something?," "Did someone show you how to do it that way?" Although the authors concluded that virtually all drawings could be traced back to an existing graphic source, they provided no data in their paper. Furthermore, I have not seen this promising line of enquiry developed in the literature. If pursued it may prove to be fruitful in understanding the extent to which comprehension of drawing models influences production in children's drawings. The alternative view that children's drawing largely develops through their discovery of their own graphic inventions may usefully be serviced by studying blind children's drawings, particularly those who have had no or limited experience with raised line drawings made by others (see chapter 3). Their drawings would provide a more direct insight into the child's natural ability at graphic invention, unadulterated by the influences of graphic cultural models. More generally, as I mentioned in chapter 4, we must refrain from conceiving that any casual relationship between comprehension and production in drawing would be only unidirectional. Research would be usefully employed in closely monitoring developmental change in drawing, and interviewing children about how they considered it to have occurred and the impact it had upon their understanding of drawing.

Another perspective on the relationship between children's production and comprehension of pictures relates to their understanding and use of pictures as symbols. In chapter 5 we saw that very young children (i.e. before children can draw representational pictures) can recognize familiar subject matter in pictures and even use a representational picture to locate a toy in a room referred to in a picture. This comprehension advantage is no doubt due to the same motor and graphic limitations in production that account for children's understanding and preference for higher levels of realism than is shown in their own drawings. But does drawing representational pictures depend upon symbolic understanding?

There has been a debate into the origins of cave art that may be relevant to this question. Of course pictures first had to be created by our ancestors before they were seen. But did the earliest picture makers have symbolic understanding? Most cave art depicts the animals that the cave people came into contact with. David Lewis-Williams (2002; see also Spivey, 2005) speculates that our ancestors considered these animals to be powerful and magical, and consequently incorporated them into their healing trances. These mental images in the brain were further facilitated by occurring in the light-deprived conditions of the cave. For Lewis-Williams these two-dimensional mental images would have been projected on to the cave walls, which the cave people desired to "nail-down" by painting them on the walls. His theory rejects, therefore, the notion that our ancient ancestors were trying to create two-dimensional pictures of the three-dimensional world (i.e. a view that depends upon them having a symbolic mind), but proposes instead that they were attempts to represent the two-dimensional images they were already "seeing" in the brain.

Although I am not suggesting that children's early representational drawing is made in trance-like states (!), this particular theory of the purpose of cave art suggests that we can produce pictures without first understanding that something can stand for something else. Do children with weak symbolic understanding draw representational pictures? Studies on the representational drawing of children with autism, a disorder that is noted for poor symbolic understanding, have shown that their representational drawing is no worse than found in the drawings from children matched on mental age (see chapter 3).

This suggests, therefore, that the deficits peculiar to autism (such as a weaker understanding of symbolism) may not detrimentally affect the making of symbolic pictures. Although it may be difficult to obtain samples of children who are devoid of symbolic understanding, it would be interesting to examine the relationship between symbolic understanding and representational drawing in typically developing children. For example, is there an association between early signs of symbolic understanding and early representational drawing?

Whatever the relationship between symbolic understanding and representational drawing the acquisition of a symbolic mind is an important milestone for the child. In my discussion of children's understanding of pictures as symbols in chapter 5 I discussed false picture tasks that seem to indicate that children up to 4 years of age may not be able simultaneously to hold in mind that pictures are objects in themselves and also refer to some other reality (i.e. the dual nature of pictures). But I went on to argue that their errors on false picture tasks have more to do with a general cognitive problem of thinking flexibly about any given entity (such as thinking about something in two ways), rather than a specific problem related to their pictorial understanding. It would be interesting to investigate in what ways this cognitive difficulty of flexibility may affect children's thinking about their own drawings. For instance, do young children struggle with switching their attention from the subject matter of their drawings and paintings to the formal properties (e.g., color, line, composition) on the page (and vice versa)?

Flexibility was also the focus of chapter 6 in my review of the representational redescription theory as it relates to the drawing domain. The theory concerns how internal representations are stored in the mind, and claims that they develop from being implicitly stored to undergoing a process in which elements of representations become more explicitly accessible to the child. Despite children's representational drawings being used as evidence for this shift in how the corresponding internal representations are stored (Karmiloff-Smith, 1990, 1992, 1999), the weight of subsequent research seriously undermines the use of drawings to illustrate the theory. Contrary to the theory, studies have consistently shown that even young children's drawings are less procedurally rigid in the order in which they draw elements of a topic, and that they can more readily manipulate their drawings of topics, than is supposed if the children had only an implicit access to their mentally stored internal representation of topics. The flexibility that children have consistently shown in this drawing literature is because to draw we need consciously to bring to mind the elements of the topic(s). Once we accept that drawing is an explicit behavioral act of producing an external manifestation of internal representations this throws up the interesting possibility that drawing induces internal representations to become more cognitively explicit to the child. So instead of conceiving drawings as behavioral manifestations of how internal representations are stored it would be more appropriate to study how the act of drawing can potentially enhance the flexibility of our internal representations. Setting children tasks of drawing subject matter from unusual angles, postures, and actions may facilitate greater flexibility in how they think about such subject matter, and is in fact a well-known classic art education technique.

The attempt of the representational redescription theory to illustrate the corresponding internal representations is a warning to researchers about the complexity of drawing, and not to consider drawings as offering clear windows to any one facet of the child. The numerous and diverse influences on drawing, both internal and external to the child, prevent an easy exercise in "reading off" from the drawing a particular cognitive aspect of the child under investigation, even when we try to design tasks to do so. The same is true for using drawing as measures of personality and emotional disturbance discussed in chapter 7, where the child's drawing ability, in particular, clouds the window towards evaluating the child's disturbance from their drawings. The difficulty of interpretation is compounded by the variety of explanations of personality and emotionality linked to any given feature (the size of the drawing is a case in point). Nevertheless, at the end of chapter 7 I outlined a potentially useful approach where the clinician generates hypotheses of disturbance (or how the child is currently experiencing it) from the child's drawings. These can then be explored further, and potentially validated, by the clinician (perhaps using other sources and measures). There may be instances where drawings provide a unique starting point to some aspect of the clinical profile of the child. This is because children may consider drawings as a "safe" ground in which to express their anxieties, fears, and disturbances compared to the more intimidating directness of some of the other tools in the clinician's armory (e.g., premature questioning of the child about his or her trauma).

In chapter 7 I commented that many British clinical psychologists report using drawings informally with their child clients, and that we need a further survey to establish what forms this practice takes. Similarly, it is unclear how drawings from children are used in legal settings. My impression is that when paper and drawing materials are made available to children who are being interviewed by the police, they are typically provided merely for the amusement of the child rather than being part of the formal interview. I suspect this is due to a suspicion on behalf of the police regarding the subjective nature of interpreting drawing, and a concern that they themselves are not trained to make appropriate evaluations. But as I discussed in chapter 8 it is not so much the drawings themselves that make them judicially beneficial, but the verbal recall they stimulate from the child. The literature has consistently shown that children can recall up to twice as much information of an event they have experienced if they are asked to draw it as well. There needs to be a greater collaboration between researchers and the police concerning these research findings, as well as the worrying findings that indicate that when children draw false reminders and inaccurate details provided by the interviewer the act of drawing actually increases the chance of the child recalling such misinformation. From such collaboration we may be able to find optimum and safe ways of using drawings in police interviews of children that prove to be a useful stimulus for children's recall in legal contexts.

The potential of the act of drawing in helping children verbally report experiences completes a mutually beneficial relationship between drawing and language that could be further exploited in practice and research. Earlier in this chapter I mentioned the benefits to be gained in understanding children's drawings by asking them to comment on them. It seems to me at least that interviewers in judicial (and possible clinical) settings are not fully utilizing drawings as cues for children to talk about their experiences, while researchers' understanding of children's drawings is being hampered by only rarely asking the children to talk about their drawings.

You may have noticed a general theme in many of the points I have made in this final chapter, namely the need for a more holistic and integrative approach to studying children's making and understanding of drawings and pictures. My ideas for future directions are not detailed research programs in themselves, but a call for researchers and practitioners to develop lines of enquiry and practice that consider and inform the wider context of children's making and understanding of their pictorial world. By doing so we will not only gain a greater and richer understanding of this important domain of children's activity, but also discover further, and argue for, its relevance in the child's overall development and education.

Note

1 Not forgetting more generic byproducts, such as improving the child's concentration, patience, confidence, and self-esteem in their art achievements, as well as art being an enjoyable activity for many children.

Further Reading

I hope you have found this book stimulating and interesting. I have certainly enjoyed writing it. The process took me on a journey through the literature which I hope through my telling of what I found has helped you in your own journey of studying this fascinating topic. It is perhaps inevitable, however, that any journey cannot take in all the sights to be seen, and with time and space constraints ingrained in writing a book, not all of the literature and ideas can be covered in a single work. With this in mind I would like to recommend three books to those who wish to study this area further.

Cox, M. V. (2005). *The pictorial world of the child*. Cambridge, UK: Cambridge University Press.

Lange-Küttner, C., & Vinter, A. (Eds.). (2008). *Drawing and the non-verbal mind: A life-span perspective*. Cambridge, UK: Cambridge University Press.

Milbrath, C., & Trautner, H. M. (Eds.). (2008). *Children's understanding and production of pictures, drawing, and art: Theoretical and empirical approaches*. Cambridge, MA: Hogrefe and Huber.

References

Abell, S. C., Wood, W., & Liebman, S. J. (2001). Children's human figure drawings as measures of intelligence: the comparative validity of three scoring systems. *Journal of Psychoeducational Assessment, 19,* 204–215.

Abell, S. C., Von Briesen, P. D., & Watz, L. S. (1996). Intellectual evaluations of children using human figure drawings: An empirical investigation of two methods. *Journal of Clinical Psychology, 52,* 67–74.

Adi-Japha, E., Levin, I., & Solomon, S. (1998). Emergence of representation in drawing: The relation between kinematic and referential aspects. *Cognitive Development, 13,* 25–51.

Allison, B., & Hausman, J. (1998). The limits of theory in art education. *Journal of Art and Design Education, 17,* 121–127.

Alschuler, R. H., & Hattwick, L. B. W. (1947). *Painting and personality.* Chicago: University of Chicago Press.

Anastasi, A., & Foley, J. P. (1936). An analysis of spontaneous drawings by children in different cultures. *Journal of Applied Psychology, 20,* 680–726.

Anastasi, A., & Urbina, S. (1997). *Psychological testing* (7th ed.). New York: Macmillan.

Anning, A. (2002). A conversation around young children's drawing: The impact of the beliefs of significant others at home and at school. *International Journal of Art and Design Education, 21,* 197–208.

Archer, R. P., Maruish, M., Imhof, E. A., & Piotrowski, C. (1991). Psychological test usage with adolescent clients: 1990 survey findings. *Professional Psychology: Research and Practice, 22,* 247–252.

Arnheim, R. (1974). *Art and visual perception: A psychology of the creative eye.* London: Faber and Faber.

Aronsson, K., & Andersson, S. (1996). Social scalings in children's drawings of class-room life. A cultural comparative analysis of children's drawings in Africa and Sweden. *British Journal of Developmental Psychology*, *14*, 301–314.

Aronsson, K., & Junge, B. (2000). Intellectual realism and social scaling in children's art: Some critical reflections on the basis of Ethiopian children's drawings. In L. Lindström (Ed.), *The cultural context. Comparative studies of art education and children's drawings*, (pp. 135–159). Stockholm: HLS Förlag.

Arrowsmith, C. J., Cox, M. V., & Eames, K. (1994). Eliciting partial occlusions in the drawings of 4 year olds and 5 year olds. *British Journal of Developmental Psychology*, *12*, 577–584.

Ashwin, C. (1975). *Art education: Documents and policies, 1768–1975*. London: Society for Research into Higher Education.

Ashwin, C. (1981). Pestalozzi and the origins of pedagogical drawing. *British Journal of Educational Studies*, *29*, 138–151.

Baird, G., Charman, T., Baron-Cohen, S., Cox, A., Swettenham, J., Wheelwright, S., Drew, A. (2000). A screening instrument for autism at 18 months of age: A 6-year follow-up study. *Journal of the American Academy of Child and Adolescent Psychiatry*, *39*, 694–702.

Bahn, P. G. (1996). Foreword. In J. M. Chauvet, E. B. Deschamp, & C. Hillaire (Eds.), *Dawn of art: The Chauvet cave* (pp. 7–12). New York: Harry N. Abrams.

Baker-Ward, L., Gordon, B. N., Ornstein, P. A., Larus, D. M., & Clubb, P. A. (1993). Young children's long-term retention of a paediatric examination. *Child Development*, *64*, 1519–1533.

Barham, L. S. (2002). Systematic pigment use in the Middle Pleistocene of South-Central Africa, *Current Anthropology*, *43*, 181–190.

Barlow, C. M. (2002). *Rigidity in children's drawings and its relationship with representational change*. Unpublished doctoral dissertation, Department of Psychology, Staffordshire University.

Barlow, C. M., Jolley, R. P., & Hallam, J. L. (submitted). Optimising the drawing method to facilitate young children's recall.

Barlow, C. M., Jolley, R. P., White, D. G., & Galbraith, D. (2003). Rigidity in children's drawings and its relation with representational change. *Journal of Experimental Child Psychology*, *86*, 124–152.

Barnes, E. (1893). A study of children's drawings. *Pedagogical Seminary, 2*, 451–463.

Barnes, R. (2002). *Teaching art to children 4–9*. London: Routledge/Falmer.

Barnett, A., & Henderson, S. E. (1992). Some observations on the figure drawings of clumsy children. *British Journal of Educational Psychology*, *62*, 341–355.

Baron-Cohen, S., Leslie, A. M., & Frith, U. (1985). Does the autistic child have a "theory of mind"? *Cognition, 21,* 37–46.

Barrett, M., & Eames, K. (1996). Sequential developments in children's human figure drawing. *British Journal of Developmental Psychology, 14,* 219–236.

Barrouillet, P., Fayol, M., & Chevrot, C. (1994). Le dessin d'une maison. Construction d'une echelle de developpement. *Annee Psychologique, 94,* 81–98.

Barrera, M. E., & Maurer, D. (1981). The perception of facial expressions by the three-month-old. *Child Development, 52,* 203–206.

Beilin, H., & Pearlman, E. G. (1991). Children's iconic realism: Object versus property realism. In H. W. Reese (Ed.), *Advances in child development and behaviour* (Vol. 23, pp. 73–111). New York: Academic Press.

Bekhit, N. S., Thomas, G. V., & Jolley, R. P. (2005). The use of drawing for psychological assessment in Britain: Survey findings. *Psychology and Psychotherapy: Theory, Research and Practice, 78,* 205–217.

Bekhit, N. S., Thomas, G. V., Lalonde, S., & Jolley, R. P. (2002). Psychological assessment in clinical practice in Britain. *Clinical Psychology and Psychotherapy, 9,* 285–291.

Bell, Q. (1963). *The schools of design.* London: Routledge and Kegan Paul.

Berk, L. E. (2006). *Child development* (7th ed.). Boston, MA: Allyn and Bacon.

Berti, A. E., & Freeman, N. H. (1997). Representational change in resources for pictorial innovations: A three-feature analysis. *Cognitive Development, 12,* 501–522.

Bertrand, J., Mervis, C. B., & Eisenberg, J. D. (1997). Drawing by children with Williams syndrome: A developmental perspective. *Developmental Neuropsychology, 13,* 41–67.

Bialystok, E. (2000). Symbolic representation across domains in preschool children. *Journal of Experimental Child Psychology, 76,* 173–189.

Bialystok, E., & Martin, M. M. (2003). Notation to symbol: Development in children's understanding of print. *Journal of Experimental Child Psychology, 86,* 223–243.

Bjorklund, D. F. (1987). How age changes in knowledge base contribute to the development of children's memory: An interpretative review. *Developmental Review, 7,* 93–130.

Blatchford, P. (1997). Pupils self assessments of academic attainment at 7, 11 and 16 years: Effects of sex and ethnic group. *British Journal of Educational Psychology, 67,* 169–184.

Booth, R., Charlton, R., Hughes, C., & Happé, F. (2003). Disentangling weak coherence and executive dysfunction: Planning drawing in autism and attention-deficit/hyperactivity disorder. *Philosophical Transactions of the Royal Society B-Biological Sciences, 358,* 387–392.

Bovet, D., & Vauclair, J. (2000). Picture recognition in animals and humans. *Behavioural Brain Research*, *109*, 143–165.

Bowler, D. M., Briskman, J., & Grice, S. (1999). Experimenter effects on children's understanding of false drawings and false beliefs. *Journal of Genetic Psychology*, *160*, 443–460.

Brady, M. S., Poole, D. A., Warren, A. R., & Jones, H. R. (1999). Young children's responses to yes-no questions: Patterns and problems. *Applied Developmental Science*, *3*, 47–57.

Bremner, J. G., & Moore, S. (1984). Prior visual inspection and object naming: Two factors that enhance hidden feature inclusion in young children's drawings. *British Journal of Developmental Psychology*, *2*, 371–376.

Bremner, J. G., Morse, R., Hughes, S., & Andreasen, G. (2000). Relations between drawing cubes and copying line diagrams of cubes in 7- to 10-year-old children. *Child Development*, *71*, 621–634.

Brooks, M. R., Glenn, S. M., & Crozier, W. R. (1988). Pre-school children's preferences for drawings of a similar complexity to their own. *British Journal of Educational Psychology*, *58*, 165–171.

Bruck, M., Melnyk, L., & Ceci, S. J. (2000). Draw it again Sam: The effect of drawing on children's suggestibility and source monitoring ability. *Journal of Experimental Child Psychology*, *77*, 169–196.

Buckalew, L. W., & Bell, A. (1985). Effects of colors on mood in the drawings of young children. *Perceptual and Motor Skills*, *61*, 689–690.

Bull, R. (Ed.) (2001). *Children and the law: The essential readings*. Oxford, UK: Blackwell.

Burgess, A. W., & Hartman, C. R. (1993). Children's drawings. *Child Abuse & Neglect*, *17*, 161–168.

Burgess, E. (1988). Sexually abused children and their drawings. *Archives of Psychiatric Nursing*, *2*, 65–73.

Burkitt, E. (2004) Drawing conclusions from children's art. *Psychologist*, *17*, 566–568.

Burkitt, E., & Barnett, N. (2006). The effects of brief and elaborate mood induction procedures on the size of young children's drawings. *Educational Psychology*, *26*, 93–108.

Burkitt, E., Barrett, M., & Davis, A. (2003a). The effect of affective characterisations on the size of children's drawings. *British Journal of Developmental Psychology*, *21*, 565–584.

Burkitt, E., Barrett, M., & Davis, A. (2003b). Children's colour choices for completing drawings of affectively characterised topics. *Journal of Child Psychology and Psychiatry*, *44*, 445–455.

Burkitt, E., Barrett, M., & Davis, A. (2004). The effect of affective characterisations on the use of size and colour in drawings produced by children in the absence of a model. *Educational Psychology*, *24*, 315–343.

Burkitt, E., Barrett, M., & Davis, A. (2005). Drawings of emotionally characterised figures by children from different educational backgrounds. *International Journal of Art and Design Education, 24,* 71–83.

Burkitt, E., Tala, K., & Low, J. (2007). Finish and English children's colour use to depict affectively characterised figures. *International Journal of Behavioral Development, 31,* 59–64.

Burns, R. C., & Kaufman, S. H. (1970). *Kinetic Family Drawings (K-F-D).* Oxford, UK: Brunner/Mazel.

Burt, C. (1921). *Mental and scholastic tests.* London: P.S. King and Son.

Butler, S., Gross, J., & Hayne, H. (1995). The effect of drawing on memory performance in young children. *Developmental Psychology, 31,* 597–608.

Callaghan, T. C. (1999). Early understanding and production of graphic symbols. *Child Development, 70,* 1314–1324.

Callaghan, T. C. (2000). Factors affecting children's graphic symbol use in the third year. Language, similarity, and iconicity. *Cognitive Development, 15,* 185–214.

Callaghan, T. C. (2008). The origins and development of pictorial symbol functioning. In C. Milbrath & H. M. Trautner (Eds.), *Children's understanding and production of pictures, drawings and art: Theoretical and empirical approaches.* Cambridge, MA: Hogrefe & Huber.

Callaghan, T. C., Rochat, P., MacGillivray, T., & MacLellan, C. (2004). The social construction of pictorial symbols in 6- to 18-month-old infants. *Child Development, 75,* 1733–1744.

Camara, W. J., Nathan, J. S., & Puente, A. E. (2000). Psychological test usage: Implications in professional psychology. *Professional Psychology: Research and Practice, 31,* 141–154.

Campbell, R. (2004, September). *Some neglected early work on children's drawing ability.* Paper presented at the British Psychological Society Developmental Section Conference, Leeds, England.

Carline, R. (1968). *Draw they must: A history of the teaching and examining of art.* London: Edward Arnold.

Caron-Pargue, J. (1992). A functional analysis of decomposition and integration in children's cylinder drawing. *British Journal of Developmental Psychology, 10,* 51–69.

Carothers, T., & Gardner, H. (1979). When children's drawings become art: The emergence of aesthetic production and perception. *Developmental Psychology, 15,* 570–580.

Cashel, M. L. (2002). Child and adolescent psychological assessment: Current clinical practices and the impact of managed care. *Professional Psychology: Research and Practice, 33,* 446–453.

Catte, M. (1998). *Emotional indicators in children's human figure drawings: an evaluation of the draw a person test.* Unpublished doctoral dissertation, University of York, UK.

Catte, M., & Cox, M. V. (1999). Emotional indicators in children's human figure drawings. *European Child and Adolescent Psychiatry, 8,* 86–91.

Celani, G. (2002). Human beings, animals and inanimate objects: What do people with autism like? *Autism, 6,* 93–102.

Chakrabarti, S., & Fombonne, E. (2001). Pervasive developmental disorders in preschool children. *Journal of the American Medical Association, 285,* 3093–3099.

Chan, D. W., & Lee, H. C. B. (1995). Patterns of psychological test usage in Hong Kong in 1993. *Professional Psychology: Research and Practice, 26,* 292–297.

Charman, T., & Baron-Cohen, S. (1993). Drawing development in autism: The intellectual to visual realism shift. *British Journal of Developmental Psychology, 11,* 171–185.

Childs, G. (1991). *Steiner education in theory and practice.* Edinburgh, UK: Floris Books.

Chomsky, N. (1986). *Knowledge of language.* New York: Praeger.

Claparède, E. (1907). Plan d'expériences collectives sur le dessin des enfants [Plan for collective experiment on the drawing of children]. *Archives de Psychologie, 6,* 276–278.

Clark, A. B. (1897). The child's attitude toward perspective problems. In E. Barnes (Ed.), *Studies in art education* (Vol. 1, pp. 283–294). Stanford, CA: Stanford University Press.

Clements, W., & Barrett, M. (1994). The drawings of children and young people with Down's syndrome: A case of delay or difference? *British Journal of Educational Psychology, 64,* 441–452.

Clottes, J. (1996). Epilogue. In J. M. Chauvet, E. B. Deschamp, & C. Hillaire (Eds.), *Dawn of art: The Chauvet cave* (pp. 89–128). New York: Harry N. Abrams.

Cohen, J. (1988). *Statistical power analysis for the behavioral sciences* (2nd ed.). Hillsdale, NJ: Lawrence Erlbaum.

Costall, A. (1989, September). *Another look at Luquet: Stages in our understanding of children's drawings.* Paper presented at the meeting of the British Psychological Society Developmental Section, University of Surrey, Guildford, UK.

Costall, A. (1995). How meaning covers the traces. In N. H. Freeman & M. V. Cox (Eds.), *Visual order: The nature and development of pictorial representation* Cambridge, UK: Cambridge University Press.

Costall, A. (1997). Innocence and corruption: Conflicting images of child art. *Human Development, 40,* 133–144.

Costall, A. (2001). Introduction: A closer look at Luquet. In G.-H. Luquet, *Children's drawings* (A. Costall, Trans. and Ed.; pp. vii–xxiv). London and New York: Free Association Books.

Court, E. (1989). Drawing on culture: The influence of culture on children's drawing performance in rural Kenya. *Journal of Art & Design Education, 8*, 65–88.

Court, E. (1992). Researching social influences in the drawing of rural Kenyan children. In D. Thistlewood (Ed.), *Drawing research and development* (pp. 51–67). Harlow: Longman/NSEAD.

Coutts, G., & Dougall, P. (2005). Drawing in perspective: Scottish art and design teachers discuss drawing. *International Journal of Art and Design Education, 24*, 138–148.

Cox, M. V. (1978). Spatial depth relationships in young children's drawings. *Journal of Experimental Child Psychology, 26*, 551–554.

Cox, M. V. (1981). One thing behind another: Young children's use of array-specific or view-specific representations. In N. H. Freeman & M. V. Cox (Eds.), *Visual order: The nature and development of pictorial representation.* Cambridge, UK: Cambridge University Press.

Cox, M. V. (1986). Cubes are difficult things to draw. *British Journal of Developmental Psychology, 4*, 341–345.

Cox, M. V. (1989). Children's drawings. In D. J. Hargreaves (Ed.), *Children and the arts* (pp. 43–58). Milton Keynes, UK: Open University Press.

Cox, M. V. (1991). *The child's point of view* (2nd ed.). London: Harvester Wheatsheaf.

Cox, M. V. (1992). *Children's drawings.* Harmondsworth, UK: Penguin.

Cox, M. V. (1993). *Children's drawings of the human figure.* Hove, UK: Lawrence Erlbaum.

Cox, M. V. (1998). Drawing of people by Australian Aboriginal children: The intermixing of cultural styles. *Journal of Art and Design Education, 17*, 71–79.

Cox, M. V. (2000). Children's drawing of the human figure in different cultures. In L. Lindstrom (Ed.), *The cultural context: The comparative studies of art education and children's drawing.* Stockholm: Stockholm Institute of Education Press.

Cox, M. V. (2005). *The pictorial world of the child.* Cambridge, UK: Cambridge University Press.

Cox, M. V., & Catte, M. (2000). Severely disturbed children's human figure drawings: Are they unusual or just poor drawings? *European Child and Adolescent Psychiatry, 9*, 301–306.

Cox, M. V., & Cotgreave, S. (1996). The human figure drawings of normal children and those with mild learning difficulties. *Educational Psychology, 16*, 433–438.

Cox, M. V., & Eames, K. (1999). Contrasting styles of drawing in gifted individuals with autism. *Autism, 3*, 397–409.

Cox, M. V., & Hodsoll, J. (2000). Children's diachronic thinking in relation to developmental changes in their drawings of the human figure. *British Journal of Developmental Psychology, 18*, 13–24.

Cox, M. V., & Howarth, C. (1989). The human figure drawings of normal children and those with severe learning difficulties. *British Journal of Developmental Psychology, 7*, 333–339.

Cox, M. V., Koyasu, J., Hiranuma, M., & Perara, J. (2001). Children's human figure drawings in the UK and Japan: The effects of age, sex and culture. *British Journal of Developmental Psychology, 19*, 275–292.

Cox, M. V., & Martin, A. (1988). Young children's viewer centred representations: Drawings of a cube placed inside or behind a transparent of opaque beaker. *International Journal of Behavioural Developments, 11*, 233–244.

Cox, M. V., & Mason, S. (1998). The young child's pictorial representations of the human figure. *International Journal of Early Years Education, 6*, 31–38.

Cox, M. V., & Maynard, S. (1998). The human figure drawings of children with Down Syndrome. *British Journal of Developmental Psychology, 16*, 133–137.

Cox, M. V., & Perara, J. (2001). Children's use of the height and size cues to depict a projective depth relationship in their pictures. *Psychologia, 44*, 99–110.

Cox, M. V., Perara, J., & Xu, F. (1998). Children's drawing ability in the UK and China. *Psychologia, 41*, 171–182.

Cox, M. V., Perara, J., & Xu, F. (1999). Children's drawings in the UK and China. *Journal of Art and Design Education, 18*, 173–181.

Cox, M. V., & Rowlands, A. (2000). The effect of three different educational approaches on children's drawing ability: Steiner, Montessori and traditional. *British Journal of Educational Psychology, 70*, 485–503.

Craig, J., Baron-Cohen, S., & Scott, F. (2001). Drawing ability in autism: A window into the imagination. *Israel Journal of Psychiatry Related Science, 38*, 242–253.

Dai, X. Y., Zheng, L. X., Ryan, J. J., & Paolo, A. M. (1993). [A survey of psychological test usage in Chinese clinical psychology and comparisons with the United States]. *Chinese Journal of Clinical Psychology, 1*, 47–50.

Dalley, T., (Ed.) (1984). *Art as therapy.* London: Routledge.

D'Angiulli, A., Kennedy, J. M., & Heller, M. A. (1998). Blind children recognizing tactile pictures respond like sighted children given guidance in exploration. *Scandinavian Journal of Psychology, 39*, 187–190.

Danvers, J. (2003). Towards a radical pedagogy: Provisional notes on learning and teaching in art and design. *International Journal of Art and Design Education, 22,* 47–57.

Darwin, C. (1859). *The origin of species.* London: John Murray.

Darwin, C. (1877). A biographical sketch of an infant. *Mind: A Quarterly Review of Psychology and Philosophy, 2,* 285–294.

Davis, A. M. (1983). Contextual sensitivity in young children's drawings. *Journal of Experimental Child Psychology, 35,* 478–486.

Davis, J. H. (1991). *Artistry lost: U-shaped development in graphic symbolisation.* Unpublished doctoral dissertation, Graduate School of Education, Harvard University.

Davis, J. H. (1997a). Drawing's demise: U-shaped development in graphic symbolisation. *Studies in Art Education: A Journal of Issues and Research, 38,* 132–157.

Davis, J. H. (1997b). The what and whether of the U: Cultural implications of understanding development in graphic symbolisation. *Human Development, 40,* 145–154.

Davison, L. E., & Thomas, G. V. (2001). Effects of drawing on children's item recall. *Journal of Experimental Child Psychology, 78,* 155–177.

Deák, G. O., Ray, S. D., & Pick, A. D. (2004). Effects of age, reminders, and task difficulty on young children's rule-switching flexibility. *Cognitive Development, 19,* 385–400.

DeLoache, J. S. (1987). Rapid change in the symbolic functioning of very young children. *Science, 238,* 1556–1557.

DeLoache, J. S. (1991). Symbolic functioning in very young children: Understanding of pictures and models. *Child Development, 62,* 736–752.

DeLoache, J. S. (2000). Dual representation and young children's use of scale models. *Child Development, 71,* 329–338.

DeLoache, J. S. (2002). Symbolic development. In U. Goswami (Ed.), *Blackwell handbook of childhood cognitive development* (pp. 206–226). Oxford, UK: Blackwell.

DeLoache, J. S. (2004). Becoming symbol-minded. *Trends in Cognitive Sciences, 8,* 66–70.

DeLoache, J. S., & Burns, N. M. (1994). Early understanding of the representational function of pictures. *Cognition, 52,* 83–110.

DeLoache, J. S., Miller, K. F., & Rosengren, K. S. (1997). The credible shrinking room: Very young children's performance with symbolic and non-symbolic relations. *Psychological Science, 8,* 308–313.

DeLoache, J. S., Peralta de Mendoza, O. A., & Anderson, K. (1999). Multiple factors in early symbol use: Instructions, similarity and age in understanding a symbol-referent relation. *Cognitive Development, 14,* 299–312.

DeLoache, J. S., Pierroutsakos, S. L., Uttal, D. H., Rosengren, K. S., & Gottlieb, A. (1998). Grasping the nature of pictures. *Psychological Science*, 9, 205–210.

DeLoache, J. S., Strauss, M. S., & Maynard, J. (1979). Picture perception in infancy. *Infant Behaviour and Development*, 2, 77–89.

Department for Education and Employment (1999). *Art and design: The National Curriculum for England*. London: Department for Education and Employment, and Qualifications and Curriculum Authority.

Deregowski, J., & Strang, P. (1986). On the drawing of a cube and its derivatives. *British Journal of Developmental Psychology*, 4, 323–330.

Deruelle, C., Rondan, C., Mancini, J., & Livet, M-O. (2006). Do children with Williams syndrome fail to process visual configural information? *Research in Developmental Disabilities*, 27, 243–253.

DiLeo, J. (1970). *Young children and their drawings*. New York: Brunner/Mazel.

Du Bois, C. (1944). *The people of Alor: A social-psychological study of an East Indian island*. Minneapolis: University of Minnesota Press.

Dykens, E. M., Rosner, B. A., & Ly, T. M. (2001). Drawings by individuals with Williams Syndrome: Are people different from shapes? *American Journal on Mental Retardation*, 106, 94–107.

Eames, K., & Cox, M. V. (1994). Visual realism in the drawings of autistic, Down's syndrome and normal children. *British Journal of Developmental Psychology*, 12, 235–239.

Edwards, C. A., & Fornham, B. D. (1989). Effects of child interview method on accuracy and completeness of sexual abuse information recall. *Social Behavior and Personality*, 17, 237–247.

Efland, A. (1990). *A history of art education: Intellectual and social currents in teaching the visual arts*. New York: Teachers' College Press.

Eisen, M. L., Quas, J. A., & Goodman, G. S. (2002). *Memory and suggestibility in the forensic interview*. Mahwah, NJ: Lawrence Erlbaum.

Ekman, P. (1982). *Emotion in the human face* (2nd ed.). New York: Cambridge University Press.

Eno, L., Elliot, C., & Woehlke, P. (1981). Koppitz emotional indicators in the human-figure drawings of children with learning problems. *The Journal of Special Education*, 15, 459–470.

Falk, J. D. (1981). Understanding children's art: An analysis of the literature. *Journal of Personality Assessment*, 45, 465–472.

Farran, E. K., Jarrold, C., & Gathercole, S. E. (2003). Divided attention, selective attention and drawing: Processing preferences in Williams syndrome are dependent on the task administered. *Neuropsychologia*. 41, 676–687.

Farylo, B., & Paludi, M. (1985). Research with the Draw-A-Person test: Conceptual and methodological issues. *The Journal of Psychology, 119,* 575–580.

Fayol, M., Barrouillet, P., & Chevrot, C. (1995). Judgement and production of drawings by 3–10-year-olds: Comparison of declarative and procedural drawing knowledge. *European Journal of Psychology of Education, 10,* 303–313.

Fenson, L. (1985). The transition from construction to sketching in children's drawings. In N. H. Freeman & M. V. Cox (Eds.), *Visual order: The nature and development of pictorial representation* Cambridge, UK: Cambridge University Press.

Fineberg, J. (1997). *The innocent eye: Children's art and the modern artist.* Princeton, NJ: Princeton University Press.

Fineberg, J. (1998). *Discovering child art: Essays on childhood, primitivism and modernism.* Princeton, NJ: Princeton University Press.

Fivush, R., & Hammond, N. (1990). Autobiographical memory across the preschool years: Toward reconceptualising childhood amnesia. In R. Fivush and J. Hudson (Eds.), *Knowing and remembering in young children* (pp. 223–248). New York: Cambridge University Press.

Flannery, K. A., & Watson, M. W. (1991). Perceived competence in drawing during middle childhood years. *Visual Arts Research, 17,* 66–71.

Flavell, J. H. (1963). *The developmental psychology of Jean Piaget.* Princeton, NJ: Van Nostrand.

Flavell, J. H., Beach, D. R., & Chinsky, J. M. (1966). Spontaneous verbal rehearsal in a memory task as a function of age. *Child Development, 37,* 283–99.

Flavell, J. H., Flavell, E. R., & Green, F. L. (1983). Development of the appearance-reality distinction. *Cognitive Psychology, 15,* 95–120.

Flavell, J. H., Green, F. L., & Flavell, E. R. (1986). Development of knowledge about the appearance-reality distinction. *Monographs of the Society for Research in Child Development, 51,* 1–87.

Fodor, J. A. (1983). *Modularity of mind.* Cambridge, MA: MIT Press.

Fodor, J. A. (2000). *The mind doesn't work that way: The scope and limits of computational psychology.* Cambridge, MA: MIT Press.

Fombonne, E. (2003). Epidemiological surveys of autism and other pervasive developmental disorders: An update. *Journal of Autism and Developmental Disorders, 33,* 265–284.

Forrest, M., & Thomas, G. (1991). An exploratory study of drawings by bereaved children. *British Journal of Clinical Psychology, 30,* 373–374.

Fortes, M. (1940). Children's drawing among the Tallensi. *Africa, 13,* 293–295.

Fortes, M. (1981). Tallensi children's drawing. In B. Lloyd & J. Gay (Eds.), *Universals of human thought*. Cambridge, UK: Cambridge University Press.

Fowler, C. (1996). *Strong arts, strong schools*. New York: Oxford University Press.

Freeman, N. H. (1972). Process and product in children's drawing. *Perception, 1*, 123–140.

Freeman, N. H. (1975). Do children draw men with arms coming out of their head? *Nature, 254*, 416–417.

Freeman, N. H. (1980). *Strategies of representation in young children: Analysis of spatial skills and drawing process*. London: Academic Press.

Freeman, N. H. (1986). How should a cube be drawn? *British Journal of Developmental Psychology, 4*, 317–322.

Freeman, N. H. (1995). The emergence of a framework theory of pictorial reasoning. In C. Lange-Küttner and G. V. Thomas (Eds.), *Drawing and looking* (pp. 135–146). London: Harvester.

Freeman, N. H. (2000). Communication and representation: Why mentalistic reasoning is a lifelong endeavour. In P. Mitchell & K. Riggs (Eds.), *Children's reasoning and the mind* (pp. 349–366). Hove: Psychology Press.

Freeman, N. H. (2004). Aesthetic judgement and reasoning. In E. W. Eisner & M. D. Day (Eds.), *Handbook of research and policy in art education*. Mahwah, NJ: Lawrence Erlbaum and National Art Education Association.

Freeman, N. H., & Cox, M. V. (1985). *Visual order: The nature and development of pictorial representation*. Cambridge, UK: Cambridge University Press.

Freeman, N. H., & Janikoun, R. (1972). Intellectual realism in children's drawings of a familiar object with distinct features. *Child Development, 43*, 1116–1121.

Freeman, N. H., & Parsons, M. J. (2001). Children's intuitive understanding of pictures. In B. Torff & R. J. Sternberg (Eds.), *Understanding and teaching the intuitive mind* (pp. 73–91). London: Erlbaum.

Frith, U. (2003). *Autism: explaining the enigma* (2nd ed.). Malden, MA: Blackwell.

Fuller, G. B., Preuss, M., & Hawkins, W. F. (1970). The validity of the human figure drawings with disturbed and normal children. *Journal of School Psychology, 8*, 54–56.

Gardner, H. (1980). *Artful scribbles*. New York: Basic Books.

Gardner, H. (2006). Reply to David Pariser. In J. A. Schaler (Ed.), *Howard Gardner under fire: The rebel psychologist faces his critics* (pp. 336–341). Chicago: Open Court Press.

Gardner, H., & Winner, E. (1982). First intimations of artistry. In S. Strauss (Ed.), *U-shaped behavioral growth*. New York: Academic Press.

Gayton, W. F., Tavormina, J., Evans, H. E., & Schuh, J. (1974). Comparative validity of Harris and Koppitz scoring systems for human-figure drawings. *Perceptual & Motor Skills, 39*, 369–370.

Geist, A. L., & Carroll, P. N. (2002). *They still draw pictures: Children's art in wartime from the Spanish Civil War to Kosovo*. Urbana, IL: University of Illinois Press.

Georgopoulos, M. A., Georgopoulos, A. P., Kuz, N., & Landau, B. (2004). Figure copying in Williams syndrome and normal subjects. *Experimental Brain Research, 157*, 137–146.

Gibson, R. (2003). Learning to be an art educator: Student teachers' attitudes to art and art education. *International Journal of Art and Design Education, 22*, 111–120.

Ginsburg, K. R. (2007). The importance of play in promoting healthy child development and maintaining strong parent-bonds. *American Academy of Pediatrics, 119*, 182–191.

Golomb, C. (1981). Representations and reality: The origins and determinants of young children's drawings. *Review of Research in Visual Arts Education, 14*, 36–48.

Golomb, C. (1992). *The child's creation of a pictorial world*. Berkeley, CA: University of California Press.

Golomb, C. (2002). *Child art in context: A cultural and comparative perspective*. Washington, DC: American Psychological Association.

Golomb, C. (2004). *The child's creation of a pictorial world* (2nd ed.). Mahwah, NJ: Lawrence Erlbaum.

Golomb, C., & Barr-Grossman, T. (1977). Representational development of human figure in familial retards. *Genetic Psychology Monographs, 95*, 247–266.

Gombrich, E. H. (1995). *The story of art* (16th ed.). London: Phaidon Press.

Goodenough, F. L. (1926). *Measurement of intelligence by drawings*. Yonkers-on-Hudson, NY: World Book Company.

Goodman, N. (1976). *Languages of art*. Indianapolis, IN: Hackett.

Goodnow, J. J. (1977). *Children's drawings*. London: Fontana.

Goodnow, J. J., Wilkins, P., & Dawes, L. (1986). Acquiring cultural forms: Cognitive aspects of socialization illustrated by children's drawings and judgments of drawings. *International Journal of Behavioural Development, 9*, 485–505.

Gopnik, A. (1996). The scientist as child. *Philosophy of Science, 63*, 485–514.

Gopnik, A., & Rosati, A. (2001). Duck or rabbit? Reversing ambiguous figures and understanding ambiguous representations. *Developmental Science, 4*, 175–183.

Grant, J. P., & Sendak, M. (1993). *I dream of peace: Images of war by children of former Yugoslavia*. New York: HarperCollins.

Grauer, K. (1998). Beliefs of preservice teachers towards art education. *Studies in Art Education, 39*, 350–370.

Green, L., & Mitchell, R. (1998). The effectiveness of an initial teacher training partnership in preparing students to teach art in primary school. *Journal of Art and Design Education, 17*, 245–254.

Gross, J., & Hayne, H. (1998). Drawing facilitates children's verbal reports of emotionally laden events. *Journal of Experimental Psychology: Applied, 4*, 163–179.

Gross, J., & Hayne, H. (1999). Drawing facilitates children's verbal reports after long delays. *Journal of Experimental Psychology: Applied, 5*, 265–283.

Gross, J., Hayne, H., & Poole, A. (2006). The use of drawing in interviews with children: A potential pitfall. In J. R. Marrow (Ed.), *Focus of child psychology research* (pp. 119–144). New York: Nova Publishers.

Haeckel, E. (1906). *The evolution of man*. London: Watts & Co. (Original work published 1874).

Hamilton, S. S. (2002). Evaluation of clumsiness in children. *American Family Physician, 66*, 1435–1440.

Hammer, E. F. (1958). *The clinical application of projective drawings*. Springfield, IL: Charles C. Thomas.

Hammer, E. F. (1969). DAP: Back against the wall. *Journal of Consulting and Clinical Psychology, 33*, 151–156.

Hammer, E. F. (1997). *Advances in projective drawing interpretation*. New York: Harcourt, Brace World.

Hammond, N. R., & Fivush, R. (1991). Memories of Mickey Mouse: Young children recount their trip to Disney World. *Cognitive Development, 6*, 433–448.

Harris, D. B. (1963). *Children's drawings as measures of intellectual maturity*. New York: Harcourt, Brace World.

Harter, S. (1982). The perceived competence scale for children. *Child Development, 53*, 87–97.

Henderson, J. A., & Thomas, G. V. (1990). Looking ahead: Planning for the inclusion of detail affects relative sizes of head and trunk in children's human figure drawing. *British Journal of Developmental Psychology, 8*, 383–391.

Henshilwood, C. S., Sealy, J. C., Yates, R., Cruz-Uribe, K., Goldberg, P., Grine, F. E. et al. (2001). Blombos Cave, Southern Cape, South Africa: Preliminary report on the 1992–1999 excavations of Middle Stone Age levels. *Journal of Archaeological Science, 28*, 421–448.

Hetland, L., & Winner, E. (2004). Cognitive transfer from arts education to nonarts outcomes: Research evidence and policy implications. In E. W. Eisner & M. D. Day (Eds.), *Handbook of research and policy in art education* (pp. 135–161). Mahway, NJ and London: Lawrence Erlbaum Associates and National Art Education Association.

Hickman, M. E. (1985). *The implications of discourse skills in Vygotsky's developmental theory.* In J. V. Wertsch (Ed.), *Culture, communication and cognition: Vygotskian perspectives.* Cambridge, UK: Cambridge University Press.

Hobson, R. P. (1986). The autistic child's appraisal of emotion. *Journal of Child Psychology and Psychiatry, 27,* 671–680.

Hochberg, J., & Brooks, V. (1962). Pictorial recognition as an unlearned ability. *American Journal of Psychology, 75,* 624–628.

Hodgson, D. (2002). Canonical perspective and typical features in children's drawings: A neuroscientific appraisal. *British Journal of Developmental Psychology, 20,* 565–579.

Howe, M. L., & O'Sullivan, J. T. (1997). What children's memories tell us about recalling our childhoods: A review of storage and retrieval processes in the development of long-term retention. *Developmental Review, 17,* 148–204.

Hudson, J. A. (1990). The emergence of autobiographical memory in mother-child conversation. In R. Fivush & J. A. Hudson (Eds.), *Knowing and remembering in young children* (pp. 166–196). New York: Cambridge University Press.

Hudson, J. A., Fivush, R., & Kuebli, J. (1992). Scripts and episodes: The development of event memory. *Applied Cognitive Psychology, 6,* 483–505.

Ilgaz, H., & Aksu-Koç, A. (2005). Episodic development in preschool children's play-prompted and direct-elicited narratives. *Cognitive Development, 20,* 526–544.

Ivanoff, E. (1909). Recherches expérimentales sur le dessin des écoliers de la Suisse Romande: correlation entre l'aptitude au dessin es les autres aptitudes. [Experiments on the drawing of Swiss school children: the correlation between drawing aptitude and other capacities]. *Archives de Psychologie, 8,* 97–156.

Ives, S. W. (1984). The development of expressivity in drawing. *British Journal of Educational Psychology, 54,* 152–159.

Jahoda, G. (1981). Drawing styles of schooled and unschooled adults: A study in Ghana. *Quarterly Journal of Experimental Psychology Section A: Human Experimental Psychology, 33,* 133–143.

Johnson, M. H., and Morton, J. (1991). *Biology and cognitive development: The case of face recognition.* Oxford, UK: Blackwell.

Joiner, T. E., Schmidt, K. L., & Barnett, J. (1996). Size, detail, and line heaviness in children's drawings as correlates of emotional distress: (more) negative evidence. *Journal of Personality Assessment, 67,* 127–141.

Jolley, R. P. (1991). *Children's ability to draw in perspective two partial occlusion scenes.* Unpublished undergraduate dissertation, University of York, England.

Jolley, R. P. (1995). *Children's production and perception of visual metaphors or mood and emotion in line drawings and art.* Unpublished doctoral dissertation, University of Birmingham, School of Psychology, Birmingham, UK.

Jolley, R. P. (2004). Review of G-H Luquet (1927, 2001) Children's Drawings [Le Dessin Enfantin]. (Alan Costall, Trans. and Intro.). *History and Philosophy of Psychology, 6,* 81–83.

Jolley, R. P. (2008). Children's understanding of the dual nature of pictures. In C. Lange-Küttner & A. Vinter (Eds.), *Drawing and the non-verbal mind: A life-span perspective* (pp. 86–103). Cambridge, UK: Cambridge University Press.

Jolley, R. P., Apperley, A., & Bokhari, S. (2002, September). *Drawing improves young children's recall of video information.* Paper presented at the British Psychological Society Developmental Section Conference, University of Sussex, Brighton, UK.

Jolley, R. P., Cox, M. V., & Barlow, C. M. (2003, September). *What develops and why in British children's expressive drawings.* Paper presented at the British Psychological Society Developmental Section Conference, Coventry, UK.

Jolley, R. P., Fenn, K., & Jones, L. (2004). The development of children's expressive drawing. *British Journal of Developmental Psychology, 22,* 545–567.

Jolley, R. P., Knox, E., & Foster, S. (2000). The relationship between children's production and comprehension of realism in drawing. *British Journal of Developmental Psychology, 18,* 557–582.

Jolley, R. P., Knox, E., & Wainwright, R. L. (2001, September). *The relationship between production and comprehension in drawing.* Paper presented at British Psychological Society Developmental and Education Sections' Joint Annual Conference. Worcester, UK.

Jolley, R. P., O'Kelly, R., & Barlow, C. M. (in preparation). The development of expressive drawing in children with autism.

Jolley, R. P., & Rose, S. E. (2008). The relationship between production and comprehension of representational drawing. In C. Milbrath & H. M. Trautner (Eds.), *Children's understanding and production of pictures, drawing, and art: Theoretical and empirical approaches* (pp. 207–235). Cambridge, MA: Hogrefe and Huber.

Jolley, R. P., & Thomas, G. V. (1994). The development of sensitivity to metaphorical expression of moods in abstract art. *Educational Psychology*, *14*, 437–450.

Jolley, R. P., & Thomas, G. V. (1995). Children's sensitivity to metaphorical expression of mood in line drawings. *British Journal of Developmental Psychology*, *12*, 335–346.

Jolley, R. P., & Vulic-Prtoric, A. (2001). Croatian children's experience of war is not reflected in the size and placement of emotive topics in their drawings. *British Journal of Clinical Psychology*, *40*, 107–110.

Jolley, R. P., Zhi, Z., & Thomas, G. V. (1998a). How focus of interest in pictures changes with age: A cross-cultural comparison. *International Journal of Behavioural Development*, *22*, 127–149.

Jolley, R. P., Zhi, Z., & Thomas, G. V. (1998b). The development of understanding moods metaphorically expressed in pictures: A cross-cultural comparison. *Journal of Cross-Cultural Psychology*, *29*, 358–377.

Jusczyk, P. (1997). *The discovery of spoken language*. Cambridge, MA: MIT Press.

Kahill, S. (1984). Human figure drawing in adults: An update of the empirical evidence, 1967–1982. *Canadian Psychology*, *25*, 269–292.

Karmiloff-Smith, A. (1990). Constraints on representational change: Evidence from children's drawing. *Cognition*, *34*, 57–83.

Karmiloff-Smith, A. (1992). *Beyond modularity*. Cambridge, MA: MIT Press.

Karmiloff-Smith, A. (1999). Taking development seriously. *Human Development*, *42*, 325–327.

Kelley, S. J. (1985). Interviewing the sexually abused child: principles and techniques. *Journal of Emergency Nursing*, *11*, 234–241.

Kellogg, R. (1969). *Analysing children's art*. Palo Alto, CA: National Press Books.

Kennedy, J. M. (1982). Metaphor in pictures. *Perception*, *11*, 589–605.

Kennedy, J. M. (1993). *Drawing and the blind: Pictures to touch*. New Haven and London: Yale University Press.

Kennedy, J. M. (1997). How the blind draw. *Scientific American*, *276*, 60–65.

Kennedy, M. L., Faust, D., Willis, W. G., & Piotrowski, C. (1994). Social-emotional assessment practices in school psychology. *Journal of Psychoeducational Assessment*, *12*, 228–240.

Kerschensteiner, G. (1905). *Die Entwicklung der Zeitnerischen Begabung*. Munich, Germany: Carl Gerber.

Kibby, M. Y., Cohen, M. J., & Hynd, G. W. (2002). Clock face drawing in children with attention-deficit/hyperactivity disorder. *Archives of Clinical Neuropsychology*, *17*, 531–546.

Kindler, A. M. (2000). Art education outside the search for deep meaning: Sometimes what matters is on the surface. *Art Education*, *53*, 39–44.

Klopfer, W. G., & Taulbee, E. S. (1976). Projective tests. *Annual Review of Psychology, 27,* 545–567.

Kogan, N., & Chadrow, M. (1986). Children's comprehension of metaphor in the pictorial and verbal modality. *International Journal of Behavioral Development, 9,* 285–295.

Kogan, N., Connor, K., Gross, A., & Fava, D. (1980). Understanding visual metaphor: Developmental and individual differences. *Monographs for the Society for Research in Child Development, 45*(1), serial no.183.

Koppitz, E. M. (1968). *Psychological evaluation of children's human figure drawings.* London: Grune & Stratton.

Koppitz, E. M. (1984). *Psychological evaluation of human figure drawings in middle school pupils.* New York: Grune & Stratton.

Kosslyn, S. M., Heldmeyer, K. H., & Locklear, E. P. (1977). Children's drawings as data about internal representations. *Journal of Experimental Child Psychology, 23,* 191–211.

Krippendorf, K. (1980). *Content analysis: An introduction to its methodology.* Beverly Hills, CA: Sage.

Kuhn, D. (1995). Microgenetic study of change what has it told us. *Psychological Science, 6,* 133–139.

Kuzmic, D. (1992). Psychic reactions to war in children of soldiers and refugees. *Psychologische Beitrage, 34,* 206–214.

La Voy, K., Pedersen, W. C., Reitz, J. M., Brauch, A. A., Luxenberg, T. M., & Nofsinger, C. C. (2001). Children's drawings: A cross-cultural analysis from Japan and the United States. *School Psychology International, 22,* 53–63.

Lambert, E. B. (2007). Diagrammatic representations and event memory in preschoolers. *Early Years, 27,* 65–75.

Lange-Küttner, C. (2004). More evidence on size modification in spatial axes systems of varying complexity. *Journal of Experimental Child Psychology, 88,* 171–192.

Lange-Küttner, C., Kerzmann, A., & Heckhausen, J. (2002). The emergence of visually realistic contour in the drawing of the human figure. *British Journal of Developmental Psychology, 20,* 439–463.

Lange-Küttner, C., & Reith, E. (1995). The transformation of figurative thought implications of Piaget and Inhelder's developmental theory for children's drawings, In C. Lange-Küttner & G. V. Thomas (Eds.), *Drawing and looking.* New York: Harvester Wheatsheaf.

Laws, G., & Lawrence, L. (2001). Spatial representation in the drawings of children with Down's syndrome and its relationship to language and motor development: A preliminary investigation. *British Journal of Developmental Psychology, 19,* 453–473.

Lee, A., & Hobson, R. P. (2006). Drawing self and others: How do children with autism differ from those with learning difficulties? *British Journal of Developmental Psychology*, 24, 547–565.

Leekam, S. R., & Perner, J. (1991). Does the autistic child have a meta-representational deficit? *Cognition*, 40, 203–218.

Leevers, H. J., & Harris, P. L. (1998). Drawing impossible entities: A measure of the imagination in children with autism, children with learning disabilities, and normal 4-year-olds. *Journal of Child Psychology and Psychiatry*, 39, 399–410.

Leffman, D., Lewis, S., & Atriyah, J. (2003). *The rough guide to China*. London: Rough Guides.

Leslie, A. M., & Thaiss, L. (1992). Domain specificity in conceptual development: Neuropsychological evidence from autism. *Cognition*, 43, 225–251.

LeVine, R. A., & White, M. I. (1986). *Human conditions: The cultural basis of educational development*. London: Routledge & Kegan Paul.

Lewis, C., Russell, C., & Berridge, D. (1993). When is a mug not a mug? Effects of content, naming, and instructions on children's drawings. *Journal of Experimental Child Psychology*, 56, 291–302.

Lewis, H. P. (1963a). Spatial representation in drawing as a correlate of development and a basis for picture preference. *The Journal of Genetic Psychology*, 102, 95–107.

Lewis, H. P. (1963b). The relationship of picture preference to developmental status in drawing. *Journal of Educational Research*, 57, 43–46.

Lewis, R. (1996). *Gendering orientalism: Race, femininity and representation*. London: Routledge.

Lewis, V., & Boucher, J. (1991). Skill content and generative strategies in autistic children's drawings. *British Journal of Developmental Psychology*, 9, 393–416.

Lewis-Williams, J. D. (2002). *The mind in the cave: Consciousness and the origins of art*. London: Thames and Hudson.

Light, P. H. & Barnes, P. (1995). Development in drawing. In V. Lee & P. das Gupta (Eds.), *Children's cognitive and language development*, Oxford, UK: Blackwell/Open University.

Light, P. H., & MacIntosh, E. (1980). Depth relations in young children's drawings. *Journal of Experimental Child Psychology*, 30, 79–87.

Lillard, P. P. (1996). *Montessori today*. New York: Random House.

Low, J., & Durkin, K. (2000). Children's conceptualisation of law enforcement on television and in real life. *Legal & Criminological Psychology*, 6, 197–214.

Lowenfeld, V. (1939). *The nature of creative activity*. New York: Macmillan.

Lowenfeld, V. (1954). *Your child and his art*. New York: Macmillan.

Lowenfeld, V., & Brittain, W. (1987). Creative *and mental growth*. New York: Macmillan.

Lubin, B., Larsen, R. M., Matarazzo, J. D., & Seever, M. (1985). Psychological test usage patterns in five professional settings. *American Psychologist, 40*, 857–861.

Lukens, H. (1896). The study of children's drawings in the early years. *Pedagogical Seminar, 4*, 79–110.

Luquet, G. H. (1913). *Les dessins d'un enfant: Thèse pour le doctorat presenté à la faculté des lettres de l'université de Lille*. Paris: Librarie Felix Alcan.

Luquet, G. H. (1927). *Le dessin enfantin*. Paris: Alcan.

Luquet, G. H. (2001). *Children's drawings*. (A. Costall, Trans.). London and New York: Free Association Books (Original work published 1927).

Machotka, P. (1966). Aesthetic criteria in childhood: Justifications of preference. *Child Development, 37*, 877–885.

Machover, K. (1949). *Personality projection in the drawings of the human figure*. Springfield, IL: Charles C. Thomas.

Magwaza, A. S., Killian, B. J., Petersen, I., & Pillay, Y. (1993). The effects of chronic violence on preschool children living in South African townships. *Child Abuse and Neglect, 17*, 795–803.

Maitland, L. M. (1895). What children draw to please themselves. *Inland Educator, 1*, 77–81.

Major, D. R. (1906). *First steps in mental growth*. New York: Macmillan.

Martin, D. (2003). *An investigation into the relationship between children's expressive and realism drawing ability and divergent thinking*. Unpublished undergraduate dissertation, Staffordshire University, England.

Martlew, M., & Connolly, K. J. (1996). Human figure drawings by schooled and unschooled children in Papua New Guinea. *Child Development, 67*, 2743–2762.

Mash, E. J., & Wolfe, D. A. (2005). *Abnormal child psychology* (3rd ed.). Belmont, CA: Thomson Wadsworth.

Matthews, J. (1984). Children drawing: Are young children really scribbling? *Early Child Development and Care, 18*, 1–39.

Matthews, J. (1999). *The art of childhood and adolescence: The construction of meaning*. London: Falmer Press.

Matthews, J. (2003). *Drawing and painting: Children and visual representation*. London: Paul Chapman.

McGarrigle, J., & Donaldson, M. (1974). Conservation accidents. *Cognition, 3*, 341–350.

Milbrath, C. (1998). *Patterns of artistic development in children: Comparative studies of talent*. Cambridge, UK: Cambridge University Press.

Millar, S. (1975). Visual experience or translation rules? Drawing the human figure by blind and sighted children. *Perception, 4*, 363–371.

Miyahara, M., Piek, J., & Barrett, N. (2006). Accuracy of drawing in a dual-task and resistance-to-distraction study: Motor or attention deficit? *Human Movement Science, 25*, 100–109.

Montangero, J. (1996). *Understanding changes in time.* London: Taylor & Francis.

Moore, V. (1986). The relationship between children's drawings and preferences for alternative depictions of a familiar object. *Journal of Experimental Child Psychology, 42*, 187–198.

Morra, S. (2002). On the relationship between partial occlusion drawing, M capacity and field independence. *British Journal of Developmental Psychology, 20*, 421–438.

Morra, S. (2005). Cognitive aspects of change in drawing: A neo-Piagetian theoretical account. *British Journal of Developmental Psychology, 23*, 317–341.

Morra, S., Angi, A., & Tomat, L. (1996). Planning, encoding, and overcoming conflict in partial occlusion drawing: A neo-Piagetian model and an experimental analysis. *Journal of Experimental Child Psychology, 61*, 276–301.

Morra, S., Caloni, B., & D'Amico, M. R. (1994). Working memory and the intentional depiction of emotions. *Archives De Psychologie, 62*, 71–87.

Morra, S., Moizo, C., & Scopesi, A. (1988). Working memory (or the m-operator) and the planning of children's drawings. *Journal of Experimental Child Psychology, 46*, 41–73.

Morris, C. A., & Mervis, C. B. (1999). Williams syndrome. In S. Goldstein & C. R. Reynolds (Eds.), *Handbook of neurodevelopmental and genetic disorders in children* (pp. 555–590). New York: Guilford Press.

Morse, R., & Bremner, G. (1998, September). Representational flexibility in young children's drawings. Poster presented at the *British Psychological Society, Developmental Section Annual Conference*, Lancaster University, UK.

Mortensen, K. V. (1991). *Form and content in children's human figure drawings: Development, sex differences and body experience.* New York: New York University Press.

Motta, R. W., Little, S. G., & Tobin, M. J. (1993). The use and abuse of human figure drawings. *School Psychology Quarterly, 8*, 162–169.

Mottron, L., Belleville, S., & Ménard, E. (1999). Local bias in autistic subjects as evidenced by graphic tasks: Perceptual hierarchization or working memory deficit? *Journal of Child Psychology and Psychiatry, 40*, 743–755.

Naglieri, J. A. (1988). *Draw a Person: A quantitative scoring system manual.* San Antonio, TX: The Psychological Corporation, Harcourt Brace Jovanovich.

Newman, R. S. (1984). Children's achievement and self-evaluations in mathematics: A longitudinal study. *Journal of Educational Psychology, 76,* 857–873.

Ninio, A., & Bruner, J. S. (1978). The achievement and antecedents of labelling. *Journal of Child Language, 5,* 1–15.

Oakland, T., & Dowling, L. (1983). The draw-a-person test: Validity properties for nonbiased assessment. *Learning Disability Quarterly, 6,* 526–534.

Oppawsky, J. (1991). Utilizing children's drawings in working with children following divorce. *Journal of Divorce & Remarriage, 15,* 125–141.

Paget, G. W. (1932). Some drawings of men and women made by children of certain non-European races. *Journal of the Royal Anthropological Institute, 62,* 127–144.

Pariser, D. (2006). Considering the U-curve. In J. A. Schaler (Ed.), *Howard Gardner under fire: The rebel psychologist faces his critics* (pp. 255–276). Chicago: Open Court Press.

Pariser, D. A., Kindler, A. M., & van den Berg, A. (2008). Drawing and aesthetic judgments across cultures: Diverse pathways to graphic development. In C. Milbrath & H. M. Trautner (Eds.), *Children's understanding and production of pictures, drawings and art: Theoretical and empirical approaches* (pp. 293–317). Cambridge, MA: Hogrefe & Huber.

Pariser, D., Kindler, A., van den Berg A., Dias, B., & Liu, W. C. (2007). Does practice make perfect? Children's and adult's constructions of graphic merit and development: A crosscultural study. *Visual Arts Research, 33,* 96–114.

Pariser, D., & van den Berg, A. (1997). The mind of the beholder: Some provisional doubts about the U-curve aesthetic development thesis. *Studies in Art Education, 38,* 158–178.

Pariser, D., & van den Berg, A. (2001). Teaching art versus teaching taste, what art teachers can learn from looking at cross-cultural evaluation of children's art. *Poetics; 29,* 331–350.

Parsons, M. J. (1987). *How we understand art: A cognitive developmental account of aesthetic experience.* Cambridge, UK: Cambridge University Press.

Pasto, T. (1967). A critical review of the history of drawing methods in the public schools of the United States. *Art Education, 20,* 2–7.

Perez, B. (1888). *L'art et la poèsie chez l'enfant* [Art and Poetry of the child]. Paris: Fèlix Alcan.

Perner, J. (1991). *Understanding the representational mind*. Cambridge, MA: MIT Press.

Perner, J., Aichhorn, M., Kronbichler, M., Staffen, W., & Ladurner, G. (2006). Thinking of mental and other representations: The roles of left and right temporo-parietal junction. *Social-Neurosciences, 1*, 245–258.

Perner, J., Leekam, S. R., & Wimmer, H. (1987). Three-year-olds difficulty with false belief: The case for a conceptual deficit. *British Journal of Developmental Psychology, 5*, 125–137.

Peterson, C., & Bell, M. (1996), Children's memory for traumatic injury. *Child Development, 67*, 3045–3070.

Peterson, C., & Siegal, M. (1998). Changing focus on the representational mind: Concepts of false photographs, false drawings and false beliefs in deaf, autistic and normal children. *British Journal of Developmental Psychology, 16*, 301–320.

Phillips, W. A., Hobbs, S. B. & Pratt, F. R. (1978). Intellectual realism in children's drawings of cubes. *Cognition, 6*, 15–33.

Piaget, J. (1929). *The child's conception of the world*. New York: Harcourt, Brace Jovanovich.

Piaget, J. (1969). *The child's conception of time*. London: Routledge.

Piaget, J., & Inhelder, B. (1956). *The child's conception of space*. London: Routledge & Kegan Paul.

Piaget, J., & Inhelder, B. (1969). *The psychology of the child*. London: Routledge & Kegan Paul.

Picard, D., & Vinter, A. (1999). Representational flexibility in children's drawings: effects of age and verbal instructions. *British Journal of Developmental Psychology, 17*, 605–622.

Pierroutsakos, S. L., & DeLoache, J. S. (2003). Infants' manual investigation of pictured objects varying in realism. *Infancy, 4*, 141–156.

Pinker, S. (1994). *The language instinct*. St. Ives, England: Penguin.

Piotrowski, C. (1999). Assessment practices in the era of managed care: Current status and future directions. *Journal of Clinical Psychology, 55*, 787–796.

Piotrowski, C., Belter, R. W., & Keller, J. W. (1998). The impact of "managed care" on the practice of psychological testing: Preliminary findings. *Journal of Personality Assessment, 70*, 441–447.

Piotrowski, C., & Keller, J. W. (1989). Psychological testing in outpatient mental health facilities: A national study. *Professional Psychology: Research and Practice, 20*, 423–425.

Piotrowski, C., & Keller, J. W. (1992). Psychological testing in applied settings: A literature review from 1982–1992. *The Journal of Training and Practice in Professional Psychology, 6*, 74–82.

Plumert, J. M. (1995). Relations between children's overestimation of their physical abilities and accident proneness. *Developmental Psychology, 31*, 866–876.

Poole, D. A., & Lamb, M. E. (1998). *Investigative interviews of children: A guide for helping professionals.* Washington, DC: American Psychological Association Press.

Potter, E. F., & Eden, K. M. (2001). *Children's motivational beliefs about art: exploring age differences and relation to drawing behaviour.* Paper presented at the annual meeting of the American Educational Research Association, Seattle, WA, April 10–14. (ERIC Document Reproduction Service No ED452134).

Pynoos, R. S., & Eth, S. (1986). Witness to violence: The child interview. *Journal of the American Academy of Child Psychiatry, 25*, 306–319.

Radkey, A. L., & Enns, J. T. (1987). Davinci window facilitates drawings of total and partial occlusion in young children. *Journal of Experimental Child Psychology, 44*, 222–235.

Rae, W. A. (1991). Analyzing drawings of children who are physically ill and hospitalized using the ipsative method. *Children's Health Care, 20*, 198–207.

Rayment, T. (2000). Art teachers' views on the National Curriculum Art: A repertory grid analysis. *Educational Studies, 26*, 165–176.

Reith, E., & Dominin, D. (1997). The development of children's drawing ability to attend to the visual projection of objects. *British Journal of Developmental Psychology, 15*, 177–196.

Ricci, C. (1887). *L'arte dei bambini.* Bologna: N. Zanichelli.

Richards, M. P., & Ross, H. E. (1967). Developmental changes in children's drawings. *British Journal of Educational Psychology, 37*, 73–80.

Richards, R. (2003). *"My drawing sucks!" Children's belief in themselves as artists.* Paper presented at NZARE/AARE Conference 2003, Auckland, NZ, November 29–December 3.

Richardson, M. (1948). *Art and the child.* London: University of London Press.

Roback, H. (1968). Human figure drawings: Their utility in the clinical psychologist's armamentarium for personality assessment. *Psychological Bulletin, 70*, 1–19.

Robinson, E. J., Nye, R., & Thomas, G. V. (1994). Children's conceptions of the relationship between pictures and their referents. *Cognitive Development, 9*, 165–191.

Romans, M. (2004). Living in the past: Some revisionist thoughts on the historiography of art and design education. *International Journal of Art and Design Education, 23*, 270–277.

Rose, S. E., Jolley, R. P., & Burkitt, E. (2006). A review of children's, teachers' and parents' influences on children's drawing experience. *International Journal of Art and Design Education, 25,* 341–349.

Rosenblatt, E., & Winner, E. (1988). The art of children's drawing. *Journal of Aesthetic Education, 22,* 3–15.

Rosenstiel, A. K., & Gardner, H. (1977). The effect of critical comparison upon children's drawings. *Studies in Art Education, 19,* 36–44.

Rosenstiel, A. K., Morison, P., Silverman, J., & Gardner, H. (1978). Critical judgment: A developmental study. *Journal of Aesthetic Education, 12,* 95–107.

Rostan, S., Pariser, D., & Gruber, H. (2002). A cross-cultural study of the development of artistic talent, creativity and giftedness. *High Ability Studies, 13,* 125–155.

Rowlands, A. L. (2003). *The use of drawing to facilitate children's event memory recall.* Unpublished doctoral thesis, University of York, England.

Rowlands, A. L., & Cox, M. V. (2002, September). *Children's drawings and facilitation of event memory: Implications for eye witness testimony.* Poster presented at the BPS Cognitive section conference, University of Kent, Canterbury, UK.

Rowlands, A. L., & Cox, M. V. (2003, September). *Does drawing facilitate young children's event memory recall? Implications for eyewitness testimony.* Paper presented at the BPS Developmental Section Conference, Coventry University, Coventry, UK.

Ruskin, J. (1857). *The elements of drawing.* London: Smith, Elder & Co.

Sabbagh, M. A., Moses, L. J., & Shiverick, S. (2006). Executive functioning and pre-schoolers understanding of false beliefs, false photographs, and false signs. *Child Development, 77,* 1034–1049.

Sabbagh, M. A., & Taylor, M. (2000). Neural correlates of theory-of-mind reasoning: An event-related potential study. *Psychological Science, 11,* 46–50.

Salmon, K. (2001). Remembering and reporting by children: The influence of cues and props. *Clinical Psychology Review, 21,* 267–300.

Salmon, K., Bidrose, S., & Pipe, M. E. (1995). Providing props to facilitate children's event reports: A comparison of toys and real items. *Journal of Experimental Child Psychology, 60,* 174–194.

Salmon, K., & Pipe, M. E. (2000). Recalling an event one year later: The impact of props, drawing, and a prior interview. *Applied Cognitive Psychology, 14,* 184–220.

Salmon, K., Roncolato, W., & Gleitzman, M. (2003). Children's reports of emotionally laden events: Adapting the interview to the child. *Applied Cognitive Psychology, 17,* 65–79.

Salsa, A. M., & Peralta de Mendoza, O. (2007). Routes to symbolization: Intentionality and correspondence in early understanding of pictures. *Journal of Cognition and Development, 8,* 79–92.

Sandow, S. (1997). The good king dagobert, or clever, stupid, nice, nasty. *Disability and Society, 12,* 83–93.

Saxe, R., & Kanwisher, N. (2003). People thinking about thinking people: The role of the temporo-parietal junction in "theory of mind". *NeuroImage, 19,* 1835–1842.

Sayıl, M. (2001). Children's drawings of emotional faces. *British Journal of Developmental Psychology, 19,* 493–505.

Schuster, B., Ruble, D., & Weinert, F. (1998). Causal inferences and the positivity bias in children: The role of the covariation principle. *Child Development, 69,* 1577–1596.

Schwartz, D. L. (1995). Reasoning about the referent of a picture versus reasoning about the picture as the referent: An effect of visual realism. *Memory and Cognition, 23,* 709–722.

Selfe, L. (1977). *Nadia: A case of extraordinary drawing ability in an autistic child.* London: Academic Press.

Selfe, L. (1983). *Normal and anomalous representational drawing ability in children.* London: Academic Press.

Sigel, I. (1978). The development of pictorial comprehension. In R. S. Randhawa & W. E. Coffman, (Eds.), *Visual learning, thinking and comprehension* (pp. 93–111). New York: Academic Press.

Sims, J., Dana, R., & Bolton, B. (1983). The validity of the Draw-a-Person test as an anxiety measure. *Journal of Personality Assessment, 47,* 250–257.

Slater, A. M., Rose, D., & Morison, V. (1984). Newborn infant's perception of similarities and differences between two and three dimensional stimuli. *British Journal of Developmental Psychology, 2,* 287–294.

Slaughter, V. (1998). Children's understanding of pictorial and mental representations. *Child Development, 69,* 321–332.

Smith, D., & Dumont, F. (1995). A cautionary study: Unwarranted interpretations of the draw-a-person test. *Professional Psychology: Research and Practice, 23,* 298–303.

Smith, L. (2002). Piaget's model. In U. Goswami (Ed.), *Blackwell handbook of childhood cognitive development* (pp. 515–538), Oxford, UK: Blackwell.

Sourkes, B. (1991). Truth to life: Art therapy with paediatric oncology patients and their siblings. *Journal of Psychosocial Oncology, 9,* 81–95.

Spensley, F., & Taylor, J. (1999). The development of cognitive flexibility: Evidence from children's drawings. *Human Development, 42,* 300–324.

Spinath, B., & Spinath, F. M. (2005). Development of self-perceived ability in elementary school: The role of parents' perceptions, teacher evaluations, and intelligence. *Cognitive Development, 20,* 190–204.

Spivey, N. (2005). *How art made the world.* London: BBC Books.

Steward, M. S., & Steward, D. S. (1996). Interviewing young children about body touch and handling. *Monographs of the Society for Research in Child Development, 61* (4, Serial No, 248).

Stiles, J., Sabbadini, L., Capirci, O., & Volterra, V. (2000). Drawing abilities in Williams syndrome: A case study. *Developmental Neuropsychology, 18,* 213–235.

Stipek, D. J. (1984). Young children's performance expectations: Logical analysis or wishful thinking? In J. G. Nicholls (Ed.), *Advances in motivation and achievement: Vol. 3. The development of achievement motivation* (pp. 33–56). Greenwich, CT: JAI Press.

Stipek, D. J., & MacIver, D. (1989). Developmental change in children's assessment of intellectual competence. *Child Development, 60,* 521–538.

Sturner, R., Rothbaum, F., Visintainer, M., & Wolfer, J. (1980). The effects of stress on children's human figure drawings. *Journal of Clinical Psychology, 36,* 324–331.

Suddendorf, T. (2003). Early representational insight: Twenty-four-month-olds use a photo to find an object in the world. *Child Development, 74,* 896–904.

Sutton, P. J., & Rose, D. H. (1998). The role of strategic visual attention in children's drawing development. *Journal of Experimental Child Psychology, 68,* 87–107.

Swensen, C. (1957). Empirical evaluations of human figure drawing. *Psychological Bulletin, 54,* 431–466.

Swenson, C. (1968). Empirical evaluations of human figure drawing 1957–1966. *Psychological Bulletin, 70,* 20–44.

Taylor, M., & Bacharach, V. R. (1981). The development of drawing rules: Metaknowledge about drawing influences performance on non-drawing tasks. *Child Development, 52,* 373–375.

Teichman, Y. (2001). The development of Israeli children's images of Jews and Arabs and their expression in human figure drawing. *Developmental Psychology, 37,* 749–761.

Thomas, G. V. (1995). The role of drawing strategies and skills. In C. Lange-Küttner & G. V. Thomas (Eds.), *Drawing and looking.* New York: Harvester Wheatsheaf.

Thomas, G. V., Chaigne, E., & Fox, T. J. (1989). Children's drawings of topics differing in significance: Effects on size of drawing. *British Journal of Developmental Psychology, 7,* 321–331.

Thomas, G. V., & Gray, R. (1992). Children's drawings of topics differing in emotional significance—effects on placement relative to a self drawing: A research note. *Journal of Child Psychology and Psychiatry, 33*, 1097–1104.

Thomas, G. V., & Jolley, R. P. (1997, September). Understanding metaphors in pictures and paintings. In *The development of the poetic mind*. Symposium conducted at the British Psychology Society Developmental section Conference, Loughbourgh, England.

Thomas, G. V., & Jolley, R. P. (1998). Drawing conclusions: An examination of empirical and conceptual bases for psychological evaluation of children from their drawings. *British Journal of Clinical Psychology, 37*, 127–139.

Thomas, G. V., Jolley, R. P., Robinson, E. J., & Champion, H. (1999). Realist errors in children's responses to pictures and words as representations. *Journal of Experimental Child Psychology, 74*, 1–20.

Thomas, G. V., & Silk, A. M. J. (1990). *An introduction to the psychology of children's drawings*. Hemel Hempstead, UK: Harvester Wheatsheaf.

Thompson, C. (1999). Drawing together: Peer influence in preschool-kindergarten art classes. *Visual Arts Research, 25*, 61–68.

Toomela, A. (1999). Drawing development: Stages in the representation of a cube and a cylinder. *Child Development, 70*, 1141–1150.

Toomela, A. (2002). Drawing as a verbally mediated activity: A study of relationships between verbal, motor, and visuospatial skills and drawing in children. *International Journal of Behavioral Development, 26*, 234–247.

Trautner, H. M., Lohaus, A., Sahm, W. B., & Helbing, N. (1989). Age-graded judgments of children's drawings by children and adults. *International Journal of Behavioural Development, 12*, 421–431.

Troseth, G. L., & DeLoache, J. S. (1998). The medium can obscure the message: Young children's understanding of video. *Child Development, 69*, 950–965.

Tryphon, A., & Montangero, J. (1992). The development of diachronic thinking in children: Children's ideas about changes in drawing skills. *International Journal of Behavioral Development, 15*, 411–424.

Tulving, E. (1983). *Elements of episodic memory*. Oxford, UK: Oxford University Press.

Uttal, D. H., Schreiber, J. C., & DeLoache, J. S. (1995). Waiting to use a symbol: The effects of delay on children's use of models. *Child Development, 66*, 1875–1889.

van Sommers, P. (1984). *Drawing and cognition*. Cambridge, MA: Cambridge University Press.

Vaughn, K., & Winner, E. (2000). SAT scores of students who study the arts: What we can and cannot conclude about the association. *Journal of Aesthetic Education*, *34*, 77–89.

Veltman, M. W. M., & Browne, K. D. (2002). The assessment of drawings from children who have been maltreated: A systematic review. *Child Abuse Review*, *11*, 19–37.

Viola, W. (1936). *Child art and Franz Cizek*. Vienna: Austrian Junior Red Cross.

Volavkova, H. (1994). *I never saw another butterfly*. Random House USA.

Walker, N. E., Lunning, S. M., & Eilts, J. L. (1996, June). *Do children respond accurately to forced-choice questions? Yes or no*. Presented at the NATO Advanced Study Institute on Recollections of Trauma: Scientific Research and Clinical Practice. Talmont Saint Hilaire, France.

Wanderer, Z. W. (1969). Validity of clinical judgments based on human figure drawings. *Journal of Consulting and Clinical Psychology*, *33*, 143–150.

Watkins, C. E., Campbell, V. L., Nieberding, R., & Hallmark, R. (1995). Contemporary practice of psychological assessment by clinical psychologists. *Professional Psychology: Research and Practice*, *26*, 54–60.

Waxman, S. R. (2002). Early word learning and conceptual development: Everything had a name, and each name gave birth to a new thought. In Usha Goswami (Ed.), *Blackwell handbook of childhood cognitive development* (pp. 102–126). Oxford, UK: Blackwell.

Weber, R. P. (1990). *Basic content analysis*. London: Sage.

Wellman, H. M., Cross, D., & Watson, J. (2001). A meta-analysis of false belief reasoning: The truth about false belief. *Child Development*, *72*, 655–684.

Werner, H., & Kaplan, B. (1963). *Symbol formation*. London: John Wiley.

Wesson, M., & Salmon, K. (2001). Drawing and showing: Helping children to report emotionally laden events. *Applied Cognitive Psychology*, *15*, 301–320.

Willats, J. (1977). How children learn to draw realistic pictures. *Quarterly Journal of Experimental Psychology*, *29*, 367–382.

Willats, J. (1985). Drawing systems revisited: The role of denotation systems in children's human figure drawings. In N. H. Freeman & M. V. Cox (Eds.), *Visual order: The nature and development of pictorial representation* Cambridge, UK: Cambridge University Press.

Willats, J. (1987). Marr and pictures: An information-processing account of children's drawings. *Archives de Psychologie*, *55*, 105–125.

Willats, J. (1992a). The representation of extendedness in children's drawings of sticks and disks. *Child Development*, *63*, 692–710.

Willats, J. (1992b). Seeing lumps, disks and sticks in silhouettes. *Perception*, *21*, 481–496.

Willats, J. (1995). An information-processing approach to drawing development: Drawing and looking. In C. Lange-Küttner & G. V. Thomas (Eds.), *Drawing and Looking* (pp. 27–43). Hemel Hampstead, UK: Harvester Wheatsheaf.

Willats, J. (1997). *Art and representation: New principles in the analysis of pictures*. Princeton, NJ: Princeton University Press.

Willats, J. (2005). *Making sense of children's drawings*. Mahwah, NJ: Lawrence Erlbaum.

Williams, S. J., Wright, D., & Freeman, N. H. (2002). Inhibiting children's memory of an interactive event: the effectiveness of a cover up. *Applied Cognitive Psychology, 16*, 1–14.

Wilson, B. (1985). The artistic tower of Babel: Inextricable links between culture and graphic development. *Visual Arts Research, 11*, 90–104.

Wilson, B. (1997). Types of child art and alternative developmental accounts: Interpreting the interpreters. *Human Development, 40*, 155–168.

Wilson, B. (2000). *Empire of signs revisited: Children's manga and the changing face of Japan*. In L. Lindstrom (Ed.), The cultural context: Comparative studies of art education and children's drawings (pp. 160–178). Stockholm: Stockholm Institute of Education Press.

Wilson, B., & Ligtvoet, J. (1992). *Across time and cultures: Stylistic changes in the drawings of Dutch children*. In D. Thistlewood (Ed.), *Drawing research and development* (pp. 75–88). Harlow, UK: Longman/NSEAD.

Wilson, B., & Wilson, M. (1976). Visual narrative and the artistically gifted. *The Gifted Child Quarterly, 20*, 432–447.

Wilson, B., & Wilson, M. (1977). An iconoclastic view of the imagery sources in the drawings of young people. *Art Education, 30*, 4–12.

Wilson, B., & Wilson, M. (1981). The case of the disappearing two-eyed profile: Or how little children influence the drawings of little children. *Review of the Research in Visual Arts education, 21*, 33–43.

Wilson, B., & Wilson, M. (1984). Children's drawings in Egypt: Cultural style acquisition as graphic development. *Visual Arts Research, 10*, 13–26.

Wiltshire, S. (1987). *Drawings*. London: J.M. Dent & Sons.

Wiltshire, S. (1989). *Cities*. London: J.M. Dent & Sons.

Wiltshire, S. (1991). *Floating cities: Venice, Amsterdam, Leningrad and Moscow*. London: Michael Joseph.

Wimmer, H., & Perner, J. (1983). Beliefs about beliefs: Representation and constraining function of wrong beliefs in young children's understanding of deception. *Cognition, 13*, 103–128.

Wing, L., & Gould, J. (1979). Severe impairments of social interaction and associated abnormalities in children: Epidemiology and classification. *Journal of Autism and Developmental Disorders, 9*, 11–29.

Winner, E. (1982). *Invented worlds: The psychology of the arts.* Cambridge, MA: Harvard University Press.

Winner, E. (1989). How can Chinese children draw so well? *Journal of Aesthetic Education, 23*, 41–63.

Winner, E. (1996). *Gifted children: Myths and realities.* New York: Basic.

Winner, E., & Cooper, M. (2000). Mute those claims: No evidence (yet) for a casual link between arts study and academic achievement. *Journal of Aesthetic Education, 34*, 11–75.

Winston, A. S., Kenyon, B., Stewardson, J., & Lepine, T. (1995). Children's sensitivity to expression of emotion in drawings. *Visual Arts Research, 21*, 1–15.

Wisniewski, J. J., & Naglieri, J. A. (1989). Validity of the draw a person: A quantitative scoring system with the WISC-R. *Journal of Psychoeducational Assessment, 7*, 346–351.

Yamagata, K. (1997). Representational activity during mother-child interactions: The scribbling stage of drawing. *British Journal of Developmental Psychology, 15*, 355–366.

Zaitchik, D. (1990). When representations conflict with reality: the preschooler's problem with false beliefs and false' photographs. *Cognition, 35*, 41–68.

Zelazo, P. D., Frye, D., & Rapus, T. (1996). An age-related dissociation between knowing rules and using them. *Cognitive Development, 11*, 37–63.

Zhi, Z., Thomas, G. V., & Robinson, E. J. (1997). Constraints on representational change: Drawing a man with two heads. *British Journal of Developmental Psychology, 15*, 275–290.

Author Index

Subject Index

Note: "n" after a page reference number refers to a note on that page.